The Impact of the First W
on International Business

T0295788

"The editors have brought together a rich collection of scholarly talent in order to provide a highly perspective on the impact of World War I, revealing fresh evidence and interpretations that will extend our understanding and provoke further research."
—John Singleton, Sheffield Hallam University, UK

People throughout the world are now commemorating the centenary of the start of the First World War. For historians of international business and finance, it is an opportunity to reflect on the impact of the war on global business activity. The world economy was highly integrated in the early twentieth century thanks to nearly a century of globalisation. In 1913, the economies of the countries that were about to go war seemed inextricably linked. *The Impact of the First World War on International Business* explores what happened to international business organisations when this integrated global economy was shattered by the outbreak of a major war.

Studying how companies responded to the economic catastrophe of the First World War offers important lessons to policymakers and businesspeople in the present, concerning, for instance, the impact of great power politics on international business or the thesis that globalisation reduces the likelihood of interstate warfare. This is the first book to focus on the impact of the First World War on international business. It explores the experiences of firms in Britain, France, Germany, Japan, China, and the United States as well as those in neutral countries such as the Netherlands, Sweden, and Argentina, covering a wide range of industries including financial services, mining, manufacturing, foodstuffs, and shipping. Studying how firms responded to sudden and dramatic change in the geopolitical environment in 1914 offers lessons to the managers of today's MNEs, since the world economy on the eve of the First World War has many striking parallels with the present.

Aimed at researchers, academics, and advanced students in the fields of business history, international management, and accounting history, this book goes beyond the extant literature on this topic namely due to the broad range of industries and countries covered. *The Impact of the First World War on International Business* covers a broad range of geographical areas and topics examining how private firms responded to government policy and have based their contributions mainly on primary sources created by businesspeople.

Andrew Smith is a Senior Lecturer in International Business at the University of Liverpool Management School, UK.

Simon Mollan is a Senior Lecturer in International Business at the York Management School, University of York, UK.

Kevin Tennent is a Lecturer in Management at the York Management School, University of York, UK.

Routledge International Studies in Business History

Series editors:
Jeffrey Fear and Christina Lubinski

For a full list of titles in this series, please visit www.routledge.com

The Impact of the First World War on International Business

Edited by Andrew Smith,
Simon Mollan, and Kevin D. Tennent

Routledge
Taylor & Francis Group

NEW YORK AND LONDON

First published 2017
by Routledge
711 Third Avenue, New York, NY 10017

and by Routledge
2 Park Square, Milton Park, Abingdon, Oxon OX14 4RN

First issued in paperback 2018

Routledge is an imprint of the Taylor & Francis Group, an informa business

Library of Congress Cataloging-in-Publication Data
Names: Smith, Andrew, 1976– editor. | Mollan, Simon, 1977– editor. | Tennent, Kevin D., editor.
Title: The impact of the First World War on international business / edited by Andrew Smith, Simon Mollan, and Kevin D. Tennent.
Description: New York, NY : Routledge, 2016. | Series: Routledge international studies in business history ; 34 | Includes bibliographical references and index.
Identifiers: LCCN 2016025155 | ISBN 9781138930032 (cloth : alk. paper) | ISBN 9781315680750 (ebook)
Subjects: LCSH: International trade—History—20th century. | International economic relations—History—20th century. | International business enterprises—History—20th century. | World War, 1914–1918—Economic aspects. | Economic history—1750–1918.
Classification: LCC HF1379 .I4594 2016 | DDC 338.8/809041—dc23
LC record available at https://lccn.loc.gov/2016025155

ISBN 13: 978-1-138-34019-0 (pbk)
ISBN 13: 978-1-138-93003-2 (hbk)

Typeset in Sabon
by Apex CoVantage, LLC

Contents

Tables and Figures

Tables

Figures

Acknowledgements

We wish to thank all the contributors for their help and timely submissions: Chris Kobrak for his feedback and advice on the papers at the workshop in London in July 2014, Neil Forbes for helping to arrange the workshop, as well as Rory Miller, Chris Corker, Takafumi Kurosawa, Samuël Kruizinga and Keith Neilson, all the staff at Routledge and our partners and families for their support while we were preparing the volume.

Contributors

Volker Berghahn is the Seth Low Emeritus Professor of History at Columbia University.

Trevor Boyns is a Professor of Accounting and Business History at Cardiff Business School.

Phillip Dehne is a Professor and Associate Chair in History at St. Joseph's College, New York.

Andrew Dilley is a Senior Lecturer in the School of Divinity, History and Philosophy at the University of Aberdeen.

Clotilde Druelle-Korn is a Lecturer in Contemporary History at the Centre de Recherches Interdisciplinaire en Historie at the University of Limoges.

Neil Forbes is a Professor of International History at Coventry University.

Eric Golson is a Teaching Fellow at SOAS, a Fellow at Oxford, and also teaches at Richmond, the American University in London, and for Coventry University.

Leslie Hannah is a Visiting Professor of Economic History at the London School of Economics.

Jason Lennard is a PhD candidate in the Department of Economic History at Lund University.

Jacqueline McGlade is an Associate Professor in the College of Economics and Political Science, Sultan Qaboos University, Oman.

Simon Mollan is a Senior Lecturer in International Business at the York Management School, University of York.

Richard Roberts is Director of the Institute of Contemporary British History and a Professor of Contemporary History at King's College London.

Andrew Smith is a Senior Lecturer in International Business at the University of Liverpool Management School.

Trevin Stratton is an Assistant Professor of International Studies at the American University in Dubai.

Kevin Tennent is a Lecturer in Management at the York Management School, University of York.

Introduction

Simon Mollan, Andrew Smith and Kevin D. Tennent

> The direct consequences [can be] listed as loss of life and limb, destruction of capital, the disruption of international trade and finance, the huge physical demand for manpower and machines, creating an irresistible pressure for reorganization and reorientation of society.[1]
>
> —Arthur Marwick, *The Deluge: British Society and the First World War* (1965), p.14.

> What the war offers is a new vantage point on the world that preceded it, the schism between one history and another . . . [this] involves the reconceptualising of time, the recognition of ruptures and the subtle retracing of the immanence of the future in the past. For against the image of 1914 as an impermeable prison wall there is an image of 1914 as a kind of porous membrane through which something trickles back, 1914–1918 reshaping the memory and the historical reality of the pre-war world.[2]
>
> —Daniel Pick, *War Machine. The Rationalization of Slaughter in the Modern Age* (1993), p.191.

Many epochal chronologies use 1914 as a beginning or an end. The year 1914 is the end of the long nineteenth century, the first era of globalisation and the era of high imperialism. It is the beginning of Eric Hobsbawm's 'age of extremes' and the twentieth century's fatal association with war (pre-war, post-war, interwar; *war*).[3] The name of the 'First World War' itself tells a story: that it was the first and that there were other global struggles to come. Contemporarily, it was known as the 'Great War' for its magnitude of horror. As such, it was a fracture in the memorial landscape. It defines and conditions how we understand phases of the past. Historiographically, the First World War has become a temporal gateway through which historians see different modernities, leading to, being destroyed by or emerging from a cataclysm of horror and death, the scale of which had not been known before.

The centenary of the outbreak of the war has been widely commemorated, both in public events and through historical work. This has been testimony to the enduring will of the generation who suffered the war to 'never forget'. This book is part of this broader public and historical discourse, a timely opportunity to consider, reconsider and evaluate the impact of the First World War, in this case, on international business. International business history, which deals with international (i.e., cross-border) or comparative business activity in history has, of course, routinely covered the impact of the war, but generally not to contribute to the historiography of the First World War or to address those years as episode or epoch of its own. An aim of this book is that international business historians join the conversation about the history of the war.

This book explores the impact that war has on international business, either as part of or susceptible to the violence of the conflict and its effects on economy and society. In this examination, the environmental context is of considerable importance. A criticism that can be made of traditional forms of business history is that it accepts the precepts of conventional microeconomics whereby ceteris paribus conditions of normality are assumed when theorising about economic action. We think that business historians have tended toward histories of strategy and management that are generally organisationally interior. Historical studies of strategy-making and business policy are narrated from an inside-the-firm perspective, where the changing external environment is a largely background influence, and change is the result of management agency. In stark contrast, we see the First World War not as change, but as a discontinuity. In total war, many aspects of life are shattered, the psychic and cultural impact being no less actual than the destruction of the physical and the social. In this volume, our contributors write violence into business history. In doing so, they move beyond a chlorinated and simplified vision of the business environment that ignores the difficult and the messy human reality.

War has been described as the 'spiritual heartland of strategy' by three of the leading figures in the field of strategic management.[4] The adoption of the rhetoric of war by the field of strategic management is, however, problematical. The notion that the practice of organised violence should serve as instructive lessons for contemporary managers is incompatible with a positive sum view of capitalism, and has the potential to shape thought and outcomes toward conflict at the expense of cooperative and peaceful visions of economic action. As this volume attests, it might be better for contemporary management to understand the how the destruction, disruption and confusion of wartime on business was experienced, and how, rather than adopting warlike strategies, the most effective responses to war by firms and managers were based on coping, incremental adaptation, getting by and working through. In contrast to theories of international business that focus on intended processes, rational choices and coherent structural adaptations that can be considered as reasonable responses to changes in the managerial or business environment, the experience of war and wartime are bewildering and phantasmagorical. When uncertainty and existential crisis abound, how did business carry on with 'business as usual'? Or indeed, did it carry on at all?

One of the investigative themes of the book is to examine how business dealt with sudden discontinuity. The unfolding of time and the writing of history are important to an understanding of how events are understood in context. The First World War is a chronological barrier through which few continuing histories flow. It has become a temporal gateway through which historians see different modernities, or indeed, fit their histories to defined epochs which may not stand in the light of breaking this barrier into pieces. We also therefore seek to explore the continuities of organisation and practice which run alongside and in parallel with the discontinuity of war itself. Holding these two notions in place simultaneously creates an analytical tension between the forces of inertia and motion. We cannot hope to always reconcile these different stories, but in telling them, we can learn of the difficult history of extreme change from which they stem.

International Business Before the First World War

To foreground the effects of the war it is necessary, first, to sketch the structures and organisational forms of international business in the pre-war era. Prior to 1914, Europe had enjoyed almost a century free of pan-continental conflict, even if its nations had been involved in a number of smaller wars. This facilitated peaceful trade and investment within the continent and broader economic conditions which allowed economic activity to prosper beyond it. During this period, several European powers had developed extensive overseas empires on every continent, to which there was a large economic (and by extension, business) component. This was the culmination of a longer, 400-year period of European expansion which had started around 1500 and which served to spread capitalism around the world. This process included both the imposition of 'hard power' through formal conquest and colonisation, particularly in Asia, Africa, Australasia and North America, and socio-economic 'soft power' moving across the boundaries of empires, for instance, building upon the former Spanish and Portuguese colonies in Latin America.[5] The expansion of the frontiers of capitalism on the coattails of European power was not just driven by the needs of industry for raw materials, but also to a large extent the export of people—what has been described as a 'settler revolution'.[6] From the early nineteenth century onwards, a series of ideological 'wests' were promoted to European emigrants and financiers—starting with the Canadian and American western frontiers (now the 'Mid-West') but then moving to California, British Columbia and the Great Plains of North America by mid-century. The Australasian colonies were also promoted as a 'west', starting with New South Wales in the early nineteenth century, before encompassing Victoria and Tasmania from the 1820s and New Zealand following the Treaty of Waitangi in 1840. The development of these lands was characterised by an initial overly optimistic 'boom' characterised by lending to create infrastructure and hoped for industrial development, before a 'bust' and, following, an 'export rescue', whereby—facilitated by the new technologies of refrigeration and freezing—the economies re-oriented towards the exportation of primary raw materials to the more developed areas of the world, notably Europe.[7] These trends applied not only to the largely English-speaking zones of settlement, such as Canada, Australia and the United States, but also to countries such as Argentina and Uruguay, and even to Russian expansion eastwards into Siberia. In many cases, this expansion was dependent upon peaceful conditions prevailing for maritime traffic, at this time dominated by the British.[8]

This dramatic expansion of the global economy and the projection of European power and Europeans overseas created opportunities for the new forms of international business that emerged to facilitate the processes of resource exploration, trade, and extraction, as well as supporting the development of infrastructure and the creation of cities and ports as trading centres.[9] As European cities grew, they served not just as markets for produce, but also places to raise finance for the support of imperial exploitation and expansion.[10] Indeed, the Victorians had come to understand—reflected in economists as dramatically diverse as Adam Smith and Karl Marx—that the circulation of capital into production and consumption was an essential component of modernisation, necessary to break with a supposedly primitive past.[11] The gradual emergence of stock market capitalism together with the introduction of limited liability laws across Europe meant that merchants could use nominally independent company registrations as vehicles for risky overseas schemes. This tendency was epitomised by the growth of the free-standing company as classified by Mira Wilkins.[12] Many thousands of FSCs were registered in European states, led by the UK, typically operating in primary industries such as mining, plantations, forestry, or cattle ranching, or tertiary industries such as railways, tramways, or utilities.[13] Such free-standing companies operated both within Europe and intercontinentally, always undertaking international business activity, either in terms of foreign direct investment and/or through trade. By circulating capital, metropolitan people were creating direct, tangible links between the old world and the new.

Furthermore, the widespread adoption of the Gold Standard by 1914 and changes to transport and telecommunications networks also promoted international business activity. Great Britain had pegged its currency to gold as far back as 1717, but in the late nineteenth century, a number of European countries also adapted the gold standard, led by Germany after unification in 1871. Sensing the economic logic of moving onto the same currency system Denmark, Norway, Sweden and the Netherlands followed suit, aiming to facilitate trade and access to credit. Austria-Hungary and Italy (apart from a period in the 1880s) did not formally adopt gold convertibility, but by 1900 had still pegged their currencies to countries that had.[14] So while there was no single currency, exchange rates were, nevertheless, predictable and stable. By 1850, London had emerged as the world's most developed international financial and commercial centre. Its financial and commodity markets, banking and commercial services, and credit and insurance systems enabled the growth of other European economies and facilitated trade and investment in Europe and across the world.[15] The period 1850–1914 saw substantial growth in European railways. The UK, France, Germany, Switzerland, the Benelux countries, northern Italy and western Austria-Hungary developed particularly dense networks.[16] Partly as a result of this and partly because of relaxed border traffic, this was also an era of the relative ease of pan-European travel, especially for business, as well as recreation.[17] The telegraph and the telephone were well established in importance by 1914, providing Europeans with communication technology which improved information flows and reduced transaction costs.[18] By 1914, the European economies were increasingly interdependent, just as the global economy was expanding and inter-connected.

This heavily globalised international economy, and especially the European economy, was one of the reasons why Norman Angell could write about the damage and futility of pan-European war in *The Great Illusion*, first published in 1909.[19] Similarly, the British Committee for Imperial Defence Sub-Committee on Trading with the Enemy investigated the possible impact of war with Germany on the British economy, reaching the conclusion that war would be economically damaging and far-reaching in its consequences.[20] Giving evidence to that committee in March 1911, Lord Revelstoke (John Baring), of Barings Bank and also a director of the Bank of England, noted the catastrophic possibility of a significant pan-European conflict:

> I can only tell you that my conviction is—and one saw threatening of it a couple of months ago—that, should a European war take place, the chaos in the commercial and industrial world would result in the ruin of most people engaged in business.[21]

So while many aspects of the impact of the war would be unimaginable for the Victorian business community, the very fact of war and its deleterious consequences for business were not entirely unforeseen, nor the global character of the international economy contemporarily unknown.[22]

The chapters in this books elaborate on the disruption of the war in great detail. This disruption can be thought of to exist in three fluid categories that interlace to form the experience of business over time. There are, first, short-run impacts. These are the immediate and more or less instantly encountered effects of wartime in Europe on business: the closures of markets and exchanges, the loss of confidence and so on. Second are some of the medium-term consequential effects of a prolonged conflict that only gradually became apparent during the war years as the dislocation of war became normalised. And third are the longer-run effects—many of them structural or institutional—the ways in which the international business environment never returned to its pre-1914 state of assumed normality, and changed to settled-on new forms and permutations once the war had ended.

In the first days of the war, immediate impacts were felt. In his chapter in this volume (Chapter 6), for example, Richard Roberts examines the closure of stock markets by confused governments unsure of how to handle the financial crisis created by the start of the war. This chapter adds to the historiography of the First World War and its impact on financial markets.[23] Such official government responses were part of a broader attempt to limit the damage of the war while at the same time protecting vital national economic interests. Belligerent nations followed a range of strategies, which were gradually tightened as the war passed from a temporary disruption to a semi-permanent state of 'normality'.[24] The United Kingdom, for instance, had begun by forcibly dissolving partnerships between British citizens and those of enemy nations while establishing supervision of businesses controlled by enemy aliens.[25] By January 1916, when £5 million worth of assets was under the supervision of the courts, these efforts were intensified, and any possibility that German-owned firms were to profit from their British operations was removed through forced liquidation, the proceeds placed in special accounts.[26] Germany followed a similar trajectory, using special ordinances to establish control of British-, French- and Russian-owned businesses by December 1914. Every major protagonist country took steps to control enemy business assets.[27] Both Britain and Germany had used emergency legislation to introduce these measures—but the French used the courts to sequester and liquidate enemy-owned businesses right from the start, holding the property as 'economic hostage'.[28] Austria-Hungary moved in a similar way to Germany; economic ministers there, perhaps aware of the value of FDI in developing the empire, were initially unwilling to move against enemy-owned assets. From late 1914, a programme of 'supervision' was introduced; this was only progressed towards compulsory administration from July 1916 onwards, and never progressed towards actual liquidation.[29] Russia perhaps introduced the most severe measures against enemy-owned businesses, formally banning the ownership of businesses by enemy aliens from September 1914, before moving to compulsory liquidation of small and medium-sized firms from January 1915 and larger firms in December.[30]

In the medium and then longer run, the First World War altered both the fiscal and monetary context of international business. Increasing taxation, necessary to finance the war, was one such instance of this. Taxation increased in every developed country.[31] The increase in taxation across different jurisdictions created the lasting problem of international double taxation. Taxation on corporations never returned to pre-war levels, as public finances took many years to recoup the cost of the conflict, and the increased role for the public sector that it had introduced. In the years following the war, London's position as the pre-eminent *commercial* centre was undermined somewhat as international companies started to re-domicile themselves to reduce their liability to taxation, and a system of international tax treaties would evolve to provide reciprocal arrangements to reduce the burden of double taxation.[32]

A further change was the abandonment of the gold standard in 1914. Although there would be a temporary and faltering return to gold in the 1920s, the currency system did not survive the depression of the 1930s. The process by which Sterling would eventually cease to be a reserve currency was also set in train, as dominion countries such as Australia and Canada were self-governing within the British imperial system. In addition to military losses, the Central Powers were further weakened by the regime of reparation that was put in place at the end of the conflict. While companies based in Allied powers would be able to claim their subsidiaries back at the end of the war, German firms lost their holdings in the US, UK, France and other Allied nations altogether, reducing Germany's FDI stock to nearly zero.[33] Even business travel now became more difficult as passport requirements were introduced around the world, and from 1917, the US started to require visitors to possess a visa.[34] The financial disruption of the First World War meant that states became more economically atomistic and the status of 'foreign companies' became a political issue, perhaps for the first time. These changes would have the effect of reducing the visibility of the free-standing type of international firm and increasing the prominence of the MNE form in the interwar years, although some FSCs continued to exist certainly until after the Second World War.[35]

The First World War and Globalisation

The global and international nature of the late Victorian economy naturally forms an important theme that runs through the chapters in this book. Whereas business history can be written from firm-level (often within and about the organisational unit, with the history of the firm itself taking on the defining chronology and problematisation), in this book it is the environment—specifically *change* in the environment—that drives the choice of chronologies and problems to address. One particular existing debate that we therefore seek to situate the book within relates to the form and timing of historical globalisation. Globalisation is both a very general and remarkably slippery concept with which to work. For ease we accept a processual view, that globalisation 'denotes the *processes* [emphasis in the original] through which sovereign nation states are criss-crossed and undermined by transnational actors with varying prospects of power, orientations, identities and networks'.[36] It follows that *economic* globalisation is characterised by the transnational activities of firms, markets and networks, and is constituted of flows of trade, capital and so on. International businesses are, then, both vectors of globalisation and subject to it. In simple terms, disruption to their ability to act internationally disrupts the processes of globalisation, or at the least, forces a reconstitution or re-ordering of those processes.

This book will challenge some of the prevailing narratives and chronologies that structure our understanding of globalisation. In the course of challenging these narratives, this book will advance our understanding of how firms adjusted their strategies in response to a global conflict whose unprecedented destructive power was largely unanticipated. Historical periodisation is important because how we order the past by naming periods influences how causation is considered. We therefore need to rigorously debate which periods we use and when particular periods and epochs begin and end.

Some historians have argued that globalisation has been characterised by a cyclical process marked by phases of globalisation and deglobalisation. In the field of economic history (as distinct from business history), 1914 is seen as the key turning point. Here, the First World War is a disruptive event that abruptly ended the pre-1914 golden age of international economic integration and initiated a period of deglobalisation, with a retreat from the relatively open economies of the pre-1914 era that were associated with free and relatively easy movement of trade, capital and people.[37]

The First World War severed many of the political, business, financial and trade connections that had driven economic globalisation since the 1850s. Within days of the outbreak of the war, blockades and submarine warfare had choked off much of the international trade of the combatant nations. Global capital flows and international financial institutions were disrupted, and stock exchanges even in neutral nations were shut. For instance, the New York Stock Exchange remained closed for four months after the outbreak of the war, even though the United States was neutral until 1917.[38] The war had a dramatic impact on the international trade and balance of payments statistics that are the main evidentiary basis for economic-historical research and it is thus not surprising that many economic historians regard 1914 as the end of a golden age of globalisation.[39]

Other academics, particularly those working in the fields of international relations and diplomatic history, have questioned the more economistic view that the First World War truly marked the end of globalisation. The thrust of this body of scholarship is that while the war certainly changed the international economy, the process of globalisation did not come to a sudden halt in the summer of 1914. In this interpretation, rather than ending globalisation, the First World War merely caused globalisation to take on different forms, and the structures which underpin the integration of activity globally to adapt.[40]

War and Corporate Organisation

Governments also further intervened in domestic economies as the conflict quickly escalated into a 'total war'. Many of these changes, such as the shortage of labour resulting from conscription, the introduction of women into the workforce and the advent of licensing hours, were largely domestic.

However, international firms, just like their domestic counterparts, found that the business models developed in peacetime were significantly disrupted by war. The macroeconomic disruptions elaborated upon above formed part of this, but total war, together with the closure of belligerent markets and the interruption of trade, led to a reorientation of industry to benefit the war effort. These disruptions could not be managed through grand strategic design, as circumstances were frequently changing, sources of supply and markets could not always be guaranteed and plant and property themselves were sometimes endangered by war. Coping strategies based on responding to circumstances and incremental adjustment instead were necessary.[41] This does not mean that individual companies always did less well through adversity; war also provided space for entrepreneurial opportunity. The First World War probably did help to encourage the growth of the Chandlerian firm, an institution already well established in the US by 1914.[42] Mass armament encouraged the development of second industrial revolution industries in relatively new fields such as steel, automotive products, electrical engineering and chemicals, and created new opportunities for older industries, such as textiles and machine tools.[43] Following the war, this led to new opportunities for global expansion in these sectors. The expansion of state intervention in business across the world was also marked during the conflict, especially in Britain, where economic policy had been in favour of free trade. As Andrew Dilley argues in this volume (Chapter 1), a new protectionist sentiment intensified. The Ministry of Munitions, created in July 1915, sought to improve efficiency and productivity in British industry, thereby promoting scientific management, elaborated in detail in Trevor Boyns's chapter in this book (Chapter 12).[44] British industrialists accepted this because they saw the war as an opportunity to reduce the productive capacity of German industry, which had become a competitor in global markets.[45] New industries that would later have implications for national competitiveness were established to replace supplies of products that Britain had previously relied on Germany for, such as industrial dyestuffs. The government sponsored a new firm, British Dyes, forcing the existing textile industry to take on its operation to ensure that 'soldiers got uniforms of the proper colour'. A synthetic ammonia plant was built to overcome the unreliable supply of Chilean nitrates. This formed the basis for the creation of Imperial Chemical Industries in 1926.[46] Other firms, such as Ferranti, would find that the overarching control of the Ministry of Munitions led them away from markets that they had targeted, such as the development of consumer electronics, towards products aimed at military markets.[47]

Though maritime warfare restricted physical trade, it also created new opportunities. The British soap multinational Lever Brothers found itself cut off from its profitable German and Austrian subsidiaries at the outbreak of war, and then from its factories in Belgium and Northern France. The firm was forced to sell its German subsidiary, and planned expansion in the Netherlands was discontinued. Fortunately, the company's newly built-up subsidiaries in the US and Japan grew during the war. Entrepreneurial opportunity also presented itself for Lever Bros. Anticipating that supplies of Danish butter and Dutch margarine to the UK would be cut off, and possessing access to supplies of palm oil through its United Africa Company subsidiary, the company was able to move into margarine production.[48] Other MNEs found their loyalties split. The British side of the Royal Dutch-Shell Oil group—a complex web of exploration, distribution and financing companies—was forced to distance itself from the Dutch component, with British executives avoiding meetings of the joint board to avoid accusations of trading with the enemy. Because the Dutch government followed a strict doctrine of neutrality, the company was able to continue trading with the Central powers, where petroleum was scarcer, and the company's historians point to the great opportunities for the increased consumption of oil that the conflict brought. Indeed, the company's flexible organisation helped it negotiate the war period successfully.[49] Managers came to accept that they would be operating within an environment where government, and increasingly, nationalism were powerful forces within the economy. These forces would persist after the war and would drive the creation of the import-substituting multinational. Typically, these companies gave their national head offices considerable managerial independence and responded to high tariff barriers by replicating manufacturing and distribution activities in each national subsidiary.[50]

The First World War therefore augured substantial changes in corporate organisation. Ascribing direct causality can be difficult; part of the problematisation of these trends is to highlight the ambiguity between direct effects and periodological divergences. Nonetheless, the rise of import-substituting, resource seeking and tariff-hopping multinationals and the beginning of the slow relative decline of the free-standing company was a substantial change (see Chapter 3 by Philip Dehne). The challenges of managing large-scale, multi-unit, multinational corporations and increasingly complex internalised (but international) supply chains were addressed by the adoption of bureaucratic managerial structures. In turn, this provided an organisational terrain within which new management knowledge could be deployed (as discussed by Trevor Boyns in Chapter 12). The increased role of the state in everything from industrial regulation to the viability of capital issuance (see Simon Mollan, Chapter 2) changed the business models that firms adopted. Changes to corporate organisation therefore were a result of how firms responded internally (that is to say, structurally and strategically) to changing external environmental and operating conditions. It is here we see most clearly one of the key contributions of this book: changes to the nature of economic globalisation forced by war became operationally enacted. In turn, international business came to be altered by events (the war) and so create a new international business environment.

Summaries of the Chapters

Several of the chapters in this collection address the theme of the impact of the First World War on the process of globalisation. As discussed above, we are generally supportive of the view that while the First World War changed the process of globalisation, it did not actually stop, let alone reverse it. Several of the chapters suggest that the war and its aftermath actually encouraged the internationalisation of firms, a development which is clearly inconsistent that the economic-historical view that globalisation stopped in its tracks in 1914.

Jackie McGlade's chapter focuses on the impact of the First World War on the R&D capabilities of DuPont, a US multinational, and the Comptoir des Textiles Artificiels (CTA), a French multinational. Her chapter supports the view that while globalisation was altered by the First World War, it did not end because of the conflict. Indeed, wartime developments, particularly knowledge sharing between these firms, appear to have contributed to the transformation of DuPont into a knowledge-based firm with a diversified market base and global operations. Wartime cooperating with DuPont also enabled CTA to expand its foreign operations, transforming itself from a multinational firm active primarily in Europe into a multiregional firm with operates in North America and other continents. McGlade's chapter draws on the late Alan Rugman's distinction between regional multinationals and global multinationals. Rugman defined global firms as multinationals with significant activities in all of the main regions of the world. Most multinationals, in his view, were simply regional firms that were active in just their home markets and nearby nations. Prior the First World War, DuPont's internal operations were essentially in the Western hemisphere: the war resulted in DuPont's expansion into Europe and thus set the firm on a trajectory towards being the multi-regional global player it is today. Similarly, its partnership with DuPont allow CTA to expand its international operations outside of Europe and into the Western hemisphere.

The chapter by Neil Forbes also undermines the notion that the outbreak of the First World War ended, rather than changed the nature of, globalisation. Indeed, Forbes shows how the financial bonds linking London to Hungary strengthened in the immediate post-war period. The breakup of the Austro-Hungarian Empire into a number of smaller states, each with its own customs frontier and currency, can be seen as supporting the thesis that the net effect of the First World War was to undermine globalisation and prompt a reversion towards autarkic. The economic history of Hungary after 1918 certainly provides many data points to support the narrative that links the First World War to deglobalisation. The 1920 Treaty of Trianon had a decided negative impact on the Hungarian economy, as the new state lost most of the territory and population that had belonged to the pre-war kingdom. As Forbes shows, a variety of domestic political-economic forces meant that the economic weakness of the new state actually increased the country's reliance on the British capital market.

Trevor Boyns challenges our thinking about the impact of the war on the process of globalisation in a subtle way. Boyns shows how the war promoted the international diffusion of US management practices across the Atlantic to Britain and France. The sharing across borders of management techniques and other business practices, and of ideas more generally, is an important element of globalisation. Prior to 1914, there were advocates of scientific management in Britain and France who advocated the adoption of American managerial methods, particularly the efficiency-seeking innovations advocated by F.W. Taylor. The pressures of producing the meet the army's voracious appetite for material intensified the demands to improve efficiency in factories. Boyns presents a highly nuanced picture of the impact of the First World War on the development of modern management practices in Britain and France. For instance, he shows that the introduction of ideas and methods of the American efficiency engineers were sometimes resisted by workers in British and French factories and that many of the specific managerial reforms during the war (such as increased standardisation) were abandoned with the return to peace. However, Boyns also documents cases in which the war did promote the rise of American-style scientific management in Britain and France. This element of his research lend credence to the view that the First World War merely changed the nature of globalisation without stopping the process.

Les Hannah's chapter shifts our attention from the strategies of firms that transacted business across borders to the impact of the war on the various national variants of capitalism. His chapter, therefore, speaks to the literature within international business history about differences between national business systems. The limited liability corporation is an organisational form that is used differently in each national business system. Hannah's previous research has explored the reasons for the differences in the rate at which various nations have adopted the business corporation as a way of organising economic life. Hannah shows that the First World War was swiftly followed by a sharp increase in the number of corporations in Germany. Hannah shows that earlier research has shown that the legal and political systems of pre-1914 Germany had been unconducive to the rise of the corporation, which meant that business corporations were relatively less important in the German economy than in Britain or the United States. Hannah shows that the defeat of Germany by the Western powers led, rather ironically, to the adoption by many German businesses of an organisational form that previously had been associated with the English-speaking, common-law, jurisdictions. The First World War, therefore, contributed to the globalisation of the corporation.

Andrew Dilley's study of the wartime activities of British Chambers of Commerce provides another way of looking at the impact of the First World War on the strategies used by British firms. Dilley shows that the war saw the abandonment of the principle of international free trade by many British businessmen. Prior to 1914, there had, of course, been a campaign in Britain for the country to follow the lead of other nations by introducing protective tariffs. This campaign was largely unsuccessful, despite the support of a small but noisy group of protectionist firms. The First World War saw a massive shift in the intellectual centre of gravity in British business away from belief in Free Trade and towards protectionism. The war saw many companies, speaking through the Chambers of Commerce, clamouring for government policies that were designed to protect them from market forces. The sheer extent of the wartime revival of protectionism and tariff reform in Britain discussed in Dilley's chapter suggests that many British businessmen were shifting towards the use of non-market strategies during the conflict.

Simon Mollan's chapter on 'the 'impact' of the First World War on business and economic development in Sudan' explains how the war put on hold the development of business activities and plans to develop colonial economies. It examines the history of the Sudan economy, the colonial government and the Sudan Plantations Syndicate as they prepared to undertake capital intensive cotton production—once hostilities had ceased and 'normal conditions' had returned. He uses this history to explore the notion of the First World War as a period-defining barrier and, in itself, as space of chronological liminality between different historical periods with distinctly different characteristics. In turn, this is used to explore slower moving change and the gradual relocation of power in the colonial setting of Sudan, in particular, the increased importance of the state over time.

Phil Dehne's chapter focuses on the impact of the war on the strategies of two giant grain trading companies in Argentina, Bunge & Born and Weil Hermanos. These firms, which had headquarters in German-occupied Belgium, nevertheless managed to profit from the war. Dehne shows that the profitability of these firms during the war was driven, in part, by surging demand for food from the Entente powers. In addition to benefitting from rising crop prices, the firms also benefitted from the war because their local managers were able to change the firm's strategies by diversifying into new lines of business and expanding from Argentina into neighbouring Latin American countries. In 1914, these firms were fairly traditional free-standing companies, with the headquarters in Belgium and all of their productive assets in a single foreign state (in this case, Argentina). By the end of the war, they had come to resemble modern multinationals in the sense that they had operations in a variety of countries.

The multinational company is frequently seen as an important component and symbol of globalisation. The common view that the First World War initiated a period of deglobalisation would, therefore, suggest that the war would have destroyed existing multinationals rather than have encouraged their formation and development. The chapter by Jason Lennard and Eric Golson challenges the idea that globalisation ended in 1914 by documenting how the war accelerated the rise of SKF, a Swedish multinational that manufactured in belligerent countries on both sides of the conflict. SKF's headquarters in Sweden was able to take advantage of wartime demand for ball bearings from the opposing armies. The war allowed this firm to develop to the point that it was the centre of worldwide trust that controlled the production of this vital product. The research by Lennard and Golson advances our understanding of how Sweden was transformed from a late-industrialising country on the periphery of Europe into a sophisticated and modern economy that was the home of a number of important multinationals. Moreover, by documenting how the war encouraged the development of this multinational, their chapter reinforces the central message of this volume, which is that the First World changed the character of globalisation rather than halting the process of globalisation.

Clotilde Druelle-Korn highlights the creation after the war of a new supranational body, the International Chambers of Commerce, which is described in this chapter as the 'League of Nations' of the commercial world. This body was closely based on the United States Chamber of Commerce, but was based in Paris and aimed to bring together businessmen internationally to create international standards and regulations to encourage the development of firms and society as a whole. This body is little studied outside of legal history, yet is seen by Druelle-Korn as an important part of the idealistic post-war movement towards peace and cooperation which would eventually break down in the 1930s. This chapter provides a counterpoint to Dilley in that while individual national Chambers of Commerce acted as lobby groups for greater protectionism, at the international level, businessmen were arguing for fewer barriers to trade. Thus, while the war disrupted globalisation, it did not stop it completely.

Volker Berghahn also investigates the aftermath of the war in his chapter, focusing on attempts to rebuild business relationships between the former belligerent powers. His study of the papers of the New York banker Frank Vanderlip reveals an attempt to restore US trade with the whole of Europe after the war in the form of a 'peace loan', possibly underwritten by the US government. This plan was not realised thanks to political opposition and the US started to look towards the Pacific Rim for trading partners instead. Lloyd George then tried to lead Western European states to fund loans to the new states of central and eastern Europe, before the US stepped in again with the Dawes Plan of 1924 to bail out an ailing Germany. This led to the involvement of IBM, Ford and General Motors in the German economy, but the plan was insufficient to prevent the collapse of the Weimar Republic. Berghahn's chapter illustrates that while the confused aftermath of the war disrupted globalisation in the traditional sense, it created new opportunities for renewed economic links, however much their good intentions were disrupted by the disastrous consequences of the Treaty of Versailles.

On the surface, Richard Roberts's chapter on the Global Financial Crisis of 1914 would tend to support the thesis that globalisation ground to a sudden halt with the outbreak of the First World War. After all, global financial networks of the sort that were disrupted by the outbreak of the war are an important part of globalisation. Indeed, such networks symbolize globalisation to many people. The century after the end of the Napoleonic Wars witnessed the emergence of a financial network centred on London but extending to virtually every city in Europe, the Americas and much of Asia. This network was crucial for the movement of goods as well as the flows of long-term capital that literally transformed the landscapes of much of the world. Robert shows that in just a fortnight, this elaborate system seized up and there were bank runs and stock exchange closures in distant corners of the globe. Roberts shows that through policy innovations improvised in London and then quickly copied in allied, neutral and belligerent countries throughout the world, the complete collapse of the system was avoided. Roberts suggests that the policies introduced in summer of 1914 were largely successful in ensuring the long-term survival of the global financial system, as they protected financial institutions and other companies from bankruptcy and liquidation. The core institutions of the global financial system thus survived to fight another day. Indeed, by 1915, the most draconian of the emergency controls had been relaxed, and a modified global financial system was starting to resume operations. Trevin Stratton provides a counterpoint to Roberts by examining the new opportunities the war and its aftermath brought to New York–based financiers. While those in Europe saw their horizons narrowed, Wall Street banks seized the opportunity to establish branches abroad to participate in the European reconstruction process. Stratton uses the board minutes of the Foreign Finance Corporation to trace this process, showing how an expansion of American commercial lending, secondary market activities and trade finance helped the US to increase its financial presence, first in Latin America and Asia, and after the 1924 Dawes Plan, also in a rebuilding Europe. To some extent US finance houses tried to fill the gap left by European based houses while shifting the US from a net debtor to a creditor nation. Stratton's chapter further illustrates the evolution of the economic globalisation process created by the war as the system reshaped itself to deal with the atomisation of national economies.

Notes

1 Arthur Marwick, *The Deluge: British Society and the First World War* (London: Macmillan, 1991), 14.
2 Daniel Pick, *War Machine. The Rationalization of Slaughter in the Modern Age* (New Haven: Yale University Press, 1993), 191.
3 Eric Hobsbawm, *Age of Extremes* (London: Abacus, 1995).
4 Chris Carter, Stewart R. Clegg, and Martin Kornberger, *A Very Short, Fairly Interesting and Reasonably Cheap Book about Studying Strategy* (London: Sage, 2008), 111.
5 Desmond Christopher Martin Platt, *Business Imperialism, 1840–1930: An Inquiry Based on British Experience in Latin America* (Oxford: Clarendon Press, 1977); Charles Jones, " 'Business Imperialism'and Argentina, 1875–1900: A Theoretical Note," *Journal of Latin American Studies* 12, no. 2 (1980): 437–44; Rory Miller, "British Free-Standing Companies on the West Coast

of South America," in *The Free Standing Company in the World Economy, 1830–1996*, eds. Mira Wilkins and Harm Schröter (Oxford: Oxford University Press, 1998), 218–51.

6 James Belich, *Replenishing the Earth: The Settler Revolution and the Rise of the Angloworld* (Oxford: Oxford University Press, 2011), 9.

7 Ibid., 86–87.

8 Paul M. Kennedy, *The Rise and Fall of British Naval Mastery* (London: Macmillan, 1983).

9 Robert Fitzgerald, *Rowntree and the Marketing Revolution, 1862–1969* (Cambridge: Cambridge University Press, 2007).

10 Cassis Youssef, "Capitals of Capital: The Rise and Fall of International Financial Centres 1780–2009" (Cambridge: Cambridge University Press, 2010); Simon Mollan and Ranald Michie, "The City of London as an International Commercial and Financial Center since 1900," *Enterprise and Society* 13, no. 3 (27 January 2012): 538–87, doi:10.1093/es/khr072; Ranald Michie, *The London Stock Exchange: A History* (Oxford: Oxford University Press, 2001); Ranald Michie, *The Global Securities Market: A History* (Oxford: Oxford University Press, 2006); Ranald Michie, *The City of London: Continuity and Change since 1850* (London: Macmillan, 1991).

11 Wolfgang Schivelbusch, *The Railway Journey: The Industrialization of Time and Space in the Nineteenth Century* (Leamington Spa: Berg Publishers, 1986), 195.

12 M. Willems, *Defining a Firm: History and Theory*, ed. Geoffrey Jones, *Transnational Corporations: A Historical Perspective* (London: Routledge, 1993); Mira Wilkins and Harm Schröter, *The Free-Standing Company in the World Economy, 1830–1996*, eds. Mira Wilkins and Harm Schröter (Oxford: Oxford University Press, 1998).

13 Charles Harvey and Jon Press, "The City and International Mining, 1870–1914," *Business History* 32, no. 3 (July 1990): 98–119, doi:10.1080/00076799000000094; Simon Mollan, "Business Failure, Capital Investment and Information: Mining Companies in the Anglo-Egyptian Sudan, 1900–13," *The Journal of Imperial and Commonwealth History* 37, no. 2 (2009): 229–48. Stanley Chapman, "British Free-Standing Companies and Investment Groups in India and the Far East," in *The Free-Standing Company in the World Economy*, eds. Mira Wilkins and Harm Schröter (Oxford: Oxford University Press, 1998), 212–15. Kevin D. Tennent, "Owned, Monitored, but Not Always Controlled: Understanding the Success and Failure of Scottish Free-Standing Companies, 1862–1910" (London: The London School of Economics and Political Science (LSE), 2009), 209–30. Ibid., 239–74. David Boughey, "British Overseas Railways as Free-Standing Companies, 1900–1915," *Business History* 51, no. 3 (May 2009): 484–500, doi:10.1080/00076790902844104. John P. McKay, *Tramways and Trolleys: The Rise of Urban Mass Transport in Europe* (Princeton, NJ: Princeton University Press, 1976). Mira Wilkins, "The Free-Standing Company, 1870–1914: An Important Type of British Foreign Direct Investment," *The Economic History Review* New Series 41, no. 2 (1988): 262, 274, http://www.jstor.org/stable/2596058.

14 Barry J. Eichengreen, *Globalizing Capital: A History of the International Monetary System* (Princeton, NJ: Princeton University Press, 1998), 17–18.

15 Mollan and Michie, "The City of London as an International Commercial and Financial Center since 1900." Youssef, "Capitals of Capital: The Rise and Fall of International Financial Centres 1780–2009."
Michie, City of London; Mollan and Michie, City of London; Cassis, Capitals of Capital.

16 Ralf Roth and Colin Divall, *From Rail to Road and Back Again?: A Century of Transport Competition and Interdependency* (Aldershot: Ashgate Publishing Ltd., 2015), 3.

17 Leo Lucassen, "A Many-Headed Monster: The Evolution of the Passport System in the Netherlands and Germany in the Long Nineteenth Century," in *Documenting Individual Identity: The Development of State Practices in the Modern World* (Princeton University Press, 2001), 235–36. Kevin D. Tennent and Alex G. Gillett, *Foundations of Managing Sporting Events: Organizing the 1966 FIFA World Cup* (Routledge: New York, 2016), pp. 11–25 discusses the pre-war growth in international sport and its disruption by the First World War.

18 Robert Millward, *State and Business in the Major Powers* (London: Routledge, 2013), 256.

19 Norman Angell, *The Great Illusion: A Study of the Relation of Military Power in Nations to Their Economic and Social Advantage* (London: McClelland and Goodchild, 1911).

20 Paul M. Kennedy, "Strategy versus Finance in Twentieth-Century Great Britain," *The International History Review* 3, no. 1 (1981): 44–61.

21 The National Archives (TNA), CAB 16/18A 'Trading with the Enemy: Report and Proceedings', Meeting 19th December, 1911, Rt Hon. Lord Revelstoke, 103–04.

22 Nicholas A. Lambert, *Planning Armageddon* (Boston, MA: Harvard University Press, 2012).

23 John Peters, "The British Government and the City-Industry Divide The Case of the 1914 Financial Crisis," *Twentieth Century British History* 4, no. 2 (1993): 126–48; Michie, *The London Stock Exchange: A History.*

24 Michael Lobban and Willem H. van Boom, "The Great War and Private Law," *Comparative Legal History* 2, no. 2 (2014): 163–83.

25 John Clement Bird, *Control of Enemy Alien Civilians in Great Britain, 1914–1918 (Routledge Revivals)* (London: Routledge, 2015), 322–23.

26 Panikos Panayi, *Enemy in Our Midst: Germans in Britain during the First World War* (London: Bloomsbury Publishing, 2014); Panikos Panayi, "German Business Interests in Britain During the First World War," *Business History* 32, no. 2 (1990): 244–58.

27 Ibid.; Kennedy, "Strategy versus Finance in Twentieth-Century Great Britain"; Lobban and van Boom, "The Great War and Private Law"; John Warneford Scobell Armstrong, *War and Treaty Legislation Affecting British Property in Germany and Austria, and Enemy Property in the United Kingdom* (London: Hutchinson & Co., 1922).

28 Lobban and van Boom, "The Great War and Private Law."

29 Armstrong, *War and Treaty Legislation Affecting British Property in Germany and Austria, and Enemy Property in the United Kingdom*, 75.

30 Lobban and van Boom, "The Great War and Private Law."

31 Simon Mollan and Kevin D. Tennent, "International Taxation and Corporate Strategy: Evidence from British Overseas Business, circa 1900–1965," *Business History* (May 2015): 1059–61.

32 Mollan and Michie, "The City of London as an International Commercial and Financial Center since 1900"; Mollan and Tennent, "International Taxation and Corporate Strategy: Evidence from British Overseas Business, circa 1900–1965."

33 Geoffrey Jones, "Globalization," in *The Oxford Handbook of Business History*, eds. Jonathan Zeitlin and Geoffrey Jones (Oxford: Oxford University Press, 2007), 147.

34 John Torpey, *The Invention of the Passport: Surveillance, Citizenship and the State* (Cambridge: Cambridge University Press, 2000).

35 Mira Wilkins, "The Free-Standing Company Revisited," in *The Free Standing Company in the World Economy, 1830–1996*, eds. Mira Wilkins and Harm Schröter (Oxford: Oxford University Press, 1998), 43.

36 Ulrich Beck, *What Is Globalization?* (Cambridge: Polity Press, 2000), 11.
37 Jeffry A. Frieden and Paul Kennedy, *Global Capitalism: Its Fall and Rise in the Twentieth Century* (New York: W.W. Norton, 2006); Anthony G. Hopkins, *Globalisation in World History* (New York: Random House, 2011); Jürgen Osterhammel and Niels P. Petersson, *Globalization: A Short History* (Princeton, NJ: Princeton University Press, 2005); Geoffrey Jones, *Multinationals and Global Capitalism* (Oxford: Oxford University Press, 2004); Adam Tooze, *The Deluge: The Great War, America and the Remaking of the Global Order, 1916–1931* (London: Penguin, 2014).
38 W.L. Silber, *When Washington Shut Down Walll Street: The Great Financial Crisis of 1914 and the Origins of America's Monetary Supremacy* (Princeton, NJ: Princeton University Press, 2007).
39 Ronald Findlay and Kevin H. O'Rourke, *Power and Plenty: Trade, War, and the World Economy in the Second Millennium* (Cambridge: Cambridge University Press, 2007), 458.
40 Tooze, *The Deluge: The Great War, America and the Remaking of the Global Order, 1916–1931*, 517; Jones, *Multinationals and Global Capitalism*, 20–23.
41 For an elaboration of coping strategies see: Robert C.H. Chia and Robin Holt, *Strategy without Design: The Silent Efficacy of Indirect Action* (Cambridge: Cambridge University Press, 2009).
42 Thomas K. Mccraw, "Alfred Chandler: His Vision and Achievement," *Business History Review* 82, Summer (2008): 207–26; Alfred Dupont Chandler, *Scale and Scope: The Dynamics of Industrial Capitalism* (Cambridge, MA: Harvard University Press, 1990).
43 Youssef Cassis, "Big Business," in *The Oxford Handbook of Business History*, eds. Jonathan Zeitlin and Geoffrey Jones (Oxford: Oxford University Press, 2007), 180–81.
44 See also John F. Wilson, *British Business History, 1720–1994* (Manchester: Manchester University Press, 1995), 141.
45 John F. Wilson, *Ferranti and the British Electrical Industry, 1864–1930* (Manchester: Manchester University Press, 1988), 120–22.
46 Geoffrey Owen, *From Empire to Europe: The Decline and Revival of British Industry since the Second World War* (London: Harper Collins, 1999), 332–35.
47 Wilson, *Ferranti and the British Electrical Industry, 1864–1930*, 120–22.
48 Charles Wilson, *The History of Unilever: A Study in Economic Growth and Social Change*, vol. 1 (London: Cassell and Company, 1954), 227–33.
49 Joost Jonker and Jan Luiten van Zanden, *A History of Royal Dutch Shell, Vol. 1: From Challenger to Joint Industry Leader* (Oxford: Oxford University Press, 2007), 149–221.
50 For example, automobile manufacturing. See Mira Wilkins and Frank Ernest Hill, *American Business Abroad: Ford on Six Continents* (Detroit: Wayne State University Press, 1964).

References

Angell, Norman. *The Great Illusion: A Study of the Relation of Military Power in Nations to their Economic and Social Advantage.* London: McClelland and Goodchild, 1911.
Armstrong, John Warneford Scobell. *War and Treaty Legislation Affecting British Property in Germany and Austria, and Enemy Property in the United Kingdom.* London: Hutchinson & Co., 1922.
Beck, Ulrich. *What Is Globalization?* Cambridge: Polity Press, 2000.

Belich, James. *Replenishing the Earth: The Settler Revolution and the Rise of the Angloworld*. Oxford: Oxford University Press, 2011.

Bird, John Clement. *Control of Enemy Alien Civilians in Great Britain, 1914–1918 (Routledge Revivals)*. London: Routledge, 2015.

Boughey, David. "British Overseas Railways as Free-Standing Companies, 1900–1915." *Business History* 51, no. 3 (May 2009): 484–500. doi:10.1080/00076790 902844104.

Carter, Chris, Stewart R. Clegg, and Martin Kornberger. *A Very Short, Fairly Interesting and Reasonably Cheap Book about Studying Strategy*. London: Sage, 2008.

Cassis, Youssef. "Big Business." In *The Oxford Handbook of Business History*, edited by Jonathan Zeitlin and Geoffrey Jones, 171–93. Oxford: Oxford University Press, 2007.

Chandler, Alfred Dupont. *Scale and Scope: The Dynamics of Industrial Capitalism*. Cambridge, MA: Harvard University Press, 1990.

Chapman, Stanley. "British Free-Standing Companies and Investment Groups in India and the Far East." In *The Free-Standing Company in the World Economy*, edited by Mira Wilkins and Harm Schröter, 202–17. Oxford: Oxford University Press, 1998.

Chia, Robert C. H., and Robin Holt. *Strategy without Design: The Silent Efficacy of Indirect Action*. Cambridge: Cambridge University Press, 2009.

Eichengreen, Barry J. *Globalizing Capital: A History of the International Monetary System*. Princeton, NJ: Princeton University Press, 1998.

Findlay, Ronald, and Kevin H. O'Rourke. *Power and Plenty: Trade, War, and the World Economy in the Second Millennium*. Cambridge: Cambridge University Press, 2007.

Fitzgerald, Robert. *Rowntree and the Marketing Revolution, 1862–1969*. Cambridge: Cambridge University Press, 2007.

Frieden, Jeffry A., and Paul Kennedy. *Global Capitalism: Its Fall and Rise in the Twentieth Century*. New York: W.W. Norton, 2006.

Harvey, Charles, and Jon Press. "The City and International Mining, 1870–1914." *Business History* 32, no. 3 (July 1990): 98–119. doi:10.1080/00076799000000094.

Hobsbawm, Eric. *Age of Extremes*. London: Abacus, 1995.

Hopkins, Anthony G. *Globalisation in World History*. New York: Random House, 2011.

Jones, Charles. "'Business Imperialism' and Argentina, 1875–1900: A Theoretical Note." *Journal of Latin American Studies* 12, no. 2 (1980): 437–44.

Jones, Geoffrey. "Globalization." In *The Oxford Handbook of Business History*, edited by Jonathan Zeitlin and Geoffrey Jones, 141–70. Oxford: Oxford University Press, 2007.

———. *Multinationals and Global Capitalism*. Oxford: Oxford University Press, 2004.

Jonker, Joost, and Jan Luiten van Zanden. *A History of Royal Dutch Shell, Vol. 1: From Challenger to Joint Industry Leader*. Oxford: Oxford University Press, 2007.

Kennedy, Paul M. *The Rise and Fall of British Naval Mastery*. London: Macmillan, 1983.

———. "Strategy versus Finance in Twentieth-Century Great Britain." *The International History Review* 3, no. 1 (1981): 44–61.

Lambert, Nicholas A. *Planning Armageddon*. Boston, MA: Harvard University Press, 2012.

Lobban, Michael, and Willem H. van Boom. "The Great War and Private Law." *Comparative Legal History* 2, no. 2 (2014): 163–83.

Lucassen, Leo. "A Many-Headed Monster: The Evolution of the Passport System in the Netherlands and Germany in the Long Nineteenth Century." In *Documenting Individual Identity: The Development of State Practices in the Modern World*, edited by Jane Caplan and John Torpey, 235–55. Princeton, NJ: Princeton University Press, 2001.

Marwick, Arthur. *The Deluge: British Society and the First World War*. London: Macmillan, 1991.

Mccraw, Thomas K. "Alfred Chandler: His Vision and Achievement." *Business History Review* 82, Summer (2008): 207–26.

McKay, John P. *Tramways and Trolleys: The Rise of Urban Mass Transport in Europe*. Princeton, NJ: Princeton University Press, 1976.

Michie, Ranald. *The Global Securities Market: A History*. Oxford: Oxford University Press, 2006.

———. *The London Stock Exchange: A History*. Oxford: Oxford University Press, 2001.

———. *The City of London: Continuity and Change since 1850*. London: Macmillan, 1991.

Miller, Rory. "British Free-Standing Companies on the West Coast of South America." In *The Free Standing Company in the World Economy, 1830–1996*, edited by Mira Wilkins and Harm Schröter, 218–51. Oxford: Oxford University Press, 1998.

Millward, Robert. *State and Business in the Major Powers*. London: Routledge, 2013.

Mollan, Simon. "Business Failure, Capital Investment and Information: Mining Companies in the Anglo-Egyptian Sudan, 1900–13." *The Journal of Imperial and Commonwealth History* 37, no. 2 (2009): 229–48.

Mollan, Simon, and Ranald Michie. "The City of London as an International Commercial and Financial Center since 1900." *Enterprise and Society* 13, no. 3 (January 27, 2012): 538–87. doi:10.1093/es/khr072.

Mollan, Simon, and Kevin D. Tennent. "International Taxation and Corporate Strategy: Evidence from British Overseas Business, circa 1900–1965." *Business History* (May 2015): 1–28. doi:10.1080/00076791.2014.999671.

Osterhammel, Jürgen, and Niels P. Petersson. *Globalization: A Short History*. Princeton, NJ: Princeton University Press, 2005.

Owen, Geoffrey. *From Empire to Europe: The Decline and Revival of British Industry since the Second World War*. London: Harper Collins, 1999.

Panayi, Panikos. *Enemy in Our Midst: Germans in Britain during the First World War*. Bloomsbury Publishing, 2014.

———. "German Business Interests in Britain During the First World War." *Business History* 32, no. 2 (1990): 244–58.

Peters, John. "The British Government and the City-Industry Divide the Case of the 1914 Financial Crisis." *Twentieth Century British History* 4, no. 2 (1993): 126–48.

Pick, Daniel. *War Machine. The Rationalization of Slaughter in the Modern Age*. New Haven: Yale University Press, 1993.

Platt, Desmond Christopher Martin. *Business Imperialism, 1840–1930: An Inquiry Based on British Experience in Latin America*. Oxford: Clarendon Press, 1977.

Roth, Ralf, and Colin Divall. *From Rail to Road and Back Again?: A Century of Transport Competition and Interdependency.* Aldershot: Ashgate Publishing, Ltd., 2015.

Schivelbusch, Wolfgang. *The Railway Journey: The Industrialization of Time and Space in the Nineteenth Century.* Leamington Spa: Berg Publishers, 1986.

Silber, W. L. *When Washington Shut Down Walll Street: The Great Financial Crisis of 1914 and the Origins of America's Monetary Supremacy.* Princeton, NJ: Princeton University Press, 2007.

Tennent, Kevin. "Owned, Monitored, but Not Always Controlled: Understanding the Success and Failure of Scottish Free-Standing Companies, 1862–1910." London: The London School of Economics and Political Science (LSE), 2009.

Tooze, Adam. *The Deluge: The Great War, America and the Remaking of the Global Order, 1916–1931.* London: Penguin, 2014.

Torpey, John. *The Invention of the Passport: Surveillance, Citizenship and the State.* Cambridge: Cambridge University Press, 2000.

Wilkins, Mira. "The Free-Standing Company Revisited." In *The Free Standing Company in the World Economy, 1830–1996,* edited by Mira Wilkins and Harm Schröter, 3–66. Oxford: Oxford University Press, 1998.

———. "The Free-Standing Company, 1870–1914: An Important Type of British Foreign Direct Investment." *The Economic History Review* New Series 41, no. 2 (1988): 259–82. http://www.jstor.org/stable/2596058.

Wilkins, Mira, and Frank Ernest Hill. *American Business Abroad: Ford on Six Continents.* Detroit: Wayne State University Press, 1964.

Wilkins, Mira, and Harm Schröter. *The Free-Standing Company in the World Economy, 1830–1996.* Edited by Mira Wilkins and Harm Schröter. Oxford: Oxford University Press, 1998.

Willems, M. *Defining a Firm: History and Theory.* Edited by Geoffrey Jones. *Transnational Corporations: A Historical Perspective.* London: Routledge, 1993.

Wilson, Charles. *The History of Unilever: A Study in Economic Growth and Social Change.* Vol. 1. London: Cassell and Company, 1954.

Wilson, John F. *British Business History, 1720–1994.* Manchester: Manchester University Press, 1995.

———. *Ferranti and the British Electrical Industry, 1864–1930.* Manchester: Manchester University Press, 1988.

Youssef, Cassis. "Capitals of Capital: The Rise and Fall of International Financial Centres 1780–2009." Cambridge: Cambridge University Press, 2010.

Part I
Shifting Globalisation
Europe's Hegemony Challenged

1   Trade After the Deluge

British Commerce, Armageddon, and the Political Economy of Globalisation, 1914–1918

Andrew Dilley

> The new protectionism differs from the old in seeking to superimpose the present war map of the world, with its divisions of belligerents, allies, and neutral upon the protectionism of 1903–5, which sought to combine protection for British industries with a closer business connection between the self-governing dominions and the mother-country.
>
> J. A. Hobson, *The New Protectionism*
> (London: T. Fisher Unwin, 1916), ix.

Globalisation ought not only be approached as a material reality, the increasing and increasingly intense connectedness of various parts of the globe, but also as a cultural phenomenon constituted through sets of ideas about the integration of the globe.[1] Such ideas are not only at the heart of the culture of globalisation, hence important in their own right, but also the way in which globalisation is imagined can play an important role in shaping actual exchanges of goods, finance, people, and ideas. Thus, when assessing the impact of the Great War on globalisation, it is necessary not only to consider the war's impact on patterns of connection and exchange, but also to chart the war's impact on ideas about economic, and indeed geopolitical, governance. To this end, this chapter considers the impact of the Great War on conceptions of global political economy in Britain and the British Empire. It explores how the war reshaped the ways in which global trade was imagined. Since international businesses lie at the intersection both of the material realities and cultural imaginaries of globalisation, the article focuses on debates on trade and tariff policy after the war amongst businessmen, re-examining the development of what J. A. Hobson called the 'new protectionism'. It argues that new protection not only signified a significant defeat for British free trade ideology, but also involved a significant re-ordering of spatial understandings of global commerce as the pre-war political economy of tariff reform transformed to accommodate Britain and her empire within a broader global liberal alliance.

Such an examination of the impact of the war on business conceptions of global geopolitical and economic globalisation can be located within, and used to critique, several broader debates about continuity and change prevalent in the literature.[2] A first, dominant paradigm emphasises the discontinuities caused by the war.[3] Thus, globalisation was on this reading unbalanced by financial exertions, productive dislocations, trade reorientations and, finally, supposedly punitive reparations.[4] Similarly, the war is argued to have destroyed or weakened European empires by promoting nationalism and weakening the imperial metropoles.[5] Thus, integration was replaced by 'fragmentation'.[6] Conversely, a revisionist paradigm stresses continuity, either arguing that the war accentuated developments already apparent prior to the war, or that these developments were less profound than they first appear. Such readings emphasise the continuation of economic integration and the surprising strength of European empires.[7] J. Adam Tooze's *After the Deluge* offers a third way, emphasising neither straightforward continuity nor disintegration, but rather arguing that the war radically reconfigured global economy and global geopolitics. Thus, he writes that the war delivered an 'unprecedented victory for a distinctive vision of world order' dominated by the US and the Western Allies, whose dominance was, if anything, reinforced by the weaknesses of the Bolshevik Russia. The British Empire, Tooze argues, was integral to this victory and 'successfully reinvented the formula of liberal empire [to] . . . claim for itself a major place in the twentieth-century world as a self-sustaining and self-legitimating unit'. However he then goes on to emphasise the failure of this vision in the interwar period—following the standard account of British imperial decline as opposed to more recent arguments emphasising the continued vitality of British imperialism.[8] This geopolitical reconfiguration was in part rooted in, and coexisted with, a similar re-distribution of global economic power, with financial and commercial might transferred across the Atlantic. Globalisation was re-ordered by the war, not reversed.[9] Generally, such debates about continuity and change focus on the impact of the war on globalisation qua integration rather than globalisation qua mentalité. Understanding the war's impact on conceptions of the political economy of becomes a crucial, and underexplored, aspect of the broader debate about its effect on globalisation.

Businesses, and in particular business associations, played a crucial role in the redevelopment of ideas of political economy in response to 'Armageddon'. As Martin Daunton and Frank Trentmann have persuasively argued, ideas of political economy are formulated in evolving public discussions, rather than emerging from a self-evident economic logic, from the rarefied reflections of academics or in isolated government offices.[10] Trentmann has emphasised the crucial role played by businessmen as a 'medium of exchange' between 'the economy and politics': 'the ways [businessmen] think, talk, and act not only help react to political economy but also help to constitute it'.[11] By the twentieth century, collective action by business associations (formal organisations mobilising businesses) lay at the vanguard of the business contribution to political economy described by Trentmann, projecting a legitimated 'voice' into broader public discourses and into the deliberations of policymakers.[12] The views of these associations are not unproblematic reflections of the potentially divided opinions of their members. Nonetheless, as political scientist James Wilson has pointed out, 'few long remain in an organisation that offers them the very opposite of what they want'.[13] Successful associations therefore must reflect broadly the interests of their members by adopting consensual positions (often through a clear institutional process). At the outbreak of the war, the chambers of commerce movement was arguably the most widespread vehicle through which businesses in Britain and the British Empire could intervene in, and shape, discussions of political economy. In the Anglophone world, chambers of commerce are voluntary associations which draw together businessmen in particular localities to campaign on matters of common interest and to provide shared services.[14] By 1914, in Britain and many of the dominions, they had formed national associations and had mobilised at the imperial and international levels.[15]

The remainder of this chapter charts the evolution of new ideas about trade after the war within the chambers of commerce movement, showing also that these ideas contributed significantly to broader discourses on political economy in Britain and the British Empire, not least amongst policymakers. Following contemporaries, notably Hobson, the term 'new protection' is adopted for this body of thought, but it must be emphasised at the outset (and again following Hobson) that new protection pursued not only domestic protection, but also a complex hierarchy of global preferential trading relations that involved the imposition of differing levels of tariffs on different trading partners based on their geopolitical allegiances. The chapter traces the evolution of this body of thought, showing that the war not only created an early turn to empire (and an earlier turn to empire than recognised in the existing literature) and the marginalisation of free trade, but also that ideas of preferential trade were quickly reformulated to reconcile domestic protection and imperial integration with the participation in a broader global alliance. The first section of the chapter shows that this imagination of global trade began at the outset of the war and became dominant by the beginning of 1916. The second section shows how new protection had to be legitimated at an imperial level given the evolving political culture of Britain's relations with the self-governing dominions. The final section explores the impact of the new protection on British and imperial policy in the later years of the war, and shows that, surprisingly, the rise of the US had a relatively limited impact on the political economy of new protection. Overall, the new protection represents a reconfiguration of British and British imperial political economy to meet the demands of a global liberal alliance of precisely the kind emphasised by Tooze. Yet, it constituted an alternate vision of the means to cement that alliance, contrary to US policy of the 'open door' in trade, through preferential trading relations. Thus, the continued prevalence of preferential trade into the cold war era raises questions about Tooze's emphasis on the US power and British decline in the post-1918 world.

Business as Usual? British Trade, Political Culture, and the War: 1914–16

The declaration of war entailed an immediate extension of state activity and significantly disrupted British trade and finance. This was not the intention of policymakers. On the outbreak of war in August 1914, Asquith's government adopted a strategy of 'Business as Usual', aiming to limit the economic dislocations caused by the war. Some scholars have argued that down to 1916, the war's impact was indeed relatively limited. Thus, John McDermott highlights the continuation of trade with the Central Powers through neutrals until the Trading with the Enemy Act of January 1916 significantly tightened the regulatory framework.[16] David French argues that the commitment to a continental war undermined the strategy 'Business as Usual' from the start, but argues that the strategy persisted until 1916.[17] Nonetheless, the 'limited' impact of the war from 1914 to 1916 is often more apparent only by comparison with the later zenith of total war. The early years of the war still saw a significant economic rupture with the *antebellum* world. As early as January 1915, the *Chambers of Commerce Journal* (the journal of the London chamber of commerce) observed that 'extraordinary strides have been taken since the war in the direction of State Socialism'.[18] Richard Roberts has ably shown how the financial and credit mechanisms of the City of London were only saved by an enormous state intervention in August 1914.[19]

The outbreak of war immediately altered the geopolitical matrix within which British and British imperial trade took place. It rendered important pre-war trades illegal at the stroke of a pen, notwithstanding McDermott's cavils. On 5 August 1914, trade with the German Empire was prohibited, and blacklists were created to prevent trading through third parties and neutral countries.[20] Equally important for economic thought, the war unleashed a wave of anti-German culture. Businesses and business associations generally shared the culture of war, and in any case would struggle to gain legitimacy if they did not reflect that culture, not least when many businesses were also suspected of profiteering.[21] Even if trade restrictions were evaded by some, such evasion was neither legal nor legitimate. Thus the war generated a new 'moral economy' (framework of judgements about the legitimacy of economic activities and exchanges).[22] From August 1914, British commerce operated in a world redivided into enemies, neutrals, allies, and empire.

The war also had a clear and almost immediate impact on global patterns of British trade. Table 1.1 presents the distributions of total British trade prior to and during the war, classified by the new wartime framework. The reconfiguration of trade as a result of the war becomes clear, and clearly

Table 1.1 Distributions of British Trade, 1909–1929

	Empire (a)	Allies (b)	Russia	US	Neutrals (c)	Enemies
All Trade (including re-exports)						
1909–1913	24.1%	20.4%	5.0%	15.4%	19.7%	15.4%
1914	29.0%	17.5%	4.3%	17.3%	20.4%	11.5%
1915	29.3%	18.9%	3.7%	23.2%	22.1%	2.9%
1916	29.5%	19.5%	3.6%	24.1%	20.6%	2.8%
1917	28.4%	19.6%	4.3%	26.7%	17.8%	3.2%
1918	29.1%	17.9%	0.4%	30.9%	17.2%	4.6%
1915–1918	29.0%	19.0%	3.0%	26.2%	19.4%	3.4%
Difference: 1909-13–1915-8	+4.9%	–1.5%	–2.0%	+10.8%	–0.3%	–12.0%
Imports						
1909–1913	21.1%	20.1%	6.1%	18.7%	18.2%	15.7%
1914	25.5%	15.7%	4.3%	21.2%	21.5%	11.8%
1915	28.4%	11.9%	2.7%	29.8%	24.1%	3.1%
1916	29.1%	10.9%	2.1%	32.9%	21.8%	3.2%
1917	30.5%	8.3%	1.8%	37.1%	19.0%	3.4%
1918	29.0%	8.8%	0.5%	41.3%	15.9%	4.4%
1915–1918	29.2%	10.0%	1.8%	35.3%	20.2%	3.5%
Difference: 1909-13–1915-8	+8.1%	–10.1%	–4.3%	+16.6%	+2.0%	–12.2%
Exports (excluding re-exports)						
1909–1913	34.5%	17.6%	3.1%	6.7%	23.6%	14.5%
1914	38.4%	18.6%	3.4%	8.1%	21.1%	10.4%
1915	35.8%	31.0%	3.6%	7.1%	19.5%	3.0%
1916	33.3%	32.3%	5.0%	6.6%	20.2%	2.5%
1917	26.9%	38.0%	8.9%	6.1%	17.0%	3.2%
1918	30.1%	38.6%	0.1%	4.9%	21.0%	5.4%
1915–1918	31.5%	35.0%	4.4%	6.1%	19.4%	3.5%
Difference: 1909-13–1915-8	–2.9%	+17.4%	+1.3%	–0.6%	–4.2%	–10.9%

Source: Adapted from Mitchell, B. R. and P. Deane, *Abstract of British Historical Statistics* (Cambridge, 1976), Overseas Trade 12, pp. 313–3.

a)   Includes British North America, West Indies, India, Australia, New Zealand, and the Non-Mediterranean Africa
b)   Includes Asia, excluding British India and Burma; excludes Russia, US, and Argentina.
c)   Includes Argentina.

originates from the outset of the war, not 1916. The proportion of trade with the empire increased overall from 24.1% to an average of 29%, with the big shift occurring in 1914 and 1915. Within this, an expansion in imports (particularly from Canada) balanced out a more varied trajectory for exports. Trade with the Allies remained constant overall, but imports contracted and exports expanded, reflecting both British financing and supply operations, not least on the Western Front. Unsurprisingly, direct trade with enemies fell dramatically and virtually instantly. Proportions of trade with the US expanded throughout the war, with the largest single advances in imports in 1914 and 1915, while the proportion of exports to the US remaining at pre-war levels. There were slight expansions in exports to neutrals from pre-war levels early in the war, which may well represent covert trading with the enemy, but also the indirect supply of allies, particularly Russia through Scandinavia. Moreover, changes in the level of exports through neutral countries hardly suggest that sufficient British trade flowed through these channels to perpetuate anything like pre-war exchanges with enemy powers. From the outset of war, it was emphatically not trade as usual. The war itself redivided the world. Economic thought rapidly responded.

British Commerce and the Moral Economy of Global Trade: 1914–16

The chambers of commerce movement offered the primary vehicle through which responses to shifting trade and the new global moral economy of war were articulated. Of all business associations in Britain, they had the broadest membership, a membership which expanded significantly during the war.[23] Since 1860, the UK movement possessed an umbrella organisation: the Association of Chambers of Commerce of the UK (ACCUK). In 1914, Prime Minister Herbert Asquith described the ACCUK as 'the most authoritative and trustworthy exponent of the commercial interests'. Asquith himself had a close relationship with the ACCUK president, Leeds manufacturer Sir Algernon Firth.[24] The leading UK chamber, the London chamber of commerce, also enjoyed high-level connections. Lord Desborough, the chamber's president from 1916, was a classic 'gentlemanly capitalist': a member of the Buckinghamshire landed gentry, former MP, and ex-Tariff Reformer who possessed royal connections and in 1915 attended Asquith's daughter's wedding.[25] During the war, chambers of commerce acquired new, formal, links to government. For example, in July 1915, the Board of Trade appointed an Advisory Committee on Commercial Intelligence composed of five leading chambers men: Firth; Stanley Machin and Sir Albert Spicer (both prominent in the London Chamber); Ebenezer Parkes (Birmingham); and A. J. Hobson (Sheffield).[26]

The chambers of commerce movement had also mobilised at the imperial level before 1914. From 1886, the London chamber convened periodic 'Congresses of Chambers of Commerce of the Empire' which drew representatives of over 100 chambers, particularly from Britain and the dominions to discuss aspects of political economy. In 1911 a permanent association, the British Imperial Council of Commerce (BICC) was founded to pursue the resolutions of these congresses. The council, located in the offices of the London chamber, combined representatives of British and other imperial chambers, overseen by an executive committee dominated by leading members of the British chambers of commerce movement including, during the war, Desborough (BIIC president from 1914), Stanley Machin (BICC chairman from 1914), and Algernon Firth.[27]

An early impact of the advent of war was to initiate a heightened sense of a distinctive imperial political economy. Existing accounts, which have overlooked the BICC almost entirely, have tended to suggest that a turn to empire in economic thought took place largely in the later years of the war, with the emergence of new pressure groups from 1916, such as the Empire Resources Development Committee, the British Empire Producers Association, and the British Commonwealth Union. This increased activism is generally seen as a response to policy discussions which culminated in the 1918 publication of the reports of the Dominions Royal Commission and Lord Balfour of Burliegh's Committee on Industrial and Commercial Policy (of which more below).[28] In fact, the BICC took an early lead in instigating a pan-imperial debate about the future of imperial commerce prior to significant engagement amongst governments. Desborough and Machin wrote to chambers across the Empire on 25 September 1914 to capitalise on what the *Chamber of Commerce Journal* described as 'the present opportunity of rendering the Empire more self-centred industrially and commercially, and placing our empire trade on a more lasting basis'.[29] Desborough reminded chambers of the BICC motto, 'Unity in Commerce and Unity in Defence', and argued that in the dominions' 'splendid and spontaneous offers of armed assistance to the motherland' there existed 'a fitting opportunity . . . to place our inter-empire trade on a more lasting basis'.[30] Machin predicted that the empire would become 'more self-contained industrially and commercially'.[31] These communications entered, even initiated, discussion of trade relations in chambers of commerce and in the press across the empire. Thus, in Australia, the *West Australian* in Perth praised the 'commendable promptitude' of the BICC while the Newcastle (NSW) *Mining Herald* thought the circulars would 'receive wide publication and be debated in the press'.[32] The 1915 BICC annual report reproduced received extensive responses from the antipodes, South Africa, Canada, India, and the West Indies.[33] By then, a new assault had begun on Britain's long-standing adherence to free trade.

The wartime revival of protectionism and tariff reform in Britain has long been recognised. The veteran new liberal free trader J. A. Hobson wrote an extensive critique of what he dubbed 'new protectionism' in 1916, of which he though chambers of commerce to be leading instigators.[34] More recently, Andrew Marrison has charted the revival of domestic protectionism, not least in the chambers of commerce movement, although he places greater emphasis on the role of W. A. S. Hewins (Unionist MP, former Tariff Reformer, and chair of the Unionist Business Committee) than in the following account.[35] Frank Trentmann has argued the war not only revived tariff reform but altered the discourse: retaliatory tariffs designed to secure trading concessions gave way to a producer-orientated discourse focused on fostering key industries.[36]

The new protectionism reconceptualised global trade in response to wartime exigencies in ways underemphasised by Trentmann and Marrison but recognised by Hobson. In particular, as Figure 1.1 illustrates, new protectionism replaced the pre-war Tariff Reformers' partition of the world between the domestic, imperial, and foreign economies (the basis of schemes of imperial preference) with a more complex distinction between domestic, imperial, allied, neutral, and enemy partners, 'five concentric circles' (as Hobson put it) each to be given different levels of favour after the war.[37] Thus, new protectionism adapted the pre-war tariff reformers' tool of preferential tariffs, originally conceived to reconcile British and dominion protectionism with the promotion of imperial unity by economic means. It represented not only a reorientation of domestic political economy towards the producer, but the development of an economic means by which British and British imperial integration could be reconciled with membership of the kind of broader global liberal alliance described by Tooze. Even if, as free traders alleged, the idea of trading preferences legitimated a desire for protection, the means by which this legitimation had to be effected would remain revealing.[38] The war not only rebalanced

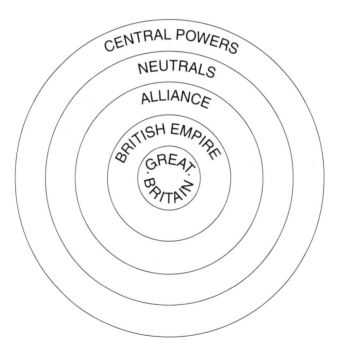

Figure 1.1 The New Protectionist Vision of a New Global Trading Order

Source: Hobson, J. A. *The New Protectionism*. (London: T. Fisher Unwin, 1916), 39.

discussions of political economy in Britain away from free trade, but in ways shaped by the moral hierarchy of war.

Chambers of commerce played an important and independent role in fomenting the new protection, including in developing its global moral economy.[39] As early as January 1915, the Barnstable Chamber of Commerce discussed the dangers of a revival of German competition after the war.[40] In April, in his presidential address to the ACCUK annual meeting, Algernon Firth expressed the essence of the global imaginary which would characterise new protection when he argued that, 'it was certain that the country would never agree to treat our enemies on the same lines as those who were our allies (cheers) nor would it consent that those who had rallied to the flag from distant parts of the empire should be treated as if not linked up to us by the same material ties'.[41] Such attacks on free trade remained controversial enough for the ACCUK to compromise and call a Royal Commission to consider Britain's 'fiscal system' given the 'conflicting opinions' of commercial men.[42] The discussion of trade after the war and the formulation of schemes of new protection became supercharged in autumn 1915. Rumours spread of post-war German plans to dump goods in allied markets. In November 1915, the ACCUK made representations to Asquith, McKenna, and Runciman to voice these concerns. In December 1915, the publication of the report of the Secret Congress of Central European Economic Associations in Vienna added fears of an exclusionary German-dominated trading bloc in *MittelEuropa*. Demands for a concerted allied countermeasures multiplied.[43]

The London chamber played a prominent role in devising mechanisms for a concerted pan-imperial and allied response to German economic competition. A special meeting of the chamber's governing council in November 1915 passed a resolution calling for 'a customs union between the British Empire, the Allies, and such neutral nations as may be willing'. Notwithstanding that 'such action would be contrary to principles of free trade', the customs union would be 'designed for the promotion of preferential trade between the contracting parties and in restraint of trade with Germany and her allies'. The sub-committee instigated extensive discussions within the chamber's subsections (which represented particular interests).[44] As a result, in 1916, the London chamber published three reports on trade after the war. The second report, published in May 1916, was particularly significant in offering detailed proposals to give effect to the principles of new protection through *ad valorum* tariffs on 'wholly manufactured goods', 'semi-manufactured goods', 'raw and manufactured foodstuffs' (raw materials were to be admitted free) which were to be levied at differential rates on members of the empire, 'present allies', 'friendly neutrals', 'other neutrals', and enemy countries.[45] Global politics and global economics were to be combined after the war.

In early 1916, the British chambers movement publicly committed to the principles of new protection. On 31 January 1916, the Lord Mayor of London and the London chamber convened a 'crowded meeting of businessmen' in the Guildhall which passed resolutions emphasising, as the Lord Mayor put it, that 'misguided relations' with Britain's enemies must never again be replicated. In particular, Lord Desborough for the BICC moved a resolution calling for 'closer co-operation with the dominions and allies'.[46] In early February, The Advisory Committee of the Board of Trade on Commercial Intelligence published a report calling for the protection of specific industries, while noting a strong desire for imperial preference.[47] On 23 February, the directors of the Manchester chamber of commerce (the great bastion of Cobdenism) resigned after members voted to reject a motion reaffirming free trade.[48] In early March 1916 the ACCUK annual meeting, attended by 500 delegates representing 100 chambers, passed resolutions demanding dialogue with the dominions on imperial preference and calling for:

(a) For preferential reciprocal trading relations between all parts of the British Empire;
(b) For reciprocal trading relations between the British Empire and the allied counties;
(c) For the favourable treatment of neutral countries;
(d) For restricting by tariffs or otherwise, trade relations with all enemy countries.[49]

Dissenting business voices such as those of the 'Manchester martyrs' could still be heard, not least in the pages of *The Economist*, but were a minority.[50] By the spring of 1916, new protection had become the dominant discourse within the British chambers of commerce movement. Bonar Law used his closing address meeting of the ACCUK on 3 March to announce an Economic Conference of the Allies to be held in Paris in June 1916 to discuss trade relations during and after the war.[51] The possibility that the British government would instigate the various elements of new protection seemed close. This naturally turned attention to the attitudes in the empire.

The Empire, New Protection, and the Imperial Business Conference of 1916

The global scheme embodied in new protection could not easily be adopted by the British government without the consent of the self-governing dominions of the British Empire: Canada, Australia, New Zealand, South Africa, and Newfoundland. Since the mid-nineteenth century, all had enjoyed tariff autonomy, and all had, by 1914, incorporated imperial preferences into their tariff schedules.[52] Moreover, the war had accentuated the pre-war conception of the dominions as increasingly equal partners with a legitimate voice in the governance of the empire.[53] This constitutional reality was recognised both by business lobbies and by the British government. The *Chamber of Commerce Journal* judged that dominion governments were, by 1916, clearly seen to have 'earned an indisputable right to share in the councils of empire'.[54] Thus dominion consultation, perhaps consent, was necessary if an allied economic bloc were to be formed on new protectionist lines. When a deputation from the ACCUK raised the subject of trade after the war with Asquith, the Prime Minister replied that Britain and the empire must present a 'united front in peace and in war' and hence it was necessary to act in 'concert with . . . our Allies and Dominions'.[55] In recognition of the interest of the dominions, the British delegation to the Allied Economic Conference included Canadian Minister of Commerce George Foster and Australian Prime Minister W. M. Hughes.[56]

Given the autonomous role of the dominions, those lobbying in pursuit of new protection needed to demonstrate support across the empire. The British Imperial Council of Commerce was the most prominent vehicle through which such pan-imperial support could be demonstrated. Although the BICC's London-based executive passed a resolution in February 1916 for a 'joint declaration [to be] made by allied nations in favour of a mutual economic policy after the war', a clear demonstration of support in imperial, especially, dominion chambers was clearly desirable on new protection as well a number of other wartime issues requiring discussion at imperial level (such as double taxation, shipping, regulation, and the treatment of 'aliens').[57] In October 1915, the BICC executive resolved to hold a smaller 'strictly business meeting', arranged to take place in June 1916.[58] The *Chamber of Commerce Journal* explained the necessity 'of ascertaining the views of Empire chambers' to ensure that there was 'no lack of preparation in responsible quarters for a decision on the practical issues which are bound to be raised on the termination of the war'.[59] The announcement of the Allied Economic Conference in June 1916 gave the proposed Imperial Business Conference a new significance.

The BICC executive made efforts to ensure the conference attained a high profile and was seen to be representative. The agenda was circulated across the empire in December 1915, and chambers appointed delegates, often expatriates resident in London. The agenda was extensively debated and overseas chambers communicated their views to these London representatives.[60] When the Winnipeg board of trade complained that Canadian representation was 'unable to carry the weight which the situation demanded', delegates from the Dominion Trade Commission (due to visit Britain under the leadership of George Foster) were invited to participate.[61] As Figure 1.2 shows, all sections of the Empire were represented at the conference, particularly the UK (with London providing about a third of UK delegates) and the dominions. BICC and conference president Lord Desborough described the conference as 'fully representative'.[62]

'New protection' dominated the first two days of the four-day conference. A memorandum by BICC chairman Stanley Machin explained that the '[fiscal question] while still inter-imperial has been widened by the obligation which the empire feels to its allies', continuing that 'the Imperial Government can only act effectively in this matter in consultation with the other Governments of the Empire'. Opening the debate, Machin

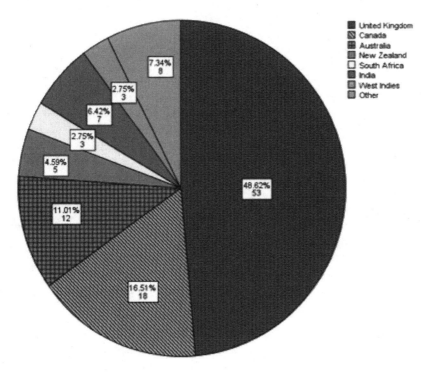

Legend:
- United Kingdom
- Canada
- Australia
- New Zealand
- South Africa
- India
- West Indies
- Other

48.62% 53
16.51% 18
11.01% 12
4.59% 5
2.75% 3
6.42% 7
2.75% 3
7.34% 8

Figure 1.2 Origins of Chambers Represented at the Imperial Business Conference,
by Number of Delegates

Source: *Imperial Business Conference Proceedings*, 1916, 1–5

argued that through a system of differential tariffs, it would be possible to 'build a system which would enable us to draw our Empire into one great whole though preferential treatment, to give the sympathetic treatment to our Allies which they had most justly earned; and that would enable us to treat benevolent neutrals in a fair and reasonable way; but above all, that would enable us to keep our unscrupulous and vicious enemies forever in their proper place'. Memoranda highlighted support for Allied preference from the Melbourne and Port Elizabeth chambers, from the Association of New Zealand Chambers of Commerce, and amongst the British expatriate-dominated chambers of commerce in India.[63] During the debate, Gilbert Anderson (for Canterbury, New Zealand), Edward R. Davson (West Indies), and Albert H. Sytner (Port Elizabeth, South Africa) spoke in favour of the position taken by the Machin. J. M. Woods of the Ontario Board of Trade (as chambers of commerce were called in Canada) offered Canadian support, explaining that the Canadian Trade Commission sought to increase Canada's trade with the empire but then to ensure that 'what they could not get from the empire should come from its allies'.[64] With dominion support clear, the conference endorsed the ACCUK resolution on Trade After the War in order that there might be (as Algernon Firth put it) 'uniformity in their demands'. The conference accepted this, with an overwhelming majority of chambers supporting the ACCUK position. Only four delegates dissented from the gospel of new protection. All did so in an individual capacity, without the support of their chambers. They were often criticised by former Free Traders such as D. F. Pennefather, MP and representative of the Liverpool chamber, who explained that 'the war had born them into a new world, and they must face that new world, and the new facts of it with fresh minds. They must obliterate all the old party catchwords'.[65]

The Imperial Business Conference of June 1916 revealed the degree to which, in business circles in Britain and the dominions, free trade had been marginalised and the degree to which the spatial imagination of tariff reformers had also been revised to differentiate allies, neutrals, and enemies. The conference endorsed the reconceptualisation of imperial preference to accommodate the global liberal order, embedding the empire in a broader global matrix and endorsing the connection between global trade and global power.

New Protection, Chambers of Commerce, and Imperial Policy: 1916–1918

By 1916, the basic principles of new protection and allied preference became the official position of the chamber of commerce movement. Thereafter, the focus of chambers associations shifted to the realisation of the goals of new protection in policy. The Imperial Business Conference achieved a high profile. It coincided with two major war events. It became a prominent venue for public mourning for Lord Kitchener, whose death prevented Asquith from addressing the conference delegates on 6 June. While speaking to the conference the next day, Arthur Balfour declared that British 'victory' at the battle of Jutland had ended the possibility of a German invasion. The conference's representative status was widely acknowledged, with press and policymakers considering it to be a major expression of business opinion. *The Times* argued that ministers 'in accepting invitations to luncheon' had 'recognised the importance of the meeting'. The views of the 'commercial world' had been 'expressed in the plainest terms'. 'The government', it continued, 'had not been unimpressed by all this and has been moved from the purely negative attitude first adopted to the Paris Conference'.[66] When W. M. Hughes (Australian Prime Minister) spoke to the conference, he praised the way in which delegates had 'cleared the path' and 'shown the way' on trade after the war.[67] After the conference, Desborough visited Asquith in Downing Street to discuss its resolutions.[68] The BICC executive sent the resolutions on trade to the entire British delegation to the Allied Economic Conference Delegation (Hughes, Foster, Lord Crewe, and Andrew Bonar Law) prior to their departure for Paris, as well as to Asquith, the dominion prime ministers, and the Secretary of State for India.[69] Certainly by mid-1916, British imperial policymakers could be in no doubt of the dominant thinking in business circles about the future of trade after the war.

The Allied Economic Conference of July 1916 recommended co-ordinated allied action against the Germans after the war. The conference seemed to demonstrate the influence of British new protection and of the chambers' campaign. The *Chamber of Commerce Journal* observed that the Paris delegates had made recommendations 'on similar lines to the Empire Business Conference'.[70] Discussion of new protection now moved into government circles. In response to the Paris Resolutions, the British government set up a Committee on Commercial and Industrial Policy, chaired by Lord Balfour of Burleigh, of which the *Chamber of Commerce Journal* complained that neither merchants nor representatives of the dominions were represented.[71] The committee deliberated through 1917 and issued an early pronouncement in favour of imperial preference in 1917, before publishing two reports in 1918.[72] Chambers of commerce featured prominently in the published evidence, and the final report directly quoted the ACCUK resolution on trade after the war (subsequently endorsed by the BICC).[73] The 1918 *BICC Annual Report* directly juxtaposed the resolutions of the 1916 business conference and the final report—that this was even possible suggests the correlation between official and business discourses on political economy. There were, however, differences in the details. Firth observed that the Balfour Committee was 'in general accord' with the 1916 conference but lambasted Balfour's 'timidity' in various areas, particularly on the extent of *post-bellum* trade restrictions.[74]

Increased contact and consultation between the British and dominion governments provided opportunities for chambers of commerce, through the BICC, to shape the political agenda at imperial level. In 1917, the dominion premiers were incorporated into an Imperial War Cabinet. Two Imperial War Conferences were held in 1917 and 1918.[75] The BICC lobbied for imperial preference to be placed on the conference's agenda on the basis of the interim report of the Balfour of Burleigh Committee.[76] Very few outside bodies were mentioned in the proceedings, making it all the more telling that in 1917, the Newfoundland premier called on the 1917 conference to get in touch with 'industrial bodies, such as chambers of commerce'.[77] The agendas of both conferences reflected areas of concern amongst the chambers. Desborough noted that the 1917 conference's agenda 'embodied so much of what the council had been advocating'.[78] In particular, in 1917, a resolution passed supporting imperial preference 'having due regard to the interests of our allies', although the details were to be finalised after the war.[79] Thus, new protection was thus cautiously endorsed at the imperial as well as the UK level.

By the close of 1917, the geopolitical tectonics underpinning schemes for trade after the war had shifted. In that year, the US declared war on Germany, and the Bolshevik Revolution ended Russia's involvement. US entry into the war had several effects on the global vision of new protection. First, it altered the matrix of economic calculations, for now the category of allied trade included a major source of British imports, and the most significant competitor of the dominions in British markets and of Britain in dominion markets. The reconciliation of domestic protection, imperial integration, and allied loyalty became less easy. Second, the global vision of embodied in wartime new protection ran counter the longstanding support of the United States for an 'open door' in trade, not free trade but equal and undiscriminating access to markets. The US entered the war as an 'associate power' precisely to avoid commitments to existing allied war aims and policy, including the resolutions of the 1916 Allied Economic Conference.[80] The US had a different conception of the alchemy by which global economic and geostrategic affinities would be combined. Indeed, in its continued advocacy of the open door in combination with protection, US political economy was in many ways less well geared towards reconciling global trade with the emergent liberal alliance described by Tooze than its British counterpart. The open door, like classic Cobdenite free trade, implied a much firmer division between great power rivalry and global economic exchange.

Nonetheless, new protection's global scheme persisted largely unaltered in chambers of commerce discourse. Indeed, the principles of preference and discrimination were increasingly to other areas such as taxation or shipping.[81] Possibly, the implications of American hostility were not yet clear. Often, little recognition was given to US associate status: in 1918, the ACCUK welcomed the US to the 'ranks of the allies'. However, *The Economist* well understood the contradiction between Wilson's position and the new protectionist schemata.[82] Only in the last year of the war were the assumptions of new protectionism even questioned in the London Chamber of Commerce. In a private memorandum, secretary Charles Musgrave observed that 'the defection of Russia and the accession of the United States has introduced a new factor which has yet to be considered'. Nonetheless, Musgrave judged it 'premature' to revise the 1916 recommendations, and concluded that 'as regards the British empire itself the case is stronger today than at any previous time'. He added that 'whatever may be determined by the Allied powers as regards their future commercial relations, freedom of action within the British Empire will doubtless be preserved'.[83] The last comment is telling. Musgrave assumed that Britain and her empire would remain free actors able to pursue an alternate political economy of Tooze's global liberal order.

The empire, and hence imperial political economy, remained sufficiently independent for an alternate vision of a global liberal order to remain plausible down to 1939. While British electorates pulled away from imperial preference in the 1920s, pressure from the dominions remained until a formalised system of imperial preference that was adopted at the Ottawa Economic Conference. The subsequent dilution of that system through bilateral deals in the mid-1930s with friendly powers including Denmark, Argentina, and the US itself was entirely consistent with the 'Empire first, friends next' approach embodied in the new protection of the First World War.[84] Only another world war, and the 1947 General Agreement on Tariffs and Trade, would finally delegitimise the heady combination of geopolitics and economics that suffused the new protection.[85]

Conclusion

British and imperial businesses were not merely passive respondents to the shifts in economic globalisation brought about by the war. Their associations, particularly the pan-imperial chambers movement, operated at the intersection of trade and politics and hence were powerfully placed to contribute to this shift in ideas of global political economy. Through their discussions of and lobbying on trade after the war, they were active agents in the remaking on of the economic mentalité of globalisation, reconstituting political economy in response to the war, in tandem with, or even in advance of, policymakers.

The outbreak of war initiated a reconfiguration of ideas about the political economy of global trade in Britain and the Empire. The world became redivided along the lines dictated by the outbreak of hostilities to produce a new moral economy differentiating trading partners between allies, neutrals, and enemies which complemented but also complicated the pre-war distinction between imperial and foreign trade. The war revived schemes of imperial preference, but also saw then reconciled with this new wartime dispensation. The device at the heart of Edwardian schemes of tariff reform, the preferential tariff, had evolved to reconcile the autonomy (and protectionism) of the dominions with a broader imperial allegiance. It was natural to extend this device to allies and neutrals who were not merely autonomous, but separate states. Indeed, the concern of preferential tariffs with the maintenance of economic independence made them perfect devices to weld together a desperate geopolitical alliance. This reconfiguration, which took place in the first half of the war, influenced and inflected policy discussions at the British and imperial levels from the 1916 Allied Economic Conference through to the end of the war. The confluence of British protectionism and preferentialism, which chambers of commerce did so much to facilitate and promote, persisted into the interwar years, finally climaxing with the creation of a formalised system of imperial preference at Ottawa in 1932 and in its subsequent revision.

This chapter offers significant support to Tooze's argument that the war reconfigured rather than undermined globalisation. As Tooze claims, British imperialism was indeed reinvented to become a component of a broader global liberal alliance; in new protection, we see the political economy of that reinvention working out in visions of future British trade. The shift began virtually from the outset of the war, reflecting both wartime culture and shifting patterns of trade, and by 1916, the new protection was framing policy discussions. Yet, new protection was a competing British vision of global order, one which was incompatible with the US doctrine of the open door. For all of Tooze's emphasis on British decline and US power, this vision of the British Empire at the heart of a global liberal alliance persisted through the interwar period, combining global economics and geopolitics in a distinctive manner premised on, and hence suggestive of, the continued autonomy (indeed significance) of British imperialism in this reconfigured but still globalised world.

Notes

1 R. Robertson, *Globalization: Social Theory and Global Culture* (London: Sage Publications, 1992).
2 S. Constantine, M.W. Kirby, and M.B. Rose, "Introduction: The War, Change and Continuity," in *The First World War in British History*, ed. S. Constantine, M.W. Kirby, and M.B. Rose (London: Edward Arnold, 1995).
3 For the classic statement, see A. Marwick, *The Deluge: British Society and the First World War* (London: Bodley Head, 1965).
4 J.A. Frieden, *Global Capitalism: Its Fall and Rise in the Twentieth Century* (London: W.W. Norton & Co., 2006), 127–54.
5 R. Hyam, *Britain's Declining Empire: The Road to Decolonisation, 1918–1968* (Cambridge: Cambridge University Press, 2006); A.J. Stockwell, "The War and the British Empire," in *Britain and the First World War*, ed. J. Turner (London: Unwin Hyman, 1988).
6 I.M. Clark, *Globalization and Fragmentation: International Relations in the Twentieth Century* (Oxford: Oxford University Press, 1997); M. Daunton, "Britain and Globalisation since 1850: II. The Rise of Insular Capitalism, 1914–1939," *Transactions of the Royal Historical Society (Sixth Series)* 17 (2007).
7 A.G. Hopkins sees the period after 1945, not 1918, as the period of major transition in the history of globalisation. See A.G. Hopkins, "Introduction: Globalization, an Agenda for Historians," in *Globalization in World History*, ed. A.G. Hopkins (London: Pimlico, 2002), 7.
8 J. Darwin, "Imperialism in Decline? Tendencies in British Imperial Policy between the Wars," *The Historical Journal* 23, no. 3 (1980); P.J. Cain and A.G. Hopkins, *British Imperialism, 1688–2000*, 2nd ed. (Harlow: Longman, 2001).
9 J.A. Tooze, *The Deluge: The Great War and the Remaking of Global Order 1916–1931* (Milton Keynes: Penguin, 2014), 6, 15, 375.
10 M.J. Daunton and F. Trentmann, "Worlds of Political Economy: Knowledge, Practices and Contestation," in *Worlds of Political Economy : Knowledge and Power in the Nineteenth and Twentieth Centuries*, ed. M.J. Daunton and F. Trentmann (Basingstoke; New York: Palgrave Macmillan, 2004).
11 Trentmann, Frank. "The Transformation of Fiscal Reform: Reciprocity, Modernization, and the Fiscal Debate within the Business Community in Early Twentieth Century Britain." *The Historical Journal* 39, no. 04 (1996): 1005–48 at 1008; see also F. Trentmann, "Political Culture and Political Economy: Interest, Ideology and Free Trade," *Review of International Political Economy* 5, no. 2 (1998).
12 R.J. Bennett, *The Local Voice: The History of Chambers of Commerce in Britain, Ireland, and Revolutionary America, 1760–2011* (Oxford: Oxford University Press, 2011), 3, 49–55. Membership could be motivated by ancillary benefits. See M. Olson, *The Logic of Collective Action. Public Goods and the Theory of Groups* (Cambridge: Harvard University Press, 1965).
13 J.Q. Wilson, *Political Organizations* (Princeton, NJ: Princeton University Press, 1995), 26.

14 Bennett, *Local Voice*.

15 A. Dilley, "The Politics of Commerce: The Congress of Chambers of Commerce of the Empire, 1886–1914," *SAGE Open* 3, no. 4 (2013).

16 John McDermott, "Trading with the Enemy: British Business and the Law During the First World War: Canadian Journal of History," *Canadian Journal of History* 32, no. 2 (1997).

17 D. French, "The Rise and Fall of Business as Usual," in *War and the State: The Transformation of British Government 1914–1919*, ed. K. Burk (London: Allen & Unwin, 1982).

18 *Chambers of Commerce Journal (CCJ* hereafter), January 1915, 1.

19 R. Roberts, *Saving the City: The Great Financial Crisis of 1914* (Oxford: Oxford University Press, 2014).

20 *CCJ*, September 1914, 289–92.

21 P. Panayi, "German Business Interests in Britain During the First World War," *Business History* 32, no. 2 (1990); J. Maltby, "Showing a Strong Front: Corporate Social Reporting and the 'Business Case' in Britain, 1914–1919," *The Accounting Historians Journal* (2005); J.-L. Robert, "The Image of the Profiteer," in *Capital Cities at War: Paris, London, and Berlin, 1914–1919*, eds. J. Winter and J.-L. Robert (Cambridge: Cambridge University Press, 1997).

22 The term was first used in E.P. Thompson, "The Moral Economy of the English Crowd in the Eighteenth Century," *Past & Present* no. 50 (1971).

23 A.R. Ilersic, *Parliament of Commerce: The Story of the Association of British Chambers of Commerce, 1860–1960* (London: Newman Neame, 1960), 174; Bennett, *Local Voice*, 607–8; J.H. Turner, "The Politics of 'Organised Business' in the First World War," in *Businessmen and Politics*, ed. J.H. Turner (London: Heinemann, 1984).

24 Quoted in Ilersic, *Parliament of Commerce*, 164.

25 Ian F.W. Beckett, "Grenfell, William Henry, Baron Desborough (1855–1945)," in *Oxford Dictionary of National Biography*, eds. H.C.G. Matthew and Brian Harrison (Oxford: Oxford University Press, 2004); *Times*, 19 February 1915, 11; ibid., 4 March 1915, 11; ibid., 1 December 1915, 11. On gentlemanly capitalism, see Cain and Hopkins, *British Imperialism, 1688–2000*, 38–50. But see also M.J. Daunton, "'Gentlemanly Capitalism' and British Industry, 1820–1914," *Past and Present* no. 122 (1989). On the London's power, see Bennett, *Local Voice*, 311–14.

26 A. Marrison, *British Business and Protection, 1903–1932* (Oxford: Clarendon, 1996), 232; Bennett, *Local Voice*.

27 Dilley, "Politics of Commerce."

28 D. Killingray, "The Empire Resources Development Committee and West Africa 1916–20," *The Journal of Imperial and Commonwealth History* 10, no. 2 (1982): 121–41; J.A. Turner, "The British Commonwealth Union and the General Election of 1918," *English Historical Review* 93, no. 368 (1978); W.K. Hancock, *Survey of British Commonwealth Affairs: Volume Two: Problems of Economic Policy, 1918–1939*, 2 vols. (London: Oxford University Press, 1942), vol. ii, 94–110.

29 *CCJ*, November 1914, 389; London Metropolitan Archive (LMA hereafter) CLC/B/082/MS18282/1: British Imperial Council of Commerce (BICC hereafter), *Annual Report*, 1915, 19–20.

30 Launceston, *Examiner*, 19 November 1914, 7.

31 *North Otago Times*, 5 February 1915, 7.

32 *West Australian*, 25 November 1914, 7; *Mining Herald*, 9 November 1914, 4.

33 BICC, *Annual Report*, 1915, 22–30; also *CCJ*, December 1914, 414–15.

34 J.A. Hobson, *The New Protectionism* (London: T. Fisher Unwin, 1916). On Hobson's thought during the war, see P.J. Cain, *Hobson and Imperialism: Radicalism, New Liberalism, and Finance 1887–1938* (Oxford: Oxford University Press, 2002), 202–06.

35 Marrison, *British Business*, 222 and passim. There is little direct evidence that chambers of commerce were as closely influenced by Hewins as Marrison implies.
36 Trentmann, 'Transformation of Fiscal Reform'.
37 Hobson, *The New Protectionism*, 38.
38 *Economist*, 21 September 1918, 360.
39 Cline's account of British post-war planning, as we shall see, wrongly characterises chambers of commerce as purely protectionist. See P. Cline, "Winding Down the War Economy: British Plans for Peacetime Recovery, 1916–1919," in *War and the State : The Transformation of British Government 1914–1919*, ed. K. Burk (London: Allen & Unwin, 1982), 163.
40 *CCJ*, March 1915, 102.
41 Ibid., April 1915, 252, 129.
42 Ibid., April 1915, 134.
43 Marrison, *British Business*, 228–31.
44 LMA CLC/B/082/MS16459/006: London Chamber of Commerce (LCC hereafter), *Council Minute Book*, 17 November 1915, 9 December 1915, 175–78, 180.
45 *CCJ*, June 1916, 151; LMA CLC/B/082/MS16459/007: LCC, *Council Minute Book*, 25 May 1916, 12–13.
46 Ibid., March 1916, 77–78.
47 Ibid., February 1916, 77–80.
48 *Times*, 24 February 1916, 5.
49 LMA CLC/B/082/MS18293: *Report of Proceedings at the Business Conference* (*Imperial Business Conference Proceedings* hereafter), 6–8 June 1916, Appendix A, 155.
50 See *Economist*, 8 April 1916, 673.
51 *Economist*, 4 March 1916, 442–43; W.A.S. Hewins, *The Apologia of an Imperialist: Forty Years of Empire Policy*, 2 vols. (London: Constable & Co., 1929), 65.
52 A.A. Den Otter, "Alexander Galt, the 1859 Tariff and Canadian Economic Nationalism," *Canadian Historical Review* 58 (1982); E. Sullivan, "Revealing a Preference: Imperial Preference and the Australian Tariff, 1901–1914," *Journal of Imperial and Commonwealth History* 29, no. 1 (2001).
53 W.D. McIntyre, *The Commonwealth of Nations: Origins and Impact, 1869–1971* (Minneapolis: University of Minnesota Press, 1977), 175–85.
54 *CCJ*, May 1916, 127–28.
55 *Times*, 8 March 1916, 6.
56 *CCJ*, May 1916, 127.
57 BICC, *Minute Book*, 24 February 1916, 74.
58 LMA CLC/B/082/MS18283/001: BICC, *Minute Book 1913–1927*, 20 October 1915, 68.
59 *CCJ*, 12 January 1916, 261.
60 Wellington, *Evening Post*, 7 January, 1916, 7; Launceston, *Enquirer*, 11 February 1916; BICC, *Annual Report*, 1917, 19; *Sydney Morning Herald*, 6 April 1916, 11.
61 BICC, *Minute Book*, 24 February 1916, 75–76.
62 *Imperial Business Conference Proceedings*, 8–9.
63 Ibid., 153–56, 169, 174, 180.
64 Ibid., 15, 17–23, 29.
65 Ibid., 31, 34, 40, 47, 58, 68, 71.
66 *Times*, 12 June 1916, 7.
67 *Imperial Business Conference Proceedings*, 137–39, 141–45, 150.
68 *Times*, 8 June 1916, 9.
69 BICC, *Annual Report*, 1916, 8–19.
70 *CCJ*, July 1916, 179.

71 Ibid., August 1916, 197.
72 CD. 8482: *Resolutions passed by the Committee on Commercial and Industrial Policy*; CD. 9034: *Interim Report of the Committee on Commercial and Industrial Policy*, 1918; CD. 9035, *Final Report of the Committee on Commercial and Industrial Policy*, 1918.
73 CD. 9035, *Final Report*, 39–40, 62.
74 BICC, *Minute Book*, June 1918, 22–23.
75 McIntyre, *Commonwealth of Nations*, 177.
76 BICC, *Minute Book*, 22 February 1917, 93.
77 CD. 8566, *Imperial War Conference, 1917*, 10.
78 BICC, *Minute Book*, June 1917, 94.
79 CD. 8566, *Imperial War Conference, 1917*, 7.
80 Tooze, After *The Deluge*, 15–16, 67.
81 *CCJ*, January, June 1917, 3, 145, May 1918, 120.
82 *Economist*, 10 August 1918, 175–76. See *CCJ*, May 1918, 119.
83 LMA CLC/b/150/MS16495/8: LCC, *Council Minute Books*, 9 May 1918, 47–48.
84 I.M. Drummond, *Imperial Economic Policy, 1917–1939*. (London: Allen and Unwin, 1974).
85 F. McKenzie, *Redefining the Bonds of Commonwealth, 1939–1948 : The Politics of Preference* (Basingstoke: Palgrave Macmillan, 2002).

References

Bennett, Robert J. *The Local Voice: The History of Chambers of Commerce in Britain, Ireland, and Revolutionary America, 1760–2011.* Oxford: Oxford University Press, 2011.

Cain, P. J. *Hobson and Imperialism: Radicalism, New Liberalism, and Finance 1887–1938.* Oxford: Oxford University Press, 2002.

Cain, P. J., and A. G. Hopkins. *British Imperialism, 1688–2000.* 2nd ed. Harlow: Longman, 2001.

Clark, Ian M. *Globalization and Fragmentation: International Relations in the Twentieth Century.* Oxford: Oxford University Press, 1997.

Cline, Peter. "Winding Down the War Economy: British Plans for Peacetime Recovery, 1916–1919." In *War and the State: The Transformation of British Government 1914–1919*, edited by Kathleen Burk, 157–81. London: Allen & Unwin, 1982.

Constantine, Stephen, Maurice W. Kirby, and Mary B. Rose. "Introduction: The War, Change and Continuity." In *The First World War in British History*, edited by Stephen Constantine, Maurice W. Kirby and Mary B. Rose, 1–8. London: Edward Arnold, 1995.

Darwin, John. "Imperialism in Decline? Tendencies in British Imperial Policy between the Wars." *The Historical Journal* 23, no. 3 (1980): 657–79.

Daunton, M. J. "'Gentlemanly Capitalism' and British Industry, 1820–1914." *Past and Present* no. 122 (1989): 119–58.

Daunton, M. J., and Frank Trentmann. "Worlds of Political Economy: Knowledge, Practices and Contestation." In *Worlds of Political Economy: Knowledge and Power in the Nineteenth and Twentieth Centuries*, edited by M. J. Daunton and Frank Trentmann. Basingstoke and New York: Palgrave Macmillan, 2004: 1–23.

Daunton, Martin. "Britain and Globalisation since 1850: Ii: The Rise of Insular Capitalism, 1914–1939." *Transactions of the Royal Historical Society (Sixth Series)* 17 (2007): 1–33.

Den Otter, A. A. "Alexander Galt, the 1859 Tariff and Canadian Economic Nationalism." *Canadian Historical Review* 58 (1982): 151–78.

Dilley, Andrew. "The Politics of Commerce: The Congress of Chambers of Commerce of the Empire, 1886–1914." *SAGE Open* 3, no. 4 (October 1, 2013): 1–12.

Drummond, Ian Macdonald. *Imperial Economic Policy, 1917–1939*. London: Allen and Unwin, 1974.

French, D. "The Rise and Fall of Business as Usual." In *War and the State: The Transformation of British Government 1914–1919*, edited by Kathleen Burk, 7–31. London: Allen & Unwin, 1982.

Frieden, Jeffry A. *Global Capitalism: Its Fall and Rise in the Twentieth Century.* London: W.W. Norton & Co., 2006.

Hancock, W. K. *Survey of British Commonwealth Affairs: Volume Two: Problems of Economic Policy, 1918–1939.* 2 vols. London: Oxford University Press, 1942.

Hewins, William Albert Samuel. *The Apologia of an Imperialist: Forty Years of Empire Policy.* 2 vols. London: Constable & Co., 1929.

Hobson, J. A. *The New Protectionism.* London: T. Fisher Unwin, 1916.

Hopkins, A. G. "Introduction: Globalization, an Agenda for Historians." In *Globalization in World History*, edited by A. G. Hopkins, 1–10. London: Pimlico, 2002.

Hyam, Ronald. *Britain's Declining Empire: The Road to Decolonisation, 1918–1968.* Cambridge: Cambridge University Press, 2006.

Ilersic, Alfred Roman. *Parliament of Commerce: The Story of the Association of British Chambers of Commerce, 1860–1960.* London: Newman Neame, 1960.

Killingray, David. "The Empire Resources Development Committee and West Africa 1916–20." *The Journal of Imperial and Commonwealth History* 10, no. 2 (1982): 194–210.

Maltby, Josephine. "Showing a Strong Front: Corporate Social Reporting and the 'Business Case' in Britain, 1914–1919." *The Accounting Historians Journal* 32, no. 2 (2005): 145–71.

Marrison, Andrew. *British Business and Protection, 1903–1932.* Oxford: Clarendon, 1996.

Marwick, Arthur. *The Deluge: British Society and the First World War.* London: Bodley Head, 1965.

McDermott, John. "Trading with the Enemy: British Business and the Law during the First World War: Canadian Journal of History." *Canadian Journal of History* 32, no. 2 (1997): 201–19.

McIntyre, W. David. *The Commonwealth of Nations: Origins and Impact, 1869–1971.* Minneapolis: University of Minnesota Press, 1977.

McKenzie, Francine. *Redefining the Bonds of Commonwealth, 1939–1948: The Politics of Preference.* Basingstoke: Palgrave Macmillan, 2002.

Olson, Mancur. *The Logic of Collective Action: Public Goods and the Theory of Groups.* Cambridge: Harvard University Press, 1965.

Panayi, Panikos. "German Business Interests in Britain During the First World War." *Business History* 32, no. 2 (April 1, 1990): 244–58.

Robert, Jean-Louis. "The Image of the Profiteer." In *Capital Cities at War: Paris, London, and Berlin, 1914–1919*, edited by Jay Winter and Jean-Louis Robert, 104–32. Cambridge: Cambridge University Press, 1997.

Roberts, Richard. *Saving the City: The Great Financial Crisis of 1914.* Oxford: Oxford University Press, 2014.

Robertson, Roland. *Globalization: Social Theory and Global Culture*. London: Sage Publications, 1992.

Stockwell, A. J. "The War and the British Empire." In *Britain and the First World War*, edited by John Turner, 36–53. London: Unwin Hyman, 1988.

Sullivan, E. "Revealing a Preference: Imperial Preference and the Australian Tariff, 1901–1914." *Journal of Imperial and Commonwealth History* 29, no. 1 (2001): 35–62.

Thompson, E. P. "The Moral Economy of the English Crowd in the Eighteenth Century." *Past & Present* no. 50 (1971): 76–136.

Tooze, J. Adam. *The Deluge: The Great War and the Remaking of Global Order 1916–1931*. Milton Keynes: Penguin, 2014.

Trentmann, Frank. "The Transformation of Fiscal Reform: Reciprocity, Modernization, and the Fiscal Debate within the Business Community in Early Twentieth Century Britain." *The Historical Journal* 39, no. 4 (1996): 1005–48.

———. "Political Culture and Political Economy: Interest, Ideology and Free Trade." *Review of International Political Economy* 5, no. 2 (January 1, 1998): 217–51.

Turner, J. A. "The British Commonwealth Union and the General Election of 1918." *English Historical Review* 93, no. 368 (1978): 528–59.

Turner, J. H. "The Politics of 'Organised Business' in the First World War." In *Businessmen and Politics*, edited by J. H. Turner, 1–19. London: Heinemann, 1984.

Wilson, James Q. *Political Organizations*. Princeton, NJ: Princeton University Press, 1995.

2 The 'Impact' of the First World War on Business and Economic Development in Sudan

Simon Mollan

I remember when lunching with Mr Asquith a day or two after the declaration of war, when I said goodbye, he said 'I want you to go ahead with the Gezira cotton growing scheme in spite of the war'. I was only too ready to do so but Kitchener thought it necessary on financial grounds to close down the work of building the dam, though we have made some progress in excavating parts of the main canal.

— Reginald Wingate, Governor General of the Anglo-Egyptian Sudan, to David Lloyd George, August 1916.[1]

This chapter considers the 'impact' of the First World War on international business and economic development in the Anglo-Egyptian Sudan from three perspectives. First, the effect on an important firm—the Sudan Plantations Syndicate—that operated in Sudan across the period; second, the impact on business-government relations; and third, how the delays to a large-scale infrastructure project changed the political-economy of the colonial state and in many ways conditioned the developmental trajectory of the country for decades to come. The chapter begins with a discussion of the historiographical context of business and economic activity in Sudan, noting the wider investment climate that prevailed before and after the First World War. The second section of the chapter examines the delays and rising costs of the capital-intensive infrastructure project to build the Gezira Scheme, and the changing role of the Sudan Plantations Syndicate, the Sudan government, and the Imperial government in London to the provision of capital for the project. The third section of the chapter offers a brief firm-level history of the Sudan Plantations Syndicate across the war years. The broader contribution of the chapter is to highlight that the First World War period was, interpretively, a liminal phase which seems to exist between two distinct and identifiable periods. In recognising this liminality, we can better avoid narratological and historiographical whiggism, a danger inherent in pre-supposing that the war must have had 'impact'. Indeed, as I will show, the main 'impact' that the First World War had on business and economic development in Sudan was to delay previously planned projects. As the actors involved (state and business) did not know how long the war would last or what the outcome would be, one of the mains effects of the war was to create stasis. As disabling as this was, I conclude that there was no sharp periodological divergence caused by the war or sudden change to the business environment. Rather, they were an artefact of the continuities and gradual changes of the war period itself.

Historiography, Chronology, and Sources

Classical theories of later British imperialism,[2] as well as later refinements of this genre (in particular, the work of Cain and Hopkins)[3], place an emphasis on the importance of capital export from Britain to the wider world to British imperialism, whether considered as a formal or informal process. There are a number of very well-known studies that explore the relationship between capital export and imperialism in the period to 1914.[4] The onset of war in 1914 is seen as epochal for good reasons in many fields. This is also true in terms of international investment, the history of which largely moves from traditional economic and business history (exemplified by the historical authors cited above) to the histories of colonial development.[5] This reflects shifts in the historiographical questions attributed to different periods. To oversimplify for the purposes of this chapter, the pre-1914 period is the era of the Gold Standard, free trade, and the organic and insatiable desire of the Victorian investor for new markets and the zeal of entrepreneurs for new opportunities. In contrast, the period 1914–1945 which followed was characterised by the retreat from the free-market ideal of the pre-1914 period, was pockmarked with crises and war, yet contained in the advent of colonial development policy the first early (and faltering) attempts at the conscious economic development of what became known as the Developing World. Crucially these attempts at colonial development were state-centred. I acknowledge that these are somewhat crude narratives of periodisation, but there is a strong sense in which they are widely adopted and, as such, obviously have merit.

It is also possible that as a result 1914 becomes an analytical dividing line, across which few studies seek to trace both continuity *and* change. Accepting for the sake of argument that the delineation articulated above does in fact indicate a change in the texture and nature of the international business environment, there is a place and need to examine how international firms experienced this change, before and after 1914. In this chapter, this will be explored by examining that the onset of war caused both delay and increased cost of the financing of cotton growing in the Anglo-Egyptian Sudan.

The historical interpretation I make is that the effect of the war was to increase the cost of borrowing, so inducing the colonial state to take on a closer and vital role in the provision of finance, creating a lasting bond (and tension) between British business operating in Sudan and the Sudan government. I then use this to examine the agential relationship between business and the colonial state. I argue (with reference to the case) that changes to finance were part of a broader change in the perceived role of business by colonial officials as well as interested businessmen, and that the war was a factor in changing this relationship. However, the pace of business and economic development in Sudan had not been rapid *before* the war. Colonies such as Sudan were sufficiently problematic as economic environments to mean that it is at least questionable whether economic development could have occurred without the intervention of the state. Finally, I use the study to comment on the impact of war (in general) on the structure of international business, something that has been only lightly touched on in the international business and strategy literature.[6]

This chapter is based primarily on archival research carried out as part of a PhD project. At the Sudan Archive at Durham University Library, the papers of Reginald Wingate (Governor General of Sudan) and the extant records of the Sudan Plantations Syndicate were used. At the National Archives in London, the Foreign Office files relating to Egypt and Sudan were used, and at Birmingham University Library, the records of the British Cotton Growing Association were also consulted.

Historical Context

Sudan was colonised by the British in 1898, establishing in 1899 the Anglo-Egyptian Condominium, which nominally and legally established the joint claims of Britain and Egypt over Sudan. This was, however, largely a fiction. Both Sudan and Egypt were run by the British and even after nominal Egyptian independence in 1922 British influence remained very strong over both countries. Specifically, in Sudan, the British were unequivocally in control of the state apparatus that they themselves had created. As in many British colonial possessions, attempts were made to develop the economy as means of paying for colonial administration and to sustain the imperial project there.

Initially, there were hopes that capital investment to develop the economy of Sudan would occur organically, reflecting many of the assumptions about late Victorian investment in the wider world. However, the failure of a number of mining enterprises in the early years of the century taught a brutal lesson to policymakers about the viability of business in Sudan, a sparsely populated and climatically harsh territory that did not offer abundant entrepreneurial opportunities.[7] By at least 1910—fully one decade after the establishment of empire in Sudan—the conclusion has been reached that without state support, commercial enterprise capable of economic development was all but impossible.

The one significant possibility that had emerged in the period before 1914 was to grow cotton. A pilot cotton growing enterprise had been formed, which by 1914 had established the credibility of growing long-staple

Egyptian cotton. This firm—the Sudan Plantations Syndicate (SPS)—had been formed in 1904 and was, structurally, a British Free-Standing Company in the mode of Mira Wilkins.[8] The firm was itself actually embedded into a broader network, consisting mainly of South African mining companies.[9] The delays caused by the war led to the disruption of the plans for widespread cotton growing based on the large-scale irrigation of a region (the Gezira; hence Gezira Scheme). Eventually, the Gezira Scheme became operational in 1924/25, with the SPS providing management.[10]

The Disruption of War: Finance and the Gezira Scheme

After formation in 1904, the SPS sought to establish whether commercial cotton growing in Sudan was viable. Initially, only a small area of land was irrigated, and a system of tenant farming was developed.[11] This was judged a success by 1909 and provided the operational basis for the management of the whole eventual Gezira Scheme.[12] By 1913 the company's board had concluded that a large-scale cotton growing scheme was feasible and were in the process of negotiating an agreement with the Sudan government to jointly develop the scheme.[13] In the proposed agreement, the company was to be given the entire management of the operational Gezira Scheme for ten years, with the possibility of a five-year extension.[14] Towards the end of 1913 the SPS began to invest further in the buildings, canals, agricultural implements, and ginning factories needed for cotton growing.[15] A "Government of Sudan Loan Act" was passed in 1913 by the Imperial Government in Westminster and amended in 1914.[16] This allowed three million pounds to be raised in a loan to be guaranteed by the Treasury. Initially, £1,300,000 was allocated for irrigation, while £1,600,000 was for railway building. This was later amended to £2,000,000 for irrigation and £800,000 for railway building.[17] This money was to be raised in the City of London by the Sudan Plantations Syndicate at three and a half per cent; in return the Sudan Plantations Syndicate was to be given control of the management of the Gezira Scheme.[18]

So it was that by the time of the outbreak of the First World War the SPS and the Sudan government had jointly formed plans to develop cotton growing in Sudan. At the last meeting held in the Sudan Plantation Syndicate's buildings in the City of London before the outbreak of war it was reported that both parties 'appeared to be mutually agreed on practically all points', and in January 1915 a meeting between senior government and Syndicate officials concluded by looking forward to resuming negotiations 'at the point where they were broken off' once 'normal conditions' returned.[19] Popular expectations, at least initially, were that the war would be short.

For the first two years of the war the relationship between the SPS and the Sudan government remained static and largely as it had been in 1914. In the negotiations that were suspended by the onset of the war it was envisaged that the SPS would be essential to raising capital on the London market to enable the Gezira Scheme to be constructed. The 'Sudan Government Loan Ordinance 1915' was passed by the Sudan government's Governor General's Council in May 1915.[20] This established that the envisaged expenditure for the Gezira Scheme was to be £2,000,000 for irrigation, £800,000 for railways, and £200,000 for contingencies.[21] The SPS was still to have a role in raising this sum from the London capital market. Meetings between the Sudan government and the SPS to prepare for development of the scheme continued, but there was little or no actual progress.[22]

In May 1916, the Legal Secretary of the Sudan Government—Edgar Bonham-Carter—reported to Reginald Wingate (the Governor General of Sudan) regarding proposals to update and possibly change the terms of the Gezira Agreement in consultation with Donald McGillivray, the Managing Director of the Sudan Plantations Syndicate.[23] Meetings in the early summer ensured that by the 23rd August the questions relating to the area and irrigation had been settled to the satisfaction of both parties, and SPS directors were told that it was 'practically certain that the Government would not insist on the Syndicate's obligation under the draft agreement of finding the original £500,000 at par'. McGillivray added that 'there was also every reason to expect that a full twelve years run, instead of eight years with a qualified option for a further four years would be granted'.[24] At the same meeting, it was reported that the Sudan government had referred to the Imperial government in London over the issue of the Loan Acts (1913/14) that authorised the loans that had not been issued. In October 1916 McGillivray was authorised by the Board of the Syndicate to offer the Sudan government £500,000 via two-year Sudan Government Treasury Bonds at seven and half per cent on the understanding that the Gezira Agreement was soon to be completed to the 'mutual satisfaction' of both parties.[25] While subscribers for this sum had for the most part already been found (the board reported), the SPS noted that their function in the loan raising process might change and the Imperial government might issue the money direct to the Syndicate themselves. In January 1917 the government rejected the offer from the SPS. The reason was that the position had changed, the directors noting that although 'the Syndicate might be invited to give their assistance towards finding the funds if required, it was understood that no financial responsibility of any kind would attach to them in connection therewith'.[26]

In a meeting to discuss the provision of funds under the Government of the Sudan Loan Acts held in the Foreign Office in late June 1917, Edgar Bernard, the Financial Secretary of the Sudan government, pointed out that the effect of wartime borrowing by the Imperial government in London had raised the interest rate for government securities with a Treasury guarantee. This, Bernard explained, necessitated an early decision as to how the Scheme was to be financed upon the cessation of war, though the Sudan government were also aware that the British government was unlikely to act until the war was over. The Sudan government used this meeting as an opportunity to point out that the other widespread financial effect of the First World

War—inflation—had increased the projected cost of the Gezira Scheme, the scale of which, they argued, should be increased in any case.[27] Thus, though originally the SPS planned to raise the funds, after the outbreak of war, they had made it clear that 'the rate of interest at which a private company could raise the necessary funds would be high and it would possibly be in the interest of the government, the Syndicate, and the cultivators alike that the necessary capital should be raised as part of the general Government Loan'.[28]

The Syndicate's *obligation* to raise £500,000 at par was finally cancelled in the summer of 1917 with the understanding that the SPS would help the Sudan government raise money in the City.[29] Subsequent discussions of finance were postponed on the advice of Lord Lovat—Chairman of the Sudan Plantations Syndicate—who insisted that the renegotiation of the Gezira Agreement needed to be completed before they proceeded.[30] At this point, the SPS evidently still assumed that they would be vital to the raising of capital at this time, offering to raise £500,000 in the City in light of the reluctance of the Treasury to make guaranteed capital available in wartime.[31] However, this offer was not taken up. In December 1918 another offer to raise capital on behalf of the Sudan government was made by the Syndicate; the government again declined.[32]

Throughout 1917, there were many meetings between the government and the Syndicate to agree the terms of the relationship, with an apparent intensification towards the summer and autumn.[33] In late June a meeting was held at the Foreign Office to discuss what was to be done about the Loan Acts that had been passed before the war, with representatives present from both the Treasury and the Board of Trade. The Treasury was relieved that the Sudan government did not require the money immediately, since all financial resources were reserved for the war effort.[34] Nevertheless, Bonham-Carter remained convinced that Sir Malcolm Ramsey, the Treasury's representative, was supportive and 'sympathetic' to Sudan's needs. The Treasury seems to have been genuinely keen on the plans to develop Sudan. Additionally, at a subsequent meeting, Sir Albert Stanley promised the Board of Trade's support to the Sudan government in any application to the Treasury to update the terms of the pre-war Loan Acts.[35]

In early October 1917 the Foreign Office contacted Reginald Wingate to inform him that Bernard would be required to attend a meeting with the President of the Board of Trade prior to plans for the Gezira Scheme being submitted to the Chancellor of the Exchequer.[36] Fredrick Eckstein (an SPS director) commented that:

> During the past summer, as indicated in the Directors' Report, the Sudan Government sent to the country eminent delegates for the purpose of bringing our Agreement with them up to date and also for the continuation of the Gezira district. I am happy to say that all our negotiations—and there were a great many meetings—were conducted in a mutually satisfactory and cordial manner, and that both objects

were achieved, so that the Sudan Government is in the position of continuing irrigation works.[37]

Central to these negotiations was the issue of cost. In July 1917 McGillivray estimated the cost of the capital requirements of the Gezira Scheme to be £840,000.[38] The civil engineer Murdoch MacDonald, who concurred, supported this figure. In the passage below, MacDonald lays out the significant items of cost:

All the calculations have been based on the assumption that there will be 100,000 acres of cotton in the first minimum scheme, 100,000 acres of green crop and 100,000 acres of fallow land. The necessary works were, as Mr Bonham-Carter has told you, to cost £2,000,000. As a matter of fact that was the original estimate which Lord Kitchener and myself agreed that the works should cost. The site of the dam had already been settled, and he asked me to examine the various proposals that had been put forward. I had to prepare an estimate for them, and the estimate was, as Mr Bonham-Carter said, £2,000,000. But at the time Lord Kitchener intended that the canal should be for only 120,000 feddans[39] altogether. His lordship intended, as the schemes went on, gradually to widen the canal, whereas in my estimates now before you the intention is to provide in the original figures for what Lord Kitchener intended to do as the works went along. That has rather increased them, and the total now, as compared with the original figure of £2,000,000 is £2,300,000. But we have spent some money already in starting and stopping the works and, as you gentlemen will appreciate, that is not a very remunerative sort of undertaking; if you are bound to lose something of the money dealt with in that way; so that I have allowed in all £2,550,000 thus the total cost of the dam will be £1,750,000 and the canal £800,000, or £2,550,000 for both. There are some smaller works which others will undertake. Those smaller works are field works including probably the provision of ginning factories and farm implements. £540,000 has been allowed for those, making a total altogether of just under £3,100,000. But interest has to be added during construction and until what is considered the paying stage is reached. In the figures that have already been given to you in the note that Mr Bonham-Carter referred to, you will find that the total has been put at £4,000,000. Practically £1,000,000 has been added for interest. £785,000 has been added for interest on the first item of page 2 in the note at the top, and lower down there is another item of £164,000 for interest. The £840,000 item is reduced by £300,000 as per the note below, so that really the cost will be about £4,000,000, or, if you add the amount of money which banking people would handle in a banking fashion to tenants, £300,000 the total would come to practically £4,400,000.[40]

However, estimates varied widely. One source estimated the cost of the irrigation of the Gezira plain to be £2,550,000, minor canalisation at £840,000; interest on both of the above before production stage was reached to be £950,395 with 'repayment to the National Bank of Egypt of the balance of the El Obeid Railway' at £740,000, bringing the total to £5,080,395. The Sudan government wished to repay the loan owed to the National Bank of Egypt because as a commercial loan, it could be called in with only six months' notice.[41] What was needed in Sudan—it was argued—was not the immediate provision of large amounts of capital, but a 'steady flow' to 'enable well considered schemes, which promise to be profitable, to be taken in hand, and carried through without unnecessary delays'.[42] Another source advised that the total capital required for the development of cotton growing in Sudan to be £6,600,000, comprising of £3,700,000 for irrigation of Gezira, Tokar, and Kassala, £2,160,000 for railway development, and £740,000 for the repayment of the debt owed to the National Bank of Egypt.[43]

However, by late 1918, the Sudan government believed that the overall cost of development was in fact much higher. Lee Stack, as acting Governor General of the Sudan Government, wrote to Reginald Wingate (by this time in Egypt as High Commissioner) to ask that the Sudan government should renew their negotiations with the Treasury for the amendment of the Government of the Sudan Loan Acts 1913 and 1914. Stack wanted to change the agreement so that the Treasury guaranteed the loans for 5½ per cent interest, that the repayment period was doubled from thirty to sixty years, with the overall cost of development to be some £9,000,000.[44]

Stack argued that though it was not the intention of the Sudan government to begin the process of development in all of the schemes, it was 'thought desirable to include them now in the schedule to obviate the necessity for a further application to the Treasury and the passing of a new act'.[45] Wingate wrote to Arthur Balfour, the Foreign Secretary, to state that he was in full agreement that the loan arrangements be changed in line with Stack's wishes.[46] The following month, Sir Murdoch MacDonald cabled the Sudan government to inform them that the estimates for the labour costs of the cotton producing development works were significant underestimates, possibly increasing the required amount by over one and a half million.[47] Indeed, the pressure from the Imperial government at this time seems to have been to ensure that the finance for the Scheme was fully costed and provided in full by any loan that was to be issued. A decision to reject an offer made by the SPS to raise £6,670,000 using the Treasury guarantee in December 1918 was taken in part because the amount was inadequate to fully fund the Scheme; it was also thought that to accept the offer would require new Acts of Parliament, and an additional worry expressed was that in order to meet the difference, money might have to be raised on the open market without a guarantee.[48]

In December 1918 it was reported at the SPS Ordinary General Meeting that 'the draft agreement, as far as we have been able to complete it, has this year been approved by the Sudan Government'.[49] This ratified negotiations between the two parties the previous autumn that had given the government increased influence over any changes to the marketing of cotton. In some ways this also marks a point at which it is possible to say that the government actors (the Sudan government and Imperial government) had reached ascendancy relating to raising capital for the scheme following a gradual process in that direction stretching over the war years. From this point onwards the role of the SPS in the Gezira Scheme was to be chiefly related to organisation, management, and the marketing of cotton in return for a share in the profits of the scheme.[50]

In January 1919 the National Debt Commissioners agreed to new bonds being issued to cover a sum of £500,000 advanced before the First World War, which relieved the pressure to repay the amount, due as it was in that month.[51] At the same time, the Treasury dealt a slight blow to the Sudan government's hopes of developing cotton growing in Sudan with a fully financed capital issue. Though the Treasury agreed to amend the Sudan Loan Acts from before the war, they only would do so by expanding the guarantee from £3,000,000 to £5,000,000. Additionally, they did not think that the markets in the City of London would find acceptable the proposed sixty-year period for the repayment of capital. The Treasury's justification was that 'in view of the pressure on the United Kingdom for capital expenditure on urgent reconstruction matters [the] Treasury note that it is not proposed to start works other than the Gezira Scheme now and consider that that the above provision should meet requirements'.[52] Stack responded, saying that 'the Sudan Government regret that H.M. Treasury are unable to see its way to making any application to Parliament at the present moment for authority to guarantee a loan amounting to £9,000,000 and that the Act now in question must be strictly limited to such a sum'.[53]

On the 11th of October 1919 the 'Sudan Guaranteed Loan Ordinance 1919' was passed, which approved that £6,000,000 was made available for the 'works of the Gezira Scheme including repayment of temporary loans raised under Government of Soudan Acts 1913 and 1915' (sic) which totalled £4,900,000, with £700,000 additionally allocated for development of the railway system in Sudan and £400,000 allocated for the irrigation of the Tokar region. Reuter's reported that this loan was floated on 20th October 1919.[54] The scheme was subsequently developed, opening in 1925.

The Impact of the First World War on the Sudan Plantations Syndicate

Evaluating the impact of the war on the SPS as a business needs to be set in the context of what the firm had been attempting to do in the years before 1914. As is indicated above, the SPS initially was central to the plans to raise capital for the Gezira Scheme, and though this fell away, it indicates part of the company's strategy of the preceding years. Headquartered as it was in the

City of London premises of the Wernher Beit/Corner House mining finance house, the SPS was organisationally connected with City finance—and many of its directors reflected this link. As such, then, in the years following formation in 1904, the SPS was a typical speculative investment vehicle of the pre-1914 era—the Classic British Free-Standing Company.[55] As a company, its function was essentially to develop an entrepreneurial project to the point where it became economically active. Thereafter, the company clearly intended to operate and manage any resulting cotton growing.

In order to do that the SPS had developed a number of pilot farms in Sudan. As a result, even in the war years before the Gezira Scheme itself had been established, the SPS did produce marketable cotton. The SPS began to produce enough cotton to sell on the world market by the end of 1913.[56] By early 1915, some 7,500 feddans were cultivated, with 2,181 four-hundred-pound bales of cotton shipped to Liverpool. Frederick Eckstein was able to inform the shareholders that:

> As regards our prospects for the coming year, I can see no reason why the present war should interfere with the cultivation of cotton. What the price of cotton will be, nobody can tell, but it must necessarily depend to a greater extent on the areas put under cotton in other parts of the World. Both America and Egypt plant early in the spring, whereas in the Sudan planting starts in mid-summer.[57]

By the beginning of 1917 the Syndicate had even begun to plan to extend the cultivated land.[58] However, though the SPS managed to consolidate the irrigation systems and cotton growing farms that were established before the war, in reality, they were engaged in little more than a holding operation during the war. This conclusion helps periodise the Syndicate's business history. To 1913/14 it proceeded on the basis of a close and (ultimately) supportive relationship with the Sudan government, with the likely prospect of the Gezira being developed quite quickly after the passing of the Loan Acts in 1912/13. From 1914 these plans went into abeyance, the prospects of success increasingly poor, albeit tempered by some consolidation of what had already been achieved. How, then, did this affect the internal governance of the firm?

From an operational point of view the war years were marked by gradual progress. In April 1915 the Syndicate agreed to sell all its cotton through the British Cotton Growing Association.[59] The process of moving cotton from Sudan to London was co-ordinated via the London offices of the Syndicate. They issued bills of lading whereby samples of the cotton were sent to the London office, while the consignments of cotton were sent directly to Liverpool. The cotton was sold there on behalf of the Syndicate by the British Cotton Growing Association, who used the firm of Kelly and Company as their brokers. The British Cotton Growing Association was also used to insure the cotton. Sudan cotton was typically sold in the market for Egyptian cotton (it being of a similar grade for the most part), but the Syndicate certainly examined whether it should be marketed as part of the American futures market.[60] In August 1916, it was estimated that the total forthcoming crop would be 3,800 kantars 'American' and 24,200 kantars 'Egyptian'; as a result, the Syndicate decided to hedge their position by taking futures on one half of the crop.[61]

However, the war badly affected the market for the Syndicate's cotton as the world price dramatically fell, so much so that by 1915, the 'market was practically closed.'[62] As Eckstein commented in December 1915: 'I regret to say that the bulk of our cotton was sold at the lowest prices ever realised by this Syndicate since we started growing cotton. This, as you will understand is entirely due to the war'. In July 1917, McGillivray commented that over the previous six seasons, Sudan cotton had been sold in Liverpool on average ¾d per pound above the price of ' "Fully Good Fair" Brown Egyptian'. This was an enduring trend in the performance of Sudan cotton in comparison with cotton from elsewhere.[63] By early 1918 as the prices of cotton began to rise, the Syndicate benefited accordingly.[64]

The SPS had been capitalised by a share issue on the London Stock Exchange. The balance sheet of the company indicates that the capital of the company grew across the war years (see Figure 2.1). However, these increases must be set against the inflation that affected sterling in this period. As the graph above shows, though the capital of the Syndicate increased quite markedly, its real value declined. In 1919 the capital value of the Syndicate reported on the balance sheet had increased to £498,687, but this would only be worth £210,361 at 1906 prices.[65] The capital position of the SPS was therefore weaker at the end of the war than at the beginning.

The SPS invested in infrastructure requiring significant capital expenditure in the years to 1914 (see Figure 2.2). This was largely spent on the

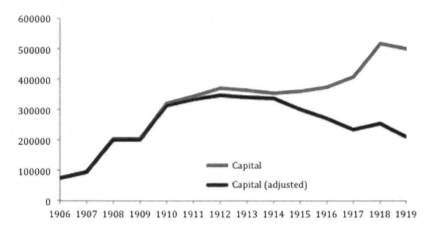

Figure 2.1 Capital (Balance Sheet) (£), Sudan Plantations Syndicate, 1906–1919. Adjusted to 1906 prices.

Source: SAD 415/8/1-152.

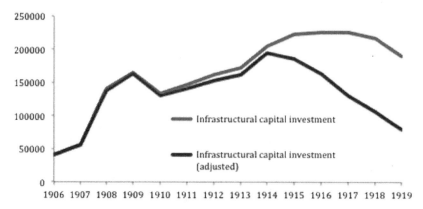

Figure 2.2 Infrastructural Capital Investment (£), Sudan Plantations Syndicate, 1906–1919. Adjusted to 1906 prices.

Source: SAD 415/8/1–152.

costs of the concession and the land, general development, buildings and furniture, canalisation, pumping installation, agricultural implements, and cotton ginning factories. Again, though the nominal value of that investment on the company balance sheet increased, inflation once again eroded the real value during the war.

Against the backdrop of a difficult international climate and depreciating capital asset values, then, the Syndicate sought to retain investor confidence by issuing dividends. Prior to the war the Syndicate issued a dividend in December 1913 of 12½%, and managed to issue a dividend of 5% in 1914 at the end of 1914 before the full disruption of the war and the collapse in market confidence was felt. In 1915 another 5% dividend was issued despite the continuation and increased intractability of the conflict.[66] There were no dividends issued in 1916 or 1917, but in early 1918, a dividend of 10% was issued; at the end of 1918, a 25% dividend was announced. Yet this should be seen as a sign of relative weakness, because the Syndicate made little profit in this period and could ill afford to haemorrhage capital.[67]

Conclusions

Before 1914 the Sudan government intended to work with the SPS to access the capital markets in London and as a means of providing business organisation and management to run cotton growing in Sudan. However, by the end of the war, the SPS was unable to undertake its financial role. The costs of the Gezira Scheme had escalated at the same time that the costs of raising capital in London had also increased. By 1918/19 only the state—in this case, the Sudan government acting in concert with the Imperial (British) government in London—could arrange the necessary long-term capital to finance the Gezira Scheme. As such, therefore, there was a financial reversal as a result of the war whereby the SPS was increasingly dependent finance put in place by the state. This inversion of the previous relationship was to shape the economic development of Sudan quite significantly and was to alter the government's long-term relationship with the SPS, who now became solely the providers of organisation and management relating to the Gezira Scheme. So this is *partly* a story about the relative decline of business in empire and the rise of the power of colonial states.

A further theme is the pressure that was brought to bear from Lancashire for more cotton, and the continuity of vision offered by the Sudan government to satisfy this need. In 1917 Arthur Hutton of the British Cotton Growing Association (and a director of the SPS) asked Murdoch MacDonald about the future viability of the project and the need to support the cotton industry in Great Britain, stating that 'Lancashire is likely to be hard pressed for cotton and one does not want to see any promising scheme delayed, if one can bring sufficient pressure to bear on the government to enable them to find the money'.[68] This view echoed that given by the British Cotton Growing Association as communicated to the Board of Trade in February of the same year.[69] As was the case before the First World War, the British Cotton Growing Association and other interest groups put pressure on the British government to develop cotton growing in Sudan. In February 1917 the *Financial News* reported that representatives of the British Cotton Growing Association and a host of other organisations[70] resolved that 'irrigation works for the development of the Gezira Plain should be pushed on with the least possible delay'.[71] This can be seen as the influence of a powerful corporate lobby, but it is also a plea for a kind of corporate welfare that is enabled by the assistance of the state.

The position of the Sudan government when representing their case to the Imperial government was that capital-intensive development backed by the state was the best way to ensure general imperial development and trade. As Bonham-Carter wrote of a meeting with Lord Balfour of Burleigh: 'I suggested to him that the best way to encourage inter-imperial trade as far as the colonies and protectorates are concerned was for the Imperial Government to facilitate the provision of capital for schemes of development'.[72] Edgar Bernard argued that the Gezira Scheme had already been begun and that the interlude of the First World War had been highly inconvenient but was not in itself enough to consider that the Scheme ought or needed to be re-approved: 'we have been delegated to come here from the Sudan and lay these schemes before the government, not as new schemes but with reference to their increased cost and the altered conditions for obtaining the necessary funds to finance them brought about by war'.[73] In this way, then, the developmental track of the Gezira Scheme marks a form of continuity, albeit one where the role for the state was intensified. The reliance on large-scale government-backed debt was to be the modus operandi for imperial development as a whole in the interwar period, and arguably prefigured the debt-development traps of dependency seen in the post-colonial era. In Sudan, the singular and unique relationship between the government and the Sudan Plantations Syndicate had tied the two together in an economic project which required vast and increasing sums of money, committed Sudan to development via one cash crop, and embedded and reaffirmed an increasingly symbiotic and interdependent relationship between business and government.

The effect of the First World War on business and investment in Sudan is in many ways a question what *did not happen* as well as what did happen, at least during the wars years themselves—as viewed through the evidence presented here.[74] In terms of economic and business development, the war was a period of stasis. Little was achieved. Yet at the same time, much changed in the power relationships that defined the relative positions and roles of business and the state. Conversely, the SPS was positioned to have a central role in cotton growing in Sudan before the First World War, and it maintained a central position in the cotton growing plans after the war. Indeed, the SPS eventually managed the Gezira Scheme until 1950. The 'impact' (which implies force and collision) of the First World War was therefore actually rather subtle: change *and* continuity. In the case of British business in Sudan, there was no *sharp* chronological dividing line formed by the war. Nonetheless, it is in the war years that the state-centred development model that dominated the interwar period can be seen slowly emerging. At the same time, the power and influence of British business overseas and the power of the City of London as a source of dynamic corporate entrepreneurialism and market-led finance can be seen—albeit dimly—to begin to decline somewhat. From the perspective of the story told here, the First World War can be seen as a kind of liminal phase of pause through which other, larger macro-structural changes to the international political economy of business and investment, indeed, of imperialism, can be seen for the first time.

Notes

1 Sudan Archive, Durham University Library (SAD) 112/5/8–10 Wingate to Lloyd George (Secretary of State for War), 14th August 1916.
2 John Atkinson Hobson, *Imperialism: A Study*, vol. 3 (London, 1902); Vladimir Il'ich Lenin, *Imperialism: The Highest Stage of Capitalism* (London: Resistance Books, 1999).
3 Peter J. Cain and Anthony G. Hopkins, *British Imperialism: 1688–2000* (London: Pearson Education, 2002).
4 Sidney Pollard, "Capital Exports, 1870–1914 Harmful or Beneficial?*," *The Economic History Review* 38, no. 4 (1985): 489–514; Mira Wilkins, "The Free-Standing Company, 1870–1914: An Important Type of British Foreign Direct Investment," *The Economic History Review* New Series 41, no. 2 (1988): 259–82, http://www.jstor.org/stable/2596058; Charles Harvey and Jon Press, "The City and International Mining, 1870–1914," *Business History* 32, no. 3 (July 1990): 98–119, doi:10.1080/00076799000000094; Desmond Christopher

Martin Platt, *Britain's Investment Overseas on the Eve of the First World War: The Use and Abuse of Numbers* (Basingstoke: Macmillan, 1986); Desmond Christopher Martin Platt, *Business Imperialism, 1840–1930: An Inquiry Based on British Experience in Latin America* (Oxford: Clarendon Press, 1977); Christopher Schmitz, "The Nature and Dimensions of Scottish Foreign Investment, 1860–1914," *Business History* 39, no. 2 (April 1997): 42–68, doi:10.1080/00076799700000050; Lance Davis, "The Late Nineteenth-Century British Imperialist: Specification, Quantification and Controlled Conjectures," in *Gentlemanly Capitalism and British Imperialism*, ed. Raymond E. Dumett (London: Longman, 1999), 82–112; Lance Davis and Robert Huttenback, *Mammon and the Pursuit of Empire: The Political Economy of British Imperialism, 1860–1912* (Cambridge: Cambridge University Press, 1986).

5 (For example, Fieldhouse, 1999; Havinden & Meredith, 1993; Kesner, 1981).

6 Morris Kalliny and Jane LeMaster, "Before You Go You Should Know: The Impact of War, Economic, Cultural, and Religious Animosity on Entry Modes," *Marketing Management Journal* 15, no. 2 (2005): 18–28.

7 Simon Mollan, "Business Failure, Capital Investment and Information: Mining Companies in the Anglo-Egyptian Sudan, 1900–13," *The Journal of Imperial and Commonwealth History* 37, no. 2 (2009): 229–48.

8 Mira Wilkins, "The Free-Standing Company Revisited," in *The Free Standing Company in the World Economy, 1830–1996*, eds. Mira Wilkins and Harm Schröter (Oxford: Oxford University Press, 1998), 3–66; Wilkins, "The Free-Standing Company, 1870–1914: An Important Type of British Foreign Direct Investment.".

9 Robert V. Kubicek, *Economic Imperialism in Theory and Practice: The Case of South African Gold Mining Finance 1886–1914* (Durham, NC: Duke University Press, 1979).

10 Mollan, "Business, State and Economy: Cotton and the Anglo-Egyptian Sudan, 1919–1939".

11 SAD 415/9/3 2nd Meeting of the Board of Directors of the Sudan Plantations Syndicate, 8th October 1904; SAD 419/9/13 9th Meeting of the Board of Directors of the Sudan Plantations Syndicate, 19th October 1905; Victoria Bernal, "Cotton and Colonial Order in Sudan: A Social History with Emphasis on the Gezira Scheme," in *Cotton Colonialism and Social History in Sub-Saharan Africa*, eds. A. Isaacman and R. Roberts (London: James Currey, 1995), 100.

12 SAD 415/9/40 Ordinary General Meeting of the Sudan Plantations Syndicate, 8th October 1908; BUL CGA 2/1/3 'The Sudan Plantations Syndicate Ltd and the Kassala Cotton Company Ltd and their work in the Anglo-Egyptian Sudan', (Reprinted from the 45th Annual Report of the British Cotton Growing Association, 1950), 3–4.

13 SAD 416/1/24 6th Ordinary General Meeting of the Sudan Plantations Syndicate, 18th December 1913.

14 SAD 416/1/16–17 98th Meeting of the Board of Directors of the Sudan Plantations Syndicate, 10th September 1913.

15 SAD 416/1/21 105th Meeting of the Board of Directors of the Sudan Plantations Syndicate, 4th December 1913; SAD 416/1/28 109th Meeting of the Board of Directors of the Sudan Plantations Syndicate, 30th January 1914.

16 Parliamentary Bill; (220) 1913 ii. 911 to authorise the Treasury to guarantee the Payment of Interest on a Loan to be raised by the Government of the Sudan; Parliamentary Bill; (271) iii. 97 to amend the Schedule to the Government of the Soudan Loan Act, 1913.

17 Parliamentary Bill; (271) iii. 97 to amend the Schedule to the Government of the Soudan Loan Act, 1913.

18 SAD 201/5/72 'Note as to the effect of war on the raising of the capital required for the Gezira Irrigation Scheme', 14th August 1916; SAD 416/1/17 Director's Minutes, Sudan Plantations Syndicate, 10th September 1913
19 SAD 416/1/46 Minutes of an adjourned Ordinary General Meeting of the Sudan Plantations Syndicate, 13th January 1915.
20 FO 141/633/6 Wingate to Colonel Sir Henry McMahon, High Commission, Cairo, 8th June 1915; E.E. Bernard, 'The Sudan Government Loan Ordinance 1915: Explanatory Note'.
21 FO 141/633/6 E.E. Bernard, 'The Sudan Government Loan Ordinance 1915: Explanatory Note'.
22 SAD 416/1/49 132nd Meeting of the Board of Directors of the Sudan Plantations Syndicate, 8th July 1915; SAD 416/1/55 137th Meeting of the Board of Directors of the Sudan Plantations Syndicate, 21st December 1915.
23 SAD 112/5/1 Bonham-Carter to Wingate 17th May 1916.
24 SAD 416/1/63 146th Meeting of the Board of Directors of the Sudan Plantations Syndicate, 23rd August 1916.
25 SAD 416/1/66–67 150th Meeting of the Board of Directors of the Sudan Plantations Syndicate, 19th October 1916.
26 SAD 416/1/66–67 150th Meeting of the Board of Directors of the Sudan Plantations Syndicate, 19th October 1916; SAD 416/1/80 155th Meeting of the Board of Directors of the Sudan Plantations Syndicate, 24th January 1917; SAD 112/9/2–8 'Note of Meeting held on 2nd August 1917 at Sir A.L. Webb's office between the Sudan Government delegates and the representatives of the Sudan Plantations Syndicate'.
27 FO 141/633/6 Memo: 'Sudan Cotton Producing Scheme' (14th August 1917), 2; FO 141/633/6 'Note on the Capital Required by the Sudan Government for the Gezira Irrigation Scheme and for certain other projects' (14th May 1917), 1–4.
28 FO 141/633/6 'Note on the Capital', 6.
29 SAD 112/9/43 'Note of Meeting held on 2nd August 1917 at Sir A.L. Webb's office'.
30 SAD 112/9/24–25 'Minutes of a Meeting held at the offices of the Sudan Plantations Syndicate Ltd on 11th September, 1917, between the Sudan Government Delegates and the Board of Directors of the Syndicate'.
31 SAD 112/8/21 Eckstein to Bernard, 12th September 1917; SAD 112/8/22 Eckstein to McGillivray, 12th September 1917; SAD 112/8/26–29 Bernard to Wingate, 14th September 1917.
32 FO 141/633/6 Telegram: Murdoch MacDonald to Keown-Boyd, High Commission, Cairo, 24th December 1918.
33 SAD 416/1/80 155th Meeting of the Board of Directors of the Sudan Plantations Syndicate, 24th January 1917; SAD 112/9/23–38 'Minutes of a Meeting held at the Offices of the Sudan Plantations Syndicate Ltd on 11th September 1917 between the Sudan Government Delegates and the Board of Directors of the Syndicate'.
34 SAD 112/8/1–2 Bonham-Carter to Wingate, 9th July 1917.
35 SAD 112/8/5 H.P. Hamilton, H.M. Treasury, to Bonham-Carter, 18th July 1917; SAD 112/8/1–2 Bonham-Carter to Wingate, 9th July 1917; the meeting was on 4th July 1917.
36 SAD 112/9/39 Foreign Office to Wingate, 3rd October 1917.
37 SAD 416/1/96 Ordinary General Meeting of the Sudan Plantations Syndicate, 20th February 1918.
38 SAD 416/1/83–84 McGillivray to Bonham-Carter, 4th July 1917.
39 A feddan roughly approximates to one acre of land, or about 4,200 square metres.
40 SAD 112/10/12–13 Sir Murdoch MacDonald quoted in 'Minutes of evidence taken before the Board of Trade Committee on the Growth of Cotton in the British Empire', 1st August 1917.

41 FO 141/633/6 Memo: 'Sudan Cotton Producing Scheme' (14th August 1917),3; FO 141/633/6 'Note on the Capital', 7.

42 FO 141/633/6 'Note on the Capital', 7.

43 FO 141/633/6 'Note on the Capital', 9. ·

44 FO 141/633/6 Stack to Wingate, 24th November 1918; £3,780,000 for irrigation in Gezira, Tokar, and Kassala; £2,160,000 for railway expansion, £2,310,000 for interest and £740,000 for the buyback on the National Bank of Egypt Loan.

45 FO 141/633/6 Stack to Wingate, 24th November 1918.

46 FO 141/633/6 Wingate to Balfour, 29th November 1918.

47 FO 141/633/6 Telegrams: Bernard to Stack, 5th December 1918; Telegram, Stack to Bernard, 6th December 1918; Telegram High Commission, Cairo, Egypt, to Foreign Office, London, 10th December 1918; Sudan Government to High Commission, Cairo, 31st December 1918.

48 FO 141/633/6 Telegrams: Murdoch MacDonald to Keown-Boyd, High Commision, Cairo, 24th December 1918.

49 SAD 416/1/106 Ordinary General Meeting of the Sudan Plantations Syndicate, 20th December 1918.

50 Simon Mollan, "Business, State and Economy: Cotton and the Anglo-Egyptian Sudan, 1919–1939," *African Economic History* 36 (2008): 95–124.

51 FO 141/633/6 Telegram: Foreign Office to High Commission, Cairo, 15th January 1919.

52 FO 141/633/6 Telegram: Foreign Office to High Commission, Cairo, 19th January 1919.

53 FO 141/633/6 Stack to His Excellency, High Commissioner in Cairo, 27th March 1919.

54 FO 141/633/6 'The Sudan Guaranteed Loan Ordinance 1919'; FO 141/633/6 Letter from Ministry of Justice, Cairo, to 'The Residency', High Commission, Cairo, 20th October 1919.

55 Mira Wilkins and Harm Schröter, *The Free-Standing Company in the World Economy, 1830–1996*, eds. Mira Wilkins and Harm Schröter (Oxford: Oxford University Press, 1998); Wilkins, "The Free-Standing Company, 1870–1914: An Important Type of British Foreign Direct Investment"; Rory Miller, "British Free-Standing Companies on the West Coast of South America," in *The Free Standing Company in the World Economy, 1830–1996*, eds. Mira Wilkins and Harm Schröter (Oxford: Oxford University Press, 1998), 218–51; Simon Mollan and Kevin D. Tennent, "International Taxation and Corporate Strategy: Evidence from British Overseas Business, circa 1900–1965," *Business History*, (May 2015): 1–28, doi:10.1080/00076791.2014.999671.

56 SAD 416/1/23 6th Ordinary General Meeting of the Sudan Plantations Syndicate, 18th December 1913.

57 SAD 416/1/45–46 Minutes of an adjourned Ordinary General Meeting of the Sudan Plantations Syndicate, 13th January 1915.

58 SAD 416/1/80 155th Meeting of the Board of Directors of the Sudan Plantations Syndicate, 24th January 1917.

59 SAD 416/1/47 129th Meeting of the Board of Directors of the Sudan Plantations Syndicate, 15th April 1915.

60 SAD 416/1/55–57 137th Meeting of the Board of Directors of the Sudan Plantations Syndicate, 21st December 1915.

61 SAD 416/1/64 146th Meeting of the Board of Directors of the Sudan Plantations Syndicate, 23rd August 1916; SAD 416/1/66–67 150th Meeting of the Board of Directors of the Sudan Plantations Syndicate, 19th October 1916.

62 SAD 112/9/4 'Confidential Memorandum No. 60 of the British Cotton Growing Association by J. Arthur Hutton to Under Secretary of State Colonial Office', 15th December 1915.

63 Mollan, "Business, State and Economy: Cotton and the Anglo-Egyptian Sudan, 1919–1939."
64 SAD 416/1/96 Ordinary General Meeting of the Sudan Plantations Syndicate, 20th February 1918.
65 All data here is deflated to 1906 prices. All conversions undertaken using EH-NET GDP-deflator: http://eh.net/hmit/ukcompare/.
66 SAD 416/1/22 105th Meeting of the Board of Directors of the Sudan Plantations Syndicate, 4th December 1913; SAD 416/1/46 Minutes of an adjourned Ordinary General Meeting of the Sudan Plantations Syndicate, 13th January 1915; SAD 416/1/54 136th Meeting of the Board of Directors of the Sudan Plantations Syndicate, 2nd December 1915.
67 SAD 416/1/94 159th Meeting of the Board of Directors of the Sudan Plantations Syndicate. 30th January 1918; SAD 416/1/105 163rd Meeting of the Board of Directors of the Sudan Plantations Syndicate, 10th December 1918.
68 SAD 112/10/21 J. Arthur Hutton quoted in 'Minutes of evidence taken before the Board of Trade Committee on the Growth of Cotton in the British Empire', 1st August 1917.
69 SAD 112/6/21 Cutting from *The Financial News*, 15th February 1917, 'Board of Trade's Encouraging Answer to Influential Deputation'.
70 The Federation of Master Cotton Spinners' Associations, the Cotton Spinners and Manufacturers Association, the Wigan and District Cotton Employees Association, the Amalgamated Association of Operative Cotton Spinners, the Amalgamated Association of Cord and Blowing Room Operatives, the Amalgamated Weavers Association, the Operative Cotton Spinners Provincial Association (Bolton) and the Chambers of Commerce of Bradford, Glasgow, Liverpool, Manchester and Oldham.
71 SAD 112/6/21 Cutting from *The Financial News*, 15th February 1917.
72 SAD 112/8/1–2 Bonham-Carter to Wingate, 9th July 1917.
73 SAD 112/10/28 E.E. Bernard quoted in 'Minutes of evidence taken before the Board of Trade Committee on the Growth of Cotton in the British Empire', 1st August 1917.
74 It is a considerable limitation that I have not examined here the human impact of the First World War on the SPS or Sudan government employees, or the Sudanese who worked on the pilot farms or lived in the communities that the SPS's business activities touched.

Bibliography

Bernal, Victoria. "Cotton and Colonial Order in Sudan: A Social History with Emphasis on the Gezira Scheme." In *Cotton Colonialism and Social History in Sub-Saharan Africa*, edited by A. Isaacman and R. Roberts, 96–118. London: James Currey, 1995.

Cain, Peter J., and Anthony G. Hopkins. *British Imperialism: 1688–2000*. London: Pearson Education, 2002.

Davis, Lance. "The Late Nineteenth-Century British Imperialist: Specification, Quantification and Controlled Conjectures." In *Gentlemanly Capitalism and British Imperialism*, edited by Raymond E. Dumett, 82–112. London: Longman, 1999.

Davis, Lance, and Robert Huttenback. *Mammon and the Pursuit of Empire: The Political Economy of British Imperialism, 1860–1912*. Cambridge: Cambridge University Press, 1986.

Fieldhouse, David Kenneth. *The West and the Third World: Trade, Colonialism, Dependence, and Development.* Oxford: Blackwell, 1999.

Frimpong, Yaw, Jacob Oluwoye, and Lynn Crawford. "Causes of Delay and Cost Overruns in Construction of Groundwater Projects in a Developing Countries; Ghana as a Case Study." *International Journal of Project Management* 21, no. 5 (2003): 321–26.

Harvey, Charles, and Jon Press. "The City and International Mining, 1870–1914." *Business History* 32, no. 3 (July 1990): 98–119. doi:10.1080/00076799000000094.

Havinden, Michael Ashley, and David George Meredith. *Colonialism and Development: Britain and Its Tropical Colonies 1850–1960.* London: Routledge, 1993.

Hobson, John Atkinson. *Imperialism: A Study.* Vol. 3. London, 1902.

Kalliny, Morris, and Jane LeMaster. "Before You Go You Should Know: The Impact of War, Economic, Cultural, and Religious Animosity on Entry Modes." *Marketing Management Journal* 15, no. 2 (2005): 18–28.

Kesner, Richard M. *Economic Control and Colonial Development: Crown Colony Financial Management in the Age of Joseph Chamberlain.* Oxford: Clio Press, 1981.

Kubicek, Robert V. *Economic Imperialism in Theory and Practice: The Case of South African Gold Mining Finance 1886–1914.* Durham, NC: Duke University Press, 1979.

Lenin, Vladimir Il'ich. *Imperialism: The Highest Stage of Capitalism.* London: Resistance Books, 1999.

Miller, Rory. "British Free-Standing Companies on the West Coast of South America." In *The Free Standing Company in the World Economy, 1830–1996,* edited by Mira Wilkins and Harm Schröter, 218–51. Oxford: Oxford University Press, 1998.

Mollan, Simon. "Business Failure, Capital Investment and Information: Mining Companies in the Anglo-Egyptian Sudan, 1900–13." *The Journal of Imperial and Commonwealth History* 37, no. 2 (2009): 229–48.

———. "Business, State and Economy: Cotton and the Anglo-Egyptian Sudan, 1919–1939." *African Economic History* 36 (2008): 95–124.

Mollan, Simon, and Kevin D. Tennent. "International Taxation and Corporate Strategy: Evidence from British Overseas Business, circa 1900–1965." *Business History* (May 2015): 1–28. doi:10.1080/00076791.2014.999671.

Platt, Desmond Christopher Martin. *Britain's Investment Overseas on the Eve of the First World War: The Use and Abuse of Numbers.* Basingstoke: Macmillan, 1986.

———. *Business Imperialism, 1840–1930: An Inquiry Based on British Experience in Latin America.* Oxford: Clarendon Press, 1977.

Pollard, Sidney. "Capital Exports, 1870–1914 Harmful or Beneficial?*" *The Economic History Review* 38, no. 4 (1985): 489–514.

Schmitz, Christopher. "The Nature and Dimensions of Scottish Foreign Investment, 1860–1914." *Business History* 39, no. 2 (April 1997): 42–68. doi:10.1080/00076799700000050.

Stewart, Frances. "War and Underdevelopment: Can Economic Analysis Help Reduce the Costs?" *Journal of International Development* 5, no. 4 (1993): 357–80.

Wilkins, Mira. "The Free-Standing Company Revisited." In *The Free Standing Company in the World Economy, 1830–1996,* edited by Mira Wilkins and Harm Schröter, 3–66. Oxford: Oxford University Press, 1998.

———. "The Free-Standing Company, 1870–1914: An Important Type of British Foreign Direct Investment." *The Economic History Review* New Series 41, no. 2 (1988): 259–82. http://www.jstor.org/stable/2596058.

Wilkins, Mira, and Harm Schröter. *The Free-Standing Company in the World Economy, 1830–1996*. Edited by Mira Wilkins and Harm Schröter. Oxford: Oxford University Press, 1998.

3 Profiting Despite the Great War
Argentina's Grain Multinationals

Phillip Dehne

The First World War transformed many aspects of global commerce, but no trade transformed exactly like the global trade in food. Western European countries had run food deficits for decades as the transatlantic trade grew in the late Victorian period. As a commodity that none of the belligerents could live without, food supplies gained a new strategic importance during the war.[1] As the war progressed, food for Britain, France, and Italy continued to pour in from across the Atlantic, much of it from the United States and Canada, but with significant amounts from Argentina.

The most important of the large companies that controlled the highly profitable Argentine trade identified as German and thus attracted the attention of those in charge of Britain's "blockade"—in twenty-first century terms, Britain's economic war. This chapter shows how, despite facing the opprobrium of the government and business community of Great Britain, the greatest commercial power of the day and one with tremendous traditional influence in Argentina, the giant grain trading companies like Bunge & Born and Weil Hermanos continued to operate and profit in neutral Argentina throughout the war. To do so, they utilized classic business strategies of diversification, vertical integration, and government lobbying. Each also needed to follow wartime strategies of chicanery and subterfuge to avoid the Entente's coalition economic sanctions. In at least the case of Bunge & Born, changes mandated by wartime circumstance led the company to permanently shift its center from Europe to Argentina.

In helping to describe the wartime resilience and innovation of these German-tainted grain multinationals, this chapter utilizes the concept of Global Value Chains (GVCs). GVCs are the long-distance connections between creators and consumers, with each step of production, development, financing, and marketing a different link in the chain. Historians of Latin America have fruitfully utilized the idea of commodity chains when discussing the export trade of certain Latin American products like coffee, nitrates, and rubber, in which specific Latin American countries (at least for a time) held global supply dominance.[2] Depending on the product and the period, commodity chains can consist of many companies at a variety of places on the chain, or just a few. Theorists of Global Value Chains identify five different forms of "chain governance" under which the flow of trade occurs, with governance becoming more centralized as one moves from market, to modular, to relational, to captive, and finally, to hierarchical structures.[3] Following the instincts of historical literature on fin de siècle imperialism and dependency, the Global Value Chain perspective traditionally focuses on the imbalances between center and periphery, and the dominance of Global North companies (and consumers) over the producers of primary goods in the Global South.[4] Many writers on GVCs focus on the expansion of "lead firms" headquartered and run from a developed country, strongly vertically integrated throughout the links of the chain, and dominant in both power and value creation over peripheral producers. However, recent writers describing commodity chains in Latin America have become more flexible in their sense of power relations, seeing constant transformation in the variety of increasingly capitalist markets for various goods, a flexibility that some have termed Global Production Networks rather than the more nefarious-sounding Global Value Chains.[5] This chapter indicates ways that the German grain giants used the opportunities and demands created by the war to dominate new links of the transformed but not shattered transatlantic wheat value chain. While creating new networks of trade within Argentina and with other countries in the region, the war caused lead firms like Bunge & Born to permanently shift their organizations away from Europe. By explaining how the First World War affected the operations of these companies, this chapter shows how the history of globalization spans, rather than breaks, during the war years.

* * *

In the standard view of the history of globalization, the First World War abruptly halted and then rolled back the century-long trend of constantly expanding free trade and the internationalization of markets for goods and finance, a global economic and cultural integration that resulted from the West's industrial revolution. The idea of 1914 as the pivotal moment between globalization and non-globalization was supported by the apparently sharp post-war transformation in European politics and economics. On the left, many believed that capitalism and internationalization during the fin de siècle fed an imperialist march to war, but more broadly, the war provoked a widespread backlash against "pre-war beliefs and assumptions" that at their most extreme rejected free-market capitalism as either fragile or immoral.[6] From this perspective, the fracturing of free-market globalization during the Great War fed into the anti-globalization movements of the 1930s embodied in the quests of Hitler and Stalin for imperial autarky.[7] Similarly in South America, according to Bill Albert, during the Great War more "insidious" controls by foreign governments brought an abrupt end to an era of free trade, which in turn created a backlash that created significant support for a fundamentally anti-globalization politics during and after the war.[8]

However, more recently, some historians have stressed ways that 1914 transformed globalization rather than destroying it. Adam Tooze argues that the war pushed economic globalization into a different form of politics, one neither fascist nor communist, but rather internationalist. The successful experiences of coalition warfare, combining controls of strategic resources (in particular shipping and food purchasing) bred the possibility that in the future, similar international cooperation focused on the health of the economies of all the states might become the norm.[9] On the level of commerce in specific industries or trades, one can perceive the war "as a story of progressions and mutations" rather than as an abrupt interruption.[10] Michael Miller has shown that from the perspective of global maritime trade, the First World War both stimulated "greater globalism in multiple ways" and "confirmed the interconnectedness of trade."[11] In the words of Steven Topik and Allen Wells, for the global economy as a whole between 1914–1945 "the organizational structures—the sinews—for trade and new technologies remained."[12]

Historians of the Argentine wheat trade have fit it into the paradigm of 1914 as the fundamental end to globalization. On what is often perceived as the periphery of the world system of global trade that boomed in the decades before the war, Argentina seemed under the control of global (and particularly London-based) capitalists, including banks, investors, and international merchants.[13] In 1914, the very existence of the Argentine grain trade, and the country's trade in food in general, was a relatively recent phenomenon, part of the expansion of global grain and meat markets in the late nineteenth century. The vast pampas of lightly populated Argentina had long appeared a potential breadbasket for the Old World, but the country only began significant wheat production in the 1890s after railways developed to connect the fertile hinterlands with Argentina's ports and ships were built to send the food abroad inexpensively.[14] These networks also encouraged immigrants to come from southern Europe to work on Argentine farms.[15] When it came to grain exports from Argentina, by the early twentieth century, a handful of firms headquartered in European states directed the lucrative chain of transactions between Argentina's farmers and purchasers in Europe. By 1914, such European-based companies loaned funds to farmers across the pampas, signed the long-term shipping agreements that made the railways in Argentina such successful investments, borrowed and invested money with the European banks in Argentina, hired the ships from the various European-based owners, and lined up wholesale buyers in Europe.[16]

And then the Great War hit, directly and immediately affecting this grain trade and these multinational companies. Jeremy Adelman finishes his illuminating comparative history of Canadian and Argentine wheat farming at the "termination date" of 1914, when the war "signaled at least a temporary end of the era of free trade in grains."[17] In the ensuing war years, according to Roger Gravil, the structures and directions of the Argentine grain trade lost all characteristics of free trade, coming fully under the domination of foreign governments. Gravil argues that the British were able to crush the participation of Germans in the Argentine trade through blacklisting efforts in that restricted access of these companies to British shipping and finance in 1916, and through their eventual official takeover of grain purchasing and the coercion of a favorable loan from the Argentine government to finance the shipment of wheat to Europe.[18]

The grain giants attacked by the British were a type of multinational company perhaps unique to that trade. By 1914, grain was among the most global of businesses, with tremendous competition between buyers and sellers around the world and with very low differentials between prices from one place to another.[19] The grain multinationals of Argentina were not "free-standing companies" set up in Europe to take advantage of specific investment opportunities abroad. Rather these firms had undertaken trade within Europe before they expanded their operations abroad. The canny late-nineteenth-century decisions of Weil Brothers and Bunge & Born to conduct business in Argentina took advantage of their skills in marketing and networking, fitting these companies into the classic definition of multinational enterprises.[20] According to Michael Miller, in the Argentine grain trade, "nearly all the largest firms were highly cosmopolitan," incorporated in one country, but with offices in a variety of European and South American cities, often led by partners and managers from multinational families.[21] The grain giants were privately held, a company structure that remains surprisingly common in the global grain trade even a hundred years later, and which in this case does not seem to have bred entrepreneurial stagnation as it did in some other sectors during the early twentieth century. But as a result of their structure, looking at the operations of these companies is not as easy as one might imagine. Bunge & Born still operates in Argentina, and indeed, after the Great War developed into the company that more than any other marked Argentina's twentieth century, but it has long been an intensely private company owned by a handful of families and does not ordinarily permit access to its archives.[22] As a result, it is uncertain what records they hold from the 1914–18 era, but it might not be much. South America is a region notorious among business historians for the evaporation of early-twentieth-century company archives.[23] Instead, this chapter utilizes a body of sources generated by the British government and in particular by its legation and consular officials in Argentina, and also by the British Chamber of Commerce in Buenos Aires. These Britons were probably the people paying the most attention to these companies' activities during the war, and although they were perhaps in some cases prone to paranoia about the activities of Germans in Argentina, among them were men like the British minister in Buenos Aires, Sir Reginald Tower, and others capable of gathering real evidence and coming to rational and realistic conclusions about the wartime activities of these grain companies. From this outside perspective we can get a suggestive description of the ways these multinational companies operated during the war.

On the face of it, the grain commodity chain in Argentina looked much like those in other South American primary exports, such as Peruvian guano and Chilean nitrates, a hierarchical GVC dominated by foreign-based merchant companies that controlled the critical knowledge and credit networks sending the goods overseas. In these trades, exporters in South America were simply the agents of North American and European-based importers who traded in various producing countries and set the prices. But the Argentine grain trade was more advanced and complicated than Chilean nitrates or Brazilian rubber, and had traditionally much less government intervention than Chile in its nitrates or Brazil in its coffee. Argentine grains also faced a world market with far less elasticity in demand than that for optional (?!) coffee.[24] In Argentine grains there were complicated local futures markets in both Rosario and Buenos Aires through which merchants in each city bought and sold grain destined for local consumers. Virtually untouched by the grain multinationals before 1914, the futures markets provided a significant alternative grain market to the one focused on the export trade.[25]

European-headquartered companies like Bunge & Born, Weil Hermanos, Louis Dreyfus & Company, and General Mercantile Company spent the decade before the war expanding into different activities down the Argentine links in the wheat commodity chain. These huge grain exporters began to finance and direct some of the purchasing agents (*acopiadores*) strung along the railway lines who purchased from the farmers. They made long-term contracts with the railways for discounted freight fares and contracted with international steam lines and tramp steamers on both long-term and spot bases in the huge ports of the Rio de la Plata. They controlled large amounts of their own capital (Bunge & Born had perhaps £2 million of its own capital in Argentina by 1914) and also could access significant credit lines at all of the European and British banks and the Argentine Banco de la Nación.[26] They took great advantage of the laying of transoceanic cables across the Atlantic, which enabled buyers in London and Europe to direct grain-laden ships from one port to another. They sent ships "to orders" from Argentina to the mid-Atlantic pit stop of St. Helena, where telegraphed orders enabled the European-based companies to take advantage of divergences in local grain prices, an action that in turn helped to even out global food prices and create a truly global market for food. Command of such new communications technologies "smoothed the ascent" of such big businesses around the world in the late nineteenth century, enabling them to either cut out or more closely direct the middlemen.[27]

After the war began in August 1914, the global wheat trade remained centered on fulfilling the needs of European consumers, whose demand for overseas food grew as the agricultural output of war-torn Europe shrunk. Throughout at least the end of 1915, the grain multinationals in Argentina continued to made profits simply by continuing to send their grain to

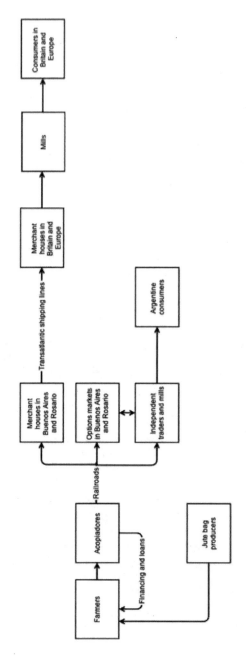

Figure 3.1 Wheat Commodity Chain in Argentina Before 1914

Europe and Britain. Due to the long-term contracts they had signed with a variety of shipping lines before the war, the German-leaning companies controlled perhaps as much as 75% of the shipments bound for Britain in 1915.[28] During 1915, they also opened up vast direct trade with countries that had never before imported Argentine grain. Bunge & Born and General Mercantile Co. concluded transactions of an astonishing quarter million tons of maize per month in mid-1915 with neutral Scandinavian ports; assumedly, it would be shipped hence to Germany.[29] The war was changing other aspects of these companies' transatlantic nature. European home offices of these Argentine grain firms were now in German-occupied territory (both Bunge & Born and Weil Brothers were headquartered in Belgium, although the latter held significant direct family connections to Frankfurt).[30] Their European offices were thus cut off from communicating freely with Argentina via British-owned transatlantic telegraphy or even by the much slower mails, which were now easily intercepted by the British blockade authorities, who controlled the sea passages from Europe.

The physical barriers of the front lines and the British blockade were enhanced by financial and commercial sanctions placed on these companies in February 1916, when the British government issued its first Statutory Blacklist of enemy companies in neutral American states. The Statutory List economic warfare program cut off these companies' access to Allied banking and merchant shipping, which seemed the most pivotal and lucrative links in the commodity chain, by the end of that year. In a final blow to these companies simply continuing "business as usual," the Entente openly jettisoned its own free markets in a wide variety of things in 1916, from commodities like meat and grains to services like shipping and banking. To ensure continued food for their armies and civilians, in late 1916, the British centralized their control of national grain purchases and also began developing interallied control of British, French, and Italian flagged shipping, parceling out shipping space to their strategic priorities.[31] When it was created in October 1916, the Royal Commission on Wheat Supplies initially made purchases through existing Allied cereal firms. Then at the end of 1917, the Royal Commission appointed a Resident Commissioner (the Anglo-Argentine ranch magnate Herbert Gibson), who undertook purchases at set minimum prices that were publicized to the farmers, but with sales through Allied firms as buying agencies.[32] The British firms, once rivals whose overall business had been dwarfed by the huge German-led companies, now became buying agencies with the prices offered by the Commission publicized directly to farmers rather than set through competition between the different *acopiadores* and trading companies. In publicly setting prices they would pay to farmers, the British Wheat Commission attempted to compete with the established multinational grain companies by reaching directly to the farmers. British control of shipping and their centralization of Allied grain purchasing would appear to have given the Argentine grain export market many facets of a "hierarchical" value chain, with the ultimate buyer holding overwhelming control. In the judgment of Roger Gravil, the lack of alternative markets for their grain production made Argentina more dependent than ever on Britain and its Allies, forcing the Argentine government to extend credit to the Allies simply to avoid the collapse of their own agricultural economy.[33]

At least in theory, such wartime circumstances should have enabled the Allies to drive the German-led grain exporters out of business. Yet despite all of these handicaps faced by the grain multinationals, throughout the war, the big grain companies in the River Plate continued to thrive. For at least nine or ten months after these firms inaugurated the Statutory List as the first listees, these grain multinationals simply continued to trade across the Atlantic on neutral Dutch ships to the Netherlands and Scandinavia.[34] At least some of these shipments from Bunge & Born and Weil Hermanos were undoubtedly destined for Germany. Finally, at the end of 1916, the fundamentally different purchasing regime created by the British Wheat Commission and firmer controls on allocation of shipping stopped the grain multinationals from undertaking direct trade across the Atlantic.

Yet despite facing growing problems retaining their core transatlantic business, the companies found new opportunities. Fifteen months after Bunge & Born entered the blacklist, Tower could only ruefully admire the way they still conducted business operations "in apparently undiminished volume."[35] They reinforced their control of existing links of the supply chain and developed new profitable networks within Argentina and in the region. There was undoubtedly some pro-German partisanship by the grain multinationals, but more than that, these companies showed a desire to take advantage of any new opportunities to make money during the war.

For one thing, the grain companies found they could still dominate in the Argentine countryside. When Sir Reginald Tower visited Bahia Blanca in May 1917, the British Vice-Consul there complained that most of the wheat in the district was in the hands of Bunge & Born and Weil Brothers, and that despite the high prices prevailing, local purchasers who wanted seed wheat would have to buy from those companies.[36] Through 1918, many Argentine farmers remained dependent on these firms for credit to run their farms and even simply to manage their everyday lives. Bunge & Born financed shops in country districts, allowing farmers who did not have enough capital to obtain goods from the shops, pledging payment in grain at harvest time.[37] Throughout the war, the German grain companies remained in control of the links of the value chain closest to many of the farmers themselves, and took advantage of these in new ways.

Within Argentina, all the grain multinationals also traded far more than ever before in the very liquid grain options markets. These had earlier been focused almost entirely on internal Argentine trade, but during the war, blacklisted companies found they could use the options markets to sell grain they owned to straw purchasers in cahoots with the blacklisted firm, and from there on to other potentially unaware purchasers. Grain options markets continued to operate in Argentina, with companies moving grain from owner to owner in ways that easily camouflaged the activities of the grain giants. Much of this eventually found its way to the primary buyer, the British Wheat Commission itself. In ironic proof of the uses of the option markets, Weil Brothers was among the firms castigated after the war by some in the German-Argentine community for doing "brisk business" in grains with the Allies during the war.[38] If one perceives it in less partisan terms, as undoubtedly the companies' canny managers were capable of doing, one might note that this was simply an indirect way of continuing the company's profitable trade with Europe. Wanting to ramp up Britain's economic warfare effort, the British Minister in Buenos Aires, Sir Reginald Tower, exploded in perplexed anger when British firms acting as purchasing agents in Argentina argued in January 1917 that they could not fill the orders of the Wheat Commission if they were forbidden to buy on the options markets.[39] As they lacked Bunge & Born's connections to agents in the countryside, the markets of Rosario and Buenos Aires were the only places for such British firms to purchase cereals. Only when the Argentine government temporarily forbade wheat exports did the British Chamber of Commerce in Argentina feel willing to accept a temporary prohibition on their members' options activities.[40]

During the war, the German grain multinationals also diversified their operations within Argentina. As Argentine grains were shipped in jute bags, Bunge & Born began selling used bags in 1917, and the next year started manufacturing and selling new bags, gaining raw jute supplies from India via both willing and clueless intermediaries.[41] They continued their pre-war expansion into the internal Argentine grain markets by gaining control of more grain elevators. The development of such grading and sorting facilities further connected the company directly to some Argentine farmers, and the elevator facilities were often run alongside mills that produced flour for local consumers.[42] After buying one local mill, Bunge & Born then used it as a cloak to purchase more milling machinery from Switzerland.[43]

They also moved more heavily into regional markets, in particular engaging in more direct trade with Brazil. A significant "coastal" trade developed during the war, on both smaller neutral steamship lines and on sailing ships. These ships ignored British attempts at control, refusing to show their manifests to the British Consulate before they left Buenos Aires for Uruguay or Brazil with grain from Bunge & Born.[44] Some ships may have been purchased during the war by the grain firms themselves. All of the investors in the Uruguayan-flagged SS "Santos" were employees of Bunge & Born.[45] Despite their affiliations, such ships could simply ignore the strictures of the British Ships Blacklist if they didn't need British coal, which through 1916 at least they could still purchase from the local German Coal Depot.[46] It soon became notorious that northward shipments were entirely in the hands of Bunge & Born, with neither Argentine nor Brazilian authorities (both neutral until Brazil joined the war in late 1917) willing to do anything to stop it, and with British supplies of coal insufficient to force the small shipowners into submission.[47]

In part, the grain traders took advantage of the domestic political circumstances of the South American countries. During the war, the Brazilian government made the local Lloyd Brasileiro line focus its limited fleet on working to maintain coastal shipping to Argentina for wheat, with haulage rates for wheat set by the government at the same level as before the war. Undoubtedly with the rise in global demand for shipping, Lloyd Brasileiro lost much potential revenue.[48] Pedraja suggests that this Brazilian policy was compelled by the desires of Brazilian officials to avoid food riots, but it certainly benefited the large German-Argentine wheat exporters. The exact degree of expansion of the grain and flour trade to Brazil during the war is unknown, but it is notable that Brazil's overall imports from Argentina nearly doubled in value between 1917 and 1918, even as those from Brazil's other two largest trading partners, the US and Britain, plateaued.[49] Even after Brazil entered the war, their economic warfare measures proved easy to elude. In February 1918, Sir Reginald Tower, the British Minister in Buenos Aires, listed a dozen known cloaks for Bunge & Born's expanding business with Brazilian flour mills.[50] Bunge & Born took the war as an opportunity to further expand its investments in Brazil, particularly in Brazil's import trade and flour milling.

It wasn't just in Brazil where the multinational grain companies appeared to have more diplomatic clout than the British government. A Bunge & Born-owned flour mill in Argentina apparently persuaded the Argentine government to allow significant flour shipments to Brazil in May 1917, at the exact time when the Argentine government had supposedly prohibited wheat exports, claiming that the crop might not be sufficient to feed Argentina itself.[51] After some efforts by Tower with the Argentine Minister of Agriculture, it was determined that a British mill in Rio would be allowed to export to Brazil 11,400 tons of wheat it owned ready to load in Buenos Aires, but at the same time, the Ministry of Agriculture allowed another 13,600 tons of wheat and 45,000 tons of flour were to be sent to Brazil.[52] Some British authorities believed that the Argentine export ban was itself caused not by real shortages but rather due to the machinations and "tampering" of the grain companies with members of the administration of the new Argentine president Hipolito Yrigoyen.[53]

Bribes may not have been exchanged, but the German grain companies in 1918 did go into the unusual business of loaning money to the Argentine government, with Bunge & Born and Weil Hermanos engaging in seven loans of over a million dollars each to the Argentine government. Tower considered the 5.5–6% rates as lower than most commercial houses would usually want as a return on their capital, but it may have been more than a mere financial investment.[54] In another move into finance, Weil Hermanos in 1916 began a new financial operation, selling Argentine "cédulas" (government mortgage bonds) smuggled from Germany and profiting from the exchange.[55] By the end of the war, the British commercial attaché estimated that £60m of these were in circulation in Argentina, "three-quarters of which were held abroad before the war."[56] It's unknown how much Weil Brothers or the other German grain multinationals profited from their move into financial services, but they certainly did profit.

In February 1917, Weil Hermanos capitalized on the anti-British feeling among many in Argentina by publishing a circular "urging growers to resist exploitation" of the British, an amazing argument for a company itself often seen as the exploiter of growers.[57] Their open intrusion into the Argentine grain market made Britain an easy target for blame if prices fell below producers expectations (as in March 1916) or if prices rose too high for seed-buying farmers and flour-buying consumers (as in early 1917).[58] In July 1917, Weil's manager in Rosario boldly walked into the British Consulate demanding to know why his name had been placed on the Statutory Blacklist. He was Argentine, after all. "A commercial German seems to be always naturalized Argentine," Tower complained to the Foreign Office.[59] But after all, they were increasingly Argentine. Extending significant advances to wheat producers around Bahia Blanca in March 1916 was not simply Bunge & Born's attempt to somehow corner a vast market, as feared by some Britons, but also ensured that they would have sufficient wheat for their local mills. The grain giants might be accused of making money, but unlike the British, they could also reasonably claim to be looking out for the needs of local consumers.

Could the British have done more to destroy and replace the German grain multinationals? The censorship was tight, and they were probably almost completely successful in cutting regular communications between the European headquarters and the Argentine branches of the firms. Yet the local management of these companies found themselves quite capable of making profitable strategic decisions on their own. Britain might have decided to impose a moratorium on all Allied purchases and shipments of Argentine wheat, corn, and linseed, effectively severing the commodity chain by sending the merchant ships under its control to other global ports. But clipping the supply chain would not only cause significant problems in South America, it would also bring hardship in the Allied countries themselves. Throughout the Great War, the Allies always felt they needed as much Argentine grain as they could get. Demand for Argentine grain spiked at certain points during the war, particularly in late 1917 to early 1918 when it was apparent that North American supplies would be significantly lower than hoped and when revolutionary Russia (and in particular the region's breadbasket, Ukraine) dropped out of global grain markets entirely. The obvious limitation of global resources, including both the food and the means of transporting it across the oceans, haunted the Allied governments and they sensibly believed that the Argentine supplies were particularly favorable both in availability and location (not nearly so distant as those from Australia or India, for example).[60] Statistics bear this out—when the grain crops of Argentina were hurt by drought in 1917, the Allies imported

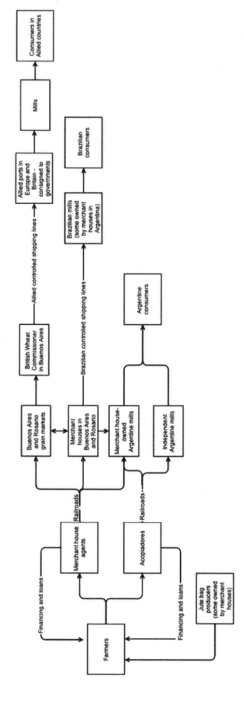

Figure 3.2 Wheat Commodity Chain by 1918

15% of their wheat from Australia and 11% from India, but when the Argentine crops recovered the next season, those two territories of the British Empire together shipped less than 9% of the Allied requirements, while Argentina went up from 8.7% to 15.6%.[61] Australian supplies were available but extremely inconvenient. As a result, the Allies had little leverage over either the Argentine government or over the fundamental structures of the Argentine grain trade. The Argentine government, adhering to strict neutrality throughout the war, made no moves to do anything to hurt the grain merchants targeted by Allied economic warfare. To ensure continued supplies, the Allies had to attenuate their economic warfare prohibitions against trading with these "enemies" by declaring them "rehabilitated" or simply failing to do all that might be done to hurt them.[62] In the eyes of their non-German competitors immediately after the war (some, like Dreyfus, themselves significant multinational grain traders), the huge, German-linked companies Weil Hermanos, Bunge & Born, and General Mercantile had made "huge profits in their local operations and with neutrals" throughout the war, with the war perhaps even allowing them to advance their position in the highly lucrative South American grain trade.[63] Astonishingly, these companies were able to continue to develop and control links in the commodity chain, and create new regional commodity chains servicing Latin American consumers, even during a vicious global conflict in which many of these companies were directly targeted by the Entente's economic war.

* * *

During the First World War, the Argentine wheat trade fundamentally and permanently changed, but the war did not end the globalization of the trade. The war caused the "lead firms" once headquartered in Europe to shift their capital and management down along the chain to Argentina, even while also nurturing the creation of new commercial chains within and between South American states. Their ability to "transfer resources across national borders," the hallmark of a multinational, remained intact.[64] Their voluminous business within Argentina enabled these companies to redirect some of their capital and expertise on a regional level during the war, adapting to the new reality of the war more nimbly than British and other competitors they had left in the dust over the previous decade. The value chains that governed Argentina's grain exports were constantly being restructured, with wartime market and non-market forces far different from those of the pre-war years propelling these changes. By 1919, some of these companies had given up any pretense that they were headquartered in Europe. Cut off from nominal owners in war-torn Europe, Buenos Aires was where the decisions of the grain firms were being made throughout the war and after. The local management proved canny in their decisions, and although Weil Brothers maintained its Frankfurt ties after the war (although still making most of their profits in Argentina), Bunge & Born became in effect fully Argentine. The prominent

German Alfredo Hirsch, its Buenos Aires manager throughout the war years, became its global chief through to the mid 1950s, by which time it was acknowledged as the largest trading company south of the equator.[65] Jorge Schvarzer, the historian of Bunge & Born, believes that the "Argentinization" of the company took place gradually over the course of decades.[66] It should be noted instead that the First World War compelled the change, making it definitively Argentine in a rather abrupt fashion. In such ways, the Great War actually prepared these nimble and innovative companies for success in the uncertain post-war markets, when the desires of rather conservative British multinational companies to return to "business as usual" failed to come to terms with the fact that in the there was no going back to the old ways.

The story of Argentina's wheat market during the First World War exemplifies how Global Value Chains constantly transform, shifting from one form of governance to another, and one geographical center to another. As the war raged in Europe, multinational grain firms decisively shifted managerial authority, capital, and virtually all of their work to their branches on the global periphery. Focusing their management and capital in Buenos Aires and Rosario, these companies found that even during the war they could manage the global chains for their own benefit, even when opposed by the British and then by the Allied governments. Unsurprisingly, the grain market in Argentina moved away from a fairly market-based global value chain, especially as the Allied governments became the primary buyers during the war. However, what is notable is how the Argentine grain trade moved towards one in which producers, the farmers on the pampas, were increasingly "captive" to the dominant buyers—not the end buyers, the Allied governments, but rather the grain merchants themselves. In other words, during the war, the South American links in the value chain multiplied and became more firmly dominated than ever before by those large multinational companies. After the end of the war, the Allied governments searching for ways to feed the starving masses of post-war Germany believed that the German wheat companies in Argentina still had more than enough capital to help finance shipments of grain to the starving masses of post-war Germany.[67] These companies quickly restarted their old direct trade abroad, but now this exporting bonanza rested atop a more significant than ever network of trade, investment, and finance across the eastern coast of South America.

Historians of the Great War have often focused on the way that increased government controls on trade by the core countries hurt the dependent economies of the global periphery. However, the case of Argentina's grain highlights how the war made people and governments in the global core more reliant than ever before on available suppliers of critical goods. During the war, the free global market in grain was obliterated by government efforts at financing, purchasing, distributing, and stockpiling food, with the state focused more than ever before on ensuring the nutritional well-being of its citizens by intervening directly in hitherto free markets like those for global grain.[68] This official focus on nutrition and health was ironic, considering how the war aimed overall to create death and destruction. There is also irony in the way that a wartime situation that maximized state intervention among the core states in the end led to the wartime development of periphery-based "lead firms" that would long thereafter dominate the lucrative grain trade of South America. Theorists on global value chains have often suggested that it is a core-centered, buyer-driven process. This notion correlates well with an overall sense of the history of the early twentieth century (including during the Great War) as one where dependency and imperialism characterized core-periphery relations. But in the case of the grain trade of Argentina, this was simply not true. One might see historical parallels between this process of entrepreneurial innovation within Argentina during the Great War and the present move of Chinese manufacturers becoming lead firms in their own right, rather than simply producers for Western multinationals.[69] Despite and even because of the turmoil brought on by war, these grain multinationals showed tremendous flexibility in adjusting to the new circumstances, making business decisions based not on sentiment or national loyalty but rather on opportunity. They were definitely not beholden to their European roots.

This chapter supports the notion that the First World War transformed the phenomenon of globalization in the Argentine grain trade rather than destroying it. Most histories of international business focus on the peacetime normal, ignoring the ways that warfare often permanently transforms the decisions and strategies of multinational companies.[70] The wartime successes of these companies, which created new networks and expanded their dominance into new links of the global value chain, provide us with examples of the resilience and adaptability of that epitome of early twentieth century capitalism, the multinational enterprise. Belying the idea that the First World War even temporarily halted global capitalism, such multinational companies as these grain firms operated as "preservers of globalization" in the decades after 1914.[71]

Notes

1 On the importance of food during the First World War, see Offer, *The First World War: An Agrarian Interpretation.*, and Barnett, *British Food Policy during the First World War.*

2 Topik, Marichal, and Zephyr, *From Silver to Cocaine: Latin American Commodity Chains and the Building of the World Economy, 1500–2000.*

3 These five forms of governance are outlined in much of the Global Value Chain literature, including on the GVC organization's Duke University-hosted website, www.globalvaluechains.org, and in Gereffi, Humphrey, and Sturgeon, "The Governance of Global Value Chains."

4 Gereffi, *Commodity Chains and Global Capitalism*; Neilson, Pritchard, and Yeung Wai-chung, "Global Value Chains and Global Production Networks in the Changing International Political Economy: An Introduction."

5 Topik, Marichal, and Zephyr, "Introduction: Commodity Chains in Theory and in Latin American History"; Henderson, "Global Production Networks and

the Analysis of Economic Development." On the usefulness and flexibility of the "network" metaphor, see Osterhammel, *The Transformation of the World: A Global History of the Nineteenth Century*, 710.

6 Trentman, *Free Trade Nation: Commerce, Consumption, and Civil Society in Modern Britain*, 190.

7 Osterhammel, *The Transformation of the World: A Global History of the Nineteenth Century*, 710.

8 Albert, *South America and the First World War: The Impact of the War on Brazil, Argentina, Peru and Chile*, 121, 312–318.

9 Tooze, *The Deluge: The Great War and the Remaking of Global Order 1916–1931*.

10 Miller, *Europe and the Maritime World: A Twentieth Century History*, 12.

11 Ibid., 11.

12 Topik and Wells, *Global Markets Transformed: 1870–1945*, 261.

13 Cain and Hopkins, *British Imperialism, 1688–2000*.

14 Scobie, *Revolution on the Pampas: A Social History of Argentine Wheat, 1860–1910*; Osterhammel, *The Transformation of the World: A Global History of the Nineteenth Century*; Barsky and Gelman, *Historia Del Agro Argentino: Desde La Conquista Hasta Fines Del Siglo XX*.

15 Lewis, *British Railways in Argentina 1857–1914: A Case Study of Foriegn Investment*, 45; Osterhammel, *The Transformation of the World: A Global History of the Nineteenth Century*, 157; Adelman, *Frontier Development: Land, Labour and Capital on the Wheatlands of Argentina and Canada 1890–1914*, 106.

16 Scobie, *Revolution on the Pampas: A Social History of Argentine Wheat, 1860–1910*, 92–93.

17 Adelman, *Frontier Development: Land, Labour and Capital on the Wheatlands of Argentina and Canada 1890–1914*, 4–5.

18 Gravil, "The Anglo-Argentine Connection and the War of 1914–1918."

19 Hooker, *The International Grain Trade*, 10–13; Topik and Wells, *Global Markets Transformed: 1870–1945*, 123.

20 Wilkins and Schröter, *The Free-Standing Company in the World Economy, 1830–1996*, 4–5, 14.

21 Miller, *Europe and the Maritime World: A Twentieth Century History*, 223–24.

22 The unavailability of the Bunge & Born archive is legendary and has been commented on by a number of historians, including Schvarzer, *Bunge & Born: Crecimiento Y Diversificación de Un Grupo Económico*, 9–11.

23 Platt, "The British in South America—an Archive Report," 495; Jacob, "Review of 'Bunge & Born: Crecimiento Y Diversificación de Un Grupo Económico' by Jorge Schvarzer."

24 On the income and price elasticity of demand for Brazilian coffee, see Topik and Samper, "The Latin American Coffee Commodity Chain: Brazil and Costa Rica," 135. Also, Topik and Wells, *Global Markets Transformed: 1870–1945*, 131.

25 On the Bolsa do Cereales, see Scobie, *Revolution on the Pampas: A Social History of Argentine Wheat, 1860–1910*, chap. 4.

26 Dehne, "The Resilience of Globalization during the First World War: The Case of Bunge & Born in Argentina," 229. Scobie, *Revolution on the Pampas: A Social History of Argentine Wheat, 1860–1910*, chap. 4. Johns, "The Making of an Urban Elite: The Case of Rosario, Argentina, 1880–1920," 159.

27 Osterhammel, *The Transformation of the World: A Global History of the Nineteenth Century*, 721. For a florid contemporary description of the grain exporters' use of their telegraph-delivered knowledge of global prices when making purchases from Argentine farmers, see Huret, *La Argentina: De Buenos Aires Al Gran Chaco*, 564–65.

28 Letter from confidential source in Buenos Aires, 14 October 1915, in FO 833/17.

29 Mackie to Tower, 25 July 2015, FO 118/363.
30 Detlev Claussen describes the wartime lives of the young Felix Weil and his astoundingly wealthy father Hermann, one of the founders of Weil Hermanos, both of whom lived in Frankfurt during the war and after. Felix was one of the early leaders of the Frankfurt School of neo-Marxist sociology and philosophy, and although he always remained close with his surprisingly leftist father, he held bitter hostility towards "the immoral practice of grain speculation"; in Claussen, *Theodor W. Adorno: One Last Genius*, 80–82.
31 Burk, "Wheat and the State during the First World War," 124–27.
32 *First Report of the Royal Commission on Wheat Supplies with Appendices, Cmd. 1544*, 21. Appendix 5.
33 Gravil, "The Anglo-Argentine Connection and the War of 1914–1918," 74–75.
34 Consul-General Mackie report to Tower of 20 September 1916, in Tower's No. 402 FTD of 22 September 1916. (FO 118/399)
35 Tower to FTD No. 377 of 30 June 1917, 22 August 1917, FTD 140701. FO 833/17.
36 Tower No. 194 Com'l of 13 May. 11 June, No. 116063, FO 368/1691.
37 WTID weekly bulletin No. 135, 13 June 1918. ADM 137/2919.
38 Newton, *German Buenos Aires, 1900–1933: Social Change and Cultural Crisis*, 48.
39 Special Meeting (with Tower in attendance) of the Council of the British Chamber of Commerce in Buenos Aires, 11 January 1917.
40 Council resolution, 21 June 1917.
41 FO 118/433 Consul Dickson to Tower No. 170 of 21 November 1917, in Tower to FTD No. 661 of 25 November 1917. FO 118/468, Tower to FTD No. 83 of 14 February 1918. Council meeting of Thursday, 21 March 1918.
42 FO 118/469, Tower to FTD No. 367 of 14 July 1918.
43 FO 118/433, Tower to FTD No. 464 of 8 August 1917.
44 FO 118/399, Consul-General Mackie to Tower, 11 September 1916.
45 FO 505/355, Consul-General Mackie to Mitchell Innes in Montevideo, 13 June 1916.
46 FO 118/399, Consul-General Mackie to Tower, 20 September 1916.
47 FO 118/400, Consul-General Mackie to Tower on 8 November 1916.
48 De La Pedraja, *Oil and Coffee: Latin American Merchant Shipping from the Imperial Era to the 1950s*, 48–49.
49 "A report on the general economic and financial conditions of Brazil for the year 1919 by Mr. E. Hambloch, commercial secretary to H.M. embassy," Rio de Janeiro, Cmd. 840 (1920), 53.
50 FO 118/468, Tower to FTD No. 114 of 25 February 1918.
51 FO 368/1690, (91900) Tel No. 180 of 5 May 1917, from Wheat Commission to Tower, via the FO.
52 FO 368/1690, (90858) Tower to FO tel. No. 184 Com'l of 4 May 1917.
53 FO 368/1690, FO tel. No. 123 Com'l to Tower (71374A), 5 April 1917.
54 FO 118/469, Tower No. 423 to F.T.D., 16 August 1918.
55 FO 833/16, Tower to FTD No. 417 (89262), para. 3, 30 September 1916.
56 "Report on the economic and industrial situation of the Argentine Republic for the year 1919, by Mr. H.O. Chalkley, commercial secretary to H.M. legation," Buenos Aires, Cmd. 895 (1920), 11.
57 FO 368/1690, FO tel. No. 123 Com'l to Tower (71374A), 5 April 1917.
58 FO 368/1478, (80318) 28 Apr. 1916, Tower to FO No. 140 Com'l of 30 March 1916.
59 MT 23/540/T42028/16, No. 364 Com'l (191125), 9 November 1915.
60 Surface, *The Grain Trade during the World War: Being a History of the Food Administration Grain Corporation and the United States Grain Corporation*, 186–87, 295–98.

61 Ibid., 23.
62 For an interesting discussion of the many variables that can shape state strategies of economic warfare, see Levy and Barbieri, "Trading with the Enemy during Wartime," 31–33.
63 FO 118/514, Letter from H. Ford of the Centro de Exportadores de Cereales on 14 February 1919, with copy of the cable sent by the Allied grain firms to David Lloyd George of 13 February 1919.
64 Roach, "A Primer on Multinational Corporations," 30.
65 "The Beneficent Octopus."
66 Schvarzer, *Bunge & Born: Crecimiento Y Diversificación de Un Grupo Económico*, 69–73.
67 Bane and Lutz, "22 January 1919 Memo by Herbert Hoover "on German and Austrian Trading in South America," 56–57.
68 Barnett, *British Food Policy during the First World War*, xiv.
69 Gereffi, "Global Value Chains in a Post-Washington Consensus World".
70 Dai, "Caught in the Middle: Multinational Enterprise Strategy in Interstate Warfare," 357.
71 Jones, *Entreprenurship and Multinationals*, 6.

Primary Sources

Admiralty files—ADM 137/2919.
Foreign Office files—FO 118/363, FO 118/399, FO 118/400, FO 118/433, FO 118/468, FO 118/469, FO 118/514, FO 368/1478, FO 368/1690, FO 368/1691, FO 505/355, FO 833/16, FO 833/17.
Ministry of Transport and Related Bodies files—MT 23/540/T42028/16.
The National Archives, Kew, UK.

Secondary Sources

Adelman, Jeremy. *Frontier Development: Land, Labour and Capital on the Wheatlands of Argentina and Canada 1890–1914*. Oxford: Oxford University Press, 1994.
Albert, Bill. *South America and the First World War: The Impact of the War on Brazil, Argentina, Peru and Chile*. Cambridge: Cambridge University Press, 1988.
Bane, Suda Lorena, and Ralph Haswell Lutz, eds. "22 January 1919 Memo by Herbert Hoover 'on German and Austrian Trading in South America'." In *The Blockade of Germany After the Armistice 1918–1919: Selected Documents of the Supreme Economic Council, Superior Blockade Council, American Relief Administration, and Other Wartime Organizations*. Stanford: Stanford University Press, 1942, 24–25.
Barnett, L. Margaret. *British Food Policy during the First World War*. Boston: George Allen & Unwin, 1985.
Barsky, Osvaldo, and Jorge Gelman. *Historia Del Agro Argentino: Desde La Conquista Hasta Fines Del Siglo XX*. Buenos Aires: Grijalbo Mondadori, 2001.
"The Beneficent Octopus." *Time*, October 19, 1962.
Burk, Kathleen. "Wheat and the State during the First World War." In *Strategy and Intelligence: British Policy during the First World War*, edited by Michael Dockrill and David French. London: The Hambledon Press, 1996.

Cain, Peter J., and A. Hopkins. *British Imperialism, 1688–2000.* Harlow: Longman, 2002.

Claussen, Detlev. *Theodor W. Adorno: One Last Genius.* Cambridge, MA: Belknap Press, 2008.

Dai, L. "Caught in the Middle: Multinational Enterprise Strategy in Interstate Warfare." *Competitiveness Review: An International Business Journal Incorporating Journal of Global Competitiveness* 19, no. 5 (2009): 355–76.

De La Pedraja, René. *Oil and Coffee: Latin American Merchant Shipping from the Imperial Era to the 1950s.* Westport, CT: Greenwood Press, 1998.

Dehne, Philip. "The Resilience of Globalization during the First World War: The Case of Bunge & Born in Argentina." In *The Foundations of Worldwide Economic Integration: Power, Institutions and Global Markets, 1850–1930.* Cambridge: Cambridge University Press, 2013.

First Report of the Royal Commission on Wheat Supplies with Appendices, Cmd. 1544, 1921.

Gereffi, G., J. Humphrey, and T. Sturgeon. "The Governance of Global Value Chains." *Review of International Political Economy* 12, no. 1 (2005): 78–104. doi:10.1080/09692290500049805.

Gereffi, Gary. "Global Value Chains in a Post-Washington Consensus World." *Reivew of International Political Economy* 21, no. 1 (2014): 9–37.

———. *Commodity Chains and Global Capitalism.* Westport, CT: Greenwood Press, 1994.

Gravil, Roger. "The Anglo-Argentine Connection and the War of 1914–1918." *Journal of Latin American Studies* 9, no. 1 (1977): 73–76.

Henderson, Jeffrey. "Global Production Networks and the Analysis of Economic Development." *Review of International Political Economy* 9 (2002): 436–64.

Hooker, Albert A. *The International Grain Trade.* London: Sir Isaac Pitman & Sons, 1936.

Huret, Jules. *La Argentina: De Buenos Aires Al Gran Chaco.* Paris: E. Fasquelle, 1913.

Jacob, Raúl. "Review of 'Bunge & Born: Crecimiento Y Diversificación de Un Grupo Económico' by Jorge Schvarzer." *Business History Review* 82 (2008): 613.

Johns, Micheal. "The Making of an Urban Elite: The Case of Rosario, Argentina, 1880–1920." *Journal of Urban History* 20, no. 2 (1994): 155–78.

Jones, Geoffrey. *Entreprenurship and Multinationals.* Cheltenham: Edward Elgar, 2013.

Levy, Jack S., and Katherine Barbieri. "Trading with the Enemy during Wartime." *Security Studies* 13, no. 3 (2004): 1–47.

Lewis, Colin M. *British Railways in Argentina 1857–1914: A Case Study of Foriegn Investment.* London: Athlone, 1983.

Miller, Michael B. *Europe and the Maritime World: A Twentieth Century History.* Cambridge: Cambridge University Press, 2012.

Neilson, Jeffrey, Bill Pritchard, and Henry Yeung Wai-chung. "Global Value Chains and Global Production Networks in the Changing International Political Economy: An Introduction." *Review of International Political Economy* 21 (2014).

Newton, Ronald. *German Buenos Aires, 1900–1933: Social Change and Cultural Crisis.* Austin and London: University of Texas Press, 1977.

Offer, Avner. *The First World War: An Agrarian Interpretation.* Oxford: Clarendon Press, 1991.

Osterhammel, Jürgen. *The Transformation of the World: A Global History of the Nineteenth Century*. Princeton: Princeton University Press, 2014.

Platt, D. C. M. "The British in South America—an Archive Report." In *A Guide to Manuscript Sources for the History of Latin America and The Carribean in the British Isles*, edited by Peter Walne. Oxford: Oxford University Press, 1973.

Roach, Brian. "A Primer on Multinational Corporations." In *Leviathans: Multinational Corporations and the New Global History*, edited by Alfred Dupont Chandler and Bruce Mazlish. Cambridge: Cambridge University Press, 2005.

Schvarzer, Jorge. *Bunge & Born: Crecimiento Y Diversificación de Un Grupo Económico*. Buenos Aires: CISEA/Grupo Editor Latinoamericano, 1989.

Scobie, James. *Revolution on the Pampas: A Social History of Argentine Wheat, 1860–1910*. Austin: University of Texas Press, 1964.

Surface, Frank. *The Grain Trade during the World War: Being a History of the Food Administration Grain Corporation and the United States Grain Corporation*. New York: Macmillan, 1928.

Tooze, Adam. *The Deluge: The Great War and the Remaking of Global Order 1916–1931*. London: Penguin, 2014.

Topik, S., and A. Wells. *Global Markets Transformed: 1870–1945*. Cambridge, MA: Harvard University Press, 2014.

Topik, Steven, Carlos Marichal, and Frank Zephyr. *From Silver to Cocaine: Latin American Commodity Chains and the Building of the World Economy, 1500–2000*. Durham, NC: Duke University Press, 2006.

———. "Introduction: Commodity Chains in Theory and in Latin American History." In *From Silver to Cocaine: Latin American Commodity Chains and the Building of the World Economy, 1500–2000*. Durham, NC: Duke University Press, 2006.

Topik, Steven, and Mario Samper. "The Latin American Coffee Commodity Chain: Brazil and Costa Rica." In *From Silver to Cocaine: Latin American Commodity Chains and the Building of the World Economy, 1500–2000*. Durham, NC: Duke University Press, 2006.

Trentman, Frank. *Free Trade Nation: Commerce, Consumption, and Civil Society in Modern Britain*. Oxford: Oxford University Press, 2008.

Wilkins, Mira, and Harm Schröter. *The Free-Standing Company in the World Economy, 1830–1996*. Oxford: Oxford University Press, 1998.

Part II

New Opportunities

Trans-Border Innovations in Wartime

4 Swedish Business in the First World War

A Case Study of Ball Bearings Manufacturer SKF

Eric Golson and Jason Lennard *

Introduction

Sweden was a late industrialiser, held back by a small internal market. By contrast, Germany had been Europe's premier metal mining and heavy industrial goods supplier from 1870 onwards. Despite Sweden's growth and access to specialty metals, it had not been able to compete with the large market advantage of the Germans. All of this was changed by the First World War, when Swedish business was transformed by the country's neutrality: demand was high, international expansion was possible, patents and belligerent property were purchased and capital investment was used to expand productive capacity.[1] The war was particularly beneficial to Sweden, as it was able to sell heavy industrial goods and raw metals to both belligerent groups, although this was later offset by lower commercial trade. This industrial growth was transformative, with the war Sweden moved from a domestic player to a global one; however, there was no immediate improvement in productivity as seen in the Ford factories of the United States or elsewhere.[2] Rather, the war set the stage for long-term Swedish industrial growth with the establishment of a lead in certain strategic goods, most notably ball bearings. Taylorism and other productivity improvements came only after an SKF monopoly over ball bearings had been established as part of the actions taken by the company in the war years and just after.

Ball and roller bearings are special engineering products that use balls between two moving shafts to reduce rotational friction. The concept of the ball bearing had been around since the early days of the Industrial Revolution. Found widely today in most mechanical devices with axles, they were a relatively new invention at the turn of the century. Their heyday came after the 1850s, when increasing mechanisation made them a necessity in most motors and axles. Swedish bearings are particularly useful for high heat and high tensile strength applications because the steel used in the Swedish bearings is particularly high grade. In wartime, this makes Sweden a critical supplier for automobiles, guns and many other engines. During the First World War, Swedish bearings would play a crucial role in the development of new modern fighting equipment, including the first tank engines, airplanes and the Vickers gun.

Higher-quality ball bearings, such as those made by SKF using Swedish steel, were important for the war effort. The shafts inside motors rotate hundreds or thousands of times per minute. Even the smallest imperfection in the circular shape of the bearing or the condition of the metal used can lead to the failure of the bearing. Any such failure can lead to the disintegration of the whole bearing inside the motor, which causes the entire motor assembly to separate into pieces. If this happens while the motor is operating at high speeds, it could lead to the ejection of motor parts outside the engine and into, for instance, the skin of the aircraft (if a plane) or through the roof of the automobile. Thus, the failure of a small bearing could render the entire aircraft or automobile useless. It is therefore crucially important that the bearings be of the highest quality.[3] Swedish manufacturers have particular advantage here, as Swedish iron ore is some of the most dense and highest-quality iron ore available in the world.

Ball bearings manufacturer SKF provides one of the best examples of a Swedish company who benefitted from the war and Sweden's neutral position. SKF, as it is now known, originally *Svenska Kullagerfabriken*, is Sweden's premier manufacturer of ball bearings. Founded in 1907, the company had a natural advantage in producing ball bearings given its access to high-quality steel. However, many elements of SKF's business practices were also important. Despite the development of intense competition in the ball bearings industry during the First World War, SKF's unique organisational structure and acquisitions, purchase of the Conrad patent and monopoly power over competition pushed the company forward to be one of the premier ball bearings suppliers in the world. By the Second World War, SKF controlled the market in bearings to such an extent the company had significant pricing power and its subsidiaries in Germany were guaranteed against loss by the Allies.[4] This chapter identifies the factors which made SKF successful in this period and set the stage for the company's long-term growth. It will first review Sweden's economic development in the war; it will then discuss SKF's structural advantages and its purchase of the Conrad patent. In the penultimate section, it will review the applications of Taylorism that increased productivity and ensured its monopoly position, before concluding with an analysis of how the war impacted the growth of SKF in the long term.

Sweden and SKF's Economic Development in the First World War

Before proceeding to a discussion of SKF's advantages, it is important to give some context to Sweden's and SKF's economic development during the war. Generally speaking, the Swedish economy emerged from the war in almost the same position to which it started in terms of GDP, but this masks several important sub-trends in both GDP and industrialisation. The interim movements in GDP are important: until 1916, the war had increased exports of goods and materials, and industrial profits were particularly high in the early years. Real GDP expanded at 4 per cent on average since the onset of the conflict. However, the second half of the war saw unrestricted warfare, which hurt exports; industrial profits retreated significantly as competition became fiercer.[5] This led to a reversal of the gains and a significant deterioration in Sweden's national income.[6] However, despite the upwards and downwards gyrations in GDP, it is important to note the Swedish economy was more industrial at the end of the war than it was before it started.

Much like the macro-economy, the ball bearing industry's development during the war was rocky. Domestic and international competition was fierce throughout the war; the volume of sales increased, as did prices, in particular, but productivity gains were anaemically low. Values and quantities of ball and roller bearings are reported in Table 4.1 below. As suggested by the aggregate export figures, demand was high and prices rose almost three-fold during the course of the war. Given the demand and high prices for ball bearings in the first months of the war, six new competitors were formed by 1917. Five had weak capitalisation and were mostly built on debt. When the end of the war came, the bubble burst; the five companies were out of business. One survived the war and proved to be a notable competitor to SKF: *Nordiska Kullageraktiebolaget* (NKA), affectionately called Northball. NKA was well capitalised, with funds coming from Melcher Lyckholm, a beer magnate. Like many of SKF's competitors, NKA would eventually fail as prices collapsed. The remnants of bankrupt NKA were eventually acquired by SKF in 1925.

In terms of Swedish economic development, growth during much of the war and the immediate post-war period was extensive.[7] The entire ball bearings industry merely added machines and workers as opposed to finding new ways to improve productivity. So bad was the situation that the First World War was a period of negative total factor productivity (TFP) growth

Table 4.1 Value and Quantity of Swedish Exported Ball and Roller Bearings, 1913–18

	Value (Crowns)	Quantity (Kilograms)	Average Price per Kilo
1913	3,641,741	764,323	4.76
1914	4,022,516	579,062	6.95
1915	11,005,610	1,464,152	7.52
1916	14,189,832	1,782,961	7.96
1917	17,825,495	1,898,543	9.39
1918	21,509,876	1,570,807	13.69
Average Annual Growth Rate (%)	47.49	23.41	23.53

Sources: Sveriges Officiella Statistik, *Handel: 1913*, p. 364; Sveriges Officiella Statistik, *Handel: 1914*, pp. 371–2; Sveriges Officiella Statistik, *Handel: 1915*, p. 343; Sveriges Officiella Statistik, *Handel: 1916*, p. 344; Sveriges Officiella Statistik, *Handel: 1917*, p. 296; Sveriges Officiella Statistik, *Handel: 1918*, pp. 275–6.

for Sweden as a whole. This period of poor productivity would ultimately set the stage for growth in the 1920s. Changes in the capital stock contributed a majority to the gains made in GDP during the war (at 1.39 per cent per year). TFP growth was a negative contributor, reducing GDP growth by just over 1 per cent per year. In the face of reduced prices and high costs of production, companies like SKF then changed strategy from 1921 onwards, using capital to increase labour productivity.[8] The slump from 1919–21 was a period of consolidation for major Swedish industrial players. TFP growth was about 1 per cent per year in each of these years, accounting for just under three-quarters of the growth in GDP. Capital continued to be a steady source of growth during the period, contributing more than a percentage point each year, while labor was decisively negative.

It was not until the post-war boom that we see the productivity gains associated with mass mechanization of production: GDP growth averaged at 4.40 per cent per year between 1922 and 1929, with 2.47 per cent coming from improvements in TFP. This closely parallels the American experience. Technological change took hold in this period, utilising much of the investment which had been made during the First World War, including in areas such as electrification and transportation; overseas investments during the war were also important. Income (dividends, interest and profits) from Swedish capital invested abroad increased significantly from 15 million crowns in 1922 to 110 million in 1929.[9] Given that Sweden had been a large capital importer from around 1870 until the outbreak of the war, this may be seen as a consequence of the large capital exports that accumulated between 1914 and 1918.[10] This example is borne out nicely in SKF's purchase of the German Conrad patent for making ball bearings, which meant that instead of having capital flows going to Germany as had happened before the war, international patent holders started sending money to Sweden after the war. Because the capital flows to Sweden coincided with the industrial expansion of the 1920s suggests the SKF story is one that can be generalised for a good deal of Swedish industry.

SKF's Structure

SKFs structure during the First World War looked considerably like many German companies of the period, but this transitioned to a more traditional Chandlerian M-form company after the war. A complex chain of subsidiaries was established or purchased before 1914, totalling some 27 sales organisations and production subsidiaries in countries around the world. This number increased during the war, reaching 83 in 1920.[11] Business historian Alfred Chandler gives an almost account of the general trend at the time, which fits SKF's expansion rather ideally—namely, "in nearly all cases they become larger, first, by integrating forward (that is investing in marketing and distribution facilities and personnel); then, by moving backward into purchasing and control of raw and semi-finished material; and sometimes, though much less often, by investing in research and development."[12] Just prior to the war, SKF entered the international ball bearings market by purchasing a controlling interest in the Norma company for 2 million marks. Norma was a member of the German ball bearings cartel and the purchase allowed them access to the patents and international markets which they were previously locked out of because SKF did not have an internationally recognised patent.[13] With access to this patent and a strong domestic production operation, SKF was able to open international sales operations with direct exports from Sweden. By 1912, branch offices in France and Germany were in operation as fully limited companies. Agents were also selling SKF bearings in Russia, Spain, Poland, Bulgaria, Romania, Mexico, India, China and South Africa. Fulfilling another tenant of Chandler's business model, SKF also built a separate research and development operation at the Gothenburg factory, including a laboratory for testing and refining ball bearings.[14]

The Great War accelerated the company's development process. One of SKF's key strategies during the war was dual production operations, with local production in belligerent countries which were supplemented with Swedish home-company production. This strategy began in 1911 when SKF acquired the Skefko Ball Bearing Company in Luton, England. As seen in Table 4.2, the strategy was extended to Germany when it inaugurated its first wide-scale German production in 1914; this strategy was extended to the United States in 1915 when it opened SKF Philadelphia and France in 1918 when SKF Paris produced its first bearings. These subsidiaries did not specialise in a particular bearing type: they produced the same bearings as SKF Sweden. However, there were a number of tariff and trade advantages to having these dual operations. As domestic producers within the belligerent country, they were not subject to wartime controls such as blockades or losses due to unrestricted submarine warfare.[15] This was highly advantageous to the firm in the later years of the war as economic warfare increasingly sought to limit the provision of crucial war materiel to the two belligerent groups.[16] The biggest advances were made in the US where, in 1915, a vast factory in Connecticut was built. The US Foreign Economic Administration described the venture in the following way:

> At the outbreak of The First World War SKF saw an opportunity for development in the US. Before that time it was customary for Germany to export ball bearings to the US. Realising, however, that the British blockade would affect Germany's exports to the US, SKF centred its attention on the US market.[17]

Increased production by 1917, particularly in the United States, resulted in SKF Sweden having a smaller share of overall production, dropping from 85 per cent in 1913 to about 50 per cent of total group production by 1918.[18] Overall, the SKF group had become the biggest ball bearings manufacturer in the world.[19]

Table 4.2 Number of Bearings Manufactured by SKF Group (Millions of Units), 1913–18

	Sweden	UK	Germany	US	France	Others	Total
1913	1.1	0.2	–	–	–	–	1.3
1914	1.2	0.2	0.8	–	–	–	2.2
1915	1.7	0.3	0.3	0.3	–	–	2.5
1916	2.4	0.3	0.2	0.7	–	–	3.6
1917	2.8	0.3	0.6	1.2	–	–	4.9
1918	2.8	0.3	0.9	1.8	0.1	–	5.9
1939	16.3	8.3	39.8	4.0	9.4	0.4	78.3
1940	16.5	9.7	39.9	7.2	6.8	0.4	80.6
1941	16.9	9.7	39.0	11.3	8.1	0.5	85.5
1942	17.8	10.5	39.8	15.7	8.8	0.4	93.1
1943	21.0	9.9	48.3	19.0	7.4	0.8	106.3
1944	22.3	9.8	28.8	22.8	3.0	2.8	89.5
1945	10.5	8.2	7.2	13.8	4.8	1.1	45.6

Source: Fritz and Karlsson, *SKF*, pp. 33 and 102.

As part of its growth strategy, SKF also engaged in considerable vertical integration, another tenant of Chandler's ideal corporate organisation of the time.[20] SKF purchased Hofors Bruk, a steel mining and milling company owned by Stockholms Enskilda Bank, ensuring vertical integration and high quality of the final products. In buying Hofors, SKF was trying to secure its economic moat and wartime advantage in quality.[21] Increases in demand and production had put a strain on all raw material producers in Sweden. SKF was dependent on the goodwill of suppliers, whose quality was at best questionable or at worst untested. Although it took years to integrate Hofors directly into SKF's operations, its presence in the group gave it a decisive advantage over its competitors, as quality could be monitored and improved over the course of the entire production process, starting with the mining. Meanwhile, competitors had to rely on other, lower-quality mines for their steel. Given quality of the final product was critically important to the purchasers, this acquisition gave it a decisive advantage over its rivals.

Maintaining control of these companies in wartime could have been a problem given the desire of governments to change or expropriate factories which were deemed in the national interest; or from companies who were considered to have been working for the enemy during wartime. However, here too, SKF excelled. As a company from a neutral country, it was able to maintain production in both belligerent groups as well as exports from Sweden to those groups with only limited restrictions (such as threat of submarine warfare). But a country or a company's neutral credentials are never really enough. The belligerents regularly threatened to seize property, plant and equipment. Tight control of the subsidiaries was needed in order to ensure the company did not face expropriation of the assets.[22]

The main method of controlling these subsidiaries was two-fold: first was access to Swedish produced bearings, which could be cut-off in the event of any expropriation of any manufacturing subsidiary. Second, access to the machine tools and high-quality steel. SKF adopted a distributed production system. This meant the same bearings produced in their worldwide factories by machines supplied from Sweden. Continuous replacement of machine tool parts and the need for new machines from Sweden meant SKF Sweden could effectively cut off and make useless any subsidiary which had been expropriated or was not doing as required. The exception was the United States, where a separate company making some machine tool parts (Hubbard Machine Co.) was eventually purchased in 1919.[23] But even in this case, SKF Philadelphia, as the US subsidiary was ultimately called, was constrained from expanding manufacturing capacity despite significant government requests to do so. Reports indicate other American ball bearings manufacturers were unable to produce bearings as robust and durable as those of SKF, leaving the market undersupplied to meet government demands. This left the market dependent on Swedish imports.[24] In this way, SKF was able to work around the wartime threats faced by most firms whose products were in significant demand.[25]

SKF Russia provides the perfect example of an SKF subsidiary which was able to resist the changes occurring around it. No longer able to buy bearings from Germany, Sweden became Tsarist Russia's sole supplier of bearings during the war. Such was the demand for Swedish bearings during this period that SKF constructed a factory outside Moscow, inaugurating the previously discussed two-tiered purchasing system in Russia. Domestically made Russian supplies were used alongside imported Swedish supplies. Despite most companies having been nationalised after the October revolution, SKF's operations were maintained because the authorities knew only SKF could run the factory. SKF continued to supply machinery and receive funds from the company until it was finally nationalised in 1922.[26] Dual control allowed SKF to maintain the factory for much longer than expected.

There can be little question the war accelerated SKF's international expansion. SKF's structure changed during the war to suit its evolving strategy: the ultimate goal was to fulfil wartime demand, securing raw materials and creating an international sales force. This growth fit the traditional Chandlerian business model of the period. But the short-term demand created by the war and the actions taken by the company also suited the company's long-term expansion and the problems of protectionism in the 1920s. Supplies produced in local countries were not subject to tariffs, so while many multinationals struggled with protectionism, SKF did relatively well, shifting production from Sweden outwards. The purchase of the Conrad patent was another of these long-term moves made possible by the war, cementing SKF's control over international ball bearings production, which will be discussed in the next section.

The Conrad Patent: Royalties and Control

Acquisition and ownership of the Conrad patent by Swedish SKF gave the company a sizeable advantage against its competitors: most notably, it could charge them a licensing fee for every ball bearing they produced and restrict their operations using quotas. Before 1912, SKF had largely been restricted from the international market. The German ball bearings industry predated the Swedish one, and since 1907, the German patent for ball bearings was owned by a cartel. Membership in the patent cartel allowed for certain levels of production and spheres of interest. SKF bought into the cartel in 1912 when it purchased a controlling interest in the Norma Company for 2 million marks. Becoming part of the German cartel, the purchase allowed them access to the patents and international markets for the first time.[27]

Swedish neutrality gave SKF a huge competitive boost with respect to intellectual property. Just prior the American entry into the war, as the Entente threatened to strip Germany of its international assets and patent rights, SKF purchased the German patent. As part of the acquisition of the American Hess-Bright ball bearing company (which would have been seized by enemy control), SKF purchased the right to the Conrad patent from Deutsche Waffen & Munition-Fabriken for $600,000. This was an exceptionally low price and generated significant income immediately, possibly up to $1 million per year. As a result, the Americans estimated the value of this patent to be between twenty and sixty million dollars. This gave SKF complete control of the ball bearings patent and its associated revenues. The cartel to which SKF had previously belonged now also paid royalties to SKF. According to American sources, the purchase was paid for from royalties within months.[28]

With the purchase of the patent, SKF was now able to control its competitive environment and benefit from industrial consolidation. With ball bearings prices so high, six new domestic competitors and many international competitors were formed by 1917; of the six domestic competitors, only NKA survived the war, and then only because of Melcher Lyckholm's investment.[29] NKA followed the SKF model closely, acquiring machine tool companies, iron ore mines and international expansion alongside SKF. But NKA and other competitors did not have access to the patent rights. This would become a crucial part of SKF's strategy for defeating these competitors. Every time a ball or roller bearing was manufactured the competition had to pay royalties to SKF. This increased the competitor's cost base and improved SKF's finances at the same time.[30]

There can be little question that in the post-war period, the ownership of the patent became decisive, and by 1929, a world trust had been formed with SKF at its heart. The firm tolerated the domestic and international competitive pressures during the war, but in the immediate post-war period, the competitive situation led to an oversupply. The five Swedish concerns mentioned above closed and NKA eventually closed as well, but the international market was also crumbling. Smaller competitors were crushed by high costs and low demand. The French and German ball bearings industries had previously been the Swedes' major competitors, but the lack of industrial investment after the war meant they were no longer competitive and were in need of rationalisation. SKF purchased their main French rivals, and the entire German industry was consolidated into a trust that became known as *Vereingte Kugellagerfabriken*. SKF was a majority shareholder in this concern, providing the international patent rights previously held by some of their partners.[31] The consolidation did rationalise the industry in a positive way. During the First World War, SKF had been a relatively inefficient producer of bearings when examined, using the ideas of mass production and Taylorism. The expansion of the bearings industry as a whole had been completed without a view towards increased efficiency: given the profits were so high, there was little need for efficiency. Ever more workers were hired to meet production needs, and there were no improvements in TFP. Control of the industry in the 1920s, the seed for which was sown during the war, gave SKF the ability to set new standards of efficiency for production.

Application of Taylorism

The war was not a period in which mechanised efficiency was applied to the Swedish ball bearings industry. Industrial wages were high but lagged behind increases in ball bearings prices. Profits were quite favourable for firms. Employing more workers and acquiring more factory space during the war were the easiest ways to increase production and still maintain profits. Following gains in the first year, industrial wages always lagged so that the initial difference was maintained. The price of ball bearings increased by 19 per cent by the end of 1914, while wages only increased 2 per cent. The difference of 17 per cent represented excess profit for SKF and was sustained over time. Subsequent years of the war show the surplus between industrial wages and bearing prices as being maintained at between 13–21 per cent. SKF net profits increased, on average, by 30 per cent per annum between 1915 and 1918.[32] However, productivity stagnated throughout the war. Bearings produced per worker fluctuated between 579 and 680 and bearings per unit of machinery capital remained between 4.04 and 4.67 Swedish crowns.

The economic malaise of the immediate postwar period and the 1920s, combined with the lack of war demand, meant that SKF was in significant financial trouble. Demand for ball bearings was naturally lower with the end of the war, but production and employee counts were declining even before then: by the end of 1918, the factory in Gothenburg had shed more than a quarter of its workforce compared to eighteen months before. The situation consistently worsened, with employee numbers in 1923 ultimately falling to an eighth of their wartime peak.[33]

Losses were inevitable and were made worse by the company's relative immaturity with handling international sales. Because of the corporate structure as it existed then, profits had been booked during and immediately after the war when bearings left Sweden, something which was logical if they were sold directly from Sweden to the end user, but the company had, unfortunately, not adopted new accounting methods to account for sales through the foreign agents. So profits were booked when bearings were transferred to these agents.[34] In wartime this was fine, as inventories were tight, but in a low-demand environment, this inevitably meant booking profits for inventories which were not actually sold to an end user, but merely held by the agent pending sale.[35] The company was forced to write down the value of its inventories in the early 1920s, leading to near financial collapse. Drastic rationalisation of SKF and its controlled entities occurred. Efficiency in production became important. The sales agents were replaced by SKF-managed sales offices in 42 different countries. Goods were henceforth taken under consignment by the foreign branches to avoid any accounting issues.

Like many American firms, SKF was caught in the general move towards Taylorism in the 1920s.[36] There is no question SKF's control of the ball bearings patent in the early 1920s give it a lead over its competitors, but when demand returned to industry, improved efficiency in production gave SKF a decisive advantage. The number of high-skilled white-collar workers in the firm swelled, and the number of blue-collar workers grew slowly. Despite reductions in overall labour figures, technical personnel increased from 10,000 in 1910 to 30,000 by the beginning of the Second World War.[37] The company looked increasingly like one of Chandler's famous M-form companies, with worldwide divisions coordinated from a head-office in Sweden.[38] The "coordinating" and management elements in the Swedish office included a technical department for manufacturing the machines that produced the bearings. This office standardised all production within the worldwide group and, of course, could cut off any subsidiary from machines or from the raw materials necessary to continue production. The Swedish home office continued to be at the centre of a closely coordinated production group.[39]

Taylorism, reorganisation and a significant investment in machinery paid off substantially. As seen in Table 4.3, productivity in the Swedish factories began to increase from 1923. With just 566 employees, bearings per worker increased from a paltry 244 in 1922 to 1,236 in 1923. With full implementation of Taylor policies and significant demand in 1939, bearings per head increased to some 4,245 units per worker per year. This is nearly six times the wartime average per worker and shows the increased levels of productivity achievable because of the consolidation, rationalisation, reorganisation and investment completed in the postwar period.

Without this application of Taylorism, it would have been unlikely that the firm could have met the extreme demands placed on it in the Second World War. As seen in Table 4.2, initial production at the start of the war was about 13 times the peak rate in the First World War, and by 1943,

Table 4.3 SKF Bearings per Worker, 1914–1939

	Bearings Manufactured (Units)	Machinery and Tools (Crowns)	Employees	Bearings per Head	Machinery and Tools per Head	Machinery and Tools per Bearing
	I	II	III	IV=I÷III	V=II÷III	VI=II÷I
1914	1,100,000		1,900	579		
1915	1,700,000	6,873,000	2,500	680	2,749	4.04
1916	2,400,000	9,416,000				3.92
1917	2,800,000	13,196,000	4,300	651	3,068	4.71
1918	2,800,000	12,932,000	4,500	622	2,874	4.62
1922	200,000		820	244		
1923	700,000		566*	1,236		
1939	16,300,000		3,840*	4,245		

Sources: Fritz and Karlsson, *SKF*, pp. 33–5, 50–1, 61–2; Svenska Kullagerfabriken, *SKF 1907–57*; Steckzén, *Svenska Kullagerfabriken*, p. 236.

Notes: Asterisks (*) indicate employees imputed from available production and bearing per head values. Swedish factories only.

that number reached 18 times. Moreover, as suggested by Golson, the firm controlled most of the European ball bearings market, providing at least 58 per cent of German supplies and 31 per cent of British.[40] There was clear favouritism, with pricing differences shown first towards the Germans and then towards the Allies.[41] The company also managed to avoid sanctions and had its German assets guaranteed in exchange for a deal to limit supply shipments to Germany in 1944. Very few firms in the history of economic warfare have ever had such guarantees and consideration. The economic moat SKF developed in and from the First World War clearly protected it in the Second.[42]

Conclusion: The War and Long-Term Growth of SKF

As an American report put it, "by 1928 it was certainly evident that SKF had embarked on a world-wide domination of the ball bearings industry."[43] This dominating position had come in large part because of the transformation during the war. SKF thrived during and after the war because it had a unique product and several business advantages. Using the tools of an international organisation and two-tiered manufacturing, it was able to overcome the problems posed first by economic warfare and later by tariffs. Vertical supply chain integration with the purchase of Hofors gave SKF a quality advantage over its rivals. Purchase of the Conrad patent, made available by the war and the threat of enemy seizure, ensured it was even able to charge others royalties, guaranteeing it would profit even from its competitors' sales. In the inevitable period of oversupply after the war, the company was able to rationalise and apply Taylorism to increase productivity and profit. This industrial growth, pushed forward by the war, moved a small Swedish ball bearings manufacturer from a domestic player to a global one.

Notes

1 See Stephen Broadberry and Mark Harrison, *The Economics of World War I* (Cambridge: Cambridge University Press, 2005), 310ff; Alfred D. Chandler Jr, *The Visible Hand* (Boston, MA: Harvard University Press, 1993). We gratefully acknowledge funding from Handelsbanken, the University of Warwick and the Swiss government. For help and comments, we thank: Anders Ögren, Ben Wubs, Jari Eloranta, Lennart Schön, Les Hannah and Tobias Karlsson and participants at the Armageddon and Mammon conference as well as those at the annual conferences of the Economic and Business History Society and the European Business History Association in Manchester and Utrecht, respectively.

2 Adam Tooze, *The Deluge: The Great War, America and the Remaking of the Global Order, 1916–1931* (London: Penguin, 2014), 200ff. Swedish TFP estimates calculated from Krantz and Schön, "Swedish Historical National Accounts 1560–2010" as reported in Eric Golson and J. Lennard, "What Was the Impact of World War I on Swedish Economic Performance?," n.d.

3 Eric B. Golson, "Did Swedish Ball Bearings Keep the Second World War Going? Re-Evaluating Neutral Sweden's Role," *Scandinavian Economic History Review* 60, no. 2 (2012): 165–82.

4 Ibid.

5 Statistiska Centralbyrån, *Historisk Statistic för Sverige*, 300; Edvinsson, *Growth, Accumulation, Crisis*, 398.

6 Lennart Schön and Olle Krantz, "Swedish Historical National Accounts 1560–2010," *Lund Papers in Economic History* 123 (2012).

7 For a discussion of the sources of Swedish economic growth between 1914 and 1929 see Golson and Lennard, "What Was the Impact of World War I on Swedish Economic Performance?"

8 Ibid.

9 Erik Lindahl, Einar Dahlgren, and Karin Kock, *National Income of Swedew, 1861–1930, Part Two* (London: P.S. King & Son Ltd, 1937), 596.

10 Lennart Schön and Ken Schubert, *Sweden's Road to Modernity: An Economic History* (Stockholm: SNS förlag Stockholm, 2010), 245.

11 SKF, *Annual Report, 1920.*

12 Alfred D. Chandler, "The Emergence of Managerial Capitalism," *Business History Review* 58, no. 4 (1984): 473–503.

13 NARA, RG169/211/1, *Report of SKF.*

14 M. Fritz and B. Karlsson, *SKF-a Global Story* (Stockholm: Informationsförlaget, 2006), 27.

15 Eric Bernard Golson, "The Economics of Neutrality: Spain, Sweden and Switzerland in the Second World War" (London School of Economics, 2011).

16 Broadberry and Harrison, *The Economics of World War I*, 34ff.

17 NARA, RG169/211/1, *Report of SKF.*

18 Fritz and Karlsson, *SKF-a Global Story*, 33.

19 NARA, RG169/211/1, *Report of SKF.*

20 Chandler, "The Emergence of Managerial Capitalism."

21 NARA, RG169/211/1, *Report of SKF.*

22 NARA, RG169/211/1, *Report of SKF.*

23 Fritz and Karlsson, *SKF*, 48.

24 NARA, RG107/160/925, *The Swedish Ball Bearings Business.*
25 Broadberry and Harrison, *Economics of World War I.*
26 Fritz and Karlsson, *SKF-a Global Story*, 46.
27 NARA, RG169/211/1, *Report of SKF.*
28 NARA, RG169/211/1, *Report of SKF.*
29 Ibid., 36–40.
30 NARA, RG169/211/1, *Report of SKF.*
31 NARA, RG169/211/1, *Report of SKF.*
32 Same as Table 5.1.; Brian Redman Mitchell, *European Historical Statistics, 1750–1970* (London: Macmillan, 1978), 74.
33 SKF, *Annual Reports, 1918–1929*; NARA, RG169/211/1, *Report of SKF.*
34 NARA, RG169/211/1, *Report of SKF.*
35 Fritz and Karlsson, *SKF-a Global Story*, 49–52.
36 Chandler, "The Emergence of Managerial Capitalism."
37 Fritz and Karlsson, *SKF-a Global Story*, 59–60.
38 Chandler, "The Emergence of Managerial Capitalism."
39 NARA, RG169/211/1, *Report of SKF.*
40 Golson, "Did Swedish Ball Bearings Keep the Second World War Going? Re-Evaluating Neutral Sweden's Role."
41 Ibid.
42 National Archives, FO837/916, *Contraband Control, etc.*
43 NARA, RG169/211/1, *Report of SKF.*

Primary sources

National Archives, FO837/916, Contraband Control, etc: Ball and Roller Bearings.
National Archives and Records Administration (NARA), RG107/160/925, *The Swedish Ball Bearing Business.*
National Archives and Records Administration, RG169/211/1, *Report of SKF.*
SKF, Annual Reports, 1918–29.
Statistiska Centralbyrån, Historisk Statistic för Sverige: Del. 3. Utrikeshandel, 1732–1970 (Stockholm, 1972).
Sveriges Officiella Statistik, *Handel* (Stockholm, 1913–8).

Bibliography

Broadberry, Stephen, and Mark Harrison. *The Economics of World War I.* Cambridge: Cambridge University Press, 2005.
Chandler, Alfred D. "The Emergence of Managerial Capitalism." *Business History Review* 58, no. 4 (1984): 473–503.
Chandler, Jr., Alfred D. *The Visible Hand.* Boston, MA: Harvard University Press, 1993.
Edvinsson, Rodney. *Growth, Accumulation, Crisis: With New Macroeconomic Data for Sweden 1800–2000.* Stockholm, 2005.
Fritz, Martin, and Birgit Karlsson. *SKF-a Global Story.* Stockholm: Informations för laget, 2006.
Golson, Eric B. "Did Swedish Ball Bearings Keep the Second World War Going? Re-Evaluating Neutral Sweden's Role." *Scandinavian Economic History Review* 60, no. 2 (2012): 165–82.
Golson, Eric Bernard. *The Economics of Neutrality: Spain, Sweden and Switzerland in the Second World War.* London: London School of Economics, 2011.

Lindahl, Erik, Einar Dahlgren, and Karin Kock. *National Income of Swedew, 1861–1930, Part Two*. London: P.S. King & Son Ltd, 1937.

Mitchell, Brian Redman. *European Historical Statistics, 1750–1970*. London: Macmillan, 1978.

Schön, Lennart, and Olle Krantz. "Swedish Historical National Accounts 1560–2010." *Lund Papers in Economic History* 123 (2012): 1–34.

Schön, Lennart. *Sweden's Road to Modernity: An Economic History*. Stockholm: SNS förlag Stockholm, 2010.

Steckzén, Birger. *Svenska Kullagerfabriken: En Svensk Exportindustris Historia, 1907–1957*. Gothenburg, 1957.

Svenska Kullagerfabriken. *SKF 1907–57: En Bildrevy*. Gothenburg, 1957.

Tooze, Adam. *The Deluge: The Great War, America and the Remaking of the Global Order, 1916–1931*. London: Penguin, 2014.

5 The Great War

Matrix of the International Chamber of Commerce, a Fortunate *Business League of Nations*

Clotilde Druelle-Korn

Introduction

Business and economic historians have published relatively little on the development of international Business Interest Organizations (BIAs).[1] This chapter will improve our understanding of the history of international BIAs by examining the formation of the International Chamber of Commerce (ICC) in the immediate aftermath of the First World War. Officially founded in Paris in June 1920, the ICC became a consultative body of the League of Nations. Since 1946, it has been connected to the United Nations. Throughout its history, this organization has maintained a low profile as it has attempted to promote international trade. Over the decades, its main activity has been the resolution of international disputes by arbitration, an efficient procedure for dealing with sensitive matters.

There is no published history of ICC other than *Merchants of Peace*, an official history written in 1938 by George L. Ridgeway. An updated version of the book was released in 1959.[2] The title is both a program and a public statement. Ridgeway was a college professor and corporate executive who worked for IBM and served on numerous committees within the US Chamber of Commerce and the State Department. In the same vein, the book has a foreword by James T. Shotwell, scholar of the History of International Relations at Columbia University. After the Paris Peace Conference, Shotwell became head of the Carnegie Endowment for International Peace. He spent years tirelessly editing the 150 volumes of a history of the impact of the Great War on the economic and social life of nations, covering 15 countries. As he said himself, "Not merely a study of its cost but of the way in which it had affected the life and thought of a generation."[3]

These two men with their respective positions interweaving the public and private spheres, goodwill and internationalism, while supporting their country's interests, embodied the spirit that produced the ICC. The institution launched at the end of the Great War was an American and European joint effort. It began as a club for businessmen from Allied nations, then extended its scope within a few years to include businessmen from other countries. The launch of the ICC gave rise to different expectations in the newly rich United States than in the war-exhausted economies of Europe. Soon, parties found common ground, promoting political and economic liberalism, sharing the will to move beyond nationalism, political speeches, endless Allied war debts and German reparation debates. The overall aim of the ICC was to facilitate international trade. In order to achieve this aim, the ICC undertook to draft a common trade language known as the Incoterms, or International Commercial Terms. This common terminology was quickly adopted in international commercial transactions as a way of reducing ambiguity and confusion.[4] The ICC also became a pragmatic broker of private and public interests and a place for a parallel system of economic and financial diplomacy under the approving gaze of the respective national governments. Officially represented in Geneva, the International Chamber of Commerce grew as the businessman's *League of Nations* within which the Americans played a leading role. Thus, the United States' alleged retreat from international engagement was more a façade than a reality. In matters of business and finance, the US government actually worked closely with organized business during the 1920s, as has been argued persuasively since the 1950s by Carl Parini, William A. Williams and Joan Hoff-Wilson.

This chapter aims to trace the history of ICC from its original inception through the decade following the Great War, to highlight its importance in understanding how firms, businessmen and their organizations recomposed themselves in the new world born from the rubble of the Great War, and how they planned to work with new international bodies, specifically the League of Nations, thus shaping a pioneering chapter in the process of international integration. It also intends to outline the value system of the ICC founders (avoiding both naivety and cynicism) and to identify the intentions and achievements of the nascent institution.

This chapter shows how the war led directly to the creation of the ICC, which brought businessmen of different nationalities together. This chapter thus helps to undermine the widespread idea that the First World War halted the process of globalization and even caused deglobalization. This chapter will suggest that the creation of the ICC in the aftermath of the First World War actually facilitated globalization. In its first decade, the ICC then undertook specific reforms that made international trade easier. Perhaps the most important of these reforms was the development of International Commercial Terms, or Incoterms.

The chapter is based on a range of primary sources. The ICC, which continues to keep a low profile, restricts access to its archive in Paris.[5] In writing the early history of this organization, it is necessary to visit other archives, including those of its member national organizations.

This chapter is based mainly on primary sources from the ICC's Parisian headquarters, US Chamber of Commerce papers, the Herbert Hoover Presidential Archives and League of Nations records. This chapter also draws on printed reports and official publications, among them ICC's house journal, which first appeared in 1924.[6] It deals specifically with the origins, ways and means of ICC and how it turned to be an international representative body during the 1920s. Then, it sketches out the networks shared by ICC and the League of Nations, and examines the similar agendas of these two organizations which supported each other with the consent of national governments. Finally, it outlines the way in which ICC handled the major financial issues of those years, and the Chamber's main achievements during its first decade of existence, before drawing a few conclusions.

A World of Opportunities, the Burden of Responsibilities

The antecedents of ICC can be traced back to the middle of the nineteenth century, when the first World Exhibitions brought millions of visitors—numerous businessmen among them—towards the European capitals and booming US cities. The journeys were often encouraged by their local Chamber of Commerce, the oldest form of business organization found all over the world. In line with such events, prominent European and American Chambers formed the habit of gathering to engage in talks about designing and promoting international standards and regulations. Formed on the initiative of the prominent Belgian industrialist and chair of the Mons Chamber of Commerce Louis Canon-Legrand (1860–1940), a loosely organized World Congress of Chambers of Commerce met in Liege (1905), Milan (1906), Prague (1908), London (1910) and Boston (1912). Approximately 1,800 to 2,000 delegates attended those conventions. The last was held in Paris in June 1914. Among the US participants were Edward A. Filene and John H. Fahey, of whom we shall hear more soon.

The early years of the First World War offered an opportunity to reconsider ways of achieving a permanent and better-coordinated worldwide organization. This time, the initiative came from the US Chamber of Commerce, the newborn nationwide organization founded in 1912 with the support of the Taft Administration.[7] Before discussing the ICC in detail, we should bear in mind how quickly businessmen's associations, backed by their governments, had drawn up international post-war trade plans, mostly related to economic war aims—as early as 1915 in Germany, France and Great Britain, even September 1914, in the case of the US National Foreign Trade Council.[8] As an example, a delegation from the American Manufacturers' Export Association toured France for several weeks in September and October 1916.[9]

In April 1919, Jean Monnet, Special Representative of the French Minister of Commerce within the Allied bodies, informed his superior that Edward A. Filene and Edward G. Miner were in France. He had been introduced to them by Thomas Lamont, the J.P. Morgan banker who was then an American Treasury Department delegate at the Peace Conference. Joined in their mission by Alfred C. Bedford, Chairman of the Board of the Standard Oil Company and Vice President of the US Chamber, they were pursuing several goals: promoting the idea of an International Chamber of Commerce, assessing the economic needs of Europe, figuring how the US could help. To achieve these goals, they suggested a mission including a delegation of prominent businessmen from France, Great Britain, Belgium and Italy who would set sail without delay for North America, at the expense of the US Chamber of Commerce, to visit their peers and explain the European financial and economic situation and their own needs.

Etienne Clémentel (1864–1936), the well-established head of the French Commerce and Industry Ministry, understood the advantages of the offer. He foresaw opportunities to push forward the controversial French economic post-war agenda, while at the same time, the delegates at the Paris Conference were negotiating the terms of the economic and financial peace treaties in a tense atmosphere. Moreover, in the spring of 1919, the Minister had just persuaded the many French trade associations to form a national organization to challenge the dominant Confédération Générale du Travail as a trade union counterpart within the future International Labor Organization. The American offer was thus also a way to promote the newborn Confédération Générale de la Production Française (CGPF) in France, by asking it to select the French delegation.[10]

In mid-October 1919, a delegation of 20 French, eight English, seven Belgian and 15 Italian businessmen, led by the French steel magnate Eugène Schneider, landed for a five-week journey through the United States. They spent a few days attending the US Chamber of Commerce congress and the massive International Trade Conference held in Atlantic City,[11] then toured the major eastern and midwestern cities. No time was left to visit the West Coast. These emissaries formed ten special committees to deal with major commodities, trade and markets, finances and transportation. They explained their needs at length and tried to figure out what they could expect from their counterparts. One committee was in charge of setting up a permanent organization. The French and Americans were the most committed to doing this and a meeting was scheduled in Paris for June 1920.

A Worldwide Organization Based in Paris and Modeled on the US Chamber of Commerce

From June 23rd to 30th 1920, a few weeks before the end of the Peace Conference, delegates from the United States (150), England (50), Belgium (25), Italy (35) and France convened in Paris for the final arrangements before the official inauguration of the *Chambre de Commerce Internationale*, or International Chamber of Commerce. Etienne Clémentel, who was a senator at the time and no longer a Cabinet Minister, had been instrumental in pushing forward the ICC idea. He was unanimously elected President, along with four Vice Presidents: Alfred C. Bedford (US), Louis Canon-Legrand (Belgium), Rolando Ricci (Italy) and Arthur Shirley Benn (Great Britain). Paris had been chosen at the request of the Americans, who argued that it was essential for the permanent organization to settle in Europe, close to Geneva and potential market opportunities. The French had suggested Washington and the English, Brussels or Paris. The function of the Chamber, as expressed in its by-laws, was

> To facilitate the commercial intercourse of countries, to secure harmony of action on all international questions affecting finance, industry and commerce, to encourage progress and to promote peace and cordial relations among countries and their citizens by the co-operation of businessmen and organizations devoted to the development of commerce and industry. The International Chamber is a confederation of the main economic forces of the countries included in its memberships united in each country by a national organization.[12]

The independence of ICC from government control or influence was strongly stated.

The rules of the agency accurately reflected the balance of power.[13] Succinctly, they were written along the lines of the US Chamber rules, with one major deviation. The American delegates would have liked direct adhesion of business and trade associations and their members to ICC. The French defended the granting of full membership to firms and trade organizations only through national committees representative of the economic life of each country. The latter point of view won the day, to the satisfaction of Etienne Clémentel who as a consequence secured the French national BIA (CGPF) he had promoted. He hoped with that provision to protect French interests better. The organization chart stated: a Council, General Meetings, National Committees, general headquarters and a Secretariat. Action was taken via conferences of experts, by referendum and through economic inquiries and publication of the results. To sum up, full membership was assigned only through the national committee. Each company cast one or more votes according to size and character and contributed proportionally to the Chamber's expenses. In addition, there were associate members—firms or individuals—without votes but entitled to the Chamber's services and to take part in its discussions.

Originally a club of businessmen from the former Allied nations, ICC quickly evolved into a worldwide organization that included the representatives of nations that had been neutral in the Great War, such as the Netherlands and Scandinavian countries. Business interests from the newly established Czechoslovakia joined the organization and in 1925, Germany joined. The tight budget of the first years was hardly sufficient for its needs. Thanks to Eugène Schneider, ICC paid a low rent to accommodate its permanent Secretariat.[14] The American Chamber provided some help, as did the French Department of Commerce, that for a few years subsidized the fledgling ICC through the French National Committee.[15] In 1926, ICC was finally able to purchase a private hotel in the Cours Albert 1er in the 8th *arrondissement* of Paris.[16] Apart from regular meetings of the Council and

General Meetings, an international congress was held every other year: London in 1921 followed by Rome (1923), Amsterdam (1925), Stockholm (1927), Amsterdam again (1929), Vienna (1933), Paris (1935) etc.

International Networks Established During the Great War Join the League of Nations and ICC

It would be judicious to study in greater detail the destinies and movements of the people involved in the many Allied bodies in London, in the numerous national War Boards, in the major relief organizations of the time, together with those who joined the League of Nations, and ran or worked for ICC. Overlapping appears to be astonishingly high. I mention only a few examples of significant migration between New York, London, Paris and Geneva. It is clear that the London Economic and Financial Allied Bureau and the Executives—for instance, the Wheat Executive—were a breeding ground for an international milieu eager to continue its duties once the war was over. After London, almost all the London staff served for months on the many Commissions at the Paris Peace Conference and on the Supreme Economic Council. Those people had learned to work together and gained a great deal of civilian expertise in international economics, logistics, finances etc. The League of Nations was a natural outcome and the next place from which international tasks and missions could be carried out. Let us consider Joseph Avenol. He was the French Treasury delegate in London during the war, Under-Secretary of the League in 1923, chosen as Secretary in 1933. From Great Britain, there was Arthur Salter, colleague of Jean Monnet in 1917–1918 on the Chartering Committee of the Allied Maritime Transport Council. In 1919 he was appointed Secretary to the Supreme Economic Council in Paris, moved to Geneva, then was installed as head of the Economic and Financial Section of the League in 1923. In France, the Department of Commerce in daily contact with the London bureau was another matrix. Several of Etienne Clémentel's assistants obtained official positions at the League Secretariat, successively handling the economic aspects of the war within the Department of Commerce, then moving to Geneva to represent French interests. Jean Monnet is the best known; there are others like Daniel Serruys, who chaired the League's Economic Committee.

In the US, the associations of businessmen represented on numerous War Boards, and bankers, such as the House of Morgan, were other breeding grounds of internationalists. The same patterns would be found among the staff of American private relief bodies like the Commission for Relief in Belgium, well marshalled by Herbert C. Hoover. These organizations were incubators for talented businessmen and philanthropists eager to with pronounced internationalist and anti-isolationist views. Moreover, many of these Americans spent time in England or France and took part in the Paris Conference. Frederick Paul Keppel is an interesting case. Besides serving as the first American commissioner to ICC, he was Secretary of the American

Association for International Conciliation before the war, unofficial adviser then Assistant Secretary of War in Washington and first Director of Foreign Operations in the American Red Cross in France.

When the results of the US mid-term elections of 1918 jeopardized the League of Nations, centerpiece of Wilson's post-war policy, the plan for an International Chamber of Commerce would have seemed more desirable both to this brand of internationalists as well as businessmen and some politicians. Looking back on the US Chamber deputation of 1919 in France, the cancellation of the American commercial attaché's trip to Paris decided after the mid-term elections was a source of concern for the American business organization spurring into action. In late 1918, prominent US BIA had spoken in favor of cancelling war debts. In Paris, Thomas Lamont was worried about the lack of economic recovery that he observed in the country. In May 1919, the banker and Herbert Hoover, who, among several positions, was a member of the Peace American Commission, sent a note to Wilson proposing the creation of a private international committee of businessmen and bankers to submit loan projects for Europe.[17] As a delegate of the Paris Conference, Etienne Clémentel was aware of a breakdown in solidarity between the Allies. He was anxious about the replacement of American public loans to France by private loans, and the question of the collaterals that would be required. He thus welcomed the American delegation, in particular Edward A. Filene, a prominent businessman and a pro-League campaigner;[18] it was good news in a tense atmosphere. What Clémentel apparently did not know was that the US mission had been officially endorsed by the US War Emergency and Reconstruction Conference of December 6th, 1918.[19] Neither the French Minister of Commerce nor the US Chamber were naive idealists or greedy robbers: they were politicians and businessmen acting to promote well-considered private and national advantages while—at least in some cases—bearing in mind a kind of ideal. Among the "Business Internationalists," to borrow Joan Hoff-Wilson's expression, we find at the forefront the names of Edward A. Filene, Thomas W. Lamont, Herbert Hoover and Owen D. Young.[20] These familiar figures in American business life were also founder members of the International Chamber, serving during the 1920s on the ICC Council and its American National Committee.

ICC and League of Nations' Mutual Interests

Until his illness in 1930, Etienne Clémentel played a pivotal role within ICC.[21] As President of the organization as well as President of its French National Committee and an influential senator, he established during those crucial years close private and official links between ICC and the League. In his daily task, he was assisted by a Secretary-General, Edouard Dolléans.[22] In the United States, the 1920 elections did not provide a clear solution for the League. Thus, on January 18th, 1921, the American delegate to ICC Council stated his wish for the Chamber to secure relations with the

League, becoming its adviser in matters of finance, industry and trade. Clémentel offered to negotiate, stipulating that the Chamber would maintain its independence[23]. Throughout the Peace Conference, the former Minister of Commerce had stood firm on a new economic order managed by the Allies and US only, monitoring raw materials—including American ones.[24] He soon had to stand down. Being a pragmatic man, he endorsed the more liberal spirit of an ICC open to all countries, even those not yet members of the League, and including former enemies. Clémentel was on good terms with Léon Bourgeois (1851–1925), the first President of the League of Nations. They were politically close, belonging to the same party, *la Gauche Radicale*, and sharing the core values of *Solidarism*, a French version of Progressivism. Moreover, as explained, Clémentel could count on many supporters in Geneva. ICC papers keep records of confidential meetings and talks between Clémentel and the League,[25] while the League's files mention number of phone calls with the ICC Secretariat.[26] In January 1922, the deal was almost done.

In 1923, the Chamber was officially invited to attend the conference on export formalities. The League's Economic Committee headed by Avenol asked for reports prepared by ICC. From then on, the Chamber was consulted as an international body (we must remember that ICC delegates in Geneva did not represent countries, only the International Chamber). For the US delegates, it was an adequate solution. In the second half of the 1920s, cooperation between the League and the Chamber became routine. While preparing the 1927 International Economic Conference, Arthur Salter told ICC he was expecting a great deal from its influence.[27] It is important to note that the relationship between ICC and the League was confined to economic and financial matters. In 1921, having formally decided that labor—a divisive topic—was not within its field of competence, the Chamber had declined an offer from the International Labor Organization's (ILO) director Albert Thomas to participate. Nevertheless, Edouard Filene was active in both: ICC and ILO.[28] Another key man was Alberto Pirelli, helping Clémentel to bridge the two institutions between Paris and Geneva. As a jurist and prominent Italian industrialist, he served at the ICC Council and at the Economic Committee of the League. In 1927, he was elected President of the International Chamber.

If the League offered ICC international visibility and influence among business associations and national governments, the League might also benefit in return from ICC, and chiefly from the US presence, as it is emphasized in a long letter sent by the American pro-League journalist Arthur Sweeter to Arthur Salter after the Rome Congress in 1923:

Dear Salter, I am enormously struck with the desirability of using Mr. Booth (the new ICC President: see below) to the limit of our capacities. [. . .] Moreover, he is very pro-league. As I have told you, it was he who, by the aid of a memorandum sent from Geneva, convinced

Secretary Hughes to modify his original rejection of the invitation to the Customs Conference and instead, to send observers. That precedent may have the greatest importance as it was followed in the case of the Customs Conference, and if I may judge by Mr. Hughes' last speech, will be followed in other conferences. The sending of observers, of course is not all that we desire, but it is the essential first step to establish confidence. Mr. Booth is now going to Washington, in a small sense as an ambassador of the League. [. . .] As I see it, therefore Mr. Booth can be of the greatest help to us. Not only will he control the International Chamber of Commerce for nearly two years more, but also he has an extreme and double importance as regards the United States. First, he can bring personal representative influence to bear on the State, Commerce and Treasury Departments, such as almost no other American in the international field. Second, by his position with the Guaranty Trust Company he can also have a good deal of influence in New York financial quarters.[29]

The American members elected to ICC Council or heading the American National Committee were indeed powerful businessmen and bankers: Willis H. Booth (Vice President of Guarantee Trust), John H. Fahey (Associated Press, Boston), Edward A. Filene, William Butterworth (President Deere and Co), Harry Wheeler (Vice President of Union Trust Co), Owen D. Young (General Electric, RCA), A. C. Bedford (Chairman Standard Oil) and Fred I. Kent (Vice President of Bankers' Trust Co.). Among the American National Committee members was the name of Herbert C. Hoover, then Secretary of Commerce and President of the American Engineering Council of Federated American Engineering Societies. Like a number of his fellows in the American Chapter, Hoover was pro-League. This position did not prevent him standing up vigorously for the payment of Allied war debts: in his opinion, the debts were not negotiable, only the repayment time and the interest rate were. As noted earlier, the 1919 US Chamber initiative had been supported by the Wilson Administration.[30] The positive attitude towards ICC endured during the Harding and Coolidge Administrations, as documented by the Herbert Hoover Commerce Papers. In view of this, we should remember that Hoover was a powerful Secretary of Commerce portrayed as the "Under Secretary of Everything." He was part of the World War Trade Commission supervising loans to foreign countries, yet on the American National Committee, he adopted a moderate position.[31] During his tenure at the Department, Hoover asked every US commercial attaché in Europe under his direction to attend each ICC Congress. He was kept informed by two channels: officially through commercial attachés, and by former close collaborators from the war years occupying major positions in business organizations. Julius H. Barnes, head of the Grain Corporation during the war, elected President of the US Chamber of Commerce in 1923, chaired the American Delegation at the ICC meeting in Rome in the same year. In his letters to Hoover, he claimed to have been "quite impressed with the ICC which has just closed. The character of men, their character and record entitled it to a considerable measure of respect."[32]

The 1920s: European Financial Recovery, War Debts and Reparations

"European needs and American interests" is the title of a long note found among the ICC papers, probably prepared for the 1919 transatlantic meeting:

> America's interest in the situation is very direct and vital. The country as a whole, on grounds of humanity and grounds of loyalty to her allies, cannot be indifferent to the suffering and demoralization of Europe. The country as a whole has a direct interest in reviving the industry and the credit of the countries which are indebted to us to the extent of many billions. Unless Europe can revive her industry and produce and sell goods, she cannot even pay the interest on her debt to us. In addition, there is a particular interest in the United States on the part of exporters and those producing goods for export, to retain the European markets. This special element of our population expects to make profits of a very substantial sort through siding in the rehabilitation of Europe.[33]

The issues are laid bare. On the last page is a list of measures that the Committee wished to consider. It comes as no surprise to find that the principles expressed were consistent with the provisions of the War Finance Corporation and those of the Edge Bill then under discussion: there was to be little or (preferably) no government initiative, but instead, private initiative and increasing confidence on the part of the public as a whole in the credit machinery to be set up.

No minutes were taken down in shorthand during the very sensitive Credit and Finance Committee sessions, contrary to the procedure on the other Atlantic City Committees.[34] The Americans and Europeans involved wanted to be efficient and pragmatic. They refused to be caught in political or public opinion poses at home or abroad. ICC followed this course of action during the 1920s. If exchange rate and monetary policy issues were crucial at the time, I have found little evidence of talks about them, unlike the discussions on debts and reparations, which were a hot topic and persistent preoccupation for all members. As early as 1920, the ICC delegate Jean Proix was invited to attend the Financial Conference organized in Brussels. The results were disappointing. However, and so, ICC set up an International Finances Committee following its London Congress in 1921, headed by the English banker Walter Leaf, later President of ICC (1925). Its object was

> to establish a permanent liaison of an international character between the Financiers of the different countries, enable them to discuss

international financial problems and to recommend any measures they consider would be conductive to a return to commercial stability and normal economic relations.[35]

Prominent leaders of the Chamber were enrolled. The aim was for ICC to be asked to cooperate with the newly established Allied Reparations Commission.[36]

Willis H. Booth and Fred I. Kent were American members on the ICC Finances Committee. At the 1923 Rome Congress, both were instrumental in promoting a well-balanced and publicized resolution, building momentum towards the Dawes plan. ICC was eager to take credit for the adoption of the Dawes plan; the reality is subtler. Nevertheless, the Chamber did play a role. The ICC Congress in Rome, hosted by Mussolini, opened on March 24th. Two months earlier, the German debt default had led to the occupation of the Ruhr by French and Belgium troops. Tensions were high. England and the United States did not favor such an extreme solution. In the midst of the crisis, Clémentel called for a rapprochement. The ICC Finances Committee, led by Fred I. Kent, worked to find ground for a practical rather than a political solution. Maurice Despret (Banque de Bruxelles), Maurice Lewandoswski (Comptoir National d'Escompte, Paris), the English banker Sir Felix Shuster, K. A. Wallenberg from Sweden, the Dutchman W. Westerman and Alfredo Pirelli agreed to draft a resolution recognizing a moral obligation to repay the debts while requesting adjustments based on Germany's real capacity to pay. The text was unanimously adopted by the ICC Congress. In order to give it more weight, the Council decided to endorse the candidacy of Willis H. Booth, Vice President of Guaranty Trust Co., to the presidency of ICC and to let Fred I. Kent speak at length in favor of the resolution.[37] Kent's address was a vibrant appeal to American businessmen, bankers and financiers. Since the national governments and American administration seemed motionless, as if frozen in political embarrassment, his fellow businessmen would have to take the lead in imagining and offering solutions. As a concrete measure, he called for a group of experts to be set up, to work on a practical plan which would then be submitted to governments.

In line with this proposal, a vast public campaign was launched in the United States towards obtaining the successful implementation of the resolution. The idea had been in the air since late 1922. In early May 1923, the ICC American National Committee was proud to announce that 420 articles had already reported on the Rome meeting. The scheme was taken up by European officials. In a letter to Herbert Hoover, A. C. Bedford alluded to discussions that had apparently taken place between Willis H. Booth and Raymond Poincaré, the French Président du Conseil. A press release from Poincaré on November 11th, 1923 explicitly referred to the Rome resolution. Bedford concluded that

[. . .] it is an open secret that Mr. Booth's intervention, as representative of the International Chamber reinforced decisively the constructive forces and influence set in motion by the suggestion of Secretary of State Hughes that such an inquiry as conducted by the Dawes Committee should be instated.[38]

The Dawes and McKenna Committees working with the Commission of Reparations resulted in the London Agreement of August 1924. At this time, Clémentel was in charge of finances in the new Cartel des Gauches Government. The agreement was in phase with the principles put forward by the Rome resolution. Altogether, 15 leading members of the ICC Council and its national chapters served on the above Committees and Commission, among them Owen D. Young, Henry M. Robinson (First National Bank, Los Angeles), Alberto Pirelli and the Belgian Albert E. Janssen. The conclusions of the report published by the ICC Economic Recovery Committee in the fall of 1923 were also included in the Dawes Plan. We will not discuss the Plan here, or how it was put into effect, backed by the US administration. However, it is obvious that ICC played a by no means insignificant role in the war debt negotiations—a role which it is nonetheless difficult to quantify.

Trade Initiatives and Arbitration

From 1921 onwards, ICC was involved in two other major issues, besides European financial recovery, that we will only mention briefly here: the preparation and adoption of rules to facilitate international trade, and commercial disputes. The ICC London Congress of 1921 voted a resolution approving the simplification of customs formalities which was supported by the League agenda. An international conference was held in Geneva from October 15th to November 3rd. ICC representatives were influential in drafting a series of predefined commercial terms. The first volume of International Commercial Terms, providing a common language for traders and trade transactions around the world, was adopted and published by ICC in 1923 and proved to be the first of many. The terms eventually became accepted by governments, legal authorities and firms.

International commercial arbitration had often been discussed among Chambers of Commerce since the nineteenth century. At an ICC meeting in Paris in 1920, a resolution was adopted advocating the establishment of an international system of commercial arbitration. A special committee set up and studied the question, considering special commodities codes (cotton and silk for instance) as well as national practices. It was not an easy issue: some nations called for legislation to enforce the terms of an arbitral award, while others preferred to rely on moral sanctions which could be exerted by business organizations on a recalcitrant member. Owen D. Young, President of the US Chamber's Arbitrary Court, and Etienne Clémentel were great supporters of arbitration, a procedure saving time and money. The former French Minister of Commerce had considerable difficulty in getting the powerful Paris Chamber of Commerce to agree. Eventually, a law recognizing the arbitration clause in a contract was passed in France in 1923. The ICC Court of Commercial Arbitration was officially launched in January 1923 in the presence of Joost Adriaan Van Hamel, Director of the Legal Section of the League. Court sessions were to be held at the ICC headquarters in Paris with Clémentel as the first President. There were 113 affiliates representing finance, trade and industry. The Court was entitled to settle disputes arising in connection with international contracts between manufacturers and traders of different countries. The Chamber laid down the principles and procedural rules of conciliation and arbitration, since then widely endorsed. In September 1923, the General Assembly in Geneva invited its members to sign a convention recognizing the validity of the arbitration clause. Alberto Pirelli, who had written his law thesis on compulsory and binding arbitration, played a key role within the League on this particular subject.[39]

Over the years, dispute resolutions and the ICC INCONTERMS turned out to be the most successful services provided by the Chamber, which also pursued its interest in trade barriers and unfair competition. These issues were destined to be major topic during the 1930s. A special ICC sub-committee was set up, working closely with the League on this purpose. The Chamber published a first, inconclusive report for the 1927 Economic Conference, followed by many others during the years to come. After the 1931 congress held in Washington, ICC endorsed cartels and ententes along the overview of governments on national economy.[40]

Conclusion: ICC during the 1920s: An Economic Diplomacy Channel and an International Forum on Globalization to Consider and Investigate

International historians have documented the important role played by businessmen such as Thomas T. Lamont and Owen D. Young, the true negotiator of the Dawes Plan.[41] Business historiography is familiar with the names of Edward A. Filene, A. C. Bedford, Willis H. Booth and Alberto Pirelli. Etienne Clémentel is well known as the Finance Minister in the Cartel Government which endorsed the 1924 London Agreement. However, these men are rarely linked together and mentioned as founding members of the International Chamber of Commerce. Yet they were not just names on an official letterhead; they devoted time and energy to ensuring the ICC's very existence and pushing forward the major economic goals of the 1920s. This new organization was long kept off the radar even for scholars focusing on the international governance and cooperation of the post-First World War era[42]—an indication that business history, economic history and international relations studies still need to be less compartmentalized.

We draw several conclusions from this study of the ICC's first decade. Its history has to be considered from within a long-term perspective. The businessmen who flocked to those conventions organized in conjunction with World Fairs were looking for standards and regulations to ease the development of firms and industrialized societies as a whole. They were aware of a more interdependent world, based on international trade and financial systems. Thus, the Great War did not deter them, but rather, the opposite. The statistical arguments often put forward as proof of the end of the golden age of globalization do not exhaust the reality.[43] The catastrophe of the First World War spurred both private and public actors into action. While fighting, they were designing separate yet convergent economic plans for the aftermath, out of which grew the International Chamber of Commerce. "The Deluge" thus reshaped globalization to an extent, although further investigation is needed to determine the scale and scope of the reshaping. However, we can make assumptions on the basis of our own research—for example, about the guaranteeing of a uniform global system of international commercial law through international terms of agreement in sale contracts and the legal service provided by the International Court of Arbitration.

To all the belligerent parties—with the notable exception of Russia—and neutrals, the new debtors and new creditors, it was soon clear that the way to prosperity was to be found through extensive foreign trade and finance with a prominent role assigned to private sector. Clémentel's draft of an economic plan excluding the Central Powers did not long resist the wishes of both old and new economic acquaintances forged among industrial societies and firms—or American willpower. The Wilsonians' idea, however vague, of a League of Nations aiming to guarantee peace throughout the world appealed to businessmen and their associations. It offered a moral vision for their economic ambitions, in line with Montesquieu's belief that "l'effet naturel du doux commerce est de porter à la paix."[44] A non-governmental body like the International Chamber of Commerce might contribute to this great vision, backing the fragile League of Nations when needed.

Within the palette of techniques and institutions devised by private and public individuals and bodies to implement politics and ideals after the Great War, ICC was pivotal. Indeed, the International Chamber became a means of coordinating foreign economic diplomacy more efficiently while fostering goals for the private sector and firms. Formally absent from Geneva, the United States were nevertheless present through several channels. One was doubtlessly the International Chamber, as an official League of Nations expert. Far from the front pages of the newspapers and heated public debates, ICC provided a meeting place to discuss, test and help to implement alternative solutions to the war debts and reparations quandary.

The International Chamber of Commerce thus served as a forum to govern a new chapter of economic globalization, besides repairing the international financial situation. It was also used as an antechamber for former enemies before joining the League of Nations in Geneva. Throughout the 1923 Rome Congress, ICC Council, working with German ICC associate members, traced a path towards a German National Committee which officially joined the Chamber on November 6th, 1925, several months before its admission to the League of Nations. If the present chapter were to focus more on the French and American partners, further research would emphasize how, and with what expectations, associate members and national committees came to join ICC, specifically those from former enemy countries and from outside Europe and North America. The men who founded ICC and ran it during the 1920s shared to some extent the same ideal, interests, purposes and ambivalences. They wore many hats: shadow diplomats acting beside their respective governments, representatives of national business organizations, often at the head of leading industrial firms or banks seeking foreign development. The degree to which collective and individual interests and ideals were able to co-exist, reconciled or in conflict, within the same person should thus be gauged. More interrogations need clarification: to what degree and for how long did members of the League of Businessmen remained aligned with the positions of their peers and national organizations who had given them mandates? In other words, were they promoting globalization only for a few firms and sectors, and were they a vanguard facing possible disaffection from their mandates, which seems to have been the case in France in the late 1920s?

It is true to say that the free trade policy promoting peace championed by the International Chamber of Commerce in the aftermath of the Great War did not do much to prevent another world conflict. The empirical research and evidence on which this chapter is based constitute additional material for a more theoretical argument about the problematic theory of capitalist peace.

Notes

1 Two important works that deal with the subject are Yann Decorzant, *La Société des Nations et la naissance d'une conception de la régulation économique internationale* (Bruxelles: P.I.E, Peter Lang, 2011), 210–13; Monika Rosengarten, *Die Internationale Handelskammer, Wirtschaftpolitische Empfehlungen in der Zeit der Weltwirtschaftskrise 1929–1939* (Berlin: Duncker-Humbolt, 2001).

2 Boston, MA: Little, Brown & Cie. The book has no citing sources.

3 Quoted by Lisa Anderson, "James T. Shotwell: A Life Devoted to Organizing Peace." http://www.columbia.edu/cu/alumni/Magazine/Winter2005/llshotwell.html

4 For International Commercial Terms, INCONTERMS is a registered trademark of ICC.

5 http://www.iccwbo.org/about-icc/
The ICC has granted limited access to some historians. For their research, see Monika Rosengarten, who had access to some papers, as well as the present author, Clotilde Druelle-Korn, *Un Laboratoire réformateur, le Département du Commerce en France et aux États-Unis de la Grande Guerre aux Années Vingt*, (Ph.D. Diss. Paris, Institut d'Etudes Politiques, 2004).

6 The first issue of ICC-CCI magazine was published in Paris, July 1924.

7 Hagley Museum and Library, Wilmington. U.S. Chamber of Commerce records, Accession 1960, Series I, Box 1. See also, Richard Hume Werking, "Bureaucrats, Businessmen and Foreign Trade: The Origins of the United Chamber of Commerce," *Business History Review* 52, no. 3 (Autumn 1978). Werking based his research on the Secretary of Commerce Papers.

8 D. Geoffrey Gamble, *The NFTC Story, 1914–2014* (Indianapolis: Dog Ear Publishing, 2014).
   Hagley Museum and Library, Wilmington. National Foreign Trade Council (NFTC) records (Accession 2345).

9 *Report to the American Manufacturers Export Association by the American Industrial Commission to France, September-October 1916* (New York: Press of Redfield-Kendrick-Odell and Co, 1917).

10 Clotilde Druelle-Korn, "Entre concurrence et structuration du champ syndical patronal: genèse et affirmation de la Confédération générale de la production française (1919–1925)," in *Genèse des organisations patronales en Europe (19ᵉ-20ᵉ siècles)*, dir. Danièle Fraboulet, Pierre Vernus (Rennes: Presses Universitaires de Rennes, 2012), 153–63.

11 U.S. Chamber of Commerce, ACC. 1960, ADD Series conferences n°3, Albert Neve, records of the Conference, 1919.

12 ICC-CCI by-law.

13 ICC Papers, Paris. BIB 51, Minutes Permanent Organization Committee, October - November 1919.

14 Eight permanent employees in 1920, 24 in 1921, 28 in 1923.

15 Archives nationales du monde du travail (ANMT Roubaix). CGPF Records, 72 AS Carton 1 Comptabilité, Grands Livres.

16 ICC Papers, BIB 50, Budgets reports 1920–1929. ICC has only recently moved to another location, 43, avenue du President Wilson, 75116 Paris.

17 Denise Artaud, *La question des dettes interalliées et la reconstruction de l'Europe 1917–1920* (Lille: University of Lille, 1978), 146–52.

18 A leading figure of the Boston department store business, William Filene's Sons Co from Boston. Edward A. Filene (1860–1937) founded the Century Foundation in 1919, today the Twentieth Century Foundation, a progressive think tank.

19 U.S. Chamber of Commerce, ACC. 1960, Series I, Box 1. Board of Directors Minutes, Sessions 1914, 1917, 1918.

20 Joan Hoff Wilson, *American Business and Foreign Policy, 1920–1933* (Lexington: University Press of Kentucky, 1971).The author doesn't mention the ICC in her insightful book.

21 From 1923, Etienne Clémentel served as Honorary President of ICC.

22 Edouard Dolléans (1877–1954), well known historian of the Union movement, he joined the French delegation to the US in 1919, then served as ICC Secretary-General from 1920 till 1932. His role at the head of the Secretariat is little known, not mentioned in the *Dictionnaire du mouvement ouvrier français*, « le Maitron ».

23 ICC Papers, BIB 50. Minutes of Executive Board meetings.

24 Georges-Henri Soutou, "Guerre et économie: le premier projet français de nouvel ordre économique mondial," *Revue Universelle des Faits et des Idées*, n°31, (avril 1977), 55–67.

25 ICC Papers, BIB 50. Minutes of Executive Board meetings.

26 League of Nations Papers, phone calls records.

27 ICC Papers, BIB 43. Trade Policy 1926–1938.

28 On Filene, Twentieth Century Fund and ILO see Thomas Cayet, *Rationaliser le travail: Organiser la production: Le Bureau International du Travail et la modernisation économique durant l'entre-deux-guerres* (Rennes: Presses Universitaires de Rennes, 2010).

29 League of Nations papers, Section 10, R 499 document 27466, dossier 24789 relative to Rome Congress 1923. Arthur Sweeter (1888–1968) to Arthur Salter, 5th December 1923. Sweetser was an American Journalist, pro league, he joined the permanent Secretariat in the League's Public information section.

30 Archives départementales Paris. Paris Chamber of Commerce Papers, CCIP I 7 60 (1), letter of the American Embassy in Paris April 1920, looking ahead the travel of the American delegation to Paris and stressed its official nature.

31 Carl P. Parrini, *Heir to Empire, United States Economic diplomacy (1916–1923)* (Pittsburgh: University of Pittsburgh Press, 1969). See Chapter VII: Loan Control: Hoover's Program to stabilize the World for Investment.

32 Herbert Hoover Presidential Library (HHPL) West Branch, IA, Commerce Papers, Box 72, Julius Barnes to Herbert Hoover, 25 March 1923.

33 ICC Papers, BIB 51, note 22 p., no author.

34 U.S. Chamber of Commerce, ACC. 1960, ADD Series conferences n°3, Albert Neve, records of the Conference, 1919.

35 International Chamber of Commerce, Digest n°40, 2/1923.

36 ICC Papers, BIB 50, Minutes of Executive Board meetings.

37 ICC Papers, BIB 50, Minutes of Executive Board meetings.

38 HHPL, Commerce papers, Box 22 International Chamber of Commerce, Bedford, 22 December 1924.

39 ICC Papers, BIB 48, Court of Arbitration 1921–1923.

40 ICC Papers, BIB 42, numerous volumes and BIB 44 studies and investigations conducted by the International Chamber and the Carnegie Foundation.

41 John M. Carroll, "Owen D. Young and German Reparations: The Diplomacy of an Enlightened Businessman," in *U.S. Diplomats in Europe 1919–1941*, ed. Kenneth Paul Jones (Santa-Barbara: ABC-Clio, 1981), 41–60.

42 Daniel Gorman, *The Emergence of International Society in the 1920s* (Cambridge: Cambridge University Press, 2012), Patricia Clavin, *Securing the World Economy: The Reinvention of the League of Nations 1920–1946* (Oxford: Oxford University Press, 2013), or Stephen A. Schuker, *The End of French Predominance in Europe: The Financial Crisis of 1924 and the Adoption of the Dawes Plan* (Chapel Hill: University of North Carolina Press, 1976). None of these books mentions the existence of the International Chamber of Commerce.

43 See Susan Berger, *Notre première mondialisation. Leçons d'un échec oublié* (Paris: La République des Idées, Le Seuil, 2003).

44 Montesquieu, *De l'Esprit des Lois*, 1758.

Bibliography

Artaud, D. *La question des dettes interalliées et la reconstruction de l'Europe 1917–1920*. Lille: University of Lille, 1978.

Berger, S. *Notre première mondialisation. Leçons d'un échec oublié*. Paris: La République des Idées, Le Seuil, 2003.

Carroll, J. M. "Owen D. Young and German Reparations: The Diplomacy of an Enlightened Businessman." In *U.S. Diplomats in Europe 1919–1941*, edited by K. P. Jones. Santa-Barbara: ABC-Clio, 1981.

Cayet, T. *Rationaliser le travail: Organiser la production: Le Bureau International du Travail et la modernisation économique durant l'entre-deux-guerres*. Rennes: Presses Universitaires de Rennes, 2010.

Clavin, P. *Securing the World Economy: The Reinvention of the League of Nations 1920–1946*. Oxford: Oxford University Press, 2013.

Decorzant, Y. *La Société des Nations et la naissance d'une conception de la régulation économique international*. Bruxelles: P.I.E, Peter Lang, 2011.

Druelle-Korn, C. "Entre concurrence et structuration du champ syndical patronal: genèse et affirmation de la Confédération générale de la production française (1919–1925)." In *Genèse des organisations patronales en Europe (19ᵉ–20ᵉ siècles)*, dir. D. Fraboulet and P. Vernus, 153–63. Rennes: Presses Universitaires de Rennes, 2012.

Gamble, D. G. *The NFTC Story, 1914–2014*. Indianapolis: Dog Ear Publishing, 2014.

Gorman, D. *The Emergence of International Society in the 1920s*. Cambridge: Cambridge University Press, 2012.

Hoff Wilson, J. *American Business and Foreign Policy, 1920–1933*. Lexington: University Press of Kentucky, 1971.

Parrini, C. P. *Heir to Empire, United States Economic diplomacy (1916–1923)*. Pittsburgh: University of Pittsburgh Press, 1969.

Ridgeway, G. L. *Merchants of Peace: The History of the International Chamber of Commerce*. Boston, MA: Little, Brown & Cie, (1938) 1959.

Rosengarten, M. *Die Internationale Handelskammer, Wirtschaftpolitische Empfehlungen in der Zeit der Weltwirtschaftskrise 1929–1939*. Berlin: Duncker-Humbolt, 2001.

Schuker, S. A. *The End of French Predominance in Europe: The Financial Crisis of 1924 and the Adoption of the Dawes Plan*. Chapel Hill: University of North Carolina Press, 1976.

Soutou, G. -H. "Guerre et économie: le premier projet français de nouvel ordre économique mondial." *Revue Universelle des Faits et des Idées* n°31 (avril 1977): 55–67.

Tooze, A. *The Deluge. The Great War and the Remaking of Global Order, 1916–1931*. London: Allen Lane, 2014

Werking, R. H. "Bureaucrats, Businessmen and Foreign Trade: The Origins of the United Chamber of Commerce." *Business History Review* 52, n°3, Corporate Liberalism (Autumn 1978): 321–41.

Williams, W. A. "The Legend of Isolationism in the 1920's." *Science and Society* 18, n°1 (Winter 1954): 1–20.

6 'A Tremendous Panic'

The Global Financial Crisis of 1914

Richard Roberts

The financial crisis of 1914 was the most geographically extensive, and possibly the most acute, global financial crisis, with some 40 countries affected. Nonetheless, no account exists, and it scarcely features in the two standard comparative works on financial crises; it is absent from Kindleberger's 'Stylised Outline of Financial Crises, 1618 to 2008' and fails to make the grade as one of Reinhart and Rogoff's seven major 'episodes of global, multicountry, and regional economic crisis' spanning 1825–26 to 2008.[1] Furthermore, the financial crisis at the start of the war has often been overlooked in the histories of individual countries' war economies, with the exception of the United States and Britain and, more recently, studies stimulated by the 100th anniversary in 2014.[2] Presumably, the neglect stems from its overshadowing by the onset of war and the collapse of the international economy in summer 1914, of which finance was a technical dimension. Moreover, the 1914 crisis was not a 'proper' financial crisis in the sense of a turning point in a boom-bust cycle. Nevertheless, the unprecedented global wave of stock market crashes, runs on banks, payment suspensions, currency notes, moratoria and the collapse of the international gold standard, constituted, in *The Economist*'s phrase, 'a tremendous panic'.[3]

The decades from the 1850s to 1914 saw the development of an international financial system involving Europe, North America, much of the British Empire and coastal commercial cities in Asia and South America. The major flows were credit for international trade, principally via bills of exchange, and capital from European savers to emerging markets through bond issues. They were intermediated by small specialist merchant banking firms and increasingly by large commercial or universal banks, as well as by stock markets and discount markets. The money centres were ever more closely connected by the electric telegraph, which was global in reach from the 1870s, and mail services carried by steamships and railways. The other vital factor was the gold standard, the key global monetary regime from the 1880s that fostered international financial and commercial transactions by minimising exchange rate risk. Then, in just a fortnight—the last week of July and first week of August 1914—the whole elaborate mechanism broke down.

International Financial System in 1914

The international financial system in 1914 comprised some 36 'money powers',[4] as indicated by scores on five indicative institutional financial criteria: (1) possession of one or more stock exchanges, (2) discount business, (3) being on the gold or gold exchange standard, (4) possession of a central bank and (5) international banking activity (see Table 6.1).

International and wholesale financial activity was concentrated in financial centres.[5] London was indisputably the world's foremost financial centre, with a second tier comprising Paris, Berlin, New York and perhaps Hong Kong.[6] Around the world, 120 cities (in 43 countries) had a stock exchange (1), identifying them as significant financial centres.[7] Some countries had multiple stock exchanges, notably the US with 13, Australia 12 and the UK 10. Stock exchanges were particularly Anglo-Saxon institutions, with America, Britain and the British Empire hosting 58 of them, half the global total. As regards discount business (trade finance) (2), some level of activity or at least interest was indicated by participation in the International Conference on Bills of Exchange held at the Hague in 1912; 37 countries sent delegations, with major dominions and colonies indirectly represented.[8] By 1914, 36 countries were on the gold or gold exchange standard (3), while 23 countries had a central bank (4).[9] Reed's study of the development of international banking centres, based on banking almanacs, provides data on this dimension from which 34 financial centres can be identified as significant in 22 countries (5).[10]

A dozen countries met all five criteria (see Table 6.2). These 'primary money powers' comprised nine Western European countries, plus the United States, Japan and, less predictably, the Netherlands East Indies. Twelve countries achieved four of the criteria. These 'secondary money powers' comprised six smaller or less developed European countries, three British Empire members and Argentina. A further twelve countries or colonies ticked three of the criteria. These 'tertiary money powers' were located in the Balkans, South America, Asia and the British Empire. Of the 36 money powers, 17 went to war in 1914, while 19 were neutral. But the distinction made little difference as regards the financial crisis that summer, as significant participants in the international financial system all were affected, as, indeed, were further countries that were less financially developed.

Table 6.1 'Money power' criteria and number of qualifying countries, c. 1914

		Countries	
(1)	Stock exchange	43	(120 exchanges)
(2)	Discount business	37	
(3)	Gold/gold exchange standard	36	
(4)	Central bank	23	
(5)	International banking activity	22	(34 international banking centres)

Table 6.2 'Money powers' c. 1914

Primary money powers—score 5
Austria*
Belgium*
France*
Germany*
Italy
Japan*
Netherlands
Netherlands East Indies
Sweden
Switzerland
United Kingdom*
United States
12

Secondary money powers—score 4
Argentina
Australia*
Canada*
Denmark
Hungary*
India*
New Zealand*
Norway
Portugal
Romania
Russia*
Spain
12

Tertiary money powers—score 3
Brazil
Bulgaria
Chile
China
Egypt
Greece
Hong Kong*
Mexico
Serbia*
South Africa*
Straits Settlement (Singapore)*
Turkey*
12

---

* belligerent in 1914

Stock Market Crashes and Closures

At 6 pm on Thursday, 23 July 1914, the Austro-Hungarian ambassador to Belgrade delivered a 'stern' note to Serbia in response to the murder of Archduke Franz Ferdinand a month earlier.[11] Austria's belligerent ultimatum, to which an answer was demanded within 48 hours, transformed the financial markets' perception of the risk of a European war, triggering a scramble for liquidity. Avalanches of sales forced the closure of markets, with selling pressure shifting to exchanges that remained open. The closures began in the heart of Continental Europe and radiated outwards. 'Black Saturday' on the Berlin bourse was a day of 'indescribable anxiety', reported the *New York Times*. 'Prices throughout the list fell with sensational, almost unprecedented rapidity'.[12] Meeting in the afternoon of Sunday, 26 July, the managements of the Vienna and Budapest bourses, which had also seen panic selling and prices at 20-year lows, suspended trading. Monday 27 July also saw the closure of Paris's junior market and the Brussels, Oslo, Stockholm and Odessa bourses.[13] On Tuesday 28 July, the Lisbon, Oporto and Madrid exchanges shut. So did Barcelona, where 'agitation' among members resulted in fistfights. Austria's declaration of war on Serbia that evening was too late for the European exchanges but triggered the first extra-European contagion with closure of the Montreal and Toronto stock exchanges. On Wednesday 29 July, with Austrian gunboats on the Danube shelling Belgrade, though the other great powers were not yet at war, the dominoes went on falling: Amsterdam, Antwerp, Berlin, Milan, Rome and St Petersburg.[14] Thursday 30 July: Zurich and Vancouver. The markets in Berlin, Paris and Copenhagen remained notionally open, but reports stressed that business was at a standstill and prices 'purely nominal'.

The closure on Friday 31 July of the London and New York stock exchanges, the world's foremost securities platforms, marked a further stage in the breakdown. The London market was shut on the insistence of members backed by the banks. They did so, explained a Melbourne broker in relation to his exchange, 'as otherwise Australia will be made a dumping ground for the world'.[15] But the New York market was closed at the behest of the US Secretary of the Treasury to prevent an external drain of gold, constituting an unprecedented political interference with Wall Street.[16] This was to forestall both a possible New York banking crisis and America's forced departure from the gold standard. Moreover, the crisis was immediately perceived by Wall Street bankers and Washington as an opportunity to challenge London's dominant position as an international financial centre and to promote the dollar as an international currency.

Following days saw shutdowns of US regional stock exchanges and of exchanges across the British Empire as the crisis travelled down the international telegraph cables. Saturday 1 August saw the closure of the five South African exchanges, four Indian exchanges and eight Latin American *bolsas*. On Monday 3 August, the crisis reached Australia, precipitating the closure of the Adelaide, Melbourne and Sydney exchanges, as well as the Shanghai and Brazilian markets.

Business on New Zealand's four stock exchanges in Auckland, Christchurch, Dunedin and Wellington was 'practically dead'. Yet there was no scramble for liquidity. 'A crisis, like the present, could not have struck us at a more favourable time', observed a local editorial, since the marketing of the year's agricultural produce had just been completed and people were flush with funds.[17] 'Sellers are not throwing shares on the market, or disposed to accept less than the ruling rates', stated the Dunedin *Evening Post*, 'but there are no buyers'.[18] Listings on New Zealand's exchanges were mostly local concerns with shares held by local investors. 'We in New Zealand are a long way from the storm centre', George Buttle, chairman of the Christchurch Stock Exchange, told members on Thursday, 6 August. 'There is no need for us to close our exchange'.[19] Indeed, they had a duty to their clients to 'maintain a fairly normal condition of values. They should act carefully, calmly and courageously'. The chairman's declaration was followed by the singing of the National Anthem and business as usual.[20]

Japan was a large debtor to London, but the breakdown of foreign exchange transmission prevented it from meeting its obligations. 'Those of us who held posts of financial responsibility during the early days of the war still remember it only too clearly', recalled Junnosuke Inouye, president of the Yokohama Specie Bank. 'It was a nerve-racking experience: we really thought this country was well down the road to bankruptcy, and I am not overstating the case when I tell you that Japan was lucky—extremely lucky—in getting through as she did without defaulting. It was one long, evil nightmare, and the memory of it still haunts my dreams'.[21] News of the closure of the London Stock Exchange triggered 'complete disorder' in Japan and closure of the Tokyo, Osaka and Yokohama markets on Monday 3 August.[22] However, the Tokyo Stock Exchange reopened the following day with 'a rise of quotations all round', and it remained open thereafter.[23] There was one other stock exchange that soldiered on—the Denver Mining Exchange. Perhaps they hadn't heard of the financial crisis in Colorado, or more likely, they figured that war was good news for mining shares.

All in all, by the middle of the first week of August, only six far-flung exchanges out of the world's 120 stock exchanges, in just three out of 43 host countries, continued to operate. The simultaneous closure of 95 per cent of the world's securities markets for around six weeks in summer 1914 was an unprecedented and unrepeated moment in world financial and economic history.

Runs on Banks

The week beginning Monday 27 July saw runs on banks across Continental Europe, particularly savings banks. Around Germany, savings banks were 'besieged by creditors'.[24] In Berlin, depositors 'began forming long queues in front of all the municipal savings banks before the banks opened, and an hour later full-fledged runs were everywhere in progress . . . deposits were paid out as fast as they were demanded without regard to the provision that depositors wishing to withdraw amounts of more than 100 marks must give notice in advance'.[25] Overall, bank deposits in Germany fell by 20 per cent.[26] In Vienna there was a 'somewhat severe' run on the First Austrian Savings Bank, the country's foremost deposit institution, with 7,000 savers withdrawing funds on Tuesday 28 July.[27] There were also runs on banks in Italy and Switzerland.[28] Dutch banks experienced a 'nasty run', and the Post Office Savings Bank availed itself of its right to delay payments to depositors for a fortnight, 'which created much inconvenience and adverse comment'.[29] Banks were also publicly criticised for selfish conduct during the crisis in Germany, Italy and Britain.

In France, banks were besieged by depositors and withdrawals totalled £120 million, equivalent to three-quarters of the £165 million gold holding of the *Banque de France*.[30] The runs were especially heavy at *Caisses d'Epagne* with savers wary of the introduction of restrictions on access to deposits as in 1870; on Friday, 31 July, to relieve the pressure on the savings banks, the government duly limited withdrawals to 50 francs (£2) per fortnight.[31] Many other countries also introduced official limits on the withdrawal of deposits in response to runs. Some specified a cash sum, others a percentage of deposits.

In the Mediterranean, Malta experienced a 'great run on the banks' on Saturday 1 August.[32] So did Constantinople, where the banks were 'literally taken by storm' by crowds demanding gold.[33] Turkey introduced a month-long general moratorium on all debts, suspended the convertibility of banknotes into specie and limited withdrawals from banks to 15 per cent of deposits. A week later, small-denomination banknotes were introduced. Since 1904, Banco di Roma had been creating a Mediterranean branch network that included Malta, Constantinople, Barcelona, Benghazi, Tripoli, Alexandria and Cairo.[34] The Alexandria and Cairo bourses closed on Thursday 30 July 'in consequence of the situation in Europe'.[35] 'Something of a panic' took hold among depositors, notably 'the local religious institutions' that all banked with Banco di Roma, who demanded their funds in gold or sterling.[36] The Banco di Roma applied to the Bank of Italy for bullion, but instead an arrangement was reached whereby the Italian central bank effectively guaranteed deposits at Banco di Roma's two Egyptian branches.[37] This is the only known instance of a deposit guarantee being deployed as a crisis containment measure in 1914.

Runs were widespread in South America, especially on European-owned banks. Chile's banks were 'paralysed' by withdrawals, and the Banco Italiano closed its doors. In Peru, the Bank of Peru and London and the Deutsche-Sudamerikanische Bank suspended payments. In Argentina, the French Bank of the River Plate closed, but the British banks and the Banco de la Nation, the government bank, continued to pay out.[38] Across the sub-continent, governments responded by promptly declaring a bank holiday that shut the banks, mostly for a week. This was extended for several days in Argentina because of the president's fatal heart attack, possibly brought on by the financial crisis. During the bank holiday, moratory legislation was introduced, and upon reopening, banks severely restricted deposit withdrawals.

In the United States, bank runs were a feature of the 'panics' of 1893 and 1907 but not in 1914, probably because of the recent creation of the Federal Reserve and robust responses by the Treasury Secretary.[39] The German-American Bank of Manhattan was an exception, presumably because of the connection of its name with a belligerent, but it survived; following America's entry into the war, it changed its name to the Continental Bank of New York.[40] Gold hoarding was not a problem in America and no restrictions were placed on the withdrawal of deposits. Canada, by contrast, which joined the war along with the rest of the British Empire, saw runs on banks across the country.[41] The hoarding of gold withdrawn from banks was rife and an inquiry reported that 'an atmosphere of incipient financial panic prevailed'.[42] In response, the convertibility of Dominion government notes into specie was suspended and banks were allowed to pay depositors in their own notes.

British colonies and dominions in Asia saw bank runs. Runs and specie hoarding in Hong Kong and Singapore led to official bans on bullion exports. The latter saw the suspension of the Chinese Commercial Bank, an important local bank, to which the colonial government made a large advance to help it reopen. India experienced a 'stampede' to convert rupee notes into silver. Banks experienced 'serious' withdrawals; the Calcutta branch of Mercantile Bank lost a third of deposits, and the Bank of Upper India failed.[43] In Australia, the New South Wales state savings bank experienced a 'small run', but conditions soon stabilised.

In Japan, Kitahama Bank suspended payments because of the crisis on the Osaka Stock Exchange. On Java in the Netherlands East Indies, 'consternation' among depositors led to heavy withdrawals of funds that resulted in bank suspensions. Java Bank, the government bank, continued to make payments but limited withdrawals. Economic activity collapsed as banks denied credit and shopkeepers refused payment except in gold and silver. Facing a 'general catastrophe' the Governor General proclaimed a general moratorium. Evidently, it worked wonders: in late August, the *Straits Times'* correspondent reported that 'Java has practically returned to its normal condition'.

Central banks were besieged by holders of banknotes seeking to change them for gold and silver coin, as they were entitled to do under the classic gold standard. In Brussels, 10,000 people mobbed Belgium's National Bank.[44] Outside the Banque de France in Paris, reported *The Times*: 'a queue of many thousands of people assembled stretching the length of several side-streets and controlled by police and Municipal Guards'.[45] *The Economist's* Berlin correspondent reported that the Reichsbank was 'besieged by

---

anxious crowds hurrying to convert their notes into gold'.[46] In London, there were long queues at the Bank of England. In Amsterdam, a crowd of 4,000 waited in front of the Netherlands Bank to change notes for cash, and it was reported that 'change for paper money is refused everywhere' and that business was at a 'complete standstill'.[47]

Overall, around four-fifths of the 36 money powers experienced runs on commercial banks or savings banks during the 1914 financial crisis with only seven exceptions—the United States, United Kingdom, South Africa, New Zealand, Denmark, Norway and Sweden; it should be noted that the European countries protected themselves with precautionary moratoriums.

Lender of Last Resort Operations

Central banks provided emergency funding to banks during the crisis through discounts and advances against good collateral. This was in accordance with their role as lender of last resort to the banking system, which by 1914 was established doctrine. The complement to liberal lending was a high interest rate for loans to encourage repayment and as a prudent precaution against likely losses. The Austro-Hungarian central bank was the first to move, raising its Bank Rate from 4 per cent to 5 per cent on Monday 27 July.[48] Others followed in fits and starts. Overall, by Wednesday, 5 August, Europe's 10 leading money powers had all increased their Bank Rate (see Table 6.3). The Bank of England was at the front of the charge with a rise of seven points. The Austro-Hungarian Bank's rate was up four points, Belgium's, three points, France and Holland, 2½ points, and Germany and Denmark two points. In a matter of days, the cost of funds tripled in Britain,

Table 6.3 Bank Rates of European Central Banks, July–August 1914

	25 July	5 August	Rate Rise	22 August
England	3	10	7	5
Austria	4	8	4	6
France	3.5	6	2.5	5
Denmark	5	7	2	6
Belgium	4	7	3	7
Norway	5	6.5	1.5	5.5
Germany	4	6	2	6
Russia	5	6	1	6
Netherlands	3.5	6	2.5	5
Romania	6	6	-	6
Switzerland	3.5	6	2.5	6
Sweden	4.5	5.5	1	5.5
Italy	5	5	-	5

Source: *Financial Times*

doubled in Austria-Hungary and almost doubled in Belgium, France, the Netherlands and·Switzerland, stunning banks and business.

The Bank of England's 'violent movement' of rates was criticised by Keynes and others as being 'quite ineffective for all purposes for which Bank Rate is usually raised' and counter-productive through its damage to public confidence.[49] Similar criticisms were levelled at the Austro-Hungarian Bank. 'The Austro-Hungarian Bank did not need to guard gold, for no bills are being granted', commented the *Oesterreichsche Volkswirt*. 'Gold cannot go out of the country, and no rise in the rate can bring it'.[50] Both central banks were accused of provoking public panic by hiking the Bank Rate to crisis level, thereby exacerbating the bank runs and the hoarding of currency.

Raising the official rate is the opposite of modern crisis management practice. A modest increase was normal procedure if the market rate went above the official rate, but the magnitudes of rises in summer 1914 were far from modest. Protection against an external drain of gold was advanced as a motive. That threat prompted Germany, Russia, Argentina, South Africa, Denmark, Norway and Sweden and many other countries to ban gold export.[51] Some did both for good measure. Austria closed its borders for gold shipment on 28 July, but afterwards raised the Bank Rate by a further three points.[52] Holland banned gold exports on Friday 31 July and then increased the Bank Rate by 1½ points.[53] The conclusion appears to be that, as in Britain, charging a high rate for funds was just part and parcel of heavy liquidity provision. Central bankers were simply muddle-headedly following what Hartley Withers, merchant banker and future editor of *The Economist*, called a 'mouldy old precedent'.[54]

Disappearance of Small Change, Currency Notes and Gold Standard Suspension

An immediate and widespread phenomenon during the last week of July was the disappearance of small change. All but the lowest denomination coins contained specie and were thus hoarded. The disappearance of small change made cash settlement impossible, hampering commercial activity. 'The financial stringency has had a serious effect upon the Halles, the central markets, owing to the impossibility of supplying change to purchasers', reported *The Times'* Paris correspondent on 31 July.[55] Meanwhile, in Berlin, Reichstag deputy Peter Hanssen tried to pay a restaurant bill with a 20 mark note. 'Haven't you any silver?' complained the 'much agitated' waiter who went to get change. Fifteen minutes later, he returned empty-handed, and Hanssen got his meal on account.[56]

There was a straightforward solution to the disappearance of change—the issue of small-denomination banknotes as substitutes. The money powers either introduced such 'currency notes' or expanded an existing currency note issue. The Banque de France, which had a substantial supply of pre-printed currency notes, began their circulation on Friday 31 July. *The*

Times reported that the 'state of famine [of coin] has been to a great extent remedied today by the welcome appearance of the small notes at 20fr. and at 5fr. Both these new forms of currency are printed on blue tinted paper'.[57] In Sweden, one-krona notes, which had been withdrawn in favour of silver coin in 1875, were reintroduced.[58] On Monday 3 August, the United States Treasury began distribution to banks of its emergency supply of currency notes that had been printed after the panic of 1907. The *New York Times* reported that they arrived in downtown Manhattan: 'in twenty big mail trucks' with armed escorts '. . . it attracted a great deal of attention'.[59] Britain, which had proscribed £1 banknotes in 1826 in response to an earlier financial crisis, hurried to print and distribute new currency notes issued by the Treasury (not the Bank of England) ahead of the reopening of the banks on Friday 7 August.

The hoarding of silver coin in Switzerland prompted authorisation of the Swiss National Bank (SNB) to issue SFr20 currency notes.[60] Subsequently, in February 1915, Adolf Jähr, the SNB's Secretary General, presented a report on the lessons of the crisis to the Executive Board.[61] One of his recommendations was the need for even smaller currency notes, down to SFr1 and SFr2 denominations. Another was that the country's statutory gold reserve cover for the note issue should be lowered from 40 per cent to 33 1/3 per cent to 'give the Bank the freedom of movement which it must have in such times to fulfil its responsibilities'. Nonetheless, he concluded, 'all in all, Switzerland and the Swiss National Bank can be proud to have triumphed over the serous crisis . . . relatively quickly and without serious ruptures'.

The international gold standard was an immediate casualty of the financial crisis through the suspension of one or more of its cardinal requirements: the convertibility of notes and gold, free international movement of gold and maintenance of the legal gold cover ratio between the note issue and gold reserves. Whether currency notes were issued by the central bank or the state, they usually meant an increase in the note issue beyond the legal limit determined by the size of the gold reserves. Such increases in the fiduciary issue violated that aspect of being on the gold standard. A more straightforward departure from the gold standard was the suspension of the convertibility of notes into specie. Russia was the first to do so on Monday 27 July, with most of Europe and Latin America following suit. In Scandinavia, for instance, the Swedish and Danish central banks were relieved of responsibility to convert on 2 August, with Norway following on 5 August.[62] By the end of the first week of August, among the 36 money powers, 28 had suspended convertibility. The handful of countries that retained at least a formal semblance of gold convertibility comprised the UK, the US, Holland, Switzerland, Japan, Australia, New Zealand and South Africa. In practice, however, through a combination of legal and administrative restrictions, all severely constrained convertibility and the free movement of gold.[63]

Moratoria

The other key financial crisis containment measure in 1914 was a so-called 'moratorium'. A moratorium was, explained the *Financial News*, a law passed in times of emergency postponing for a specified period the settlement of financial contracts: 'The delay, or period of grace allowed by the law is a "moratorium"'.[64] Several moratoria had been implemented in France during the Franco-Prussian war of 1870–71.[65] More recently, a general moratorium had been imposed by Bulgaria, Greece and Serbia during the Balkan War of 1912–13.[66] The subject of a bill of exchange moratorium was discussed 'at length' at the International Bills of Exchange Conference held at the Hague, which met in 1910 and 1912, reported Charles Conant, technical adviser to the US delegation.[67] The 1912 session, attended by 75 delegates from 37 countries, resulted in an undertaking by 30 countries, including France and Germany, though not Britain and the United States, to adopt a 'uniform law' regarding bills of exchange.[68] This constituted a major international commercial development, but implementation fell victim to the onset of the war.

The foremost objective of the moratoria of the summer of 1914 was to safeguard the banks, and their provisions authorised either a mandatory or discretionary restriction on the withdrawal of funds by depositors. It was also intended that they would forestall bankruptcies on the part of firms and individuals who were unable to make payment due to circumstances arising from the war. The moratoria of 1914 took four principal forms: stock exchange closures, bank holidays, bills moratoria and general moratoria. A bills moratorium deferred the date that bills of exchange falling due for payment had to be met until a date in the future. A general moratorium, which came in many shapes and sizes, applied widely to contracts and debts but with exemptions and variations from case to case and over time. 'Their promulgation', noted an American legal scholar in 1918, 'has been more frequent in the civil law countries of Continental Europe and Latin America than in the common-law countries of the British Empire and the United States'.[69]

The government of France had reserve powers to introduce moratoria by decree through precautionary legislation passed in January 1910 in case of 'the mobilisation of the army, an epidemic or a public calamity'.[70] The law was invoked on Friday 31 July when a bills of exchange moratorium was imposed. Further decrees were consolidated into a general moratorium on 10 August. 'This general moratorium', observed *The Economist*, 'was soon to prove itself a real stumbling-block'.[71] Indeed, it was so stringent that it even prevented further payments by subscribers to a pre-war government loan, which complicated public finances. The general moratorium contributed to Frances's economic breakdown in the opening months of the war, though its effects are impossible to separate from those of the mobilisation of three million men (including most of the staff of the Banque de France), transport chaos and the collapse of credit. 'The disorganisation of industry was appalling and unemployment was reaching . . . a dangerous level', Keynes reported to the Chancellor in a January 1915 briefing note. 'Some of these things were very badly managed in France'.[72] The moratorium was relaxed in stages over the autumn, and French banks allowed full access to deposits from 1 January 1915, which did 'much to relieve the situation'.[73] But the moratorium's complete removal proved impossible because of the protection it provided for those serving with the armed forces.

Around 40 countries introduced some form of bills of exchange moratorium, even if only on a precautionary basis, with the United States a notable exception.[74] Among the 36 money powers, 25 governments took general moratorium powers, as did at least five other countries; the eleven money powers that did not adopt (or implement) some form of general moratorium were Australia, Canada, Hong Kong, India, New Zealand and Straits Settlements (Singapore) from the British Empire, the United States, China, Japan, Spain and Germany (see below). General moratoria were as common among non-belligerents and among belligerents, reflecting the universal challenges to business and payments. Among belligerents, legislation was passed protecting those serving with the colours; Canada and New Zealand, for instance, adopted specific moratory measures to protect farmers from mortgage foreclosures. Neutrals Denmark, Sweden and Switzerland adopted measures that protected debtors from foreign creditors but not domestic ones. Adolf Jähr's report for the Swiss National Bank's Executive Board called the wartime moratoria a 'bitter necessity' and commented that generally they had not been thought through resulting in a 'bewildering plethora of poorly drafted improvised measures'. There was a clear geographical pattern; in Europe, almost every country, whether a belligerent or not, introduced a moratorium; in Latin America they were widespread; in North America and Asia, by contrast, they were largely unused.

Germany's Financial War Plan

Britain had no plans for the financial crisis of 1914 and, like other countries, met the emergency by improvisation. Germany, uniquely, had a fully fledged plan for finance in the event of war. The secret scheme had been formulated by the Reichsbank and Imperial Treasury as long ago as 1891.[75] It was assumed that the war would be short and the immediate cost would be met by government borrowing from the central bank. This would be repaid from reparations, as after the Franco-Prussian War of 1870–71. To strengthen the Reichsbank's reserves and maintain confidence in the currency, the government's 'war chest' of 120 million gold marks, derived from French reparations and housed in the Spandau Tower, would be transferred to the Reichsbank. Moreover, following acute financial pressure at the time of the Agadir crisis of 1911, when the statutory gold coverage ratio had been breached, efforts were made to increase the central bank's bullion reserves as a precaution and banks were exhorted to increase their reserves. In addition, the Reichsbank printed a large stock of various types of currency notes to be available in an emergency.

Runs on German banks and on the Reichsbank's gold, triggered the suspension of convertibility on Friday 31 July and circulation of the emergency notes. On Tuesday, 4 August, as German troops swept into Belgium, the Reichstag enacted a set of pre-formulated war finance laws.[76] Suspension of the Bank Act legalised the suspension of convertibility and the expansion of the note issue. To counter the shortage of small change, the currency and other notes were made legal tender to enhance their acceptability and encourage the deposit of coin with the banks. To meet war needs, the Reichsbank was permitted to discount Reich Treasury bills that were accorded equal status to commercial bills. Finally, to provide credit for businesses, state governments and local authorities, 'loan banks' (*Darlehnskassen*) were activated as in the crises of 1848, 1866 and 1870. Owned and operated by the Reichsbank, they provided local credit in the form of currency certificates. The overall outcome was an 'enormous' increase in Germany's paper currency issue, reflected in the 'marked depreciation' of the mark against neutral countries' currencies in autumn 1914, and that was just the beginning.[77]

The introduction of a general moratorium was raised in the Reichstag during the passage of the war finance laws, but there was concern about adverse effects on morale and credit. Moreover, the Reichsbank was determined that economic activity should not be hobbled by a general moratorium, and the draft finance laws were designed to avoid this encumbrance. President Rudolf von Haverstein told colleagues in late September: 'we must under all circumstances maintain the payment of obligations and the obligations themselves. All our preparations for the financial mobilisation were based on this, and they have proven themselves superbly, and we can be truly proud that we . . . alone among the combatants, have come through without a moratorium'.[78] Nevertheless, the strict regulations of the cheque and bills acts were modified to allow for delays caused by the war. Moreover, there were moratoria for certain financial assets, notably bills of exchange, with payments postponed to avert insolvencies and foreclosures. Formally, a general moratorium was avoided, but, commented historian Konrad Roesler, 'substantively it came pretty close'.[79] The Swiss National Bank report observed that the Germans 'cannot boast enough that they eschewed a moratorium', but, noted the SNB's Adolf Jähr, 'I have the strong suspicion that if there was a reverse on the battlefield or an enemy invasion a moratorium would be back on the table'. All in all, Germany's crisis planning meant a less disruptive financial crisis than elsewhere; the flaws, which emerged later, proved to be the overabundance of credit provision and the assumption of a short and easily financed war, not a war of attrition.[80]

Relaxation of Crisis Measures

With the eye of the financial storm having passed, it became possible to relax or even lift crisis measures. Interest rates came first, led downwards by the Bank of England, which cut the Bank Rate from 10 per cent to 5 per cent on Saturday 8 August. Over the subsequent fortnight, France, Holland, Denmark and Norway also reduced their Bank Rate. There was substantial convergence of rates compared to pre-war. On Saturday 22 August, ten of the dozen European countries whose rate was quoted in the *Financial Times* had Bank Rate in the range 5–6 per cent;[81] across the continent it was a '5 per cent war'. It is possibly significant that the two outliers, Belgium at 7 per cent and Austria-Hungary at 8 per cent, were both scenes of fighting.

When the stock exchanges closed, limited securities transactions continued to be done on a cash basis, often with novel arrangements, such as street trading, public auctions and newspaper small ads. Brokers soon pressed for exchanges to reopen to resume their livelihoods. Reopenings proceeded from mid-September, beginning on the Australian exchanges and in Singapore. October saw the reopening of Chile's exchanges and Canada's. The US regional stock exchanges resumed in November, as did the Hong Kong and Shanghai markets. On 7 December, the Paris Bourse was the first major European exchange to reopen, but little business was done. Then came New York on 12 December and London on 4 January. The latter triggered the reopening of the South African exchanges. The reopening of the Amsterdam exchange on 9 February was of more than local significance since during the war neutral Holland became an international financial entrepot between Germany, Britain, France, the United States and the wider world.[82] By spring 1915, most of the world's stock exchanges were open again, though many operated under new officially imposed restrictions on trading.

Moratoria were imposed for a limited period of time, typically a month, but were often renewed repeatedly. They were disruptive to economic activity and there was pressure from business and the public for their removal, though there might be counter lobbying for retention from bankers worried about a possible run. In some countries, moratoria were simply lifted when the situation permitted, for instance, Switzerland as early as mid-October and Britain in early November.[83] Often the terms were progressively moderated at each renewal. A refinement sometimes adopted was the replacement of a general moratorium with a so-called 'special moratorium' that provided law courts with discretionary authority to protect parties hit financially by the hostilities until after the end of the war.[84] Mostly it was not until well into 1915 that moratoria were removed or substantially relaxed. But by summer 1915, a year on from the onset of the crisis, the countries that featured in reports about on-going moratoria were mostly ones that were financially challenged well before the crisis, such as Haiti, Nicaragua, Paraguay, Bulgaria and Romania. In some countries, a moratorium became a permanent feature applying 'while the war lasts', for instance, in

Argentina, Italy and Nicaragua, or 'indefinitely', as in Belgium, Bulgaria and Romania.

Impacts and Legacy

The outbreak of the Great War was a blow for the global economy, its immediate impact being a severe downturn in activity and world GDP; for belligerents through dislocation and destruction, but also for neutrals and countries far from the battlefields through the stoppage of shipping and financial flows. Trade collapsed bringing hardship and unemployment to, for instance, cotton growers in the Southern states of America,[85] Chile's nitrate industry, Brazil's coffee producers and Switzerland's tourist industry. It is well established in modern financial crisis literature that recessions associated with financial crises are significantly more severe, resulting in 'much larger declines in real economic activity, and their recoveries tend to be slow'.[86] For European belligerents, this effect was plainly overwhelmed by other factors. As regards neutrals, a financial crisis may possibly have aggravated their downturn, but it is impossible to disentangle the impacts of the financial turmoil from the onset of war that was the fundamental factor.

It is possible that crisis management exacerbated the negative economic impact of financial crisis, notably the imposition of a stringent general moratorium that caused cash-flow problems for businesses and restrictions on bank lending to prioritise the state that caused a credit crunch for business. Keynes believed that the French general moratorium had baleful effects, and there were complaints by businessmen about Britain's general moratorium and the conduct of the banks.[87] On the other hand, the moratoria served their purpose of protecting the banks from runs and other enterprises from failure because of disruption due to the war. There was no significant bank failure anywhere—no 1914 Lehman Brothers—to take a toll of other banks and businesses. That was an achievement, though it is noteworthy that the general moratorium has subsequently been little used as a crisis containment measure. In 1931 and 2008, governments chose to bail out or nationalise troubled banks rather than to safeguard the banks by freezing the whole economy.

In each crisis, governments took the view that the financial sector was too important to fail. The 1914 financial crisis resulted in unprecedented state interference in the financial sector—with markets, banks and the central bank. Pre-war central banks, often privately owned and operating with considerable independence, were principally concerned with the gold standard exchange rate and the integrity of the currency. Departure from the gold standard removed the first function, and they became subordinate to finance ministries as agents of the state working to furnish war finance and thereby contributing to wartime inflation.

It is striking that so many countries arrived apparently independently at a similar set of policy responses to the financial crisis. While the diplomatic crisis generated copious cable traffic between foreign ministries and embassies, there is no evidence of consultation or even communication between finance ministries or central banks during the financial crisis; there were neither ties nor time to do so. Britain, the foremost money power of the day, certainly did not set an example, being the laggard in the adoption of most emergency measures. Moreover, while there was a body of writing about the role of a central bank as a lender of last resort in a crisis,[88] pre-war texts on moratoria or currency notes are sought in vain. The widespread resort to stock exchange closures, bank holidays, moratoria, currency notes and suspension of the gold standard were common on-the-hoof responses to common pressures.

Financial crises are commonly followed by a 'revulsion' phase—the term of American economist Hyman Minsky—meaning a wave of recrimination, retribution and regulation very apparent in the aftermaths of the crises of the early 1930s and 2008. Reform in the immediate wake of the 1914 crisis took the form of adjustments to wartime conditions with state interference with banks and markets, as already mentioned. After the war came endeavours to restore the international financial system to functioning order through several international economic and financial conferences, notably Brussels in 1920, and Cannes and Genoa in 1922.[89] David Lloyd George, the British Prime Minister, was a key mover with his outlook possibly coloured by his experience as Chancellor of the Exchequer during the 1914 crisis.[90] Little progress was made on the intractable issue of international indebtedness, but the gatherings helped to pave the way for the restoration of the international gold standard, reversing its demise in 1914.

The restored gold standard was short lived, collapsing in 1931. Did the experience of 1914 alert the authorities or bankers to the potential breakdown of the system for a second time in a generation? Apparently not, despite the personal experience of many financial professionals in the earlier crisis, including leading central bankers Montagu Norman of Britain, Benjamin Strong of the US, Hjalmar Schacht of Germany and Emile Moreau of France, each of whom had been caught up in the 1914 crisis.[91] The world had moved on and the global financial crisis of 1914 was regarded, insofar as it was remembered at all, as a dimension of the onset of war rather than a potentially instructive episode—as just 'a tremendous panic'.

Notes

1 Charles P. Kindleberger and Robert Z. Aliber, *Manias, Panics, and Crashes: A History of Financial Crises* (London: Palgrave, 2011), 302–11; Carmen Reinhardt and Kenneth Rogoff, *This Time Is Different: Eight Centuries of Financial Folly* (Princeton, NJ: Princeton University Press, 2009), 261.
2 See William L. Silber, *When Washington Shut Down Wall Street: The Great Financial Crisis of 1914 and the Origins of America's Monetary Supremacy* (Princeton, NJ: Princeton University Press, 2007); Teresa Seabourne, "The Summer of 1914," in *Financial Crises and the World Banking System*, eds. Forrest Capie and Geoffrey E. Wood (London: Macmillan, 1986), 77–119; Richard

Roberts, *Saving the City: The Great Financial Crisis of 1914* (Oxford: Oxford University Press, 2013); Laure Quennouelle-Corre, ed., *La Mobilisation Financiere en France et a l'Etranger* (Paris: IGPDE, 2015).

3 "War Supplement," *Economist*, 19 December 1914.
4 The term is taken from Paul Emden, *Money Powers of Europe* (London: Appleton-Century, 1938).
5 Richard Roberts, "The Economics of Cities of Finance," in *Cities of Finance*, eds. Herman Diederiks and David Reeder (Amsterdam: North Holland, 1996), 7–20.
6 See Roberts, Richard, ed., *Global Financial Centres* (Cheltenham: Edward Elgar, 1994); Youssef Cassis, *Capitals of Capital: A History of International Financial Centres, 1780–2005* (Cambridge: Cambridge University Press, 2006).
7 Ranald C. Michie, *The Global Securities Market: A History* (Oxford: Oxford University Press, 2006), 136; S.S. Huebner, "The Scope and Function of the Stock Market," *Annals of the American Academy of Political and Social Science* 35 (1910): 1–23; H. Lowenfeld, The World's Stock Markets," *Financial Review of Reviews* (October 1907): 7–15.
8 US Senate, *Bills*, 8, 359.
9 Barry Eichengreen and Marc Flandreau, *The Geography of the Gold Standard*, CEPR Discussion Paper No.1050 (October 1994), 9 (author's amendments); Forrest Capie et al. (eds.), *The Future of Central Banking* (Cambridge: Cambridge University Press, 1994), 6 (author's amendments).
10 Howard Curtis Reed, *The Preeminence of International Financial Centers* (New York: Praeger, 1981), 101–11 (countries scoring 1–3 plus author's amendments).
11 *Illustrated London News*, 1 August 1914.
12 "Bourses Shaken by Fear of War," *New York Times*, 26 July 1914; "Run on Berlin Banks," *New York Times*, 28 July 1914.
13 "Odessa Bourse Closed," *New York Times*, 31 July 1914.
14 "More Bourses are Closed," *New York Times*, 30 July 1914.
15 "Melbourne Stock Exchange Closed," *Colonist*, 4 August 1914.
16 See Silber, *Washington*.
17 "The War and New Zealand Finance," *Press*, 4 August 1914.
18 "Dunedin Stock Exchange," *Dunedin Evening Post*, 1 August 1914.
19 "The Stock Exchange: No Need to Close," *New Zealand Herald*, 7 August 1914.
20 "Auckland Stock Exchange," *Colonist*, 7 August 1914.
21 Junnosuke Inouye, *Problems of the Japanese Exchange, 1914–1926* (Glasgow: Glasgow University Press, 1931), 5–6.
22 "Tokyo Stock Market is also Closed," *Japan Times*, 4 August 1914.
23 "Tokyo Stock Market Opened Brisk," *Japan Times*, 6 August 1914.
24 "Tension in Germany," *The Times*, 29 July 1914.
25 "Run on Berlin Banks," *New York Times*, 28 July 1914.
26 Charles P. Kindleberger, *A Financial History of Western Europe* (London: George Allen & Unwin, 1984), 292.
27 "Run on Savings Banks," *Financial Times*, 29 July 1914.
28 "'Switzerland' and 'Italy'," *Economist*, 19 December 1914.
29 "Holland," *Economist*, 19 December 1914.
30 Elizabeth Johnson, *Collected Writings of John Maynard Keynes: Vol. XVI Activities 1914–1919: The Treasury and Versailles* (London: Macmillan, 1971), 43.
31 Tournie, "Crisis," 69; "French Emergency Notes in Use," *Financial Times*, 1 August 1914.
32 "Financial Crisis," *Standard*, 3 August 1914.
33 "Egyptian Financial Situation," *Financial Times*, 20 August 1914.
34 John A. Consiglio, *A History of Banking in Malta* (Valetta: Progress Press, 2006), 131; Roberto di Quirico, *Italian International Banking*, EUI Working Paper HEC No.98/7, (Florence: European University Institute, 1998), 7.
35 "Closing of the Bourses," *Egyptian Gazette*, 31 July 1914.

36 "Egyptian Financial Situation," *Financial Times*, 20 August 1914.
37 "Egyptian Financial Situation," *Financial Times*, 20 August 1914. I am grateful to Alessandro Roselli for details about this episode.
38 "Fear Run on Banks," *New York Times*, 12 August 1914.
39 Neil Shafer and Tom Sheehan, *Panic Scrip of 1893, 1907 and 1914: An Illustrated Catalog of Emergency Monetary Issues* (Jefferson, NC: McFarland, 2013); Charles Calomiris and Garry Gorton, "The Origin of Banking Panics: Models, Facts, and Bank Regulation," in *Financial Markets and Financial Crises*, ed. Glenn Hubbard (New York: NBER, 1991), 109–73.
40 "New Incorporations," *New York Times*, 7 May 1918.
41 R. Craig McIvor, *Canadian Monetary, Banking and Fiscal Development* (Toronto: Macmillan, 1961), 102.
42 *Report Royal Commission*, 22.
43 Edwin Green and Sara Kinsey, *The Paradise Bank: The Mercantile Bank of India, 1893–1984* (Aldershot: Ashgate, 1999), 38.
44 "Run on Belgian National Bank," *New York Times*, 1 August 1914; "Withdrawals in Brussels," *The Times*, 31 July 1914.
45 "Vanished Gold," *The Times*, 1 August 1914.
46 "Germany-War and Economic Life," *Economist*, 15 August 1914.
47 "The Defence of Holland," *Financial Times*, 3 August 1914.
48 "Austrian Bank Rate Up," *Daily Mail*, 27 July 1914.
49 J.M. Keynes, "War and the Financial System, August 1914," *Economic Journal* xxiv (September 1914): 460–86.
50 "War Supplement," *Economist*, 19 December 1914.
51 William Adams Brown, *The International Gold Standard Reinterpreted, 1914–1934*, vol. I (New York: NBER, 1940), 16; Claes Ahlund, ed., *Scandinavia in the First World War* (Lund: Nordic, 2012), 231.
52 Stefan von Muller, *Die Financielle Mobilmachung Ostereichs und ihr Ausbau bis 1918* (Berlin: Leopold Weiss, 1918), 28.
53 "Export of Gold to be Prohibited," *Financial News*, 1 August, 1914.
54 Hartley Withers, *War and Lombard Street* (London: Smith, Elder, 1915), 12.
55 "Vanished Gold," *The Times*, 1 August 1914.
56 Hans Peter Hanssen, *Diary of a Dying Empire* (Bloomington, IN: Indiana University Press, 1955), 18.
57 "Vanished Gold," *The Times*, 1 August 1914.
58 Gunnar Wetterberg, *Money and Power: From Stockholms Banco 1656 to Sveriges Riksbank Today* (Stockholm: Atlantis, 2009), 257.
59 *New York Times*, 4 August 1914.
60 "Business Absolutely Dead," *Financial Times*, 1 August 1914.
61 Swiss National Bank Archive [Reference to be found]. Adolf Jähr, *Die Förderung der Finanziellen Kreigbereitschaft nach den Erfahrungen des Jahres 1914*. Zurich, February 1915. I am grateful to Patrick Halbeisen of the Swiss National Bank for informing me about this document.
62 Ahlund, *Scandinavia*, 231.
63 Brown, *International*, 37.
64 "The Moratorium," *Financial News*, 8 August 1914.
65 "Moratorium: Its Purpose and Effect," *Western Mail*, 11 September 1914.
66 "Moratoriums of Balkan States," *Financial Times*, 31 July 1914; Phocas-Cosmetos, *Lendemain*.
67 Charles A. Conant, *A History of Modern Banks of Issue* (New York: Putnam, 1927), 739.
68 "U.S. Senate," *Bills*, 397.
69 Charles Kettleborough, "Moratory and Stay Laws," *American Political Science Review* 12, no. 3 (August 1918): 458–61.

70 Albert Koesner and Charles Dickson, *Moratorium*, vols. I-V. (Stockholm: Svenska Bankeningen, 1915–22), vol. I., 496.
71 "War Supplement," *Economist*, 19 December 1914.
72 Johnson, *Collected*, 45.
73 "Banking Enterprise of Our Allies," *Financial Times*, 16 February 1916.
74 See Koesner, *Moratorium*.
75 Gerd Hardach, *Financial Mobilisation in Germany 1914–1918*, EABH Papers No.14–08 (September 2014), 3.
76 Gerald D. Feldman, *The Great Disorder: Politics, Economics and Society in the German Inflation, 1914–1914* (Oxford: Oxford University Press, 1993), 26.
77 "Germany," *Economist*, 19 December 1914.
78 Feldman, *Disorder*, 32.
79 Konrad Roesler, *Die Finanzpolitik des Deutschen Reiches im Ersten Weltkreig* (Berlin: Duncker & Humblot, 1967), 44.
80 Hardach, *Financial*, 8.
81 "Bank Rate Movements," *Financial Times*, 22 August 1914.
82 See Euwe, "Financing".
83 "End of the Swiss Moratorium," *The Times*, 20 October 1914.
84 Koesner, *Moratorium*, vol. I., iii.
85 See Link, *Cotton*.
86 Stijn Claessens et al., "The Global Financial Crisis: How Similar? How Different? How Costly?," in *Financial Crises: Causes, Consequences, and Policy Responses*, eds. Stijn Claessens et al. (Washington: IMF, 2014), 229; Reinhart, *Different*, 223–39.
87 See John Peters, "The British Government and the City-Industry Divide: The Case of the 1914 Financial Crisis," *Twentieth Century British History* 4, no. 2 (1993): 126–48.
88 See Forrest H. Capie and Geoffrey E. Wood (eds.), *The Lender of Last Resort* (London: Routledge, 2006).
89 Kindleberger, *Financial*, 333–35.
90 Stephen A. Schuker, "American Policy towards Debts and Reconstruction at Genoa, 1922," in *Genoa, Rapallo and European Reconstruction in 1922*, eds. Carole Fink, Axel Frohn and Jurgen Heideking (Cambridge: Cambridge University Press, 1991), 95–130.
91 See Liaquat Ahamed, *The Lords of Finance* (London: Windmill Books, 2010).

Bibliography

Ahamed, Liaquat. *The Lords of Finance*. London: Windmill Books, 2010.
Ahlund, Claes (ed.). *Scandinavia in the First World War*. Lund: Nordic, 2012.
Brown, William Adams. *The International Gold Standard Reinterpreted, 1914–1934*, vol. I. New York: NBER, 1940.
Calomiris, Charles and Garry Gorton. "The Origin of Banking Panics: Models, Facts, and Bank Regulation." In *Financial Markets and Financial Crises*, edited by Glenn Hubbard, 109–73. New York: NBER, 1991.
Capie, Forrest et al. (eds.). *The Future of Central Banking*. Cambridge: Cambridge University Press, 1994.
Capie, Forrest H., and Geoffrey E. Wood (eds.). *The Lender of Last Resort*. London: Routledge, 2006.
Cassis, Youssef. *Capitals of Capital: A History of International Financial Centres, 1780–2005*. Cambridge: Cambridge University Press, 2006.

Claessens, Stijn et al. "The Global Financial Crisis: How Similar? How Different? How Costly?" In *Financial Crises: Causes, Consequences, and Policy Responses*, edited by Stijn Claessens et al., 209–38. Washington: IMF, 2014.

Conant, Charles A. *A History of Modern Banks of Issue*. New York: Putnam, 1927.

Consiglio, John A. *A History of Banking in Malta*. Valetta: Progress Press, 2006.

di Quirico, Roberto. *Italian International Banking*. EUI Working Paper HEC No.98/7. Florence: European University Institute, 1998.

Eichengreen, Barry and Marc Flandreau. *The Geography of the Gold Standard*. CEPR Discussion Paper No.1050 (October 1994).

Emden, Paul. *Money Powers of Europe*. London: Appleton-Century, 1938.

Euwe, Jeroen. "Financing Germany: Amsterdam's Role as an International Financial Centre, 1914–1931." In *Convergence and Divergence of National Financial Systems: Evidence from the Gold Standards, 1871–1971*, edited by Patrice Baubeau and Anders Ogren, 219–40. London: Pickering & Chatto, 2010.

Feldman, Gerald D. *The Great Disorder: Politics, Economics and Society in the German Inflation, 1914–1914*. Oxford: Oxford University Press, 1993.

Green, Edwin and Sara Kinsey. *The Paradise Bank: The Mercantile Bank of India, 1893–1984*. Aldershot: Ashgate, 1999.

Hanssen, Hans Peter. *Diary of a Dying Empire*. Bloomington, IN: Indiana University Press, 1955.

Hardach, Gerd. *Financial Mobilisation in Germany 1914–1918*. EABH Papers No.14–08 (September 2014).

Huebner, S. S. "The Scope and Function of the Stock Market." *Annals of the American Academy of Political and Social Science* 35 (1910): 1–23.

Inouye, Junnosuke. *Problems of the Japanese Exchange, 1914–1926*. Glasgow: Glasgow University Press, 1931.

Johnson, Elizabeth. *Collected Writings of John Maynard Keynes: Vol. XVI Activities 1914–1919: The Treasury and Versailles*. London: Macmillan, 1971.

Kettleborough, Charles. "Moratory and Stay Laws." *American Political Science Review* 12, no. 3 (August 1918): 458–61.

Keynes, J. M. "War and the Financial System, August 1914." *Economic Journal* xxiv (September 1914): 460–86.

Kindleberger, Charles P. *A Financial History of Western Europe*. London: George Allen & Unwin, 1984.

Kindleberger, Charles P., and Robert Z. Aliber. *Manias, Panics, and Crashes: A History of Financial Crises*. London: Palgrave, 2011.

Koesner, Albert and Charles Dickson. *Moratorium*. Vols. I-V. Stockholm: Svenska Bankeningen, 1915–22.

Link, Arthur S. "The Cotton Crisis, the South, and Anglo-American Diplomacy, 1914–1915." In *The Higher Realism of Woodrow Wilson and Other Essays*, edited by Arthur S. Link, 309–29. Nashville: Vanderbilt University Press, 1971.

Lowenfeld, H. "The World's Stock Markets." *Financial Review of Reviews* (October 1907): 7–15.

McIvor, R. Craig. *Canadian Monetary, Banking and Fiscal Development*. Toronto: Macmillan, 1961.

Michie, Ranald C. *The Global Securities Market: A History*. Oxford: Oxford University Press, 2006.

Muller, Stefan von. *Die Financielle Mobilmachung Ostereichs und ihr Ausbau bis 1918*. Berlin: Leopold Weiss, 1918.

Peters, John. "The British Government and the City-Industry Divide: The Case of the 1914 Financial Crisis." *Twentieth Century British History* 4, no. 2 (1993): 126–48.

Phocas-Cosmetos, S. P. *Au Lendemain des Guerres Balkaniques.* Paris: Librairie Payot, 1915.

Quennouelle-Corre, Laure (ed.). *La Mobilisation Financiere en France et a l'Etranger.* Paris: IGPDE, 2015.

Reed, Howard Curtis. *The Preeminence of International Financial Centers.* New York: Praeger, 1981.

Reinhardt, Carmen and Kenneth Rogoff. *This Time Is Different: Eight Centuries of Financial Folly.* Princeton, NJ: Princeton University Press, 2009.

Report of the Royal Commission on Banking and Currency in Canada, 1933.

Roberts, Richard. *Saving the City: The Great Financial Crisis of 1914.* Oxford: Oxford University Press, 2013.

———. "The Economics of Cities of Finance." In *Cities of Finance,* edited by Herman Diederiks and David Reeder, 7–20. Amsterdam: North Holland, 1996.

Roberts, Richard (ed.). *Global Financial Centres.* Cheltenham: Edward Elgar, 1994.

Roesler, Konrad. *Die Finanzpolitik des Deutschen Reiches im Ersten Weltkreig.* Berlin: Duncker & Humblot, 1967.

Schuker, Stephen A. "American Policy towards Debts and Reconstruction at Genoa, 1922." In *Genoa, Rapallo and European Reconstruction in 1922,* edited by Carole Fink, Axel Frohn and Jurgen Heideking, 95–130. Cambridge: Cambridge University Press, 1991.

Seabourne, Teresa. "The Summer of 1914." In *Financial Crises and the World Banking System,* edited by Forrest Capie and Geoffrey E. Wood, 77–119. London: Macmillan, 1986.

Shafer, Neil and Tom Sheehan. *Panic Scrip of 1893, 1907 and 1914: An Illustrated Catalog of Emergency Monetary Issues.* Jefferson, NC: McFarland, 2013.

Silber, William L. *When Washington Shut Down Wall Street: The Great Financial Crisis of 1914 and the Origins of America's Monetary Supremacy.* Princeton, NJ: Princeton University Press, 2007.

Tournie, Vincent. "The Crisis and the French Savings Banks." *The Aftermaths of Crises Savings and Savings Banks: Elements of Stability in Times of Crises?* ESBG *Perspectives* 66 (December 2013): 63–74.

U.S. Senate, *Bills of Exchange.* 63rd Congress, Senate Document No.162 (Washington, 1913).

Wetterberg, Gunnar. *Money and Power: From Stockholms Banco 1656 to Sveriges Riksbank Today.* Stockholm: Atlantis, 2009.

Withers, Hartley. *War and Lombard Street.* London: Smith, Elder, 1915.

7 Business as (Un)Usual

DuPont, Comptoir des Textiles Artificiels and the Post-First World War Internationalization of the Synthetic Products Industry

Jacqueline McGlade

Economic historians of globalization tend to portray the First World War as a disruptive event that abruptly ended the pre-1914 golden age of international economic integration and initiated a period of so-called deglobalization (i.e., regression back toward autarky).[1] It is certainly true that First World War dramatically severed many of the political, business, financial, and trade connections that had driven economic globalization since the 1850s. However, while the war certainly changed the international economy, the process of globalization did not come to a sudden halt in the summer of 1914. The diplomatic historian Adam Tooze has recently argued that rather than ending globalization, the First World War merely caused globalization to take on different forms. Indeed, he shows that the war actually increased some global economic interconnectedness, albeit in a form very different from "late Victorian globalization."[2] The business historian Geoffrey Jones has also challenged the conventional wisdom that globalization ceased as of 1914. In his study of how successive "waves of globalization" have driven the rise of the multinational enterprise (MNE), Jones notes that the first wave of MNEs lasted from c. 1880 straight through First World War and into the interwar years, cresting just prior to the worldwide financial collapse in 1929.[3] According to Jones, multinationals continued to expand after First World War even as "the first global economy disintegrated," largely bolstered by robust outlays of foreign direct investment by firms, especially in cross-border corporate ventures and acquisitions. Multinationals continued to flourish, as did "free-standing companies" (i.e., firms that had their headquarters and shareholders in one country and all of their productive assets in another).[4]

The view of Tooze and Jones that globalization did not abruptly end in 1914 is congruent with the research presented in this chapter. This case study suggests that instead of halting the rise of managerial capitalism as embodied in the MNE, First World War and the economic apocalypse of its aftermath enabled certain firms to grow through new and essential opportunities for overseas business development, trade and investment. This chapter, which focuses on the R&D capabilities of DuPont, a US multinational, and the Comptoir des Textiles Artificiels (CTA), a French multinational, supports the view that while globalization was altered by the First World War, it did not end because of the conflict. Indeed, wartime developments appear to have contributed to the transformation of DuPont into a knowledge-based firm with a diversified market base and global operations. Wartime cooperation with DuPont also enabled CTA to expand its foreign operations, transforming itself from a multinational firm active primarily in Europe into a multiregional firm with operates in North America and other continents.

Business as (Un)Usual: The Partnership of E.I. DuPont Company and Comptoir des Textiles Artificiels

Micro studies of how emerging multinationals adjusted market and organizational strategies, operations, capabilities and markets in the light of the First World War provide special insights then into the re-shaping of global capitalism after 1919. The pre- and post-First World War involvement between the E.I. DuPont Company and the French syndicate, Comptoir des Textiles Artificiels, presents such a case. It showcases the deliberate attempts on the part of both companies to continue to develop new civilian products and market along with competitive production capabilities even in the midst of a dire war.

In this way, this case runs counter to traditional business, economic and military studies that portray First World War as a "total" event in which firms fully re-oriented and redirected their energies and capacities in support of armaments production and war servicing.[5] Instead, this study shows how both firms continue to navigate along core business lines, the development of synthetic dyes and fibers, with an eye toward expanding beyond military contracting into anticipated civilian markets imagined long before the First World War.[6] While both companies benefited greatly from military contracts and wartime spending largesse, the entrepreneurial impulse of both firms to envision new civilian markets and then develop scientific, production and managerial capacities aligned with delivering such consumer products.

Overall then, the firms demonstrated, as illustrated by Geoff Jones, the kinds of long-term strategic thinking, organization and action that gave rise to their post-First World War transformation from multi-regional to multi-national firms.[7] Also reflective of Jones, the unease and uncertainty fraught by the financial, geographic and state constraints and dislocations imposed by First World War required both firms to seek out and engage in new entrepreneurial forms of partnership.[8] While enabling independent multinational growth, the association, however, also imposed on both firms inconvenient, uneasy dependencies made necessary by the loss of pre-war predictable business and markets entry pathways.

In this way, the CTA-DuPont case illuminates how post-First World War firms turned to forms of "business as unusual" in an effort to return to "business as usual" or "normalcy" conditions. In traditional corporate terms, then, this required both firms to capture new financial and markets gain and advantages, as well as maintaining dominance in position within a respective business sector, whether nationally, regionally or globally.[9]

DuPont's "Bigness": Acts of Foreign Acquisition or Indigenous Invention?

Along with the growth of both firms as multinationals, this chapter also re-examines the importance of CTA in transferring critical scientific and manufacturing knowledge to DuPont, precipitating its rise as a chemical giant in the interwar era. In doing so, this case counters traditional business studies that promote in-house R&D and products invention as the basis for DuPont rise from family firm to a vertically integrated giant chemical multinational firm since the end of First World War.[10] As a result of its relationship with CTA, particularly in the period from 1919 to 1927, DuPont subsequently acquired new patents, manufacturing organization models, production processes and technical equipment that proved critical in its launch of its transformational businesses in consumer rayon and cellophane products. Through the partnership, DuPont also gained critical access to CTA European chemical plants in France, Switzerland, Germany and Italy, which provided not only key entry points into post-First World War European consumer and business markets, but also laid the managerial and manufacturing frameworks for long-term penetration of comparable and developing consumer markets and industrial outposts worldwide.

While business historians including Alfred Chandler, David Hounshell, John K. Smith, Kathryn Steen and Charles Cheape present extensive works examining the rise of DuPont as a chemical giant and multinational firm, they only present CTA in very sketchy detail or not at all.[11] A greater understanding of CTA's role as central for DuPont's eventual rise as a synthetic products leader as well as a multinational firm offers critical insights, then, into key inter-related patterns of DuPont corporate strategic and operational dependency on foreign scientific, management and production techniques before and after the First World War. Instead of original R&D breakthroughs, then, DuPont increasingly relied, especially after 1916, on a strategy of *foreign acquisition over internal invention* in its ever-desperate pursuit of critical patents, scientific knowledge and manufacturing processes related to synthetic materials and product creation.

In this way, DuPont's strategy of foreign acquisition over indigenous creation of synthetic processes and products reflects the general finding of Raymond Vernon that the "innovative drive of U.S. businessmen" in the late 19th and early 20th c. should "not be confused with any capacity to invent," as "the function of U.S. businessmen in many instances was simply that of accepting the risks and costs associated with developing the invention and introducing it in the U.S. market."[12] Raymond Vernon also notes that relationships like the one entered into by CTA and DuPont, which along with DuPont's previous 1910 sales and patent payments agreement with the UK explosives firm Nobel,[13] bordered on international cartelization of the U.S.-European chemical products imports-exports. In this way, DuPont and its European partners shared before and after the First World War the main "objective . . . to take the uncertainties out of the market."[14]

Reflective of Vernon, the initial strategic motivation on the part of DuPont managers to pursue a partnership with CTA and other European partnerships did not emanate then from a bold, innovate push to expand DuPont as an international leader in the chemicals industry. Indeed, DuPont executives viewed foreign partnerships as an unfortunate but necessary defensive move, even if involving unfavorable payments and profit-sharing arrangements, to block any significant European encroachment in American-based synthetic products markets.

In a 1962 report for the US National Bureau of Economic Research entitled "The Origins of the Basic Inventions Underlying DuPont's Major Product and Process Innovations 1920–1950," Willard F. Muller chronicled DuPont's overreliance on European synthetic chemicals science and invention in establishing the company's top twenty-five synthetic products and chemical processes. As shown in Table 7.1, Muller demonstrated that only ten products "were based on the inventions of DuPont scientists and engineers . . .

Table 7.1 Summary of New Products and Product and Process Improvements Introduced by DuPont, By Source of Basic Invention, 1920–1949

New Product	Original Source of Basic Invention	Product/Process Improvement	Original Source of Basic Invention
Vicose rayon	CTA (France)	Duco lacquers	Du Pont
Tetraethyl lead (bromide process)	General Motors (US)	Tetraethyl lead (chloride process)	Standard Oil (US)
Cellophane	CTA (France)	Moisture-proof cellophane	Du Pont
Synthetic ammonia	Norway/France	Dulux finishes	Du Pont
Synthetic methanel	Other and Du Pont		
Acetate rayon	CTA (France)	Cordura high tenacity rayon	Du Pont
Freon refrigerants	General Motors (US)		
Titanium pigments	US/Norway/France	Rotile titanium dioxide	Du Pont
Lucite	ICI, Ltd (UK)		
Nylon	Du Pont		
Polyvinyl acetate	ICI, Ltd (UK)		
Teflon	Du Pont		
Alathon polyethylene	ICI, Ltd (UK)		
Orlon	Du Pont		
Titanium metal	Germany		
Polymeric color film	Du Pont		
Fiber V (Dacron)	Calico/ICI, Ltd (UK)		

Source: Adapted from Willard F. Muller, "The Origins of the Basic Inventions Underlying DuPont's Major Product and Process Innovations 1920–1950," National Bureau of Economic Research, Washington, DC: Government Printing Office, 1962, pp. 326–344.

and of the eighteen new products, DuPont discovered five and shared in the discovery of one other."[15] Even in terms of product and processes improvements vs. invention, Muller found DuPont lagging behind foreign firms in that of ten such improvements, only five "were DuPont originals."[16]

Muller concluded that such evidence has called into question "the frequent statement of DuPont's bigness has created a perfect environment for inventive activity . . . The record during the period of this study does not support such a generalization."[17] He bases his assertion on financial evidence as well noting that as "there has not been a proportional acceleration in the number of *important* [sic] inventions coming from its laboratories" that matched the revenue flows from those fully acquired or improved upon from European sources in the interwar period.[18]

Relying on the French: DuPont Enters the Rayon Business

The CTA story in light of Muller's analysis carries particular importance then in illuminating DuPont's over-dependency on foreign patents and scientific knowledge at all stages of its growth in the 1920s and 1930s as a multinational in the emerging synthetic chemical industry. It is at this point, however, that the CTA story complicates the studies offered by Chandler, Steen, Hounshell and Smith, and others, who largely credit DuPont's initiating in-house R&D and manufacturing capabilities for its transformational reorganization and success as a vertically and horizontally integrated multinational enterprise. Instead of indigenous invention, DuPont actually entered and ascended as a global leader in synthetic consumer products as a result of its aggressive acquisition in the interwar period of European patents, processes and scientific personnel. In addition to rapidly procuring R&D and manufacturing capabilities through financial deals, DuPont also exploited new business opportunities and advantages brought on by widespread industry disruptions and dislocations among the top British, German and French chemical firms in the aftermath of the First World War. Overall, DuPont possessed the strategic advantages over its European competitors in this era of having largely unfettered access to huge sums of capital, home and overseas markets, as well as benefitting from stable government support in contract to its European rivals struggling in the midst of post-First World War recovery efforts.

DuPont's entrance into the fledgling European industry of nitrocellulose and artificial textile fibers in the early 1920s, which after two decades of its partnership with CTA and $100 million in investment, would yield three new consumer products, rayon, cellulose acetate textile fibers and cellophane film—all that contributed greatly to the company's transformation along many lines including public identification, market diversification, corporate profitability and geographic reach. While historians David Hounshell and John K. Smith have lauded DuPont as "lead[ing] the synthetic fiber revolution . . . with nylon, Orlon and Dacron,"[19] the company actually struggled and failed to build its artificial fibers division until entering into its partnership with the French rayon firm Comptoir des Textiles Artificiels in January 1920.

However, the connection of DuPont with CTA and the emerging European artificial fibers industry at large did not immediately take shape and took four years to formalize. DuPont had first contacted the French firm Chardonnet Company, founded by scientist Count Hilaire de Chardonnet, who had invented nitrocellulose textile fibers in the 1890s, which had led to the development of several popular consumer products in the form of artificial silk by the 1910s. However, talks broke down quickly without resolution on a joint partnership.[20]

DuPont then looked to Britain for a corporate connection, where Charles F. Cross and Edward F. Bevan had developed the alternative fiber called viscose that by 1908 became known as rayon. After several failed attempts to buy from the American Viscose Company from its British owners, Courtaulds Ltd., in 1916, DuPont executives decided to reconsider nitrocellulose-based fibers as an entry point into the rapidly expanding international artificial textiles markets.[21] However, DuPont managers could not fully abandon foreign acquisition as its primary strategy, as in-house invention seemed an even more daunting breakthrough effort to achieve in the synthetic chemicals industry. Other than its modest business in artificial leathers developed out of the purchase of British patents during the First World War, DuPont by 1917 then seemed unable to either leverage through offers of investment capital and plants formation, or more importantly, invent its way into the critical new chemical field of synthetic fibers.[22]

Starting in 1913, DuPont had spent over $100,000 in financing several failed R&D ventures based in Delaware and New Jersey that executives finally "abandoned" after they "deemed [it] expedient to purchase know-how for a completely worked out process" in viscose and cellulose acetate science and production.[23] In 1919, the opportunity to acquire such wholesale operations came again from overseas, but this time not through DuPont efforts, but from the unexpected overtures of a French syndicate of artificial silk manufacturers, the CTA.

CTA: "L'aventure des Gillet. . .l'espirit entrepreneurial"

Comptoir des Textiles Artificiels, a syndicate of traditional dye and artificial silk manufacturers located throughout France, had emerged in 1913 as result of the expansionist activities of brothers Edmond, Charles and Joseph Gillet. The brothers established CTA on the business foundation set by their grandfather Francois Gillet, who built one of Europe's largest dye works in Lyon, France, from 1838 until his death in 1895.

As the "chiffre d'affaires" or chief executive of the La Société Gillet & Fils, Francois invested early on in developing R&D capabilities for his firm, especially in the invention of new dyeing techniques using synthetic organic chemicals for application in multiple fiber and cloth types.[24] Also, Francois sent his grandson Joseph-Louis to a newly established chemistry school in Wiesbaden, Germany, in 1860 with the intention of bringing back to the firm the latest scientific theories and manufacturing techniques in the creation and production of artificial dyes and synthetic fibers. By 1869, the firm had grown from "l'atelier de teinturier (custom dye house) to "un grand enterprise de la chemie," or a chemical company earning over 900,000 francs per year[25] in revenues. In 1869, this sum represent the equivalent of $4.3 million in current US dollars, an amount far exceeding the DuPont Company's net revenues of $96,560.69, or $1.6 million in current US dollars.[26]

As noted by French industrial historians Pierre Cayez and Serge Chassagne, the firm at the time of Francois's death in 1895, and now run by grandsons Edmund, Paul and Charles, had emerged as a "très grand enterprise . . . des textiles artificiels" largely due to in-house formulas, processes and techniques invented by their father, Joseph-Louis.[27] By 1902 Gillet & Fils had embarked on a wave of regional chemical plant and company purchases and mergers, resulting in the formation in 1911 of CTA,[28] which became the French-Italian-Swiss regional leader in artificial dyeing and fiber production, especially artificial silk or "rayon," as it became known as by 1916.[29] In 1922, CTA further diversified its reach into the synthetic organic chemicals products market by entering into a critical partnership in 1922 with Société Chimique des Usines du Rhône (SCUR), which had developed patents in cellulose acetate (1902) and a cellulose-based plastic called Rhoid in 1917. Under the new company, Rhodiaseta in 1922, the executive leadership of both CTA and SCUR secured[30] SCUR production facilities in Brazil and the United States gained through foreign subsidiary arrangements first set in 1919.[31]

As part of CTA's expansion activities in this period, Cayez and Chassagne also cites Joseph-Louis' efforts along with Usines de Rhône professor Victor Grignard for establishing just prior to the First World War one of France's premier chemistry instruction schools, "L'Ecole supérireure de chimie de industrielle de Lyon." When coupled with the Gillet grandsons' participation in the creation of the powerful Rhone-Poulenc industrial region in 1928[32] all of these efforts provide ample evidence of, in the estimation of Pierre Cayez, the "L'aventure des Gillet est une parfait illustration de l'esprit entrepreneurial."[33]

In this same entrepreneurial spirit and in its capacity as an international first mover in the emerging synthetic chemicals industry, CTA "sought an interview with the DuPont Company to ascertain its interest in purchasing information in viscose [fibers] . . . manufacture" as early as 1916.[34] The pursuit by the CTA syndicate of a DuPont association demonstrated a managerial aggressiveness, or in precisely French terms, *entrepreneurship*, more often attributed to post-First World War American firms looking to establish markets in European consumer markets.[35] In this case, French producers through the CTA led a move toward transatlantic expansion by seeking a firm connection into the potentially lucrative American clothing markets through a partnership with DuPont.

Catching Up at Any Cost: DuPont's Reliance on CTA Rayon and Cellophane

The 1919 CTA outreach eventually proved a monumental event in re-shaping DuPont's corporate structure as well business destiny. There is no question that the partnership that DuPont eventually forged with the CTA represented an all-important turning point in the company's long struggle[36] to "meet and keep up with the [European] competition"[37] in rayon research and production. Indeed, DuPont President Crawford Greenwalt in July 1950 in an internal company newsletter credited foreign as well as US acquisitions since 1915 as fueling "the period of DuPont's greatest growth" with "most of the purchases . . . made in the 1920s when DuPont was diversifying its chemical manufacturing and needed know-how and facilities in new lines."[38]

The story of CTA and DuPont involvement unshrouds then, not only the general intricacies of international partnerships, but a window into the many new complexities, necessary interactions and challenging realities faced by Western firms in the pre- and post-First World War global business environments. In the case of DuPont, the necessity to rapidly gain synthetic chemical scientific and manufacturing capabilities out of fear of European encroachment in emerging home markets drove new managerial strategies feverishly rooted in overseas acquisition even before the First World War. DuPont's corporate resolve further intensified as the opportunities for transatlantic growth driven by the emerging European industrial uncertainties and production vacuums after the First World War. However, repeated failures before the First World War to achieve the expansion of its corporate scientific and manufacturing capabilities posed a large barrier for DuPont if it hoped to seize the business and consumer market advantages in synthetic products looming at home and abroad. As a result, DuPont managers readily embraced the adaptation of foreign management knowledge, scientific methods and manufacturing processes over in-house innovation and means as a "catch up and pull ahead" post-war business strategy.

In this way, the CTA-DuPont partnership offers an important counter story to the evolution of post-First World War international business as largely a chronicle of the independent rise and spread of American vertically integrated firms forged through indigenous managerial innovation and products development as the predominant model and impetus for the re-birth of economic globalization, corporate modernization and business multinationalism.[39] In his 1952 study of the DuPont's Rayon Technical Division, Ferdinand Schultze verified and waxed admiringly over the deep influence and primacy of early French and CTA artificial fibers research and production in the origins of DuPont's later success:

> The fine filaments of this man-made yarn . . . stretched historically across the Atlantic to a great textile nation, France. There resides the anteced-ents of the Rayon Department, just as those of the DuPont Company; for the process on which the Company's first synthetic yarn plant was based had been developed in the French [CTA] plants . . .[40]

CTA scientists and engineers, according to Schultze, in a few short years also greatly assisted DuPont in its efforts to move, not only into rayon, but also into cellophane production—another pioneering area in which chemis-try increasing intersected with the development of new consumer products and markets.[41] While DuPont's R&D breakthroughs in the 1930s finally propelled it into its paramount industry position by the 1940s, it neverthe-less relied heavily on CTA managerial and scientific knowledge to achieve its later successes.

DuPont's frequent overreliance on and deference toward CTA in plant engineering and products manufacturing processes underscore the pre-dominance of CTA in the partnership from the start. After the rejection of the proposed British-based Courtaulds merger, DuPont Vice President Irenee DuPont, in an attempt to seek out European patents and processes in synthetic fibers, sent company liaison Colonel Leonard A. Yerkes, then Assistant Director of the Development Department, to set up an office in Paris. In late 1919, Yerkes finally acted on the 1916 CTA inquiry and met with Edmond Gillet, who represented the French syndicate, through an introduction arranged by Henry Blum, the executive director of the French firm, United Piece Dye Works. Subsequently, Yerkes crafted a series of introductory communications and meetings between Gillet and DuPont executives, most notably Walter S. Carpenter, Jr., then Director of the Development Department and later company President. After visiting a number of fledgling artificial textiles in Belgium, Switzerland and Ger-many along with France, Yerkes recommended shortly after the meeting that DuPont join in association with the CTA, which, as a conglomerate of a number of firms located in the Rhone-Poulenc region, had incorpo-rated viscose techniques in the manufacturing of its patented artificial silk textiles.[42]

As a part of an affiliate agreement struck in January 1920, the CTA won a joint interest in DuPont's synthetic fiber production in exchange for shar-ing its bobbin technology and textile drying processes. As part of the deal, DuPont established a subsidiary, the DuPont Fibersilk Company, later to become DuPont Rayon, which gave CTA a 40% stake in profits stemming from the development of a new production plant located in Buffalo, New York. The venture also garnered CTA another 24% for its initial transfer of patent and process knowledge as well as plant technology setups and provided for an option to take up to an additional 16% stake in DuPont Fibersilk company stock.[43]

From the start in 1923, CTA demonstrated a strong position of parity alongside of DuPont in making decisions and guiding the new company. According to the Fibersilk agreement, five CTA executives sat with six DuPont members on a combined board that oversaw "all [contracts and] activities, including production, sales, accounting, etc."[44] This arrangement of joint management would continue well into the mid-1930s before the DuPont Company began to patent its own technologies and processes that eventually led to significant modifications to CTA's position in the Fibersilk venture.

The predominance of French leadership in the transfer of technical and managerial production knowledge to DuPont, along with the company's high reliance on CTA guidance, remains the most striking, if not outstanding aspect of the early partnership. As chronicled in the DuPont technical reports of the time, just three short months after the 1920 agreement had been reached, French managers from the CTA-affiliated Izieux plant in Northern France journeyed to Buffalo, New York, to help set up DuPont's first viscose yarn production facility. "Substantially copying" French production machinery, factory floor layouts and chemical processes, the new DuPont Fibersilk Company produced its first success batch of artificial textile yarn by May 1921, ending in less than one year a decade of frustrating attempts by DuPont to start up rayon production.[45]

Textile industry demand for the durable new cloth soon outstripped capacities at the Buffalo plant and, between 1925–1928, DuPont had set up two additional French-styled plants: "Old Hickory" outside of Nashville Tennessee and another facility in Richmond, Virginia, which produced cellophane as well as rayon. Despite the fact that DuPont by 1930 far outpaced the CTA syndicate in terms of production volume, equal admiration and cooperation still marked the relationship. As a tribute to the DuPont-French connection, company executives choose to name the Richmond factory, the "Spruance Plant" to mark the efforts of Colonel William C. Spruance, a DuPont Vice President who had forged close ties with CTA representatives and had "only seven years before . . . negotiate[d] with the French for the purchase of cellophane technology."[46] Spruance's deal-making prowess, however, does not fully illuminate DuPont's seemingly swift movement into cellophane. Like the case of rayon, CTA aggressiveness and DuPont's overt dependency on French business guidance, scientific mentorship and technology transfer marked the start-up of cellophane production at the Nashville and Richmond plants.

DuPont Acquires Cellophane: The Second CTA Venture

As with rayon technology, the CTA held patents since 1912 under an agreement with Swiss scientist Edwin Brandenberger, utilizing his processes for cellophane production.[47] Confident in the successful tone and pace of the DuPont rayon partnership, Charles Gillet and CTA chief executive Alfred Bernheim "directed the attention of the DuPont representative [in Paris] to their new cellulosic wrapping film." An energetic and visionary executive, Bernheim had arranged for the patent relationship with Brandenberger and also set up the CTA-backed company La Cellophane Société Anonyme, complete with a Paris showroom featuring packaging displays that encased a wide range of products from convenience foods to perfumes in the new wrapping film.[48]

Intrigued by the potential of cellophane's applications in American consumer goods packaging markets, DuPont dispatched Fibersilk Chemical Director George Rocker and Sales Manager C.F. Benz several times to France to survey CTA production facilities and sales operations starting in 1922 through 1925. The Rocker and Benz reports revealed several astonishing aspects of the CTA-DuPont cellophane partnership, most notably the virtual total transfer of French technology and business practices again to jump-start an entrance into American markets.[49]

While again highly dependent on French science and production processes, DuPont entered into another subsidiary agreement with the CTA through the Spruance negotiations, ending in the creation of the DuPont Cellophane Company on June 9, 1923. The cellophane deal, while more difficult to negotiate due to DuPont's doubts over the durability of the Brandenberger processes, nevertheless netted CTA a 48% share in profits in a new cellophane manufacturing facility built by DuPont, based largely again on CTA plant blueprints, designs and equipment. As in rayon, CTA on-site technical leadership proved decisive in DuPont's first efforts to produce cellophane, as Dr. Brandenberger personally oversaw "the first sheet of cellophane to be produced in America from a casting machine" at the Buffalo, New York, plant in April 1924.[50]

In addition to production, French pioneering efforts in cellophane sales also shaped DuPont marketing strategies. In a 1925 report, C. J. Benz chronicled French innovations in cellophane usages and packaging as well as sales organization:

> Their sales organization comprises of seven salesmen in Paris, four general agents in the whole of France outside of Paris, to whom thirty-six sub-agents report . . . All of the salesmen, agents and sub-agents are paid on a straight commission except beginners, who are given a nominal salary and commission until their learned the product.[51]

DuPont executive interest proved so high in French sales organization that Benz was directed to send another report on "how much" agents received and other salary figures and considerations.[52]

Benz also detailed in his reports "substantial" cellophane wrapping of consumer convenience items, commenting in particular on baked products:

> [cakes and biscuits] not made in the States . . . and were very interesting and we brought a number of samples back with us. The Cracker

industry is a possible market for us and will add to our development of the baking business.[53]

He also noted that:

> considerable cellophane was found on Dried Fruits [sic] . . . Whether or not this . . . packaging is done in the States, will have to be found out. It will help materially to have the French experience as an aid to increase our present business . . .[54]

Benz also singled out the vast potential tapped by the French in the sanitary products market, taking particular notice of non-prescription drugs, soaps and toothbrushes wrapped in cellophane. "We are making a special effort to get to that market," Benz wrote, "using the background of the French success as a stepping stone." Overall, Benz calculated that the French cellophane business had permeated four industries, with 31% of sales in 1924 associated with baked goods, 20% in perfume packaging, 12% in chocolate and confectionary products, 11% in pharmaceuticals and another 15% in a variety of wrapping applications involved in the shipping and display of textiles and miscellaneous foodstuffs.[55]

Mimicking the French pioneering efforts, DuPont executives and agents went on to engage in the mid-1920s through the 1930s in company-changing marketing and sales forays intended to align consumer products industries with new forms of cellophane packaging, shipping and display presentations. Reports in 1926 advanced from the Spruance and Buffalo plants to DuPont Chemical Director Dr. E. B. Benger, visiting CTA plants in France, confirmed the rapid success of the second CTA-DuPont technical partnership. As one executive wrote, "Cellophane is doing very well. Sales are running ahead of the forecast, quality is excellent and we have practically no complaints."[56]

The intentionality by which CTA granted DuPont unfettered access into its rayon and cellophane businesses seems shocking in light of modern-day no-holds-barred tactics of companies to preserve technical and market advantages. While antithetical today, open and frequent accommodation of DuPont needs and requests proved to be an extremely winning strategy, however, for the CTA in its push to maximize profits and markets related to its proprietary lead in viscose science and production. Over and over in their reports, DuPont executives, engineers and scientists remarked on the high level of cooperation exerted by CTA officials. In his 1925 European trip report, C. F. Benz commented on the fact that lead CTA scientist Edwin Brandenberger had assigned the head sales manager for La Cellophane "to give us any information we might want," which included a four-day inspection of a manufacturing plant outside of Paris, "where we had the undivided attention of Mr. Ray [plant manager] and were supplied with valuable information and statistics."[57]

Acts of intentional sharing and overt transparency marked the extension of detailed technical information by CTA to inquiring DuPont plant managers, engineers and scientists as they attempted to replicate French rayon and cellophane processes in the United States. As early as 1922, DuPont chief scientist George Rocker began submitting back to Buffalo highly specific accounts of French artificial fibers production techniques facilitated by multiple visits and interviews with CTA officials located at plants throughout France and parts of Switzerland and Germany. In one such report, Rocker marveled at the superiority of CTA spinning techniques that clearly distanced French from British artificial fibers in terms of quality and strength and included "photographs . . . given to me by [CTA chief executive] Rene Bernheim showing cross sections of silk spun both by the bucket processes and the bobbin processes."[58]

Another DuPont manager, H. J. White, who accompanied Rocker a year later in a series of return visits to the CTA plants, commented that Rene Bernheim again had arranged meetings for the DuPont team with "official[s] similar to our plant manager or from the plant superintendent," who made it possible to receive information that "cover[ed] the essential points from a strictly operating viewpoint." These meetings also enable the DuPont team to engage in comparison talks with the French plant managers over the compatibility of CTA-Buffalo plant operations.[59]

The communiqués between the two companies on the cellophane deal illustrate the extraordinary cordiality and sincere concern by which the executives took each other's positions and recommendations into account, even when relations became overly strained. In writing to Colonel William C. Spruance, DuPont's chief negotiator on the cellophane, to confirm the delivery of new machinery from Lyon to Wilmington, Delaware, Mr. Rene Bernheim of the CTA Paris office reflected the spirit of camaraderie that had gotten both companies over several major difficulties endangering their partnership:

> It is a real satisfaction to us to see that our [CTA-DuPont] hopes have been fully realized and no doubt it is a feeling which must be your own at the same moment . . . In Rayon, the result of our collaboration of 10 years have been most satisfactory also . . . When so you expect to visit Europe again? You know how glad we should be to have you amongst us after so many years of friendly and confident collaboration.[60]

Bernheim also alluded to the extraordinary level of technical cooperation that had been built between the DuPont and CTA engineering and production teams: "In Rayon . . . the present position is not as bright as Cellophane but we are confident that with the improvements of qualities which are being steadily worked out in our different groups."[61]

Detailed trip reports compiled by DuPont engineers and scientists from the 1920s and 1930s attest to Bernheim's claim of the determined efforts on both sides of the Atlantic to integrate DuPont and CTA research and development findings along with production processes. Constant cordiality and accommodation marked the CTA's approach to working with the DuPont teams. One DuPont executive emoted enthusiastically during his trip to CTA plants in 1933 that "[w]e received the finest kind of treatment everywhere and were freely supplied with all available information. The members of the Comptoir organization gave us generously of their time, although they were obviously short-handed."[62] "I am very much pleased," he went on to declare, "I have never seen a group work together so well and so pleasantly, particularly when we are together practically 24 hours a day."[63] The DuPont executives also strongly appreciated the openness of CTA plant managers, engineers and scientists to share in detail any changes and improvements to their emerging rayon and cellophane operations. "Fortunately the Société Chimique des Usines des Rhone (SCUR) is a very orderly organization and their records are in excellent shape," Chemical Chief Ernest Benger exclaimed in a 1926 trip report, "[that] same spirit has found its way into Rhodiaseta [Gillet operation]." The accuracy and accessibility to a high level of engineering information and scientific data courtesy of the Gillet brothers led Benger to exclaim that "I have already figured most the of buildings" to enable a wholesale transplant of CTA rayon and cellophane production into DuPont's Buffalo, New York, and Nashville, Tennessee, plants.[64]

The value of sharing production knowledge and improvements in a concrete, ongoing fashion with the French over German and Italian rayon and cellophane producers also emerged as a strong recommendation back from the DuPont teams. "They have a number of very interesting and clever tricks about the operation," Ernest Benger noted in one of his reports, "[however] the patent situation will not be easy on account of the failure of Rhodiaseta to take patents as fast as ideas were conceived . . . [the French] are extremely active in this respect."[65] Indeed, CTA and DuPont scientists and engineers organized and then regularly exchanged laboratory and production reports before the end of the 1920s. In addition to collaborative R&D efforts, the firms went on to maintain a joint board composed of six DuPont and five CTA executives to manage the new DuPont Cellophane Company modeled after their earlier DuPont Fibersilk Company venture.[66]

By joining with CTA then, DuPont rapidly gained a ready-made transatlantic network of plants and sales operations, first in rayon, and then in cellophane. Enabled by the first CTA agreement, DuPont engineers, managers and scientists journeyed to Europe in 1922 to conduct "an investigation" of eight CTA facilities that spread out throughout France and in Switzerland.[67] Prodigious reports emanating from yearly trips provided DuPont executives with exact details, blueprints, photo layouts and scientific analysis of the various spinning and dyeing processes carried out by CTA facilities.[68] These reports proved critical in DuPont's later efforts to re-shape and expand the entirety of its artificial fibers production technology and output processes. In the case of cellophane, DuPont's association with the CTA broadened its European network even further to include plants in Germany, Belgium and

Italy.[69] Furthermore, DuPont's alliance with CTA cannot be underestimated, as company executives regularly sought advice and guidance from their new French corporate partners on how to navigate successfully through unfamiliar and difficult European business environments.

Competition Over Camaraderie: DuPont Separates from CTA

Like the case of Rayon, both companies would eventually benefit from unprecedented consumer demand for cellophane products and packaging with a 63% in the industry from 1928–1930 alone. Despite the onset of the Great Depression, sales continued to rise up 100% in 1930 and by 200% in 1931, driving new cellophane competitors into the filed on both sides of the Atlantic, most notably Belgium's Sidac against CTA and its subsidiary Sylvania against DuPont in the United States.[70]

As profits and markets grew rapidly in artificial fibers into the 1930s, so did the efforts of both CTA and DuPont to meet business demand and competition challenges. Ironically, the greatest source of tension between the two companies on the issue of competition emerged not from external but from intra-firm forces. As DuPont expanded in the early 1930s to take advantage of its long-standing foothold in South America, CTA reacted negatively, as such expansion efforts threatened operations and contracts it held in Argentina and the West Indies before the 1923 Fibersilk agreement. Also, DuPont scientists by the early 1930s devised a waterproof form of cellophane, the chemical composition of which proved significantly different from the French method, calling the arrangement of CTA-DuPont patent sharing into serious question.[71] However, DuPont regularly deferred to any pushback by CTA over its original profit-sharing arrangements, even resulting in a new agreement in 1928 that allowed CTA to recoup over $3 million in addition compensation for past deficit profits. Also, DuPont agreed to pay CTA an increase of 15% up from 4% of all future profits stemming from rayon production carried out under the original CTA patents.[72]

Despite several such attempts to maintain a close partnership, DuPont and CTA would eventually part ways, as the change to French patent laws and the coming of the First World War required CTA to increasingly secure its own independent markets and operations in France and other parts of Western Europe. Also, DuPont's gigantic strides in artificial fibers and cellophane science and technology continued to outpace the efforts of CTA. As a result, DuPont no longer needed to rely on CTA patents or equipment as it moved into its own production of branded artificial fibers such as DACRON and moisture-resistant cellophane packing past the end of the 1930s.

Conclusion

By the end of the 1920s, then, the CTA-DuPont partnership in rayon and cellophane had more than paid off for both organizations. US consumption of rayon products jumped from 8.2 million pounds in 1919 to over 130 million pounds in 1929, as DuPont Fibersilk cut substantially into the monopoly in production held by Courtaulds' American Viscose Company.[73] While disputes over the strength of CTA patents eventually led to a rupture with DuPont over the continued joint development and production of cellophane for the American market, nonetheless, both companies enjoyed a 50% return on investment within two years of their initial venture, struck in 1921.[74]

Clearly, DuPont's strategy to acquire CTA patents and processes in rayon and cellophane production instead of conducting time-consuming indigenous invention not only swiftly boosted production, but also sparked a solid start to its own R&D efforts, which finally gave the company "additional leverage . . . with its European counterparts . . ."[75] With deals developing between DuPont and a growing number of British, Belgium and German chemical and processing companies, the company had clearly learned from its experiences with CTA to build in less than a decade a viable European arm for its overseas business interests. By engaging in acts of "business as unusual," then, in this case a massive transfer of CTA scientific knowledge and technology transfer, DuPont had successfully re-cast itself in less than a decade as a global leader in the manufacture, and eventually invention, of synthetic chemical consumer products. In line with Geoffrey Jones's definition, Du Pont stood more as a "multiregional" instead of a "multinational" firm before to its relationship with CTA as its direct investments and business interests resides primarily within American continental countries.[76] The partnership with CTA enabled DuPont to evolve into a true multinational, with its presence in Europe linked to CTA's multiple plants throughout Switzerland and Italy along with France.

Conversely, the DuPont partnership propelled CTA to go beyond its multiregional locations in Europe to go multinational by entering American and Caribbean markets as well as acquiring a British foothold prior to the First World War.[77] In 1935, CTA became the parent company of "British Cellophane," a subsidiary of the British textile company Courtaulds Ltd., which had struggled in its attempts to diversify beyond rayon into cellulose products through its "Viscacelle" film brand. Leading with its superior "La Cellophane" formula, CTA directed construction in Bridgewater, Somerset, England, of a joint major production facility with Courtaulds, which employed over 3,000 workers by 1937.[78] While German occupation during the Second World War forced CTA to end its Courtaulds partnership, the firm managed to maintain its manufacturing of rayon, cellophane and other synthetic consumer products for European and American markets into the WWII postwar era.[79] In the manner of the DuPont partnership, Solvay mainly acquired CTA for its R&D operations and invention portfolio, which remained strong with over 185 independent chemical formulas, synthetic products and manufacturing patents established from the 1920s through the early 1960s.[80]

Overall, the case of CTA and DuPont reveals a picture of post-First World War business redevelopment that both diverges as well as converges with traditional scholarly views on the impact of the war on economic globalization. As most historians note, American multinationals flourished during the interwar period by filling the direct foreign investment and manufacturing vacuum left by European governments and firms, with particular growth in firms involved in motor vehicles, machinery, chemical and rubber production.[81] The rise of the United States over Britain as the central driver of world direct investment and capital markets after 1914 also re-shaped economic globalization as American multinational firms eclipsed European governments as the source of world business stimulus, consumer markets development and investment growth.[82]

While European firms like CTA possessed key advantages over its rivals in terms of proprietary scientific knowledge, innovative manufacturing processes and aggressive consumer products marketing strategies and access, it remained hampered in its growth as a vertically integrated, multinational firm by unstable political, social and economic conditions after the First World War through the Second World War. Likewise, DuPont benefited from the unsettled business conditions and financial constraints faced by its European rivals by swiftly acquiring through patents and manufacturing partnerships the scientific know-how and synthetic products development that had so frequently alluded the firm before its connection to CTA and other European firms.

However, the initial dependence of DuPont on the CTA has been underestimated in the entry of the firm into artificial fibers and cellophane production and markets. The CTA partnership proved invaluable, if not historic in nature, as it allowed DuPont in less than three decades to evolve from a firm largely confined to American continental markets to the world's leading multinational in consumer synthetic products. CTA's mentorship also assisted DuPont considerably in its efforts to connect and navigate in essential European business environments. In its role, then, as a first mover and model for DuPont, CTA also presents scholars with an important case of a "Europe to America" flow of management influence that runs counter to traditional business history studies that promote Americanization as the predominant trend in 20th c. European corporate development. Overall, scholars need to revisit the early growth of multinationals to discover cases similar to DuPont and CTA that illuminate the re-emerging conditions conducive to business globalization despite the disruptions wrought by the First World War.

Notes

1 Broadberry and O' Rourke, *The Cambridge Economic History of Modern Europe*; Frieden, *Global Capitalism: Its Fall and Rise in the Twentieth Century*; Hopkins, *Globalisation in World History*; Jones, *Multinationals and Global Capitalism: From the Nineteenth to the Twenty-First Century*; Osterhammel and Petersson, *Globalization: A Short History*; Tooze, *The Deluge: The Great War and the Remaking of Global Order 1916–1931*.

2 Ibid., 517.

3 Jones, *Multinationals and Global Capitalism: From the Nineteenth to the Twenty-First Century*, 20.

4 Ibid., 21–23. Mira Wilkins first offers the concept and definition of free standing companies in her landmark 1988 article, Wilkins, "The Free-Standing Company, 1870–1914: An Important Type of British Foreign Direct Investment." She speculates that they continued on, in a much reduced form, after 1918 in her 1998 chapter. Wilkins and Schröter, *The Free-Standing Company in the World Economy, 1830–1996*.

5 Cuff, *The War Industries Board: Business-Govenrment Relations during the First World War*; Rockoff, *Until It's Over, Over There: The US Economy in World War I*; Broadberry and Harrison, *The Economics of World War I*.

   Total production studies include Nelson, *Arsenal for Democracy*; Baime, *The Arsenal of Democracy: FDR, Detroit, and an Epic Quest to Arm an America at War*; Peck and Scherer, *The Weapons Acquisition Process: An Economic Analysis*, 108–1909, 619–20; Herman, *Freedom's Forge: How American Business Produced Victory in World War II*.

6 Dai, "Caught in the Middle: Multinational Enterprise Strategy in Interstate Warfare"; Jones, *Multinationals and Global Capitalism: From the Nineteenth to the Twenty-First Century*; Levy and Barbieri, "Trading with the Enemy during Wartime"; Natarajarathinam, Capar, and Narayanan, "Managing Supply Chains in Times of Crisis: A Review of Literature and Insights."

7 Jones, *Multinationals and Global Capitalism: From the Nineteenth to the Twenty-First Century*, 21–34. For more on the evolution of mutli-regional firms into multinationals see Wilkins, "The History of Multinational Enterprise"; Rugman and Verbeke, "A Perspective on Regional and Global Strategies of Multinational Enterprises"; Rugman and Brain, "Multinational Enterprises Are Regional, Not Global."

8 Jones, *Multinationals and Global Capitalism: From the Nineteenth to the Twenty-First Century*, 21–34.

9 Chandler, *Strategy and Structure : Chapters in the History of the American Industrial Enterprise*.

10 Chandler and Hikino, *Scale and Scope : The Dynamics of Industrial Capitalism*, 185; Hounshell and Smith, *Science and Corporate Strategy, DuPont R&D, 1902–1980*; Cheape, *Strictly Business: Walter Carpenter at DuPont*; Steen, *The American Synthetic Organic Chemicals Industry: War and Politics, 1910–1930*.

11 Chandler and Hikino, *Scale and Scope : The Dynamics of Industrial Capitalism*; Hounshell and Smith, *Science and Corporate Strategy, DuPont R&D, 1902–1980*; Cheape, *Strictly Business: Walter Carpenter at DuPont*; Steen, *The American Synthetic Organic Chemicals Industry: War and Politics, 1910–1930*.

12 Vernon, *Sovereignty at Bay: The Multinational Spread of US Enterprises*, 79.

13 Reader, "The Chemical Industry," 162–63, pegs the DuPont-Nobel Explosives, Co. Patent sharing agreement as starting in January 1920. However, DuPont records show that sales revenues and patent sharing financial payments were made by the company to Nobel as early as 1910, culminating in the signing of for-profit sharing contracts in August 1914, followed by the patent agreement after the war in 1920. EIDPDN&CO, Accession No. 228. Part I. Box 40. Correspondence Re: European Contracts, 1913–1914. Folder ID 10–41.

14 Vernon, *Sovereignty at Bay: The Multinational Spread of US Enterprises*, 83.

15 Muller, "The Origins of the Basic Inventions Underlying DuPont's Major Product and Process Innovations, 1920 to 1950," 342. DuPont

16 Ibid.

17 Ibid., 344.

18 Ibid., 343.

19 Hounshell and Smith, *Science and Corporate Strategy, DuPont R&D, 1902–1980*, 161.

20 Taylor and Sudnik, *DuPont and the International Chemical Industry*, 61. DuPont

21 HML, EIDPDN&CO, Accession no. 1850, DuPont consultant Fin Sparre to the Executive Committee, "Progress Report—Excess Plan Utilization," 15 September 1916, Coleman, *Courtaulds: An Economic and Social History, Vol. 2 Rayon*, 4–22; Hounshell and Smith, *Science and Corporate Strategy, DuPont R&D, 1902–1980*, 162.

22 Taylor and Sudnik, *DuPont and the International Chemical Industry*, 82. DuPont

23 Schultze, *The Technical Division of the Rayon Department, 1920–1951*, 27.

24 Varon, "Les Textiles Artificiels et Synthétiques."

25 Benoit, "Obituary of Francois Gillet."

26 Historical conversion tables from French francs to dollars are unavailable but the website Carpes Ho Gras retrieved at "Carpes Ho Gras" suggests that "early French franc (mid-1830s) equivalent to 25 British pounds," placing value of 900,000 French francs at 36,000 British pounds around 1869 or at 10–20 modern British pounds. The website Eliasen, "Historical Currency Conversions" pegs the historical equivalent of 1 British pound in 1869 to $2388.15 in current USD buying power. Using this formula, 900,000 francs converted to 36,000 British pounds in 1869 would have been the equivalent in modern USD of $4.29866964e+6. According to Hagley Museum and Library Reference Archivist Lucas R. Clawson, taken from his own research, DuPont's annual revenue in 1869 was $96,560.69 with the same buying power as $1.67269526e+6 in current USD. Clawson also notes, however, that DuPont's total capital in stock (all shares owned by family members) in 1869 was $620,000 without additional surplus revenue, and based on the previous surpluses gained in 1868, the company paid the total ($849,212.72) out in dividends to the stockholders in 1870. Nevertheless, CTA's overall annual earnings outpaced DuPont by almost 4 to 1 until US rayon and cellophane sales took off for DuPont in the 1930s.

27 Benoit, "Obituary of Francois Gillet."

28 Lambert-Dansette, "Histoire de L'entreprise et Des Chefs D'entreprise En France : L'entreprise Entre Deux Siècles (1880–1914)."

29 Origin of the name "rayon" for artificial silk came out of American marketing, as the word "artificial" "was not very appealing" to US consumers. After a nationwide contest yielded no attractive alternatives, a contest committee member declared: "Let's just see if we can shed a Ray of Light on this problem. Why not the word 'RAYON,' which is a derivative of a French word meaning 'rays of light'." In 1924, US and European manufacturers universally adopted rayon as an official name for the fabric. For more see Brandon, "Rayon: Is That Silk?". See also, Hatch, *Textile Science*, 181–91; Kadolph, *Textiles*, 82–87.

30 "Obituary of Edmund Gillet."

31 Solvay, "150 Years: Solvay." Both SCUR and CTA would eventually merge in 1928 into Rhône-Polenc, which after a 40-year wave of reorganizations, nationalizations, re-privatizations and mergers led Rhône-Polenc to be enfolded into the Belgian chemical conglomerate Solvay in 2011.

32 History and rise of Rhône-Polenc as an industrial region specializing in chemicals and pharmaceuticals production chronicled in LaFerrère, "Les Industries Chimiques de La Region Lyonnaise" and Varon, "Les Textiles Artificiels et Synthétiques".

33 Cayez and Chassagne, *Les Patrons Du Second Empire: Lyon et Le Lyonnais*.

34 Schultze, *The Technical Division of the Rayon Department, 1920–1951*, 5.

35 Phrase coined by 18th c. French economist Richard Cantillon that attached managerial decision-making to business risk. Jones, *Multinationals and Global Capitalism: From the Nineteenth to the Twenty-First Century*, 13–14. As an example, the term "entrepreneur" has been more regularly associated with American business culture, risk taking and innovation, when indeed it originated in a French context as codified by the work of 19th c. economists Jean-Baptiste Say and Richard Cantillon. Say, along with additional interpretations by Cantillon, posited that the word "entrepreneur described the dynamic, new spirit of French business creation and market development," in which individuals, over families and the state, "undertook an enterprise" and were "accountable for the inherent risks and the outcome." French origins of term retrieved at: "Entreprenur."

36 Company President Irene DuPont, along with executives on the Development Committee, first targeted artificial fibers as a growth area for DuPont in 1912 leading to several frustrating attempts over the next eight years to acquire from French, British and Belgian sources patents, companies and plants as a rapid route to developing its own R&D and production activities. Taylor and Sudnik, *DuPont and the International Chemical Industry*, 61, 82.

37 Hounshell and Smith, *Science and Corporate Strategy, DuPont R&D, 1902–1980*, 164.

38 HML, EIDPDN&CO, Accession no. 2632, DuPont China, Inc., Folder 17, ND 1950–1951, DuPont Supervisory Newsletter, vol. 4. no. 7. July 1950.

39 Chandler and Hikino, *Scale and Scope : The Dynamics of Industrial Capitalism*, 181–87.

40 Schultze, *The Technical Division of the Rayon Department, 1920–1951*, 3.

41 Hounshell and Smith, *Science and Corporate Strategy, DuPont R&D, 1902–1980*, 164.

42 HML, EIDPDN&CO, Accession no. 678, Series II, Part 4, Box 95, DuPont Rayon Company, Yerkes Plant, Foreign Trip Reports, 1922–1926.

43 HML. EIDPDN&CO, Accession no. 678, Series II Part 4, DuPont Fibersilk Company, File of Wm C. Spruance, Memo on Fibersilk and Cellophane Companies, 22 May 1923, Agreements, Memos and Correspondence, 1920–1933. Also see, Taylor and Sudnik, *DuPont and the International Chemical Industry*, 118.

44 HML, EIDPDN&CO, Accession no. 678, Series II Part 4, DuPont Fibersilk Company, File of Wm C. Spruance, Memo on Fibersilk and Cellophane Companies, 22 May 1923, Agreements, Memos and Correspondence, 1920–1933.

45 HML, EIDPDN&CO, Accession no. 678, Series II, Part 4, DuPont Rayon Company, Box 95, Yerkes Plant, Foreign Trip Reports, 1922–1926.Schultze, *The Technical Division of the Rayon Department, 1920–1951*, 5.

46 Ibid., 12.

47 Taylor and Sudnik, *DuPont and the International Chemical Industry*, 119.

48 Schultze, *The Technical Division of the Rayon Department, 1920–1951*, 19.

49 HML, EIPPDN&CO, Accession no. 678, Series II, Part 4, DuPont Rayon Company, Yerkes Plant, Box 95, Reports of Foreign Trips, 1922–1926.

50 Hounshell and Smith, *Science and Corporate Strategy, DuPont R&D, 1902–1980*, 172; Schultze, *The Technical Division of the Rayon Department, 1920–1951*, 19–20.

51 HML, EIPPDN&CO, Accession no. 678, Series II, Part 4, DuPont Rayon Company, Yerkes Plant, Box 95, Reports of Foreign Trips, 1922–1926, E.G. Benz, "Trip to France and England," Item 8: 1.

52 Ibid., 2–3.

53 Ibid., 2–3.

54 Ibid., 3–4.

55 Ibid., 5.

56 HML, EIPPDN&CO, Accession no. 678, Series II, Part 4, DuPont Rayon Company, Yerkes Plant, Box 96. Reports of Foreign Trips, 1926–1927, Report from Old Hickory Plant to Ernest B. Benger, 27 July 1926.

57 HML, EIPPDN&CO, Accession no. 678, Series II, Part 4, DuPont Rayon Company, Yerkes Plant, Box 95, Reports of Foreign Trips, 1922–1926, E.G. Benz, "Trip to France and England," Item 8: 5.

58 HML, EIPPDN&CO, Accession no. 678, Series II, Part 4, DuPont Rayon Company, Yerkes Plant, Box 95, Reports of Foreign Trips, 1922–1926, George Rocker, "Information Collected Abroad," Item 1.

59 HML, EIPPDN&CO, Accession no. 678, Series II, Part 4, DuPont Rayon Company, Yerkes Plant, Box 95, Reports of Foreign Trips, 1922–1926, H.J. White, "Report on Visit to Following Artificial Silk Plants in Europe," Item 7: 1.

60 HML, EIDPDN&CO, Accession no. 678, Series II, Part 4, DuPont Fibersilk Company, Letter from Rene Bernheim to William C. Spruance, 11 September 1930, File of William C. Spruance, Agreements, Memos and Correspondence, 1920–1933.

61 Ibid.

62 HML, EIDPDN&CO, Accession no. 678, Series II, Part 4, DuPont Rayon Company, Yerkes Plant, Foreign Trip Reports, 1929–1938., Box 102, "European Trip 1933", Item 12.

63 HML, EIPPDN&CO, Accession no. 678, DuPont Rayon Company, Yerkes Plant, Reports of European Trips, 1933–1937, Box 103, "European Trip-1933," Item 2.

64 Ibid.

65 Ibid.

66 HML, EIDPDN&CO, Accession no. 678, Series II, Part 4, DuPont Fibersilk Company, File of William C. Spruance, Agreements, Memos and Correspondence, 1920–1933.

67 HML, EIPPDN&CO, Accession no. 678, Series II, Part 4, Yerkes Plant, Box 95, G.W. Tuttle, "Report of Investigation of European Silk Plants," Reports of Foreign Trips, 1922–1926, Item 6.

68 Two collections chronicle the technical information and data collected by DuPont executives under the CTA partnership, HML, EIPPDN&CO, Accession no. 678, Series II, Part 4, DuPont Rayon Company, Yerkes Plant, Reports of Foreign Trips, 1922–1926 and EIDPDN&CO, Accession no. 678, Series II, Part 4, DuPont Rayon Company, Yerkes Plant, Foreign Trip Reports, 1929–1938.

69 HML, EIDPDN&CO, Accession no. 678, Series II, Part 4, Box 102, DuPont Rayon Company, Yerkes Plant, "Itinerary—R.M. Pickens," Foreign Trip Reports, 1929–1938.

70 Hounshell and Smith, *Science and Corporate Strategy, DuPont R&D, 1902–1980*, 176.

71 Schultze, *The Technical Division of the Rayon Department, 1920–1951*, 3; Hounshell and Smith, *Science and Corporate Strategy, DuPont R&D, 1902–1980*, 176.

72 Ibid.

73 Tesi, Bendigo, and Shapiro, "The Old and New in Synthetic Fibers," 58–69.

74 Taylor and Sudnik, *DuPont and the International Chemical Industry*, 118–19.

75 Ibid., 124.

76 Jones, *Multinationals and Global Capitalism: From the Nineteenth to the Twenty-First Century*, 22.

77 Boudet, *Le Monde Des Affaires En France de 1830 À Nos Jours*; Cayez, *Rhône-Poulenc, 1895–1975: Contribution À L'étude D'un Groupe Industriel*.

78 Davenport-Hines and Jones, *Enterprise, Management and Innovation in British Business, 1914–80*, 61; Lawrence, *A History of Bridgwater*.

79 Solvay, "150 Years: Solvay."
80 "Comptoir Des Textiles Artificiels: Registered Patents, 1920–1950s."
81 Frieden, *Global Capitalism: Its Fall and Rise in the Twentieth Century*, 166–67.
82 Jones, *Multinationals and Global Capitalism: From the Nineteenth to the Twenty-First Century*, 21–34.

Primary Sources

Hagley Museum and Library—E. I. DuPont de Nemours & Company Minute Books archives.

Secondary Sources

Baime, A. J. *The Arsenal of Democracy: FDR, Detroit, and an Epic Quest to Arm an America at War*. New York: First Mariner Books, 2014.
Benoit, Bruno. "Obituary of Francois Gillet." *Millénaire 3: Le Centre Resources Perspectives de Grand Lyon*, 2007. http://www.millenaire3.com/ressources/francois-gillet-1813–1895.
Boudet, J. *Le Monde Des Affaires En France de 1830 À Nos Jours*. Paris: Societe d'edition of Dictionnairres and encyclopedias, 1952.
Brandon, Karen. "Rayon: Is That Silk?" *Textile Fabric Consultants, Inc*, 2009. http://www.textilefabric.com/site/main/articles.php?id=14.
Broadberry, S, and M. Harrison, eds. *The Economics of World War I*. Cambridge: Cambridge University Press, 2005.
Broadberry, S., and K. O' Rourke. *The Cambridge Economic History of Modern Europe*. Cambridge: Cambridge University Press, 2010.
"Carpes Ho Gras." Accessed March 4, 2016. http://chanvrerie.net/history/general/currency/.
Cayez, P. *Rhône-Poulenc, 1895–1975: Contribution À L'étude D'un Groupe Industriel*. Lyon: Dunod, 1988.
Cayez, P., and S. Chassagne. *Les Patrons Du Second Empire: Lyon et Le Lyonnais*. Lyon: Picard, 2006.
Chandler, Alfred Dupont. *Strategy and Structure : Chapters in the History of the American Industrial Enterprise*. Cambridge : M.I.T. Press, 1962.
Chandler, Alfred Dupont, and Takashi Hikino. *Scale and Scope : The Dynamics of Industrial Capitalism*. Repr. 1990. Cambridge, MA: Belknap Press, 1990.
Cheape, C. W. *Strictly Business: Walter Carpenter at DuPont*. Baltimore: Johns Hopkins University Press, 1995.
Coleman, Donald C. *Courtaulds: An Economic and Social History, Vol. 2 Rayon*. Oxford: Clarendon Press, 1969.
"Comptoir Des Textiles Artificiels: Registered Patents, 1920–1950s." Accessed September 17, 2015. http://www.patentmaps.com/assignee/comptoir_textiles_artificiels_5.html.
Cuff, R. *The War Industries Board: Business-Govenrment Relations during the First World War*. Baltimore: Johns Hopkins University Press, 1973.
Dai, L. "Caught in the Middle: Multinational Enterprise Strategy in Interstate Warfare." *Competitiveness Review: An International Business Journal Incorporating Journal of Global Competitiveness* 19, no. 5 (2009): 355–76.

Davenport-Hines, R. P. T., and Geoffrey Jones. *Enterprise, Management and Innovation in British Business, 1914–80*. London: Routledge, 1988.

Eliasen, Alan. "Historical Currency Conversions." *Things I Made From Yarn*. Accessed March 4, 2016. http://www.futureboy.us/fsp/dollar.fsp.

"Entreprenur." *Wikipedia*, 2015.

Frieden, J. A. *Global Capitalism: Its Fall and Rise in the Twentieth Century*. New York: W. W. Norton, 2006.

Hatch, K. *Textile Science*. St. Paul: West Publishing Company, 1993.

Herman, Arthur. *Freedom's Forge: How American Business Produced Victory in World War II*. New York: Random House, 2012.

Herve, J., *Les Gillets de Lyon: Fortunes d'une grande dynastie industrielle* (1838–2015). Geneva: Librarie Droz, 2015.

Hopkins, A. G., ed. *Globalisation in World History*. New York: Random House, 2011.

Hounshell, D. A., and J. K. Smith. *Science and Corporate Strategy, DuPont R&D, 1902–1980*. Cambridge: Cambridge University Press, 1988.

Jones, Geoffrey. *Multinationals and Global Capitalism: From the Nineteenth to the Twenty-First Century*. Oxford: Oxford University Press, 2005.

Kadolph, S. J. *Textiles*. Upper Saddle River, NJ: Prentice-Hall, 2014.

LaFerrère, M. "Les Industries Chimiques de La Region Lyonnaise." *Revue de Géographie de Lyon* 27, no. 3 (1952): 219–56.

Lambert-Dansette, J. "Histoire de L'entreprise et Des Chefs D'entreprise En France : L'entreprise Entre Deux Siècles (1880–1914)." *Les Rayons et Les Ombres* 5 (2009).

Lawrence, J. C. *A History of Bridgwater*. Chichester, Phillimore, 2005.

Levy, J. S., and K. Barbieri. "Trading with the Enemy during Wartime." *Security Studies* 13, no. 3 (2004): 1–47.

Muller, W. F. "The Origins of the Basic Inventions Underlying DuPont's Major Product and Process Innovations, 1920 to 1950." In *The Rate and Direction of Inventive Activity: Economic and Social Factors*. Washington, DC: National Economic Research Bureau, 1962.

Natarajarathinam, M., I. Capar, and A. Narayanan. "Managing Supply Chains in Times of Crisis: A Review of Literature and Insights." *International Journal of Physical Distriubtion & Logistics Management* 39, no. 7 (2009): 535–73.

Nelson, D. *Arsenal for Democracy*. New York: Harcourt Brace, 1946.

"Obituary of Edmund Gillet." *Bulletin de L'Association Anicale Des Anciens Élèves de L'Ecolede Chimie Industrielle de Lyon* 98 (1931): 3–4.

Osterhammel, J., and N. P. Petersson. *Globalization: A Short History*. Princeton, NJ: Princeton University Press, 2005.

Peck, M. J., and F. M. Scherer. *The Weapons Acquisition Process: An Economic Analysis*. Cambridge, MA: Division of Research, Graduate School of Business Administration, Harvard University, 1962.

Reader, W. J. "The Chemical Industry." In *British Industry between the Wars: Instability and Industrial Development, 1919–1939*, edited by N. K. Buxton and D. H. Aldcroft. London: Scholar Press, 1979.

Rockoff, Hugh. *Until It's Over, Over There: The US Economy in World War I*. NBER Working Paper. Washington, DC, 2004.

Rugman, Alan, and C. Brain. "Multinational Enterprises Are Regional, Not Global." *Multinational Business Review* 11, no. 1 (2003): 3–12.

Rugman, Alan, and A. Verbeke. "A Perspective on Regional and Global Strategies of Multinational Enterprises." *Journal of International Business Studies* 35, no. 1 (2004): 3–18.

Schultze, F. *The Technical Division of the Rayon Department, 1920–1951.* Wilmington: E. I. DuPont Company, 1952.

Solvay. "150 Years: Solvay." *Press Release,* 2013.

Steen, K. *The American Synthetic Organic Chemicals Industry: War and Politics, 1910–1930.* Chapel Hill: University of North Carolina Press, 2014.

Taylor, G. D., and P. E. Sudnik. *DuPont and the International Chemical Industry.* Boston: Twayne Publishers, 1984.

Tesi, A. F., C. W. Bendigo, and A. Shapiro. "The Old and New in Synthetic Fibers." *The Analysts Journal* 8, no. 1 (1951): 58–69.

Tooze, Adam. *The Deluge: The Great War and the Remaking of Global Order 1916–1931.* London: Penguin, 2014.

Varon, H. "Les Textiles Artificiels et Synthétiques." *L'information Géographique* 13, no. 4 (1949): 145–47.

Vernon, R. *Sovereignty at Bay: The Multinational Spread of US Enterprises.* New York: Basic Books, 1971.

Wilkins, Mira. "The History of Multinational Enterprise." In *The Oxford Handbook of International Business,* edited by Alan M. Rugman, 3–38. Oxford: Oxford University Press, 2009.

———. "The Free-Standing Company, 1870–1914: An Important Type of British Foreign Direct Investment." *The Economic History Review* 41, no. 2. New Series (1988): 259–82.

Wilkins, Mira, and Harm Schröter. *The Free-Standing Company in the World Economy, 1830–1996.* Oxford: Oxford University Press, 1998.

Part III

Postwar Reconstruction and Its Financing

8 American and British Businessmen and Attempts to Reconstruct War-Torn Western Europe, 1918–1922

Volker R. Berghahn

The centenary of the outbreak of the First World War was accompanied by lively debates on who was responsible for pushing Europe and ultimately the globe into the abyss. It is now widely accepted that it was not the European business community. On the contrary, those involved in international finance, commerce and industry warned against a war among the great powers, though it should not be forgotten that they were not opposed to repression and extreme violence in the colonies in Africa, Asia and Latin America, where millions of people died before 1914. This latter point needs to be stressed to avoid a skewed understanding of the dynamics of European and American capitalism. Pondering the results of the extensive research that has been done on the evolution of colonialism and the quest for empire during the past thirty or so years, Marxist writings on the subject should not be discarded, even if it was not merely economic forces that drove the late-nineteenth-century scramble for colonies. Power-political and socio-psychological as well as cultural factors should also be considered.[1] What European and American big business did not want was a major war between the great powers of the time.

One of the frequently cited examples of this attitude is the 1910 book by the British businessman Norman Angell. Entitled *The Great Illusion*, it became a bestseller and was quickly translated into several European languages.[2] Angell certainly fervently believed that twentieth-century warfare among industrial nations would no longer produce any victors. All sides would be devastated and financially ruined. Reference should also be made to the French-Polish banker Jean de Bloch, who went even further when he published his *The Future War*.[3] In it he described very graphically what the human and material costs of a European clash of arms would be. Angell's argument appears to have resonated with European businessmen, for when the great conflict suddenly seemed imminent in July 1914, bankers in London, Paris and Hamburg spoke up against it.[4] Albert Ballin, the Hamburg shipping magnate, sailed to London in an attempt to stop the looming great-power conflict, and even in distant America, nervous bankers did not *want* to believe that rational decision-makers would wish to unleash a catastrophe.[5] As the *Wall Street Journal* put it on July 28, the day when

Austria-Hungary declared war on Serbia: "The whole world is engaged in business as never before. Industrial Germany in thirty years has far outrun military Germany. Throughout the civilized world, villages have become mill centers; towns have become cities; empires have succeeded states, and the empire of the modern world is commercial and not martial."[6]

However, this chapter is not concerned with the beginning and course of the First World War, but with how American big businessmen, Wall Street bankers and politicians in Washington responded to the catastrophe when it was finally over. It is complemented by an examination of how Britain's prime minister David Lloyd George, British industry and the City of London, before 1914 the unquestioned financial center of the world, reacted to the problems of the postwar period. To anticipate the conclusion, it did not prove possible to reach consensus on how the enormous socio-economic and political chaos that the war left behind might be sorted out, and since the attempts at "recasting of bourgeois Europe" never really succeeded, we shall also raise the question what lessons were learned from the First World War that were then applied more successfully after 1945.[7]

The final tally of 1918 was certainly depressing: After five years of ever more total war, Europe had lost some 20 million lives and its economies were greatly weakened. Following the Bolshevik seizure of power in Russia, there were widespread fears among the elites that radical left-wing revolutions would spread in western and southern Europe. The only country that had emerged economically strengthened from the conflict was the United States and its banking system. Having been a debtor nation before 1914, it had become a creditor nation that had financed the British and French war effort against the Central Powers and supplied grain and other foodstuffs to Britain. After the long-delayed American entry on the side of the Allies in April 1917, industry had been mobilized further to produce war materials that had equipped the US Army when it was finally deployed on the Western Front in the spring of 1918. Its appearance and fighting in France tipped the scales in favor of the Allies and forced the Germans to sue for peace.[8]

Once the guns had fallen silent and the Paris Peace Conference had begun, American industry was faced with the task of converting its factories to civilian production and, fearing that domestic demand was too fickle to absorb the enlarged productive capacities that the war had generated, was looking for export markets overseas. Given the destruction and the need for investments, especially of capital goods, Europe potentially constituted this market. But it needed credit, also for cranking up the most powerful engine of renewed growth: Germany, the former enemy that was being made responsible for the loss of human lives and the material destruction not only of Belgium and northern France, but of wealth in all participant countries more generally.

There are three men, one South African and two Americans, prepared to look beyond the profound Western bitterness against the Germans and articulated very perceptively what in their view needed to be done. Jan

Smuts, one of the advisers of the British prime minister at the Peace Conference, wrote as early as March 1919: "I am seriously afraid that the peace to which we are working is an impossible peace, conceived on the wrong basis; that it will not be accepted by Germany, and, even if accepted, that it will prove utterly unstable, and only serve to promote the anarchy which is rapidly overtaking Europe."[9] He was also convinced of two basic points: "1. We cannot destroy Germany without destroying Europe; 2. We cannot save Europe without the cooperation of Germany." After all, to Smuts it was a fact "that the Germans are, and will continue to be, the *dominant factor* on the Continent of Europe, and no permanent peace is possible which is not based on this fact." He recalled that the men who made the peace at the Congress of Vienna in 1815 were "wiser in their generation" when they reintegrated France into the Concert of Europe instead of ostracizing her.

There is also the statement of Ellis Dresel, who had been a member of the American delegation at Paris. After traveling in Europe, he wrote that, while opposed to a " 'forget and forgive' " policy, "close economic relations with Germany" would be "the surest guarantee against another war of revenge."[10] Finally, the words of Norman Davis are particularly insightful. He had worked for Democrat President Woodrow Wilson, but subsequently felt compelled to advise Charles Hughes, the Secretary of State of the new Republican administration in Washington, in March 1921 with the following words: "Through the highly industrial developments of Europe prior to the war, Germany has become the axis, and the rehabilitation of Europe and its continued prosperity is most dependent on that of Germany. Unless Germany is at work, France cannot be so, and the prosperity of the entire world depends on the capacity of industrial Europe to produce and purchase."[11] He continued: "Into this enters the element of credit, and credit will not be forthcoming as long as there is no stability and confidence, and until German reparation is settled constructively on the basis which will inspire confidence, the credits necessary for the reestablishment of normal conditions will not be forthcoming."

As is well known, this advice was not taken in Washington until after a further escalation of the Franco-German crisis over reparations payments and the occupation of the Ruhr industrial region by France and Belgium in January 1923. It was only in 1924 that American bankers forged the Dawes Plan, which secured a measure of stability and business confidence.[12] The credits, with which the reconstruction of Europe could at last begin, started to flow from 1925 onwards. But instead of revisiting this later phase of American-European financial and commercial relations, this chapter will deal with the proposals that an influential Wall Street banker made before Norman Davis wrote his letter, followed by examining in a final section the significance of the Washington System of 1921 and of the Genoa Conference of 1922.

This Wall Street banker was Frank Vanderlip, who for the previous twenty years had been the key executive of the National City Bank (NCB) in New York, one of the largest financial institutions of the United States, in which the Rockefellers had a major interest.[13] Apart from his long service to the financial industry, he had also held a number of powerful but strenuous official positions during the country's mobilization for war. Before joining the NCB, he had worked in journalism and had always pursued an interest in larger questions of national and international politics and business. He had also become a wealthy man who could afford to retire and act as a kind of elder statesman to the United States, as it had been gaining great influence in international affairs without having the experience of Britain, the first power in the world economy and international politics before 1914. In 1919, Vanderlip, the retiree, decided to travel, especially to Europe, where he still had many friends and colleagues from the pre-war years.

His papers are a treasure trove, full of detailed notes that he took during his travels and of letters with Americans and Europeans.[14] While the subsequent analysis is therefore based on the archive of one individual, its scope is much wider and thus offers deep insights into the world in which he moved. Some of his ideas were published in the early twenties, but they were also exchanged with people whom he knew well and with whom he had extensive conversations both in New York, on the West Coast, where he had a home, and in Europe. Of course, more work needs to be done in the field, especially on the complexities of early postwar American banking and industry as well as Washington politics. I would like to advance some arguments relating to the post-1918 trans-Atlantic political economy that, I hope, will be further investigated and tested.

In July 1914, Vanderlip had been among those who hoped that a world war could be avoided. Once the conflict had broken out, he had supported the Allied side, although he had not been keen on the United States formally to enter the war as a combatant. His pre-1914 fears notwithstanding, his wartime jobs had made him realize more fully how destructive the conflict had been for Europe. He had followed the difficulties of peace-making at the Paris conference with concern and was convinced that it would be "impossible" to return "to prewar conditions at an early stage", as he put it to US secretary of labor, W. B. Wilson.[15] At the same time, he was anxious to exploit the advantages that the United States had gained as a result of the war. Thus, in November 1918, he had submitted a plan to boost the efficiency and quality of domestic production to William Redfield, Woodrow Wilson's secretary of commerce.[16] Such a policy, he continued, would not only be of "great value to our industry and our people", but would also "be a great stride in foreign trade."

At the same time, he had a keen sense of the destruction in Europe, and in order to gain a first-hand impression of conditions across the Atlantic, he decided to undertake a tour of Europe in the early summer of 1919. Returning in July, he concluded, "with a fresh view of the suffering of Europe in my mind . . . the world is really in a very serious troubled state."[17] While in Europe, he had kept diary notes of the information that he had gathered through his network of business contacts. Having plenty of time on his hands during his sea journey back to New York, he decided to write an account on the basis of his notes that was subsequently published.

There is no space here to go into the details of Vanderlip's survey of the economic and social situation in Europe. Suffice it to say that, if the situation was bad in Britain, it got worse the farther he had gone East. "In picturing the devastating effect of the war on European industry," he wrote, ". . . one must not confine the view to the Hindenburg line" in France. Major industries in Poland had also been destroyed. The Romanian prime minister told him that the country, once a major exporter of grain, would "be able to raise this year only a sufficient amount of food for her own population." Serbia was "utterly despoiled," and even "if it were possible to show the exact percentage of the industrial life of Europe" that had been bombed and torched, it would, "vast as it is," still bear "no overwhelming relation to the whole."

Asking if and how it might be possible to overcome the difficulties, he suggested that an American manufacturer, however enterprising, would find them insurmountable as well, not least because the transportation system had also broken down and there were no raw materials. As to European industry's capacity to pay for imported finished goods, Vanderlip thought that, apart from Spain and the Scandinavian countries, no one would be able to settle their debts. Yet, the rest of Europe was in such desperate need of credit that he came home convinced that "there can be no secure peace until a way is found to supply . . . credits to all industrial centers."

It is against this background that Vanderlip developed a salvage plan in the shape of a massive credit. He thought that enough money could be raised if, apart from the United States, Switzerland, Scandinavia, Japan and some Latin American countries participated. To be sure, he realized that "the role of the American banks can play in the credit situation in Europe is of vast importance." It was a role that "they can play with security and profit," provided they held "firmly to the line of sound commercial banking." To him, it was a strategy that had to be accompanied by an American-style liberal capitalism based on "comfort and liberty" and underwritten by "the greatest of democracies, pledged to the sovereign rule of majorities."

So, even if Vanderlip's report contained plenty of gloomy news, he was confident enough to see a great opportunity for the United States and its banks, which he circumspectly put as a question: "Is New York to become the financial center of the world?"[18] In light of the power of the London City before the war, only an ignoramus, he added, would have asked this question before 1914. But "today it has become a question" for New York that must "be asked in seriousness, examined with care and answered in light of the new conditions." To be sure, the City still had many strengths, and yet he felt that Wall Street could become "the depository of a great part of the international bank balances coming from every quarter of the world." However, the issue was not just about which country would be No. 1 in international finance; it was also about industrial leadership. And last but by no means least, "we are the greatest producers of food and raw materials and minerals in the world." Accordingly, "for years to come our commodity trade balance" also seemed "likely to run several hundred million a year in our favor."

In these circumstances, no time was to be lost, in his view, to float this "international loan to Europe" not only to relieve economic distress, but also because of the threat of Bolshevism. For, "unless there is speedy action in the direction of restarting paralyzed industry, there may follow a quick march of events toward revolutionary outbreaks in any country where idleness is continued and is followed by hunger and want." There was one big hitch, though. Vanderlip seems to have been wanting to gain the participation of the Washington government. It looked like a reasonable idea for a cautious ex-banker, but it would have required Congressional legislation that, if obtainable in principle, would have taken too long to reach the statute books. Instead, his private "peace loan" would be coordinated and supervised by an International Loan Commission based "in the Peace Palace at The Hague." This body would "determine from the facts regarding the industrial situation in each of the possible borrowing countries the proportionate allocation of the parts of the total loan to each borrowing nation." Later on, the commission was also to decide, "in conjunction with representatives from the borrowing nations, the definite amounts of machinery, raw material, rolling stock etc. which should be furnished." In return, the borrower would "pledge a first lien on its customs revenue to meet the interest and amortization service of that portion of the loan allocated to that nation." Moreover, the Europeans were to issue "Receivers' certificates, that is to say that new loans should rank in front of all other indebtedness."

That Vanderlip's plans and an article in the *Wall Street Journal* that "U.S. Bankers prepare to finance Europe" had meanwhile unleashed a wider discussion is evidenced by the fact that a number of other influential people advanced their own proposals that were geared to putting struts into lending practices on the American side.[19] Redfield, by now president of the American Manufacturers Export Association, worried that without a branch banking system of its own, all American drafts would go "through banks owned by our competing countries." American businesses should therefore show "vision and courage to do a very simple thing . . . [i.e., to] put American money into American-owned and American-run and American-controlled industries around the globe." Somewhat later, John McHugh, the chair of the Commerce and Marine Division of the American Bankers Association, wanted to convert some $4 billion held by American investors in short-term bills of exchange into long-term investments in order to "open up again the flow of our [American] goods [to Europe] where they have ceased to flow." He also proposed to give the program an institutional foundation by means of an "Edge corporation organized as a debenture bank" whose debentures would attract savings from depositors in banks "outside the main centers (New York, Chicago, Cleveland, Detroit, and San Francisco)."[20]

However, it was clear to all involved that a massive loan to Europe involved a very high risk. Given the terrible state of the European economies, the chances of default by one or even several borrowers were alarmingly great. So, with bankers being risk-averse people, especially in times of crisis, the idea came to be mooted that the American taxpayer should underwrite the whole enterprise. It did not require long inquiries in Washington, however, that the country and its representatives in Congress were in no mood to enter such a deal. The "greatest of democracies pledged to the sovereign rule of majorities" was in large parts of the country either in an isolationist or an attentist mood. The course of the negotiations at the Paris Peace Conference, where the interests of the various European powers had asserted themselves against Wilsonian ideas of a new international order without old-style Machiavellian power politics, merely reinforced these popular moods. The elected members in both chambers of Congress in Washington did not dare or want to ignore them, as they could have done for the sake of trying to foster peace, stability and economic recovery across the Atlantic.[21]

It is also significant that Republicans were on their way to conquering the White House and presidential candidate Warren Harding had campaigned on the basis of typical Republican promises: tax cuts and a reduction of public debts. All this meant that Vanderlip's European "peace loan" was never floated. Instead the Europeans were put through the wringer of the crisis of 1923 before American bankers reappeared on the scene. This time they provided private loans and also helped with foreign direct investments of American manufacturing companies. The US government gave encouragement to the crafting of the so-called Dawes Plan behind the scenes, but otherwise remained passive.

And yet, this was not the end of the story of the very early 1920s. The reasons for this lie in the desperate desire of American industry to stimulate its exports. A few statistics may illustrate this. Between 1914 and 1920, iron production had doubled to 37.5 million tons and electricity generation had grown threefold. Factory space had seen a similar threefold expansion. The number of employees in the car industry alone rose by 162 percent to over 340,000. The attempt to revert to civilian production in order to satisfy domestic demand and to restock turned out to be a straw fire. Domestic output in iron and automobiles dropped by 50 percent by 1921, copper saw a decline of 80 percent. In 1919, American exports reached $5.2 billion, generating a considerable surplus. But by 1921 the figure, calculated in current dollars, had reached a low of $2.1 billion. Exports in meat and meat products were also declining and the only item that doubled in value between 1920 and 1921 were grain exports. Grain was what the Europeans could not do without and were prepared to pay for to avoid mass starvation and social unrest. While unemployment was rising, everything else in Europe had to wait for better times that came only from 1924/25 and then merely lasted till 1928/29 and the onset of the Great Slump.

This brings me to an aspect of economic reconstruction and the postwar role of the United States. With American credit to Europe stalling and European markets remaining stagnant and unable to pay for American manufactured goods, industry began to look towards the Asian markets. In 1921, official negotiations started between the United States (this time in its role as a Pacific power), Japan, China and several European powers with interests in the Pacific region.[22] These negotiations, finding no major opposition in Washington, culminated on February 6, 1922 in a Nine-Power trade agreement between the US, Britain, France, Italy, China, the Netherlands, Belgium, Portugal and Japan that secured equal access to Far Eastern markets and to that of China in particular. It is significant that this treaty was accompanied by two pacts that were designed to provide political and military security in the region. The Four-Power agreement between the United States, Britain, France and Japan guaranteed the territorial status quo. It was complemented by a Five-Power pact that limited the number of battleships in the Far East to a 5:5:3:1.75:1.75 ratio among the US, Britain, Japan, France and Italy in that order. Thus the Open Door was established in the Pacific and gave American industry an outlet for its exports, though given the underdeveloped or still restricted state of the Asian region, it was hardly a substitute for the collapsing European market.

This leads me to the final part of my analysis that takes me back to Europe and the policies of Britain under prime minister Lloyd George. Realizing that the Americans would stay out of Europe, he saw an opportunity for Britain to take the lead in Europe. There may be some truth in the argument that he developed his own plan for the reconstruction of Europe because he had rather an inflated image of himself. However, there are two other factors that are at least as important for an understanding of British policy in the autumn of 1921, at the same time when the preparations for the Washington System had begun. First, at the end of the war, British industry had even greater reconversion problems than the United States. Mobilization had been more total and many more returning veterans had to be reintegrated into the economy.[23] They had been promised that they would get their former civilian jobs back. This meant that, as a first step, women, who had risked their lives producing grenades and other war materials in the factories, had to be eased out and told to be homemakers again—a policy that inevitably led to some resistance and widespread bitterness. In comparison to July 1914, wholesale prices had increased by some 200 percent, and this made it very difficult for many working-class families to make ends meet with only one breadwinner, especially as the pay of those veterans who did find a job remained meager and was constantly threatened by unemployment. On the whole, the labor reintegration efforts proved less successful than expected. With poverty levels rising, the British government had no choice but to boost welfare programs for disabled veterans as well as for war widows and orphans, reducing whatever funds were available to stimulate the economy.

There was, as I have noted, a brief postwar boom, but it collapsed in Britain even more quickly than in the United States. Shipbuilding saw an upswing in 1919/20 but then dropped to some 38 percent from its peak in the fourth quarter of 1920. With orders declining also from other metal industries, the steel production that had reached its peak in 1917 had declined by 40 percent by the end of 1921. Similarly, ironmaking was 25 percent lower than in 1913, while coal production was even 50 percent below the level of the last year before the war. This was partly due to a strike by the miners in the spring of 1921 that lasted for three months. The strike rippled through the rest of the economy so that by June 1921 British unemployment stood at 23.1 percent. The annual average for the year was 15.3 percent. Around one million could find only part-time employment. No less than 2.1 million Britons and their families thus had to rely on welfare benefits.

In light of these conditions, it is not surprising that British industry, like its American competitor, should be looking for overseas markets. To be sure, there was the Empire and Commonwealth, in which Britain enjoyed many overt and hidden advantages. However, with Germany having been the country's best customer before the war, the question arose if there was a way of reviving old trading links, including Bolshevik Russia. The lure of the Russian market was particularly strong after the brutal civil war had come to an end and Lenin's regime had begun to adopt its New Economic Policy in order to revive the economy. Wartime central controls were reduced and domestic private initiative encouraged.

It is against this background that British industry and commerce saw opportunities, and Lloyd George as prime minister responded by designing a plan for the formation of a consortium of West European states that would mobilize some of their resources for investments in the East. It was unlikely that the Americans would join in such an enterprise, partly because they could not overcome their deep-seated suspicions of Bolshevism, for whose destruction they had even sent their own troops in support of the counter-revolution in the Russian civil war. Moreover, Wilson in particular remained suspicious of the British at the Paris Peace Conference. He felt that London delegates kept appointing "a lot of committees . . . to maintain Britain supreme commercially in the world."

When Lloyd George put his consortium plans on the table in the autumn of 1921 in the hope of including the Americans, the Republican administration, averse to any kind of commitment in Europe, promptly thought his "grand scheme for European reconstruction premature at best."[24] By the end of 1921 the American position had hardened further. While Lloyd George had presented the proposal for an international conference to launch the consortium plan as a purely economic initiative, US secretary of state Hughes came to believe that the meeting had a "wider political purpose." US secretary of commerce Herbert Hoover even suspected that the idea aimed at reasserting Britain's position "as the hub of a revived world economy and to lure Germany and Russia into the British orbit" at a time when—as we have seen—Wall Street was hoping to replace the City.[25] Another indication of the reviving Anglo-American economic rivalry was that Washington, having failed to sign the Versailles Treaty with Germany, had concluded a separate peace with Berlin on August 25, 1921.

What must have encouraged the British premier to make a move was that his French counterpart, Aristide Briand, seemed open to the consortium venture, partly because he, too, favored the reintegration of Germany into the European community of nations. Given the loans and investments that France had lost in the Russian Revolution, the inclusion of Russia also seemed to open up the prospect of talks with Moscow about this issue of repayment. A pre-conference was therefore convened at Cannes in January 1922 to discuss German and Russian participation at the larger meeting that was now scheduled to be held at Genoa in the spring. To foster Franco-British relations, the conclusion of an alliance between the two countries was also put on the agenda. However, when the French chamber of deputies rebelled against German participation and against the danger that Berlin might introduce the reparations problem, Briand was called to Paris and forced to resign on January 12. He was replaced by Raymond Poincaré, a politician who was in no mood to make any concessions to the Germans.[26]

Even though the prospects for a success of Lloyd George's consortium plans had by then become rather diminished, invitations went out for the international conference that began in Genoa in April 1922.[27] The Americans merely sent observers. A bright spot was that the British prime minister had succeeded in getting the Exports Credits Act through Parliament in London. It gave to loans floated in Britain the kinds of official guarantees that US Congress had refused when Wall Street had asked for its own massive European reconstruction loan to be underwritten by the American taxpayer, should it fail. The hope was that other participants at Genoa would similarly support the establishment of an International Corporation to open up the Russian market to European exports. Perhaps with the treaty arrangements before his eyes that had just been signed for the Pacific region, Lloyd George may also have hoped that the Consortium might be complemented by a balanced reduction of land forces similar to the agreement on naval ratios in the Far East and a non-aggression pact for Western Europe. Although the Versailles Treaty had already reduced the German army to 100,000 men, Poincaré was not prepared to contemplate reductions of the French armed forces, so this particular idea died an early death. The question of military security therefore continued to complicate all efforts to stabilize the economies of Europe.[28]

Nevertheless, the most serious setback occurred in the middle of the Consortium negotiations, when the German and Russian delegations concluded the notorious Rapallo agreement that provided not only for the expansion of *bilateral* trade but also for mutual diplomatic recognition between those two countries. There has been much research and argument about why the two sides made this deal. The Russians, with the secret links that had already been forged between the Red Army and the German Reichswehr in 1921 before their eyes, believed that having to deal with one capitalist country that moreover viewed itself, like the Soviets, an outcast of the international system, was easier than with the Consortium.[29] And for the Germans, whose economy was in even worse shape than that of Britain and the United States, there was the attraction of access to the Russian market without the worry of competition. The trouble was that the Rapallo Treaty destroyed the Consortium plan, souring Anglo-German relations and encouraging Poincaré to push his anti-German agenda even harder that, within a year, culminated in the Franco-Belgian occupation of the Ruhr industrial region and the collapse of the German economy.[30]

Given this outcome, it is illuminating to see what Frank Vanderlip found when he decided to attend the Genoa conference as a private observer.[31] Arriving in the middle of April, he quickly discovered through his contacts that two positions had emerged by the end of the first week. The pessimists thought that the prospects of finding a "quick formula for the economic reconstruction of Europe" were pretty much nil. In the view of the second group, it was "a real achievement to bring together the highest representatives of thirty-four nations and . . . to hold them together in a fairly amiable state of mind." Vanderlip was also impressed by the "great many bankers and captains of industry" who had come, very much aware of the "growing seriousness of the European situation." For him there was hence a dire need for this sort of conference, although he also believed that many more had to follow "before Europe's reconstruction is accomplished."

Lloyd George, Vanderlip reported, was putting "the greatest emphasis on the pressing need to reestablish economic relations with Russia," even if rehabilitation would take many years. Nor would the Consortium be anything more than a plan to send "goods on credit." It would also take a long time for Russia to generate sufficient surplus production to join the mutual trade pattern of Europe as a whole. At the same time, the visitor was much more concerned about the "pressing [and] menacing" problems that Germany confronted, probably also because his contacts to German participants and observers were closer. Thus, he concluded that if reparations demands remained unchanged, the country "faces inevitably financial collapse." Worse, there would be political and social consequences that would likely "be contagious."

While Vanderlip agreed that it was right for the United States not to join in the Genoa conference, he did not think "that we should not participate in a future one." He added that Washington's attitude was "one of reserve, and of conserving ammunition for a time when its use will be much more effective than at present." This was an approach "where Wall Street could learn a lesson from Washington." Defending American banks against European criticism, he thought Europeans would act like the Americans if they were in their position, i.e., "they would reserve their financial strength and then use it freely when the opportunity offered [itself] to use it more effectively for Europe's

[re]habilitation and more certainly for American prestige." He reasoned that when the "proper time" had come and Europe had got its act together, "we should contribute most liberally from our redundant stock of gold."

However, he was arguably most outspoken when it came to the "political turmoil" caused by the Rapallo Treaty. This move had led some observers to "picture the development of a vast Teutonic-Slavic coalition" and to view "the division between eastern and western Europe moving from the Vistula to the Rhine." Returning to the distress in Germany, he had learned that without a moratorium on reparations and temporary aid to buy food, the country's situation would be hopeless. The Germans who he met admitted that Rapallo had "injured their situation with the nations of western Europe"; yet while they regretted "the injury," they did "not the action." As to the United States, they stressed "that the moral force of America is the only thing that can bring order out of chaos," while also appreciating that US investments could not be expected "at the present time."

Taking stock of the Genoa conference, Vanderlip had criticisms for France and also for the Czechs, but then concluded that Lloyd George had failed because he had prepared it insufficiently. He had been motivated by too heavy a dose of opportunism and had never gained more than a superficial understanding of very complex realities. Overall, the Wall Street banker was not the only one to take a wait-and-see attitude with respect to an American commitment to European reconstruction. As we have seen, secretary of state Hughes also did not heed the advice given by Norman Davis in March 1921, and not only because his hands were tied by the Republican majorities in Congress, but also because it remained the official policy of the Harding administration.[32]

After the Franco-Belgian occupation of the Ruhr, the demise of the German economy and hyperinflation reached its peak in the fall of 1923, when one dollar could be exchanged for 4.2 trillion marks.[33] It was only now that, with the encouragement of the American administration, a Committee of Experts was constituted that eventually produced the Dawes Plan. The reconstruction of Europe finally began with American loans and direct investments by major American corporations such as General Motors, Ford and IBM. However, the stability and prosperity that came to Europe was never built on solid foundations.[34] It generated an illusory optimism that the economies of Europe had finally turned the corner and had overcome the postwar depression. This optimism would hardly have been as great had it not been for the boom that occurred in the American economy during the mid-twenties. These were the wild years when many investors thought that the sky was the limit. They were also too remote from Europe to have reliable information on the viability of many companies to observe greater caution. Some American investors bought bonds that a number of German cities had been offering. They were deemed to be better secured and, while not directly contributing to the modernization of manufacturing industry, helped improve the urban infrastructure. However, not all the money went into road building or modern public utilities. Local politicians, anxious to remain popular with their voters, also spent it on parks and public swimming pools. In retrospect, it is therefore not surprising that the bubble burst first in the United States and quickly had a snowball effect upon Europe and Germany in particular.[35]

The rest of the story is well known. The Hitler movement began to sweep the board in the early 1930s and in January 1933, a government was put in power by Hindenburg, the former Prussian field marshal and president of the Weimar Republic, that, within less than a year, built a brutal one-party dictatorship and embarked upon a massive rearmament program with the intention of launching another European war. When after Pearl Harbor, Hitler declared war on the United States, it was—given America's industrial potential—a matter of time before the Axis powers would be defeated.

The interesting question is though, if the political and economic elites had learned any lessons after 1945 from what had happened in the early 1930s. I would argue that they did. It soon became clear that Germany, despite aerial bombing, still had the potentially most powerful economy in postwar Europe. There were, it is true, influential voices that wanted to punish the Germans and to destroy their war-making potential once and for all. This time it was not only the advocates of the Morgenthau Plan, but also the protagonists of another retreat to the North American continent who were pushed back by other influential groups in Washington and in the business community.[36] These groups argued, as Davis had done in 1921, for the integration and rebuilding of (the western zones of occupied) Germany. No less importantly, this time, the reconstruction that would also trigger the reconstruction of the whole of Western Europe was not to be left to the private sector that might then be too cautious to commit its own resources to the project. Rather it was public money—American taxpayers' money—that was committed through the Marshall Plan and, against some opposition, eventually approved by Congress.[37] It is against this background that the massive international loan that Vanderlip and others rooted for 1920 is not only an intriguing and largely unknown initiative in its own right, but also one that raises the question of the capacity of elite groups to learn from the mistakes of the past.

Finally, there is a strange irony in all this that Germany should be the great beneficiary of American reconstruction policies after 1945 while Britain, the ally of the United States in two world wars against Germany, was left behind. Another irony is that Germany, which twice in the twentieth century tried to conquer the European continent by force, has now become the hegemonic power in the European Union without having firing a single shot.

Notes

1 Gopal Balakrishnan, *Debating Empire* (London: Verso, 2003); A. Dirk Moses, *Empire, Colony, Genocide: Conquest, Occupation, and Subaltern Resistance in*

World History (New York: Berghahn Books, 2008); Jürgen Osterhammel, *Colonialism: A Theoretical Overview* (Princeton, NJ: Wiener/Randle, 1997); Roger Owen and Robert B. Sutcliffe, *Studies in the Theory of Imperialism* (London: Longman, 1972).

2   Norman Angell, *The Great Illusion: A Study of the Relation of Military Power in Nations to Their Economic and Social Advantage* (London: McClelland and Goodchild, 1911).

3   Jan Bloch and William Thomas Stead, *The Future of War in Its Technical, Economic, and Political Relations* (World Peace Foundation, 1899).

4   Richard Roberts, *Saving the City: The Great Financial Crisis of 1914* (Oxford: Oxford University Press, 2013); Niall Ferguson, *The Pity of War* (New York: Basic Books, 1999).

5   Lamar Cecil, *Albert Ballin: Business and Politics in Imperial Germany, 1888–1918* (Princeton, NJ: Princeton University Press, 1967); Nicholas A. Lambert, *Planning Armageddon* (Boston, MA: Harvard University Press, 2012).

6   Wall Street Journal, 28 July 1914.

7   Charles Maier, *Recasting Bourgeois Europe. Stabilization in France, Germany and Italy in the Decade after World War I* (Princeton: Princeton University Press, 1975).

8   See, e.g. Gregor Dallas, *1918: War and Peace* (New York: Random House, 2012).

9   Quoted in: William K. Hancock and Jean Van Der Poel, *Selections from the Smuts Papers: Volume 1, June 1886-May 1902* (Cambridge: Cambridge University Press, 1966), 82–87.

10 Quoted in: Alexander Sedlmaier, *Deutschlandbilder und Deutschlandpolitik: Studien Zur Wilson-Administration (1913–1921)* (Wiesbaden: Franz Steiner Verlag, 2003), 354.

11 Quoted in: Werner Link, *Die Amerikanische Stabilisierungspolitik in Deutschland 1921–32* (Dusseldorf: Droste Verlag, 1970), 56.

12 See William C. McNeil, *American Money and the Weimar Republic* (New York: Columbia University Press, 1986).

13 On Vanderlip's career and retirement see Wall Street Journal, 4 January 1919; ibid., 6 January 1919.

14 See Columbia University Archive (CUA), Vanderlip Papers.

15 CUA, Vanderlip Papers, B-1-8, Vanderlip to Wilson, 20 May 1919.

16 Ibid., Vanderlip to Redfield, 2 November 1919.

17 Ibid., Vanderlip to Joseph T. Talbot, 7 July 1919, also for the following.

18 Frank Arthur Vanderlip, *What Happened to Europe* (New York: Macmillan, 1920).

19 Wall Street Journal, 11 April 1919.

20 On the Redfield and McHugh initiatives see Carl P. Parrini, *Heir to Empire: United States Economic Diplomacy, 1916–1923* (Pittsburg: University of Pittsburgh Press, 1969), 76ff.

21 See Margaret MacMillan, *Paris 1919: Six Months That Changed the World* (New York: Random House, 2007).

22 See Thomas H. Buckley, *The United States and the Washington Conference, 1921–1922* (Knoxville, TN: University of Tennessee, 1970); Erik Goldstein and John Maurer, *The Washington Conference, 1921–1922* (London: Frank Cass, 1994).

23 See Arthur Marwick, *Britain in the Century of Total War: War, Peace, and Social Change, 1900–1967* (Harmonsworth: Penguin, 1968); Adam R. Seipp, *The Ordeal of Peace: Demobilization and the Urban Experience in Britain and Germany, 1917–1921* (Aldershot: Ashgate Publishing Ltd., 2009).

24 Quoted in Edward M. Lamont, *The Ambassador from Wall Street: The Story of Thomas W. Lamont, JP Morgan's Chief Executive: A Biography* (Madison, WI: Madison Books, 1994), 103. Ibid. for the following quote.

25 Patrick O. Cohrs, *The Unfinished Peace after World War 1: America, Britain and the Stabilization of Europe, 1919–1932* (Cambridge: Cambridge University Press, 2006), 87.
26 Zara S. Steiner, *The Lights That Failed: European International History, 1919–1933* (Oxford: Oxford University Press, 2005), 206ff.
27 Best study of the Genoa conference remains Carole Fink and Axel Frohn (eds.), *Genoa, Rapallo, and European Reconstruction in 1922* (Cambridge: Cambridge University Press, 1991).
28 Ibid.
29 Francis Ludwig Carsten, *Reichswehr and Politics*, vol. 102 (Berkeley, CA: University of California Press, 1973).
30 Conan Fischer, *The Ruhr Crisis 1923–24* (Oxford: Oxford University Press, 2003).
31 CUA, Vanderlip Papers, D-11, folder 1, Report "No. 1", 17 April 1922, and Report "No. 2", n.d., also for the following.
32 See above, p. 175.
33 Gerald D. Feldman, *The Great Disorder: Politics, Economics, and Society in the German Inflation, 1914–1924* (Oxford: Oxford University Press, 1997).
34 Mary Nolan, *Visions of Modernity: American Business and the Modernization of Germany* (Oxford: Oxford University Press, 1994).
35 Volker R. Berghahn, *American Big Business in Britain and Germany* (Princeton, NJ: Princeton University Press, 2014), 168ff.
36 Bernd Greiner, *Die Morgenthau-Legende* (Hamburg: Hamburger Edition, 1995).
37 Michael J. Hogan, *The Marshall Plan: America, Britain and the Reconstruction of Western Europe, 1947–1952* (Cambridge: Cambridge University Press, 1989).

Bibliography

Angell, Norman. *The Great Illusion: A Study of the Relation of Military Power in Nations to their Economic and Social Advantage.* London: McClelland and Goodchild, 1911.

Balakrishnan, Gopal. *Debating Empire.* London: Verso, 2003.

Berghahn, Volker R. *American Big Business in Britain and Germany.* Princeton, NJ: Princeton University Press, 2014.

Bloch, Jan, and William Thomas Stead. *The Future of War in Its Technical, Economic, and Political Relations.* World Peace Foundation, 1899.

Buckley, Thomas H. *The United States and the Washington Conference, 1921–1922.* Knoxville, TN: University of Tennessee, 1970.

Carsten, Francis Ludwig. *Reichswehr and Politics.* Vol. 102. Berkeley, CA: University of California Press, 1973.

Cecil, Lamar. *Albert Ballin: Business and Politics in Imperial Germany, 1888–1918.* Princeton, NJ: Princeton University Press, 1967.

Cohrs, Patrick O. *The Unfinished Peace after World War 1: America, Britain and the Stabilization of Europe, 1919–1932.* Cambridge: Cambridge University Press, 2006.

Dallas, Gregor. *1918: War and Peace.* Random House, 2012.

Feldman, Gerald D. *The Great Disorder: Politics, Economics, and Society in the German Inflation, 1914–1924.* Oxford: Oxford University Press, 1997.

Ferguson, Niall. *The Pity of War.* New York: Basic Books, 1999.

Fink, Carole, and Axel Frohn (eds.). *Genoa, Rapallo, and European Reconstruction in 1922.* Cambridge: Cambridge University Press, 1991.

Fischer, Conan. *The Ruhr Crisis 1923–24*. Oxford: Oxford University Press, 2003.

Goldstein, Erik, and John Maurer. *The Washington Conference, 1921–1922*. London: Frank Cass, 1994.

Greiner, Bernd. *Die Morgenthau-Legende*. Hamburg: Hamburger Edition, 1995.

Hancock, William K., and Jean Van Der Poel. *Selections from the Smuts Papers: Volume 1, June 1886-May 1902*. Cambridge: Cambridge University Press, 1966.

Hogan, Michael J. *The Marshall Plan: America, Britain and the Reconstruction of Western Europe, 1947–1952*. Cambridge: Cambridge University Press, 1989.

Lambert, Nicholas A. *Planning Armageddon*. Boston, MA: Harvard University Press, 2012.

Lamont, Edward M. *The Ambassador from Wall Street: The Story of Thomas W. Lamont, JP Morgan's Chief Executive: A Biography*. Madison Books, 1994.

Link, Werner. *Die Amerikanische Stabilisierungspolitik in Deutschland 1921–32*. Dusseldorf: Droste Verlag, 1970.

MacMillan, Margaret. *Paris 1919: Six Months That Changed the World*. New York: Random House, 2007.

Maier, Charles. *Recasting Bourgeois Europe. Stabilization in France, Germany and Italy in the Decade after World War I*. Princeton: Princeton University Press, 1975.

Marwick, Arthur. *Britain in the Century of Total War: War, Peace, and Social Change, 1900–1967*. Harmonsworth: Penguin, 1968.

McNeil, William C. *American Money and the Weimar Republic*. New York: Columbia University Press, 1986.

Moses, A Dirk. *Empire, Colony, Genocide: Conquest, Occupation, and Subaltern Resistance in World History*. New York: Berghahn Books, 2008.

Nolan, Mary. *Visions of Modernity: American Business and the Modernization of Germany*. Oxford: Oxford University Press, 1994.

Osterhammel, Jürgen. *Colonialism: A Theoretical Overview*. Princeton, NJ: Wiener/Randle, 1997.

Owen, Roger, and Robert B. Sutcliffe. *Studies in the Theory of Imperialism*. London: Longman, 1972.

Parrini, Carl P. *Heir to Empire: United States Economic Diplomacy, 1916–1923*. Pittsburg: University of Pittsburgh Press, 1969.

Roberts, Richard. *Saving the City: The Great Financial Crisis of 1914*. Oxford: Oxford University Press, 2013.

Sedlmaier, Alexander. *Deutschlandbilder und Deutschlandpolitik: Studien Zur Wilson-Administration (1913–1921)*. Wiesbaden: Franz Steiner Verlag, 2003.

Seipp, Adam R. *The Ordeal of Peace: Demobilization and the Urban Experience in Britain and Germany, 1917–1921*. Aldershot: Ashgate Publishing, Ltd., 2009.

Steiner, Zara S. *The Lights that Failed: European International History, 1919–1933*. Oxford: Oxford University Press, 2005.

Vanderlip, Frank Arthur. *What Happened to Europe*. New York: Macmillan, 1920.

9 Mammon Unbound

The International Financial Architecture of Wall Street Banks, 1915–1925

Trevin Stratton

Introduction

The First World War is a seminal event in the periodization of waves of global integration. Economic historians often portray the war as the end of an era of globalization and the hegemony of classical liberalism.[1] The war is treated as a shift from an interconnected global economic system to a system that embraced fierce economic nationalism and autarky. Certainly, if we focus on certain regions and sectors of the global economy—European foreign direct investment, for instance—then a story of deglobalization emerges. Indeed, many of the economic connections that had previously driven globalization were severed due to the war. The Pax Britannica and the mercantilism of the European empires largely characterized the pre-war wave of globalization. It is understandable why the end of the peace, the rise of American economic power, and Woodrow Wilson's confrontation with imperialism after the war can be conflated with the end of this wave.

However, other scholars have attempted to temper the arguments resulting from such a grand historical narrative. Globalization is a somewhat nebulous term that lacks academic specificity. Adam Tooze uses a multidimensional approach by making a distinction between Wilson championing economic globalization while attempting to avoid global integration through politico-military entanglements with Europe. Tooze states: "It was an anti-militarist, post-imperialist agenda for a country convinced of the global influence it would exercise at arm's length through the means of soft power—economics and ideology."[2] A. G. Hopkins uses a similar lens by emphasizing different types of globalization. He argues that while most historical treatment of globalization focuses on economic aspects, "political, social and cultural aspects have still to be explored."[3]

A number of authors have noted that European instability was to blame for de-globalization of capital flows after the war. Kobrak, Hansen, and Kopper argue that hyperinflation represented political risk that was too high for lenders to consider the investment in the German economy.[4] Similarly, William McNeil notes that the United States' massive speculation in German marks came to a disastrous end in 1922, resulting in little American capital going to Germany for the next two years.[5] He mentions "Europe's political and economic instability kept prudent American investors from lending their money abroad until 1924."[6] Youssef Cassis[7] argues that only the stabilization of the German currency with the Dawes Plan in 1924 caused the resumption of capital flowing into Europe, while Harold James[8] points to sterling stabilization in 1925. James argues that the gold exchange standard represented the best way of providing the guarantee of stability that would allow large international capital flows to occur because investors demanded such a system.[9]

However, Hopkins remarks on the Eurocentrism of much scholarship in world history.[10] An important question to ask when assessing global integration in the history of First World War is: globalization for whom? It is natural to focus on the de-globalization of Europe resulting from the war. After all, European countries were the actors that had driven economic globalization since the nineteenth century and were the primary belligerents in the war. However, if we look beyond Europe, then a different story unfolds. Jeffry Frieden argues:

> World War I also dramatically accelerated the expansion of American enterprise in the developing areas, and especially Latin America. The Europeans practically ceased exports and overseas lending and investing in 1914, and only began again, in greatly reduced amounts, a decade later. In the interim, American investors had filled the vacuum, and conditions had been created for the subsequent change in the United States government policy.[11]

The First World War created the opportunity for the United States to globalize its economy to fill the void left after Europe's economic deglobalization. Correspondingly, the global economic connections of countries in the non-Western world shifted as the United States filled this new economic role.

Cassis specifically points to the expanding role of Wall Street in international trade financing due to the introduction of exchange controls in London.[12] He states: "Drafts in dollars tended to replace those in sterling, not only in financing American foreign trade but also that of other European countries, particularly with Latin America and the Far East."[13] Additionally, he notes that the massive expansion of the United States' merchant navy during the war—half of American freight was transported on American ships by 1920—led to a parallel development in marine insurance.[14]

This chapter corresponds with Tooze's argument that the First World War did not end globalization, but changed the nature of it.[15] The shift in the center of global finance from London to New York is an integral part of this change in economic and financial globalization. After the war, the British implemented a ban on capital exports until 1924 in an attempt to get back on the gold standard. This chapter will assess how the banks on Wall Street filled this vacuum in the global capital market and adapted to their new role in global finance through organizational changes and new types of international business. By focusing on the "nuts and bolts" of American international banking between 1915 and 1925, we can determine how American finance paved the way for more widespread projection of American economic power. As the United States ascended to economic primacy, a globalization based on European imperialism gave way to a globalization based on the American Open Door policy.

A major organizational development in the American financial services sector was the changing relationship between the government and banks. Frieden has shown how the federal government played an active role in exporting American capital abroad to the Allies during the war.[16] After the war, this role was being ceded back to the banks. James posits that many states—particularly Germany—turned to private capital markets after witnessing the political humiliation experienced by Austria and Hungary resulting from their stabilization by the League of Nations.[17] He further states that the availability of bank money caused the League to complain that its attempts at restoring fiscal rectitude were being undermined.[18] James likens the entire state of affairs to a contemporary developing country turning away from the International Monetary Fund in favor of private lenders.[19]

Mira Wilkins notes that the American government committed itself to aiding US business in world markets with the Webb-Pomerene and Edge Acts, but that federal government policies often failed to rise to the challenge of world economic leadership.[20] She states: "There remained a desire to separate the nation from a perceived economic dependency in a number of sectors and also to distance the United States from a Europe where prevailing ideas and ideologies seemed to clash with American values."[21] McNeil has extensively documented the casual attitude government officials took toward American capital exports by leaving foreign lending decisions to the banks' discretion.[22] Cassis places more agency with the banks themselves. He explains Wall Street's rise to the pinnacle of global capital markets by pointing to an abundance of savings, J. P. Morgan's role in financial diplomacy, and the expertise and networks of East Coast investment banks.[23]

It must be noted that the shift from public lending to private sector lending did not mean the American government attempted to curtail capital exports. Rather, the government came to play a more passive role in approving private foreign lending in the post-war years. The new nationalism of the banking business continued after the war, just in a different form. Additionally, it should not be assumed that this new nationalism of business equated with autarky. Previous decades of European mercantilism demonstrate that globalization and nationalism are not necessarily mutually exclusive or in a binary relationship. For the United States, the postwar context allowed financial globalization to be used as a means to achieve a strong national economy.

A second development was the formation of new types of financial organizations at the firm level to facilitate foreign lending. These took the form of investment trusts or foreign finance corporations. Between 1915 and 1925, a number of prominent bankers on Wall Street pooled their resources and expertise to form new firms engaged in foreign financing. Similarly, a number of existing firms created international arms to conduct their foreign business during this period. The result was a notable increase in the capabilities of Wall Street to embrace the United States' new leading role in global finance.

New York banks also started to engage in new foreign business. The war had stimulated new skills in currency and export trading amongst bankers on Wall Street. After the war, these skills were leveraged to increase and expand the international business of American financial firms. The postwar period saw a massive increase in the foreign branches of Wall Street banks, creating a pipeline to export American capital abroad. Using the board meeting minutes from the Foreign Finance Corporation (FFC), it is also evident that new investment banking business was sought in commercial lending, secondary market activities, and trade finance. Though a significant amount of foreign lending was provided to foreign businesses, much of this new business also facilitated new opportunities for American multinational enterprises abroad. Geoffrey Jones has demonstrated how foreign direct investment enabled multinationals to thrive in the postwar period as the global economic system was being transformed.[24]

Erecting this global financial architecture has two key implications in the historiography of the impact of the First World War on international business. First, it demonstrates that American financial globalization was running rampant even while Europe experienced economic deglobalization in many industries, American farm exports suffered, and the US Senate failed to approve American membership in the League of Nations. Secondly, this change in globalization resulted in new financial connections being made between different parts of the world. The United States was increasing its financial integration with Latin America and Asia relative to other regions of the world between 1919 and 1924. Only after the Dawes Plan comes into effect in 1924 does capital get redirected toward European reconstruction. These findings can help historians tailor their understanding of the relationship between The First World War and globalization and to consider the dynamics of integration in all of its complexity.

Federal Government Cooperation with Wall Street

During early years of the war—from 1914 to 1917—the firm J.P. Morgan & Co. primarily conducted American foreign financing. The firm was the natural representative of American international banking, having developed expertise in selling American securities to Europeans over the past several decades. However, by 1915, the House of Morgan's traditional activities were reversed as the firm found itself selling European loans to Americans. Furthermore, the financing of the Allies took a sharp turn once the United States entered the war in April 1917. Private money became unnecessary as the US government made nearly $10 billion in government-to-government loans in the war effort. In the end, 82.8% of capital exports during the war were direct loans of the US government to European governments, while only 17.2% were private loans floated in the United States.[25]

The capital export trend of government-to-government lending, such as that conducted by the War Finance Corporation, continued in the first two years after the Armistice. The extension of the loans post-armistice was to enable the European governments to carry out contracts previously made for the purchase of American goods, since the Treasury was fearful of the consequences of an immediate cancellation of the large buying orders.[26]

However, following the war the United States policymakers recognized the need to curtail government lending and shift the burden to American banks. Edge Act corporations were intended to assume the role played by the government during the war. By arranging long-term foreign financing and encouraging the development of agencies for the penetration of American capital, these new organizational structures were meant to support American enterprise abroad. Private sector foreign financing could improve the American economy without the heavy use of federal tax power experienced during the war. As a result, the exportation of capital was no longer predominantly conducted by the US government, but was rather managed in concert with a group of Wall Street bankers.

Following the war, the Edge Act was signed on December 24, 1919, which allowed national banks to engage in international banking through federally chartered subsidiaries. Prior to the amendment, American corporations were not permitted to own foreign banks. The legislation, sponsored by Senator Walter Evans Edge (R-NJ), was meant to give American banks more flexibility in competing with foreign firms. By creating subsidiary Edge Act corporations, banks and holding companies were able to engage in foreign financing while supposedly separating the risk of international operations and domestic banking activities. Following the legislation, many of the most powerful New York banks expanded their foreign financing operations through this new type of financial architecture. The federal government had amended the Federal Reserve Act to cooperate with the New York banks engaged in foreign financing to send capital abroad.

The Edge Amendment to the Federal Reserve Act made possible two organizational developments in American foreign financing. First, the Edge Act provided for the unification and combination of banking capital for the purpose of foreign acceptance banking. Multiple banks were able to combine in the ownership of corporations doing acceptance business and operating internationally through foreign branches or subsidiary corporations. Secondly, the Edge Act made possible the federal chartering of corporations that could extend long-term loans to foreign governments and corporations. Only Federal Reserve member banks were allowed to hold stock in these Edge Act corporations, and the new firms were permitted to issue debentures, bonds, and promissory notes.

McNeil has extensively documented that American banks had been in the habit of advising the State Department of any foreign loans during the war and that the review by government officials was rather lax.[27] The practice was only discontinued in the postwar period because the Wilson administration had requested that the banks no longer burden the government with the information. Yet, with the continuance of large-scale foreign financing after the war, the Harding administration had requested the resumption of the wartime practice, and the banks were happy to oblige.

On Friday, June 3, 1921, J. P. Morgan Jr. and his wife Jane met with President Harding and his wife Florence in Washington D.C. The banker and the President met to determine the future cooperation between Wall Street and the federal government in foreign financing. On June 6, Morgan sent two letters from New York—one formal and one personal—to President Harding updating him on the results of their conversation. In his formal letter he wrote:

> I have the honor to report that I have seen substantially all the people here who have anything to do with issuing foreign loans, including the following: National City Bank, Guaranty Trust Co., Bankers Trust Co., Kuhn, Loeb & Co., Brown Brothers & Co., Lee, Higginson & Co., Kidder, Peabody & Co., Dillon, Read & Co., and Equitable Trust Co. All are in complete accord with your suggestion, and agree to keep the State Department fully informed of any and all negotiations for loans to foreign governments which may be undertaken by them.[28]

In his personal letter, Morgan recounted how all of the bankers he approached had stated, "Why, of course, that is what ought to be done, and it will be a pleasure to do it" when asked about President Harding's request.[29]

In his reply, Harding expressed his appreciation that the government and bankers were cooperating with each other to facilitate the country's new role in global finance:

> It is very gratifying to be assured that you and your associates and all others who are interested in the negotiation of loans to other nations are in accord about the desirability of consulting with our State Department before being committed to any contract. I think I have already assured you that the government does not desire to interfere unnecessarily. It is important that those who speak for our country in its new financial relationship to the world should proceed in full understanding with those who are called upon to safeguard American interests.[30]

The new administration and the banks were aware of the significance of their new financial relationship with the world. They agreed to share information to ensure that international financial activities were aligned with the national interest.

The result was a drastic expansion in capital exports, particularly after the Dawes Plan was put into effect in 1924. Later defaults on this lending in Central Europe and Latin America called into question the wisdom of advancing huge sums to foreign governments that, in hindsight, they were obviously not able to pay. The bankers who were responsible for floating many of these loans admitted that there had been an unhealthy competition on the part of many financial houses to induce foreign governments and municipalities to float unneeded and unwise loans.[31]

However, bankers not only argued that they had disregarded the possible consequences in the promotion of foreign issues, but also that the State Department had given consent to unsound loans for political reasons. For example, Grosvenor M. Jones, Chief of Finance and Investment at the Department of Commerce, stated:

> The merits of a loan would be the subject of more or less discussion between the economic adviser [of the State Department] and myself; not that it made a great deal of difference except along the particular points that have been enunciated as part of our foreign loan policy, but sort of entre nous, speaking as man to man, we would exchange views as to whether we thought a certain government was overborrowing, or whether these loans looked good to us. I suppose we were amateur international bankers.[32]

The State Department, for its part, vigorously denied these claims, stating in a *New York Times* article from January 8, 1932, that it had declared a definite warning to the bankers in the fall of 1925 regarding the further expansion of German loans that went unheeded.

Nevertheless, the cooperation of the New York banks and the federal government had resulted in a new role for the United States in the international financial system. Table 9.1 demonstrates that the expansion in

Table 9.1 Distribution of American Foreign Security Issues, 1919–1925

Year	Europe	Canada*	Latin America	Asia	Total
1919	227,632,500	114,760,000	33,597,500	755,000	376,745,000
1920	247,406,000	183,512,800	48,520,400	0	479,439,200
1921	155,811,400	193,277,500	229,554,200	14,867,500	593,510,600
1922	211,161,000	168,213,000	223,329,600	111,664,800	714,368,400
1923	107,871,300	119,857,000	114,484,100	70,261,000	412,473,400
1924	525,831,100	150,924,100	186,492,200	95,168,700	958,416,100
1925	628,521,900	136,588,800	157,930,800	140,857,200	1,063,898,700

Source: Computed from US Department of Commerce, *American Underwriting of Foreign Securities* (various issues).

* Canada was often considered to be a domestic investment rather than a foreign investment. As a result, investments in Canada may be due to the domestic availability of credit in the United States.

American foreign investments was not simply diverted toward reconstructing postwar Europe, but was channeled in huge sums to developing Latin America and Asia. Much of the expansion in American foreign investments involved replacing British capital in areas where England had historically placed its own foreign investments. British bankers were recovering from the war, and American investors met the demand for foreign capital in these regions, in effect shifting the center of global finance from London to New York. These new global financial connections required American banks to create new organizational structures in order to foster the flow of capital from the United States to the rest of the world.

Investment Trusts and Foreign Banking Corporations

The international financial architecture of American banks was underdeveloped prior to the First World War. American bankers had to create new organizational mechanisms both during and after the war as Wall Street took its place as the center of global finance. Many private international bankers—often referred to as Wall Street's "gold ring"—pooled their resources to export American capital abroad. J.P. Morgan & Co. had traditionally been the leader of this group of New York bankers, and the firm played an integral role in foreign financing. Similarly, a number of banks in New York and all over the United States created new foreign banking corporations to conduct their international business.

For example, on November 12, 1919, a day after the first anniversary of the Armistice, H. P. Davison filed the certificate of incorporation for the short-lived Foreign Finance Corporation.[33] The corporation was organized under the laws of the State of New York and the certificate was filed in the office of Francis Hugo (R-NY), New York's Secretary of State.[34] Davison was a senior partner at J.P. Morgan & Co. and was widely recognized as one of the most able bankers in the United States. He organized the first meeting of the Board of Directors of the new corporation on November 24 at 3:15pm at the infamous 23 Wall Street, the headquarters of the House of Morgan.[35] Meetings were held twice a month. The location of the FFC office was diagonally across the street in room 2309 of the Bankers Trust Building at 14 Wall Street.[36]

The Foreign Finance Corporation represented some of the most powerful New York City money center banks and included some of the city's most prominent bankers (Table 9.2). Mirroring power within the financial sector, J.P. Morgan & Co. led the FFC while the institutions Bankers Trust, Guaranty Trust, National City Bank, Central Trust, and the Liberty National Bank[37] helped to coordinate the corporation's activities through membership on its Board of Directors. Indeed, J.P. Morgan & Co. was appointed the transfer agent for the capital stock of the FFC.[38] J. P. Morgan Jr. himself was Chairman of the Board.[39] Arthur M. Anderson, his partner at J.P. Morgan & Co., served as President and was charged with running the proceedings of the meetings.[40]

Table 9.2 Directors of the Foreign Finance Corporation

Name	Affiliation	Position in the Foreign Finance Corporation
J. P. Morgan Jr.	J.P. Morgan & Co.	Chairman
Arthur M. Anderson	J.P. Morgan & Co.	President
H. C. Hoskier	Unaffiliated	Vice President
Seward Prosser	Bankers Trust	Director
J. S. Alexander	National City Bank	Director
G. W. Davison	Central Trust	Director
J. A. Stillman	National City Bank	Director
Charles H. Sabin	Guaranty Trust	Director
A. H. Wiggin	Chase National Bank	Director
Harvey D. Gibson	Liberty National Bank / New York Trust Company	Director
H. P. Davison	J.P. Morgan & Co.	Director
G. F. Baker, Jr.	National City Bank	Director
A. A. Tilney	Bankers Trust	Director
George Whitney	J.P. Morgan & Co.	Director
Ernest Stauffen, Jr.	Liberty National Bank / New York Trust Company	Director
E.V.R. Thayer	Chase National Bank	Director
D. W. Morrow	J.P. Morgan & Co.	Director
F. D. Bartow	J.P. Morgan & Co.	Director
Harold Stanley	Guaranty Trust	Director
E. S. Pegram	J.P. Morgan & Co.	Secretary*
Malcolm D. Simpson	Babcock Co.	Secretary†

Source: Derived from: Minutes of the Foreign Financing Corporation, December 4, 1919 to April 20, 1920; ARC1216, Folder 160, Box 97, J.P. Morgan, Jr. Papers; Morgan Library, New York City, New York.

* Resigned as Secretary on February 16, 1920.

† Appointed Secretary on February 16, 1920.

He was paid $25,000 per year for his services.[41] Shortly after the formation of the FFC, Herman C. Hoskier was floated as a potential Vice President due to the need for an exchange expert on the board.[42] Hoskier was a British professional biblical scholar and textual critic and was unaffiliated with any major American financial institution. However, he was also the son of a well-known British merchant banker who had lent his son his name. Hoskier was elected Vice President on January 6, 1920 and received a salary of $18,000 per year.[43] He ran the proceedings of the meeting when Anderson was absent.

On January 27, it was determined that the Executive Committee of the FFC board would be comprised of: Morgan, Anderson, and D. W. Morrow from J.P. Morgan & Co.; J. A. Stillman and J. S. Alexander from the National City Bank; George W. Davison from Central Trust; and A. A. Tilney from Bankers Trust.[44]

The finances of the FFC were structured so as to facilitate foreign financing from the headquarters in New York. By December 19, 1919, the stock subscriptions of the FFC amounted to $100,000 and 1,000 shares of stock were issued.[45] On January 6, 1920, Anderson informed the board that he considered it advisable to remit funds abroad in order to have capital readily available for any business that might arise.[46] He suggested sending $600,000 to London and $300,000 to Paris.[47] A committee consisting of Morgan, Stillman, and Sabin was appointed to handle the matter.[48] Indeed, the board decided to forgo tying up too much capital in the purchase of securities in these markets.[49] The foreign financing transactions proposed were in effect purchases of exchange. Since exchange was deemed to be an attractive business at the time, the board decided it would be wiser to leave such funds as might be remitted on deposit in London or Paris.[50] By February 16, the subscribers to the capital stock had paid in $3,500,000.[51] The balance in New York was $450,000, £4,000 was in London, and F2,000,000 was in Paris.[52]

The FFC allowed banks to organize foreign financing transactions through a syndicate. The corporation created a vehicle for banks to coordinate which foreign investment banking opportunities to pursue under what terms. Anderson (or Hoskier, if the President was absent) would propose potential business during board meetings and members would vote on how to proceed.

The FFC was neither the only nor the first firm to create such an organization, simply the firm where the most data is available in the historical record. The National City Bank of New York was the forerunner in establishing an international presence. National City formed the International Banking Corporation in 1901 to carry out banking operations in the Far East.[53] However, the first foreign affiliate under the firm's name was not opened until 1915.[54] Following the war, the corporation vastly expanded its operations and had over 40 foreign branches in operation by 1925.[55]

The Asia Banking Corporation was organized by the Guaranty Trust Company to perform its banking business in Japan, China, and the Philippines.[56] Charles H. Sabin, Chairman of the Board of the Guaranty Company, was President of the Asia Banking Corporation.[57] Other directors of the corporation were affiliated with Bankers Trust, Standard Oil, the Overseas Securities Company, and the law firm Stetson, Jennings, Russell and Davis.[58] The corporation was eventually taken over by the International Banking Corporation in 1925.[59] The only other American institution that remained with branches in the Asian region was the Equitable Eastern Banking Corporation, formed by the Equitable Trust Company.

A group of New England bankers organized the International Securities Trust of America in 1921.[60] The Guaranty Trust Company began acting as trustee for the organization under an agreement dated June 1, 1923.[61] The purpose of the trust was to invest in a number of different securities and to issue its own securities against them.[62] In this manner, the organization was promoted as the first general investment trust formed in the United

States.[63] It was modeled after similar types of investment combines that had supervised the bulk of the overseas investments of the British Empire.[64] Indeed, the formation of such foreign investment corporations is indicative of the attempt to shift the global financial center from London to New York. In a letter to its shareholders from December 31, 1924, the trust reported that it had purchased small amounts of securities in 400 companies in 24 countries.[65] These included sovereign bonds, sub-sovereign bonds, and foreign corporate stocks and bonds.[66] The capitalization of the company was $65 million with a bond authorization of $45 million.[67]

The American and Continental Corporation was organized by a group of financial interests that included: Kuhn, Loeb & Co.; Dillon, Read & Co.; the International Acceptance Bank; and the French American Banking Corporation of New York.[68] According to a *New York World* article from October 14, 1924, the corporation was formed concurrently with the flotation of a German loan to finance industrial enterprises in Europe, particularly in Germany. The purpose of the corporation was to supply the necessary interim financing until such time as its loans could be replaced either through the accumulated savings of Germany, or by permanent financing through the sale of securities in the United States or abroad.[69] The authorized capital was $25 million, of which $10 million was initially subscribed. The stock of the corporation was not offered publicly according to a *New York Times* article from October 14, 1924.

The Mercantile Bank of the Americas was started in 1915 with a small capital stock subscribed by Brown Brothers & Co. and J. and W. Seligman & Co.[70] The intention was to create a pan-American bank to promote the foreign trade of the United States. Shortly thereafter, the following banks were added to the group: Guaranty Trust; the National Shawmut Bank of Boston; the Anglo-London Paris National Bank of San Francisco; and the Hibernia Bank and Trust Company of New Orleans.[71] The Bank of Central and South America was later formed by a group of powerful New York banking houses, including: J.P. Morgan & Co.; Guaranty Trust Company; Brown Brothers & Co.; Corn Exchange Bank; J. and W. Seligman & Co.; W.R. Grace & Co.; and Mechanics and Metals National Bank.[72] The bank had taken over the business of the Mercantile Bank of the Americas.[73] However, in 1925, all of the stock of the bank was sold to the Royal Bank of Canada, which took over its business.[74]

The American Foreign Banking Corporation was founded in 1917 and capitalized at $2 million, according to a *New York Times* article from July 10, 1917. The article goes on to explain the formation of the bank. The firm specialized in the financing of imports and exports. The President of the corporation was Archibald Kains, who resigned as Governor of the Federal Reserve Bank of San Francisco to assume his new duties. The stock of the bank was owned by several large national banks. Albert H. Wiggin, President of the Chase Bank, was the prime mover in the creation of the new firm. Other organizers were the Merchants National Bank of Boston; First

National Bank of Cleveland; Philadelphia National Bank; Canal Bank and Trust Company; National Bank of Commerce of St. Louis; Corn Exchange National Bank; First and Security National Bank of Minneapolis; Fifth-Third National Bank of Cincinnati; Anglo-London Paris National Bank of San Francisco; First National Bank of Milwaukee; Hayden B. Harris; Norman H. Davis of the Trust Company of Cuba; and Schmidt & Gallatin.

The American International Corporation was formed in 1915 as a financing, developing, and holding company.[75] The organization was incorporated to engage in any kind of banking, except banking and operation of public utilities.[76] The purpose of the corporation was to conduct international business and to finance and promote the development of American activities in foreign countries.[77]

Foreign Branches and Correspondent Banks

The Wall Street banks expanded their financial activities and business operations under their new organizational forms. One way in which these banks adapted to their new role in global capital markets was through foreign branch banking and relationships with correspondent foreign banks. Of course, banks could lend to foreign businesses through these branches and correspondents. However, these outposts were also useful for American multinationals attempting to gain a foothold in international markets. Therefore, these financial stations not only demonstrate an increase in the physical presence of American finance abroad, but also how Wall Street banks facilitated international business for other American industries.

Table 9.3 demonstrates the extraordinary growth in the foreign presence of American banks, both Federal Reserve member banks and foreign banking corporations. Only three years after the end of the war, a large number of foreign branches, as well as representatives of American banks and banks owned or controlled by American institutions, had appeared all over Europe, Latin America, and Asia. The number of overseas branches of American banks increased from 26 in 1913 to 181 in 1920, though later heavy losses caused this figure to decline to 107 by 1925.[78] Particularly notable is the vast expansion in the presence of American banks in Latin America and Asia. Frieden states: "As the belligerents deserted the developing world and even their own colonies in the battle for their homelands, the field was clear for American capital and manufacturing exports."[79] Indeed, the strong American presence in South America, where European interests had been dominant for centuries, as well a surprising presence in European colonies such as India, Indonesia, and Hong Kong indicate a change in the pattern of financial globalization.

While banks operated foreign bank branches to engage in foreign financing, their branching did not represent the full foreign representation of American banks or present a complete picture of how American banks maintained their foreign connections. Writing in *The Annalist*, John Oakwood

Table 9.3 Foreign Presence of American International Banks in 1922[80]

Federal Reserve Member Banks

Bankers Trust (NY)	**Branches:** • Paris, France		
Equitable Trust (NY)	**Branches:** • London, England **Representatives:** • Hong Kong, China • Berlin, Germany	• Paris, France • Bombay, India • Calcutta, India	• Mexico City, Mexico • Yokohama, Japan
Farmers Loan and Trust (NY)	**Representatives:** • London, England **Owned/Controlled:** • London, England (2)	• Paris, France	
First National Bank of Boston (Boston)	**Branches:** • Buenos Aires, Argentina	• Havana, Cuba	
Guaranty Trust (NY)	**Branches:** • Antwerp, Belgium • Brussels, Belgium	• Liverpool, England • London, England	• Le Havre, France • Paris, France
National City Bank of New York (NY)	**Branches:** • Buenos Aires, Argentina • Rosario, Argentina • Antwerp, Belgium • Brussels, Belgium • Pernambuco, Brazil • Rio de Janeiro, Brazil • Santos, Brazil • Sao Paulo, Brazil	• Santiago, Chile • Valparaiso, Chile • Cuba (21) • London, England (2) • Paris, France • Genoa, Italy • Lima, Peru	• Ponce, Puerto Rico • San Juan, Puerto Rico • Moscow, Russia • Petrograd, Russia • Montevideo, Uruguay • Caracas, Venezuela • Copenhagen, Denmark

Foreign Banking Corporations

American Foreign Banking Corporation (NY)	**Branches:** • Rio de Janeiro, Brazil • Havana, Cuba	• Mexico City, Mexico • Cristobal, Panama	• Panama, City, Panama
Asia Banking Corporation (NY)	**Branches:** • China (6)	• Manila, Philippines	• Singapore

Table 9.3 Continued

Foreign Banking Corporations

Bank of Central and South America (NY)	*Branches:* • Hamburg, Germany *Owned/Controlled:* • Columbia (7) • Costa Rica	• Nicaragua (4) • Peru (6)	• Venezuela (4)
Empire Trust (NY)	*Branches:* • London, England		
Equitable Eastern Banking Corporation (NY)	*Branches:* • Shanghai, China *Representatives:* • Hong Kong, China	• Bombay, India	• Yokohama, Japan
International Banking Corporation (NY)	*Branches:* • Rangoon, Burma • China (8) • Dominican Republic (8) • London, England • Lyons, France • Haiti • Bombay, India	• Calcutta, India • Kobe, Japan • Yokohama, Japan • Batavia, Java • Soerabaya, Java • Cebu, Philippines	• Manila, Philippines • Barcelona, Spain • Madrid, Spain • Colon, Panama • Panama City, Panama • Singapore
Mercantile Overseas Corporation (NY)	*Owned/Controlled:* • Guayaquil, Ecuador		

Source: All data derived from: *Federal Reserve Bulletin* 8 (1922), 1298–1299.

stated: "Many of those listed have in addition correspondent relations with native banks in cities in other countries, sometimes covering virtually every business center in the world; while still other banks conduct their foreign operations entirely through correspondent foreign banks."[81] National City Bank's security affiliate, the National City Company, controlled many correspondent foreign banks in addition to its affiliated foreign branches, such as the Banque Nationale de la République d'Haiti.[82] Apart from its affiliated foreign branches, Guaranty Trust also had an interest in several correspondent foreign banks, its policy being to control these banks as much as possible.[83] Alternatively, the National Bank of Commerce was one of the best-known examples of a bank that conducted most of its relations abroad through correspondent foreign banks rather than creating affiliated foreign branches.[84]

The use of correspondent banks was widely practiced by the International Acceptance Bank. The firm was organized in February 1921 with Paul M. Warburg as Chairman, F. Abbot Goodhue (Vice President of First National

Bank of Boston) as President, and P.J. Vogel (Chase National) and E.W. Davenport (Vice President of First National Corporation of New York) as Vice Presidents.[85] Foreign interests were allotted a total of one-third of the capital, split between Swiss, Dutch, Swedish, and English operators.[86] As such, the firm agreed not to establish foreign branches, but to work through correspondent banks under European control. Prominent subscribers of stock were representatives of Kuhn, Loeb (through Warburg); National City Bank (through American International Corporation); and the House of Morgan (through Goodhue).

Some of the banking corporations that were formed had no foreign branches, but were nonetheless organized to finance foreign trade or to undertake foreign financing operations. Examples of these are the First Federal Foreign Banking Association of New York, the Foreign Trade Financing Corporation of New York, and the Federal International Banking Company of New Orleans.[87]

Commercial Lending

While a physical presence abroad was certainly helpful in facilitating foreign financing, it was not altogether necessary for foreign banking corporations to engage in new international business. In the postwar period, we see American firms exporting capital abroad through commercial lending from newly created finance corporations without a foreign branch. Many of this new business involved lending to foreign companies. However, some of this capital was also given to American multinationals attempting to expand their international business opportunities.

The board meeting minutes of the Foreign Finance Corporation provide an intricate understanding of how foreign financing decisions were made. For example, the FFC was interested in Cuban financing in Latin America. Bonbright & Co. tendered a piece of business to the FFC that was presented at the board meeting of December 4, 1919. The transaction was a purchase of a Cuban sugar plantation called the Espana Mill that was being evaluated by Bonbright.[88] The cost of the evaluation was $25,000 and it was proposed that the FFC assume one-third of the cost in order to have a one-third interest in the option held by Bonbright.[89]

The FFC was also interested in financing American companies abroad. On January 27, 1920, Anderson presented a proposal for the advancement of a maximum of $5,000,000 to the International General Electric Company.[90] The General Electric Company would endorse the transaction with collateral consisting definitely of notes of its foreign branches, probably of notes of the customers of the foreign branches, and possibly the deposit of internal government bonds of the countries in which the company was selling merchandise on credit.[91] It was the sense of the board that this was desirable business provided the company could obtain an interest rate that was 1% in excess of the rate on which it could borrow from the FFC for the same period of time.[92] The board unanimously voted to give favorable consideration to the proposal.[93]

On January 6, 1920, Anderson also submitted to the board a proposed loan of an amount between $3,000,000 and $4,500,000 for the Société Anonyme de Filature de Soie of Lyon, France. The loan would run for 10 years and would be secured by first mortgage bonds of the company, whose financial condition was reported as very good. The bonds were to be secured by a mortgage on a manufacturing plant to be purchased or erected in the United States and to be convertible into stock of the Société. The rate was to be two shares of stock[94] for $1,000 of the proposed loan. The board decided to approve and proceed with the transaction. On January 27, it was reported that the company's American representative was attempting to purchase a mill in the United States.

On February 16, 1920, Hoskier submitted a proposal from Czecho-Slovakia, who had approached the Foreign Commerce Corporation on the subject of a $4,000,000 to $7,000,000 credit at six to nine months.[95] The credit was for the purchase of fertilizers against payment by Czecho-Slovakia in dollars or in goods.[96] The board agreed that there was nothing to prevent the FFC from joining in this operation if and when proper details could be worked out and the trades adequately secured.[97] The board decided that further consideration would be given to the transaction and that the opinion of the War Finance Corporation would be sought.[98]

At the February 16, 1920 board meeting a proposition from Copenhagen for a loan of $500,000 to a Danish leather and shoe factory was submitted.[99] The board regularly moved and seconded that this business be referred to J.P. Morgan & Co.[100] Indeed, J. P. Morgan, along with other private international banks, enjoyed a certain informational advantage in commercial lending during the postwar period. These firms had previous relationships with European commercial centers and could leverage these connections to obtain new business and gather information.

Secondary Market Activities

The war had stimulated skills and expertise in currency trading amongst Wall Street bankers, particularly those from the House of Morgan. The firm has taken a leading role in financing the Allied war effort and satiating the British demand for dollars. After the war, these new skills were applied in the secondary market as a new aspect of American international banking.

For example, during the first FFC board meeting on November 24, a sub-committee was appointed and eventually approved the purchase of £1,000,000 State of Sao Paulo 5% bonds of the loan of 1905.[101] However, the purchase encountered complications since the owner was the German government, who had no representation at the time with whom the FFC could negotiate.[102] At the second meeting the board regrouped and Anderson proposed the pursuit of another Brazilian transaction, a £1,200,000 5%

funding loan of 1898 listed on the London Stock Exchange.[103] The proposal was moved and unanimously carried.[104] Anderson, Alexander, and Prosser were empowered to purchase the bonds or any part thereof deemed desirable.[105] However, the prices were raised and the bonds were not bought.[106] Taking matters into his own hands, Anderson went to London to pursue the negotiations to a more definite conclusion.[107]

On February 16, 1920 the board re-approved the purchase of the Brazilian funding bonds, this time for £1,100,000.[108] The approval was for a price of 72 net, which included Morgan, Grenfell & Co.'s remuneration.[109] Anderson met with N.M. Rothschild & Sons representatives in London on the same day in order to negotiate the purchase.[110] He was prepared to consider three proposals:[111]

1) The delivery to Brazil of £200,000 of the bonds as a consideration for Brazil's stamping the remaining £900,000 of bonds payable in dollars at parity.
2) The taking over by Brazil of the entire block against which it might issue its three- or five-year notes for $3,750,000.
3) To have Brazil stamp the entire £1,100,000 bonds payable in dollars, with the FFC to undertake the sale of the stamped bonds on joint account with the Brazilian government.

As a response, N.M. Rothschild & Sons suggested that the FFC pay the Brazilian government $400,000 cash as a consideration for the stamping of the entire block of bonds payable in dollars at mint parity.[112] At the February 27 board meeting, Hoskier pointed out that the cost of the bonds to the FFC when stamped in dollars would be 57.83% under such an agreement.[113] The board instead opted to handle the matter directly with the Brazilian government through the Rio de Janeiro office of attorneys Curtis, Mallet-Prevost & Colt.[114] In the end, the FFC paid $400,000 for the stamping of a block of bonds worth £1,105,960.[115]

On March 15, the FFC board approved the re-sale of £105,960 bonds in London, netting a profit of $29,000 or 11⅜% on the investment.[116] The board also approved the sale of a further £200,000 in London and New York if the opportunity arose, though further sales in London would have to wait until the previous sale had been absorbed.[117] On March 31, Hoskier announced to the board that an additional £50,000 bonds had been sold in New York at $559 per £200.[118] The price was equal at 3.95 to a London price of 72 on an ex April coupon or 70¾ without.[119] Hoskier had drawn at 3.88 for the April coupons on the entire £1,000,000 bonds.[120] Anderson sent a letter from Europe expressing concern that negotiations with Brazil might be called off in the case that it seemed the FFC might get stuck with dollar bonds.[121] He feared that there was no market for these dollar bonds, while there was a limited market for sterling bonds in London.[122] As a result, the board assigned George Whitney the task of conferring with both the

Guaranty Trust Company and the National City Company to determine the best method for disposing of the bonds.[123] However, by April 20, Hoskier reported to the board that though the Brazilian government could not lawfully stamp the 4½% bonds of 1898 in dollars, it did indicate a desire to buy the bonds from the FFC.[124] At the board meeting, it was resolved that the FFC negotiate the sale of the remaining £950,000 bonds at a satisfactory price.[125]

On January 6, 1920, Anderson presented more Latin American business to the board with a proposition to purchase 7% preferred stock of the Havana Cigar Company in London.[126] The stock was quoted in London at 90 with a view of replacing it with a dollar issue.[127] The board voted to proceed further with the business.[128]

On December 19, 1919, Anderson also presented for consideration the purchase of short-term securities payable in sterling.[129] He suggested Second Series Japanese 4½% bonds maturing in 1925, City of Quebec bonds maturing in 1923, and Province of Quebec bonds maturing in 1928.[130] The board unanimously decided that Anderson should be authorized to purchase up to £100,000 of the Japanese bonds and £50,000 of the Quebec bonds.[131] By January 27, 1920, the FFC had purchased £25,000 of the Japanese bonds as well as £21,600 Province of Quebec bonds.[132] By March 31, Hoskier reported to the board that the Japanese bonds could be liquidated at a small profit, and the sale was authorized.[133]

The firm's European business was primarily in countries that were Allies during the First World War. On December 4, 1919, Anderson presented for board consideration a proposition to purchase New Haven French Franc Loan Bonds that were being dealt in Paris.[134] Such a proposal provided that the bonds could be stamped by the New Haven railroad as payable in dollars and could be resold in the United States by Oldham, Merrill & Co.[135] The board voted to proceed with the purchase of an amount that could be arranged with the railroad and could be sold by Oldham, Merrill & Co. of a profit not less than 2½% to the FFC.[136] However, the railroad preferred not to stamp any further bonds and the purchase was not completed.[137]

Trade Finance

Many of the private international banks on Wall Street came from the British merchant banking tradition. As such, they were intimately acquainted with export financing prior to the war. However, these firms—particularly J.P. Morgan & Co.—honed this expertise during the war effort. After the war, American multinationals were champing at the bit to export their excess supply, while European companies were seeking economic recovery through foreign markets. The experience gained financing the trade of American exports and Allied supplies during the First World War proved to be priceless in this postwar context.

For example, Anderson presented a proposal to the FFC board for a loan in connection with a possible sale of equipment by the American Car and Foundry Company to either the Belgian government or the Belgian State Railways.[138] The payment was to be made in Belgian government Five-Year Treasury Bills.[139] The American Car and Foundry Company proposed to form an export company with $5,000,000 capital stock and to issue $20,000,000 of notes without recourse to the company.[140] It was reported that some of the other American corporations, such as the American Foreign Banking Company and the Foreign Bond and Share Company, were prepared to take part in the issue of notes at an interest rate of 2% in excess of the rate at which they could borrow from the War Finance Corporation over a similar period.[141] The notes of the export company were to be collateralized by Belgian Treasury Bills.[142] The FFC board had to decide whether to share in the business to the extent of $2,500,000.[143] The board chose to give the matter further consideration until such a time when the precise character of the collateral available could be determined.[144]

Another piece of Czecho-Slovak financing was proposed on April 19, 1920. A proposal was received to participate with the newly formed Export Banking Corporation in a credit of $10,000,000 to finance the export of 39,000 bales of cotton to a Czecho-Slovak Spinners Syndicate.[145] The credit was to be on the basis of nine months' notes with interest at 6% and a ½% acceptance commission per month.[146] The notes were to be guaranteed by the government of Czecho-Slovakia and by a group of bankers in that country.[147] After a full discussion, the FFC board decided not to participate in this business.[148]

On March 15, 1920, participation was also offered to the FFC of $1,000,000 in a credit arranged for Belgium to cover shipments of grain and flour by the Grain Corporation.[149] It was explained that the Belgian government proposed to issue its 7% Treasury Bills to the extent of $10,000,000; with half of the bills running one year and the other half for two years.[150] Compensation for the bankers was to be 2% per annum and an exchange provision giving holders of the bills the option of payment in dollars or francs at a rate of 8 francs to the dollar.[151] The War Finance Corporation was to advance the funds at 6% interest against the notes of participating guarantors secured by those bills.[152] The FFC board agreed to accept the participation if successfully negotiated according to the terms indicated or with a larger participation if possible.[153] At the next board meeting Hoskier announced that the FFC had been offered an additional $1,000,000 participation.[154] It was resolved to accept the participation, making the FFC's interest in the credit of $2,000,000.[155] At the April 19 meeting Hoskier reported that the total amount of the issue had been raised to $12,000,000.[156]

However, under the regulations of the federal WFC, the FFC could not participate as bankers in the credit for the $2,000,000 reserved to it because it was not chartered as a federal Edge corporation.[157] The board resolved to proceed as a sub-participant of the Foreign Credit Corporation pending further investigation of the status of the FFC before the War Finance Corporation.[158] At the April 30 meeting, the board authorized the payment of Belgian Treasury Notes or other securities to the WFC as collateral security.[159] If the WFC still refused to make advances to the FFC, then the board authorized the purchase of Belgian Treasury Notes from the Foreign Credit Corporation.[160] The principal amount would not exceed $2,000,000 at 98½% plus interest accrued at 6% per annum, payable semi-annually.[161]

The short history of the Foreign Finance Corporation demonstrates the leading role that J.P. Morgan & Co. played in much of the foreign financing business that came the way of American banks in the immediate postwar period. J.P. Morgan & Co.'s reputation as a merchant bank, strong historical connections to British and European financing, and paramount position amongst private international banks placed it in the position to coordinate American foreign financing on Wall Street. However, the emerging problems with the WFC and the legality of the FFC forced the reorganization of foreign financing in 1920.

Conclusions

The shift in the center of global finance from London to New York provides us with two important conclusions on the impact of the First World War on international business. First, the phenomenon of financial globalization did not disappear. Rather, the source where global finance originated shifted to a new core and changed the nature of financial globalization. The preceding research demonstrates that American-led financial globalization was blossoming due to the war. The US government was encouraging American banks to engage in international banking. Foreign securities issues were increasing drastically. New financial firms were being created with the express purpose of conducting foreign business. The physical presence of American banks was expanding all over the world. An important impact of the war was that American financial firms could capitalize on the international banking expertise gained during the First World War to conduct new business in the postwar period.

Secondly, a new center of global finance meant new relationships with recipients of capital. Of course, the United States shifting from a net debtor nation to a net creditor is well known. The instability of European financial systems after the war is also well documented. Lesser known is the international financial architecture constructed by the United States in Latin America and Asia. While the historical economic interest of the United States and these regions is clear, the extent to which American banks attempted to fill the financial void left by European empires and firms is less so. American foreign securities issues in Latin America and Asia increased at a much greater rate than other regions after the war. Latin American issues even surpassed European issues between 1921 and 1923. A number of the new firms created to export American capital abroad were specifically tailored for Asia and Latin America. In 1922, the majority of foreign outposts were in Latin America and American banks had the same physical presence in Asia as in Europe at the time.

Of course, this global financial system was short lived. Eventually, the practicalities of the situation in Europe could not be addressed at arm's length and American decision-makers realized their existing entanglements. The Dawes Plan of 1924 represented a change in American postwar economic strategy. The stabilization of European economies and gradual return to gold caused the attractiveness of Latin American and Asian markets to decline. Yet, the preceding years reveal the development of an alternative American-led Open Door policy of financial globalization. Alas, this version of financial globalization eventually encountered the harsh realities of the postwar settlement.

Notes

1 Stephen Broadberry and Kevin O'Rourke, *The Cambridge Economic History of Modern Europe: Volume 2, 1870 to the Present* (Cambridge: Cambridge University Press, 2010); Charles Emmerson, *1913: In Search of the World Before the Great War* (London: Random House, 2013); Niall Ferguson, "Sinking Globalization," *Foreign Affairs* 84 (2005); Margaret MacMillan, *The War that Ended Peace: The Road to 1914* (New York: Random House, 2014).
2 Adam Tooze, *The Deluge: The Great War, America and the Remaking of Global Order, 1916–1931* (New York: Viking, 2014), 9.
3 A.G. Hopkins, "The History of Globalization—And the Globalization of History?" in *Globalization in World History*, ed. A.G. Hopkins (London: Pimlico, 2002), 30.
4 Christopher Kobrak, Per H. Hansen, and Christopher Kopper, "Business, Political Risk, and Historians in the Twentieth Century," in *European Business, Dictatorship, and Political Risk, 1920–1945*, eds. Christopher Kobrak and Per H. Hansen (New York: Berghahn Books, 2004), 14.
5 William C. McNeil, *American Money and the Weimar Republic: Economics and Politics on the Eve of the Great Depression* (New York: Columbia University Press, 1986), 48.
6 Ibid., 1.
7 Youssef Cassis, *Capitals of Capital: The Rise and Fall of International Financial Centres, 1780–2009* (Cambridge: Cambridge University Press, 2010), 154.
8 Harold James, *The End of Globalization: Lessons from the Great Depression* (Cambridge: Harvard University Press, 2002), 40.
9 Ibid.
10 Hopkins, "The History of Globalization," 30.
11 Jeffry Frieden, "The Economics of Intervention: American Overseas Investments and Relations with Underdeveloped Areas, 1890–1950," *Comparative Studies in Society and History* 31 (1989): 71.
12 Cassis, *Capitals*, 151.
13 Ibid.
14 Ibid., 154.
15 Tooze, *Deluge*.
16 Jeffry A. Frieden, *Global Capitalism: Its Fall and Rise in the Twentieth Century* (New York: W.W. Norton & Company, 2006), 131.

17 James, *End of Globalization*, 39.
18 Ibid.
19 Ibid.
20 Mira Wilkins, *The History of Foreign Investment in the United States, 1914–1945* (Cambridge: Harvard University Press, 2004), 79.
21 Ibid.
22 McNeil, *Weimar*, 25–48.
23 Cassis, *Capitals*, 155–56.
24 Geoffrey Jones, *Multinationals and Global Capitalism: From the Nineteenth to the Twenty-First Century* (Oxford: Oxford University Press, 2005).
25 Robert W. Dunn, *American Foreign Investments* (New York: B.W. Huebsch, 1926), 5.
26 Humanitarian considerations also played a part, primarily with reference to loans made to smaller European governments and those who had not engaged in war with enemies of the United States.
27 McNeil, *Weimar*, 25–48.
28 Formal Letter from Morgan to Harding, 6 June 1921; ARC1216, Folder 378, Box 108, J.P. Morgan, Jr. Papers; Morgan Library, New York City, New York.
29 Personal Letter from Morgan to Harding, 6 June 1921; ARC1216, Folder 378, Box 108, J.P. Morgan, Jr. Papers; Morgan Library, New York City, New York.
30 Letter from Harding to Morgan, 10 June 1921; ARC1216, Folder 378, Box 108, J.P. Morgan, Jr. Papers; Morgan Library, New York City, New York.
31 *Hearings before the Committee on Finance of the United States Senate*, Part I, 25.
32 *Hearings before the Committee on Finance of the United States Senate*, Part II, 724.
33 Letter from H.P. Davison to Morgan, 22 November 1919; ARC1216, Folder 160, Box 97, J.P. Morgan, Jr. Papers; Morgan Library, New York City, New York.
34 Ibid.
35 Ibid.
36 Minutes of the Foreign Financing Corporation, January 6, 1920; ARC1216, Folder 160, Box 97, J.P. Morgan, Jr. Papers; Morgan Library, New York City, New York.
37 The Liberty National Bank was acquired by the New York Trust Company in 1921. The New York Trust Company was subsequently represented on the Board of Directors of the Foreign Finance Corporation.
38 Minutes of the Foreign Financing Corporation, December 19, 1919; ARC1216, Folder 160, Box 97, J.P. Morgan, Jr. Papers; Morgan Library, New York City, New York.
39 Minutes of the Foreign Financing Corporation, December 4, 1919; ARC1216, Folder 160, Box 97, J.P. Morgan, Jr. Papers; Morgan Library, New York City, New York.
40 Ibid.
41 Minutes of the Foreign Financing Corporation, December 19, 1919; ARC1216, Folder 160, Box 97, J.P. Morgan, Jr. Papers; Morgan Library, New York City, New York.
42 Ibid.
43 Minutes of the Foreign Financing Corporation, January 6, 1920; ARC1216, Folder 160, Box 97, J.P. Morgan, Jr. Papers; Morgan Library, New York City, New York.
44 Minutes of the Foreign Financing Corporation, January 27, 1920; ARC1216, Folder 160, Box 97, J.P. Morgan, Jr. Papers; Morgan Library, New York City, New York.
45 Minutes of the Foreign Financing Corporation, December 19, 1919; ARC1216, Folder 160, Box 97, J.P. Morgan, Jr. Papers; Morgan Library, New York City, New York.

46 Minutes of the Foreign Financing Corporation, January 6, 1920; ARC1216, Folder 160, Box 97, J.P. Morgan, Jr. Papers; Morgan Library, New York City, New York.
47 Ibid.
48 Ibid.
49 Ibid.
50 Ibid.
51 Minutes of the Foreign Financing Corporation, February 16, 1920; ARC1216, Folder 160, Box 97, J.P. Morgan, Jr. Papers; Morgan Library, New York City, New York.
52 Ibid.
53 Dunn, *American*, 53.
54 Ibid.
55 Ibid.
56 Ibid.
57 Ibid.
58 Ibid.
59 Ibid.
60 Ibid., 54.
61 Ibid.
62 Ibid.
63 Ibid.
64 Ibid.
65 Ibid.
66 Ibid.
67 Ibid.
68 Ibid.
69 *Commercial and Financial Chronicle* 119 (1924): 1801.
70 *Federal Reserve Bulletin* 4 (1918): 736.
71 Ibid.
72 Dunn, *American*, 55.
73 Ibid.
74 Ibid.
75 Dunn, *American*, 55.
76 Ibid.
77 *Moody's Industrials* (1924): 1702.
78 Cassis, *Capitals*, 155.
79 Frieden, *Global*, 131.
80 All data derived from: *Federal Reserve Bulletin* 8 (1922): 1298–99.
81 John Oakwood, *Annalist* 25 (1925): 710.
82 Dunn, *American*, 53.
83 Ibid.
84 Oakwood, *Annalist*, 710.
85 "International Acceptance Bank, Inc.," *Acceptance Bulletin* (1921): 9.
86 Carl P. Parrini, *Heir to Empire: United States Economic Diplomacy, 1916–1923* (Pittsburgh: University of Pittsburgh Press, 1969), 96.
87 Ray B. Westerfield, *Banking Principles and Practice, Vol. 2* (New York: Ronald Press, 1921), 309.
88 Minutes of the Foreign Financing Corporation, December 4, 1919; ARC1216, Folder 160, Box 97, J.P. Morgan, Jr. Papers; Morgan Library, New York City, New York.
89 Ibid.
90 Minutes of the Foreign Financing Corporation, January 27, 1920; ARC1216, Folder 160, Box 97, J.P. Morgan, Jr. Papers; Morgan Library, New York City, New York.

91 Ibid.
92 Ibid.
93 Ibid.
94 Which was being quoted at approximately F4,500 to F5,000.
95 Minutes of the Foreign Financing Corporation, February 16, 1920; ARC1216, Folder 160, Box 97, J.P. Morgan, Jr. Papers; Morgan Library, New York City, New York.
96 Ibid.
97 Ibid.
98 Ibid.
99 Minutes of the Foreign Financing Corporation, February 16, 1920; ARC1216, Folder 160, Box 97, J.P. Morgan, Jr. Papers; Morgan Library, New York City, New York.
100 Ibid.
101 Minutes of the Foreign Financing Corporation, December 4, 1919; ARC1216, Folder 160, Box 97, J.P. Morgan, Jr. Papers; Morgan Library, New York City, New York.
102 Minutes of the Foreign Financing Corporation, December 19, 1919; ARC1216, Folder 160, Box 97, J.P. Morgan, Jr. Papers; Morgan Library, New York City, New York.
103 Minutes of the Foreign Financing Corporation, December 4, 1919; ARC1216, Folder 160, Box 97, J.P. Morgan, Jr. Papers; Morgan Library, New York City, New York.
104 Ibid.
105 Ibid.
106 Minutes of the Foreign Financing Corporation, December 19, 1919; ARC1216, Folder 160, Box 97, J.P. Morgan, Jr. Papers; Morgan Library, New York City, New York.
107 Ibid.
108 Minutes of the Foreign Financing Corporation, February 16, 1920; ARC1216, Folder 160, Box 97, J.P. Morgan, Jr. Papers; Morgan Library, New York City, New York.
109 Ibid.
110 Ibid.
111 Ibid.
112 Ibid. Exchange based on the gold content of the currencies.
113 Minutes of the Foreign Financing Corporation, February 27, 1920; ARC1216, Folder 160, Box 97, J.P. Morgan, Jr. Papers; Morgan Library, New York City, New York.
114 Ibid.
115 Minutes of the Foreign Financing Corporation, February 27 to March 15, 1920; ARC1216, Folder 160, Box 97, J.P. Morgan, Jr. Papers; Morgan Library, New York City, New York.
116 Minutes of the Foreign Financing Corporation, March 15, 1920; ARC1216, Folder 160, Box 97, J.P. Morgan, Jr. Papers; Morgan Library, New York City, New York.
117 Ibid.
118 Minutes of the Foreign Financing Corporation, March 31, 1920; ARC1216, Folder 160, Box 97, J.P. Morgan, Jr. Papers; Morgan Library, New York City, New York.
119 Ibid.
120 Ibid.
121 Ibid.
122 Ibid.

123 Ibid.
124 Minutes of the Foreign Financing Corporation, April 20, 1920; ARC1216, Folder 160, Box 97, J.P. Morgan, Jr. Papers; Morgan Library, New York City, New York.
125 Ibid.
126 Minutes of the Foreign Financing Corporation, January 6, 1920; ARC1216, Folder 160, Box 97, J.P. Morgan, Jr. Papers; Morgan Library, New York City, New York.
127 Ibid.
128 Ibid.
129 Minutes of the Foreign Financing Corporation, December 19, 1919; ARC1216, Folder 160, Box 97, J.P. Morgan, Jr. Papers; Morgan Library, New York City, New York.
130 Ibid.
131 Ibid.
132 Minutes of the Foreign Financing Corporation, January 27, 1920; ARC1216, Folder 160, Box 97, J.P. Morgan, Jr. Papers; Morgan Library, New York City, New York.
133 Minutes of the Foreign Financing Corporation, March 31, 1920; ARC1216, Folder 160, Box 97, J.P. Morgan, Jr. Papers; Morgan Library, New York City, New York.
134 Minutes of the Foreign Financing Corporation, December 4, 1919; ARC1216, Folder 160, Box 97, J.P. Morgan, Jr. Papers; Morgan Library, New York City, New York.
135 Ibid.
136 Ibid.
137 Minutes of the Foreign Financing Corporation, December 19, 1919; ARC1216, Folder 160, Box 97, J.P. Morgan, Jr. Papers; Morgan Library, New York City, New York.
138 Minutes of the Foreign Financing Corporation, January 27, 1920; ARC1216, Folder 160, Box 97, J.P. Morgan, Jr. Papers; Morgan Library, New York City, New York.
139 Ibid.
140 Ibid.
141 Ibid.
142 Ibid.
143 Ibid.
144 Ibid.
145 Minutes of the Foreign Financing Corporation, April 19, 1920; ARC1216, Folder 160, Box 97, J.P. Morgan, Jr. Papers; Morgan Library, New York City, New York.
146 Ibid.
147 Ibid.
148 Ibid.
149 Minutes of the Foreign Financing Corporation, March 15, 1920; ARC1216, Folder 160, Box 97, J.P. Morgan, Jr. Papers; Morgan Library, New York City, New York.
150 Ibid.
151 Ibid.
152 Ibid.
153 Ibid.
154 Minutes of the Foreign Financing Corporation, March 31, 1920; ARC1216, Folder 160, Box 97, J.P. Morgan, Jr. Papers; Morgan Library, New York City, New York.

155 Ibid.
156 Minutes of the Foreign Financing Corporation, April 19, 1920; ARC1216, Folder 160, Box 97, J.P. Morgan, Jr. Papers; Morgan Library, New York City, New York.
157 Ibid.
158 Ibid.
159 Minutes of the Foreign Financing Corporation, April 30, 1920; ARC1216, Folder 160, Box 97, J.P. Morgan, Jr. Papers; Morgan Library, New York City, New York.
160 Ibid.
161 Ibid.

References

Broadberry, S., and K. O'Rourke. *The Cambridge Economic History of Modern Europe: Volume 2, 1870 to the Present.* Cambridge: Cambridge University Press, 2010.

Cassis, Y. *Capitals of Capital: The Rise and Fall of International Financial Centres, 1780–2009.* Cambridge: Cambridge University Press, 2010.

Dunn, R. W. *American Foreign Investments.* New York: B. W. Huebsch, 1926.

Emmerson, C. *1913: In Search of the World before the Great War.* London: Random House, 2013.

Ferguson, N. "Sinking Globalization," *Foreign Affairs* 84 (2005).

Frieden, J. A. *Global Capitalism: Its Fall and Rise in the Twentieth Century.* New York: W. W. Norton & Company, 2006.

———. "The Economics of Intervention: American Overseas Investments and Relations with Underdeveloped Areas, 1890–1950," *Comparative Studies in Society and History* 31 (1989): 71.

Hopkins, A. G. "The History of Globalization—And the Globalization of History?" In *Globalization in World History*, edited by A. G. Hopkins. London: Pimlico, 2002.

James, H. *The End of Globalization: Lessons from the Great Depression.* Cambridge: Harvard University Press, 2002.

Jones, G. *Multinationals and Global Capitalism: From the Nineteenth to the Twenty-First Century.* Oxford: Oxford University Press, 2005.

Kobrak, C., P. H. Hansen, and C. Kopper. "Business, Political Risk, and Historians in the Twentieth Century." In *European Business, Dictatorship, and Political Risk, 1920–1945*, edited by Christopher Kobrak and Per H. Hansen. New York: Berghahn Books, 2004.

MacMillan, M. *The War that Ended Peace: The Road to 1914.* New York: Random House, 2014.

McNeil, W. C. *American Money and the Weimar Republic: Economics and Politics on the Eve of the Great DePression.* New York: Columbia University Press, 1986.

Parrini, C. P. *Heir to Empire: United States Economic Diplomacy, 1916–1923.* Pittsburgh: University of Pittsburgh Press, 1969.

Tooze, A. *The Deluge: The Great War, America and the Remaking of Global Order, 1916–1931.* New York: Viking, 2014.

Westerfield, R. B. *Banking Principles and Practice, Vol. 2.* New York: Ronald Press, 1921.

Wilkins, M. *The History of Foreign Investment in the United States, 1914–1945.* Cambridge: Harvard University Press, 2004.

10 The Flows of International Finance After the First World War

The Bank of England and Hungary, 1920–1939

Neil Forbes

This chapter analyses the disruptive effects of the First World War on the flow of international finance with particular reference to Hungary in the 1920s and 1930s.[1] At the end of the First World War, the succession states of the Austro-Hungarian Empire were confronted with the dismantlement of internal markets and communication networks. Furthermore, in many cases, the post-war boundary settlements exacerbated rather than resolved tensions over national minority populations. The conditions imposed on Hungary at the Treaty of Trianon, in 1920, seemed particularly harsh: in comparison to the pre-war kingdom, the new state lost nearly three-quarters of its territory and the majority of its population. In spite of attempts at stabilisation and reconstruction, Hungary remained economically weak. The enduring legacy of the Great War in central Europe was one of irredentism, economic weakness, and national humiliation. In the wake of the Great Depression and Financial Crisis, an existing tradition of authoritarianism in Hungary provided a platform for the rise of a form of nationalist dictatorship.

Notwithstanding these conditions, Britain's banking authorities made strenuous efforts throughout the period to direct financial resources towards Hungary. These efforts had the effect of strengthening the financial bonds between Britain and Hungary. International financial linkages are an important part of globalisation. In the historiographical literature that considers such questions, the First World War is commonly seen as having stopped or even reversed the process of globalisation. This chapter, however, presents a contrary view by showing how in the case of Hungary, the conflict caused this region of central Europe to become increasingly connected to London. Behind the efforts to promote British lending to Hungary lay the guiding hand of the Bank of England. Historians have looked at the way the Bank's Governor, Montagu Norman, exercised considerable influence in the early 1920s and argued that he became less influential as a result of the Financial Crisis.[2] But, the extent of his involvement throughout the 1930s in pursuing a vision of what collaboration between central banks could achieve has not been fully considered. Norman's role in foreign, financial affairs is, perhaps, a manifestation of what Adam Tooze describes as the search for a new way to secure international order—a progressive vision too easily criticised 'as symptomatic of the delusions of liberal idealism and as doleful overtures to appeasement'.[3]

There are several factors that help to explain the nature of the Bank's commitment. At the intergovernmental level, little attention was given in the years after 1918 to questions of stabilisation and reconstruction. Similarly, the British government never established a clear and settled policy towards central and Eastern Europe. The First World War left a residue of hostility towards former enemy powers; in some political circles, there was a particular dislike of Hungary's Magyars. To set against this, however, there were also fears that economic distress in the region would open the way for Bolshevism to spread. When this particular danger began to dissipate, there seemed to be few, vital British interests in the region and, from the mid-1920s, Hungarian issues began to receive less attention in foreign-policy terms.

In the absence of a coordinated policy directed at the intergovernmental or even national level, the lead to promote economic and financial reconstruction in the succession states was taken by a number of 'sub-state actors', such as financial experts who acted under the auspices of the League of Nations.[4] In this regard, Montagu Norman was a key figure.[5] His conduct of financial diplomacy in the 1920s has been described as dynamic, resourceful and passionate.[6] For although the British Treasury had become the most influential government department in determining policies related to international finance, it was Norman who was active in attempts from 1921 to put together stabilisation loans for Austria, Czechoslovakia, and Hungary when inflationary pressures mounted and economic collapse was in prospect.[7]

Of necessity, the economies of the succession states looked to external sources for finance as they had neither foreign-exchange resources nor the opportunity to accumulate capital by themselves. The First World War fractured existing financial networks; the importance of Vienna as a financial centre declined while that of London, Paris, and New York grew.[8] Nevertheless, there were particular reasons why Hungary should have looked to the City for international finance: one London house, NM Rothschild & Sons, had strong, historic connections with Hungary; the bank was supportive of the new state and was to act as its principal financial agent in the interwar years.[9]

Furthermore, internationalisation of this kind coincided with one of Norman's goals—to re-establish the City as the premier centre for the world's financial and economic systems. In the case of central and eastern Europe, it was highly undesirable that the door should be left wide open for the French or even the Italians to become the dominant commercial power. However, Norman's ambitions were much broader than this. With his cosmopolitan and internationalist background, he developed and held to a vision of central banking whatever the political constraints in Britain or ideological divisions in Europe.[10]

Whatever antipathy Norman harboured against the politics of socialism, in some respects, the foreign-policy objectives of Britain's first Labour

Government were closely aligned to the Governor's aspirations. In early May 1924, Philip Snowden, the Chancellor of the Exchequer, wrote to Norman about the great progress that had been made with the League of Nations scheme for reconstruction in Hungary. With this set of proposals now signed at Geneva, Snowden argued that the time had come when it was necessary to provide credits for the Hungarian government. The Dawes Loan which was being prepared would, it was hoped, modify the objections that were held in parts of the City to aspects of the Hungarian scheme.

But, with the failure to enlist the interest of Wall Street in participating in the loan, it soon became apparent that the whole plan was endangered. Snowden believed the position was critical: he feared for the stability of central Europe and the prestige of the League. But he was also confident that such considerations would weigh heavily in the City—especially the desire to retain the reputation Britain had gained for fostering reconstruction. He wrote again to Norman to 'venture, therefore, as a question of public policy and in what I regard as quite exceptional circumstances, to ask your support and aid'.[11] The following month, under the auspices of the Council of the League, Hungarian assets were released from Reparations liens thereby opening up the way for the stabilisation loan to be issued. The loan was floated by a private banking syndicate led by NM Rothschild & Sons and a little under £8 m was taken up, mostly through London.

With the establishment of economic reconstruction in central Europe, a period of optimism in international relations prevailed in the second half of the 1920s. No one seemed to question, publicly at least, the commonly held view that Hungarian stabilisation had been successful and that it had set the conditions for a return to economic prosperity. Historians, however, have shown how such contemporary views were misguided, if not deluded. Given that persistent structural problems made the servicing of external debt an ever-increasing burden, creditors, in general, do not appear to have acted with high levels of responsibility in their lending policies.[12] Whatever the benefits were of establishing sound money, there was little progress in re-building the Hungarian economy. Whilst the loan may have served the political purpose of bolstering the régime's prestige, much of the money was put to non-productive uses, such as paying amortisation installments on old debts and developing the bureaucracy.[13] Altogether, the League of Nations failed to look at the economic viability of the Hungarian state in the round.[14]

It seems highly unlikely, in any case, that a re-structuring of the Hungarian economy would have been possible before the onset of the Great Depression. As Hungary depended to a large extent on agricultural exports to generate overseas earnings, the condition of the state's finances was bound to deteriorate with the decline in world commodity prices in the course of 1929. In May 1929, Montagu Norman cabled George Harrison, President of the Federal Reserve Bank of New York, to point out that while it would be possible to arrange credits or advances among European Central Banks for Hungary and Germany, the ultimate need was for dollars. Norman maintained that the requirements of the National Bank of Hungary had to be met somehow, and he asked for Harrison's views. Demonstrating either a gift for prescience or a sense of foreboding, Norman concluded, 'Generally the situation appears difficult and I need your personal ideas regarding American and European policies'.[15]

Norman followed this up by despatching Harry Arthur Siepmann, Special Adviser at the Bank of England, to the continent in June 1929. He was given strict instructions: he was told to do his utmost in Paris to reach a reasonable basis for credit with New York and Paris and one other central bank. If successful, he was instructed, when in Munich, to urge Dr. Popovics—President of the National Bank of Hungary—to take up the credit. The Bank of England was prepared to offer an installment on its own account. Norman was very keen that nothing should be done to avoid driving Popovics into the arms of private bankers.[16]

But, even into the summer of 1929, Hungary had indeed continued to arrange loans from foreign banks. In July, Hambros Bank in London issued seven and a half per cent Sterling Land Mortgage Bonds to a total value of £0.5 m on behalf of the City of Budapest Municipal Savings Bank; the Hungarian Commercial Bank of Pest raised £0.3 m, also through London; the Union of Hungarian Credit Associations arranged a credit of $6 m over 14 months, via the New York Trust Company, in order to finance the export of Hungarian agricultural products. But the most important of all the credit arrangements undertaken at this point was the discount of the second installment, amounting to $11,040,000, of the Swedish Match Loan made by NM Rothschild & Sons.[17]

The Bank of England did arrange a small credit, in conjunction with the Banque de France and other participants, to the National Bank in June 1929. But this was advanced on commercial terms—at an interest rate of seven and a half per cent or two per cent above the official discount rate of the participants, whichever was the higher. When Hjalmar Schacht, President of the Reichsbank, found out that the Bank of England had not asked him to join the syndicate or even told him that the credit was being mobilised, he expressed his great dissatisfaction to Siepmann. The excuse offered in response was that the advance had been arranged quickly and quietly because the Hungarians did not want it to be broadcast that they were in need of a credit.[18]

When Siepmann met Popovics again, this time in Karlsruhe in early October, he had become concerned at how the technical dangers of Hungary's position were being increased by the underlying trend of events. In other words, it was clear that the economic difficulties were being exacerbated by political developments. Siepmann then travelled to Paris to meet Béla Imrédy, recently appointed as a Director of the National Bank of Hungary. Taking place in the background were the negotiations for a re-structuring of reparations payments—the Young Plan. Siepmann rejected any notion that the Bank of England would allow itself to be used as an instrument for exerting political pressure on Hungary. On the other hand, Siepmann warned Imrédy that Hungary would be assuming a great responsibility if, instead of being prepared to compromise, the state held fast to old grievances and remained an obstacle to the adoption of the Young Plan. In such circumstances, it was said, the attitude of the Bank of England would not have remained unaffected.[19]

In the course of 1930, NM Rothschild & Sons took the lead in trying to prepare the ground for a long-term Hungarian State Loan. The Governor told Lionel de Rothschild that the needs of stabilisation ranked ahead of all others. But, following the ratification of the Young Plan at the Hague Conference at the beginning of the year, the priority for Norman and the Bank of England was the marketing of the Young bonds and also the setting up of the Bank for International Settlements. Furthermore, the Hungarian government was granted dispensation by the Reparations Commission only after protracted and difficult negotiations. Consequently, whilst Norman was ready to give moral support for any international loan, he advised that French and American participation would be highly desirable. Eventually, in late October 1930, Norman informed the Rothschilds that he saw no reason why they should not go ahead, and a Hungarian State Loan was arranged, but on a much smaller scale than originally envisaged.[20] In early 1931, the Governor thought the Hungarian state should be able to get by with no new money and that proceeding with any new negotiations for short-term loans would be very ill advised.[21]

But the coming of the Financial Crisis in the summer of 1931 caused a caesura in all of the accepted norms and practices of international finance. For the authorities in Britain, and especially for the Bank of England, the crisis threatened to destroy the nascent international structure of central banking which had been so painstakingly built up in the 1920s. The crisis demanded a volte-face in policy and the newly established Bank for International Settlements (BIS) was mobilised to mount emergency support for the Hungarian National Bank; a credit of $5 m was granted on 6 June, with a repayment date of 18 September. This represented an advance for a syndicated short-term credit of $10 m, in which $2 m was extended each by the Bank of England, the Banque de France, and the Federal Reserve Bank, whilst the Banca d'Italia contributed $1 m, and seven other banks participated in the consortium with smaller amounts.[22]

However, as the crisis deepened, it very quickly became evident that the credit was not sufficient. By 26 June, the National Bank of Hungary had lost all of its *Devisen*. It had, as its sole reserve, gold to the value of £4 m, of which £1 m was in the name of BIS. So a second credit was hastily arranged for $11 m; on this occasion the Bank of England, the Federal Reserve and BIS each contributed $3 m, with the Banca d'Italia and the other banks making up the rest of the credit.[23]

As confidence began to collapse, capital flight from central Europe threatened to bring about the destruction of the entire international financial system. This imposed unprecedented institutional demands on central banks and placed those at the head of such institutions under untold personal strain. The Bank of England had, by early July 1931, granted credits amounting to $53,500,000 to maintain the currencies of Germany, Austria, and Hungary. Although, as Norman told Harrison, this was quite as much as was convenient, it was possible that more would be necessary to avoid financial collapse. But, in this context, the Governor attempted to draw a distinction between lending that supported central European governments, especially those with budgetary problems, and a revolving fund which would be used to avoid financial breakdown. To Norman, extending a loan that gave comfort to state authorities was a 'political' act and a question for governments, not central bankers. But although this philosophy continued to underpin Norman's vision, such fine distinctions between politics and finance were rendered nugatory as the international crisis developed in the course of the decade.[24]

Although Montagu Norman realised the extent and nature of Hungary's problems, he was convinced that the National Bank could have done little to avert them. As he told Popovics, the Hungarian central bank continued to deserve, therefore, to be given every confidence and support. But for this to be managed effectively, international co-operation had to be secured—above all through the involvement of the United States. George Harrison, at the Federal Reserve, shared this view but was unable to persuade the private New York bankers of the seriousness of the Hungarian position. This left Norman despondent: he confessed that 'what I fear is that the solution of these difficulties lies, like their origin, beyond the range of Central Banking'.[25]

As the global economic crisis evolved, Norman recognised that whatever the lead taken by the London authorities, the paramount need was for co-ordinated action at the level of international politics. There was little appetite amongst London banks for a new placing of Hungarian Treasury Bonds. But NM Rothschild & Sons would have arranged such an issue if the Bank of England had instructed the bankers to do so: in the carefully mannered world of the City, it would have been sufficient for the Rothschilds to tell their friends that the Governor would have liked to see the operation done. Yet, as much as he might wish circumstances were otherwise, Norman would not countenance further financial assistance to Hungary. The British Foreign Office was also sympathetic to Hungary's plight; the Hungarian minister in London was informed that the Bank of England was aware of this and that the British government would have welcomed any action which the Bank might have found possible to take to relieve the situation. At the same time, it was pointed out that decisions over action rested solely with the Bank: intervention by the government would have been impossible. As Sir Robert Vansittart, Permanent Under-Secretary at the Foreign Office, told Norman, the Hungarian Chargé d'Affaires had been calling but he 'seemed to realise that little was to be hoped from the City'.[26]

Indeed, the City was distracted by other concerns over the summer of 1931. With the crisis in the confidence of international investors focusing on London, capital took flight and Britain was forced to suspend the Gold Standard. The requirement to manage the currency had largely unforeseen consequences: a new equilibrium was established that provided a basis for economic recovery. By way of contrast, the position of Hungary continued to worsen, and the state appeared to be on the edge of bankruptcy. At the end of November 1931, Baron Korányi, the Hungarian Finance Minister, arrived in London with the unwelcome news that his government was about to announce a transfer moratorium—a suspension on payments to international private creditors.

The private bankers were confronted with an unpalatable choice between accepting a forced renewal of their short-term credits—predominantly Hungarian Treasury Bonds—or dealing with the consequences of a Hungarian default. The attempt to negotiate a standstill agreement was led by NM Rothschild & Sons. But the way New York viewed the crisis diverged considerably from the way it was seen in London. By the beginning of 1932, the negotiations had become deadlocked.

In general, all the private bankers felt that the priority given to the League loan and the BIS credit, which had just been renewed, was most unfair. Whilst, for example, the principal and interest on the central bank credit was payable in fine gold or US gold dollars, the private bankers feared that they were likely to get nothing.[27] City bankers believed that it was all the more important, therefore, that immediate steps were taken to arrange an orderly settlement; they warned the Americans that if this proved not to be the case, disastrous results would ensue. Anthony de Rothschild asked the Governor to intercede with Sir Otto Niemeyer, a member of the Financial Committee of the League of Nations, in order to pass on the City's views. Norman agreed to do so, though he did not want to arbitrate between respective claims. But Niemeyer reacted furiously against what he took to be an attack by the Americans on the repayment of League loans. He told one New York bank, Speyer & Co, that 'it would be well to apply judicious cold water' to such ideas. Niemeyer reasoned that any failure to honour obligations under the League loans would fatally undermine what was left of Hungary's credit standing.[28]

The London creditors finally signed a Hungarian Standstill Agreement on 14 March 1932, but, unlike its much bigger German counterpart, it was not an international agreement. Ironically, the 'policy of preference' which discriminated in favour of League loans did not operate in practice because Hungary's shortage of foreign exchange was so acute, not even these obligations could be honoured. In July 1932, the BIS informed the Bank of England that Hungary was unable to repay any part of the $20 m credit to the National Bank. The credit was renewed for a further three months—a pattern which repeated itself throughout the following years.[29]

By the beginning of 1933, the authorities in Britain could begin to hope that the country had weathered the worst of the economic storm. In terms of international politics, however, the consequences of the Depression and Financial Crisis afforded policymakers no grounds for optimism: with Hitler's appointment as Chancellor of Germany, nationalist and extremist ideology was massively bolstered throughout Europe. Abortive attempts to achieve any meaningful international disarmament foreshadowed the failure, in the mid-1930s, to restrain fascist aggression by means of collective security under the auspices of the League of Nations. Similarly, plans to bring about stabilisation collapsed at the World Economic Conference in 1933 and, in the acrimonious aftermath, schisms turned to open breaches and the fracturing of the world economic order.

Given this outlook, what remained of the institutional architecture that gave structure to international finance and payments seemed at least to offer some chance for co-ordinated action. The BIS and central banks had attempted to prevent currency disorders from spreading by giving credit to weaker members. In some cases, these credits were thought to be sound even if, because of national transfer difficulties, there appeared to be little prospect of repayment in the immediate future. The problem was that when such credits became frozen, they formed part of a large volume of short-term indebtedness which blocked the channels of trade. For the Bank of England, nothing was more urgent in the international financial arena than dealing with this indebtedness, as it limited the freedom of movement of central banks in their own markets.

The Bank considered the Hungarian credits to be a desperate case. Siepmann could not think of another country whose entire exports were insufficient to pay the service on its foreign debt. He noted that the Standstill creditors were apparently content to prolong the agreement, which had no effect other than to protect the debtor while the creditor systematically wrote off his asset. This was hardly surprising, since the private investors knew that the National Bank of Hungary owed $25 m. But, in Siepmann's view, continuing along such a path led nowhere: there was a deadlock which he believed could be broken only by the BIS and the central bank creditors.[30]

When, in October 1933, Montagu Norman made one of his regular visits to Basle, for a meeting of the Directors of the BIS, he took with him ideas for a consolidation of the Hungarian Credits. The plan required Hungary to make an initial repayment of nearly $4 m and created National Bank of Hungary Gold Dollar Cash Certificates, with interest set at one per cent.[31] The consolidation was successfully concluded, and Popovics wrote to express his thanks to Norman for his great service to Hungary. In turn, the Governor, cautious as ever, sought and received reassurance from Siepmann that the Bank of England's position was now complete and safe.[32]

However, nothing could be held to be certain in an era when the ideological divisions in Europe were becoming progressively wider and the governing régime in Hungary was growing more authoritarian. The consolidation scheme was designed to run for three years. In early 1935, Siepmann remained convinced that the Bank of England did not have to write down its claim on the National Bank of Hungary to anything less than par: he maintained that the claim was 100 per cent good for valuation purposes. At the same time, he admitted that they did not know the date at which the claim could be realised in full. However, he drew comfort from taking the long view: he reminded the Chief Cashier that, 'Fortunately, Central Banks survive long enough to pay, and to collect, their debts'.[33]

Indeed, it is in this context that the policy of Britain's financial authorities during the 1930s towards states where liberal democracy had been overthrown must be located. In states where government was in the hands of a régime which was politically unsavoury, and the principles of a market economy abandoned, trust continued to be placed in the institutions of central banking. But, depending on a central bank as a guarantor that international financial commitments would be honoured at some indeterminate point in the future rested, in large measure, on investing belief in the individual central banker concerned.[34]

Consequently, when it became apparent in late 1934 that Popovics would have to retire because his health was deteriorating, the Bank of England became anxious over the question of his successor. Governor Norman despatched Siepmann to Budapest to investigate the possibilities. But the Bank did not want to be seen to be interfering. As Norman privately informed Leon Fraser, the BIS President, Siepmann had been instructed to go about his work quietly, unsuspected by anybody and not letting himself be seen more than he could help.[35] Travelling incognito was an act which Norman himself sometimes liked to perform. During his visit, Siepmann saw nothing to reassure him that political or economic conditions in Hungary were improving. On the contrary, what impressed him most were the 'radical faults' with the country, which he believed could not be eradicated. He told his Bank of England colleagues that 'Standards, habits, temperament, tradition combine to produce a state of affairs which does not pass muster, if it is judged as we should judge ourselves'.[36]

In early 1935, under the Gömbös régime, Hungary moved closer still to fascism. Béla Imrédy, who had been Hungary's Finance Minister, succeeded Popovics, in February 1935, as President of the National Bank. But his appointment coincided with a sharp deterioration in Hungary's economic position. Bruce, the BIS Adviser attached to the National Bank, reported that conditions had suddenly become critical and that there was panic because of foreign-exchange shortages; drastic reductions in import allocations were required. In asking for help, the new régime claimed the moral support of the BIS. But no basis for an arrangement could be found and Bruce feared that this meant the end of co-operation and of his usefulness as Adviser.[37] Yet, the Bank of England moved swiftly to try to reassure Budapest that its attitude towards Hungary remained the same as it had been since the 1920s. Siepmann wrote to Imrédy that, 'We have not been able, on this occasion, to find the cash but we hope that this will not lead you to change your mind about us'.[38]

Implicit in this expression of regret is the worry that Hungary would, of necessity, gravitate towards Germany's economic orbit, to the point where it would be impossible to escape. At this stage, however, the Hungarian government continued to look to the West for financial aid. In June 1935, Imrédy visited the London Rothschilds for talks on re-negotiating the Standstill Agreement. He also saw Montagu Norman to discuss in secret a proposal to devalue the Pengö—the Hungarian currency. The National Bank President wanted to know whether London would help with a credit if one were required to facilitate devaluation. Norman was adamant in rejecting such a possibility: foreign creditors would not have been able to justify an increase in their already considerable holdings of assets frozen in Hungary.[39]

One area in which Norman was determined to act was in resolving the problem of the Standstill bills. Acceptances amounting to £3 m had been carried by the market since 1931 and had been taken by the Bank of England only because of what was thought of as the national emergency. By 1936, the Governor considered the time was not far off when they could be eliminated from the market. He suggested that a private word could be given to the Acceptors and the Discount Market, followed up with a warning that the Bank would cease to take the bills. The plan was postponed when it emerged that certain houses would have been seriously affected. Finally, notice was given that the bills would no longer be eligible for discount at the Bank after 15 July 1937.[40]

But, to achieve this, Norman was prepared to mount, in secret, a special operation. In May 1937, the Bank considered whether to advance an unsecured or partly secured credit to the National Bank of Hungary. This could not be justified, of course, on ordinary banking grounds. Rather, it would have been a way to liquefy the Standstill bills and to provide a practical example of central banking co-operation. It might even have opened up possible routes to secure a much bigger prize—a solution of German indebtedness. Sir Otto Niemeyer believed that if the decision was taken to grant a credit, it needed to be taken solely on the grounds of London's interest in ending the Standstill. He advised that they should not seek any security at all, other than the undertaking of the National Bank of Hungary to repay over the agreed period.[41] In the event, however, the operation was unnecessary: an agreement was reached between the London creditors and the Hungarian debtors. On 3 November 1937, Norman was able to report to the Committee of Treasury that the whole amount of Hungarian Standstill bills—to the value of £3,379,000—had been taken off the market.[42]

In the last year or two before the outbreak of the Second World War, any discussion of financial support for Hungary came up against the ideological blockage of a state system that was one step away from establishing a full-blown fascist dictatorship. In May 1938, Cameron Cobbold—a future Governor of the Bank—met Imrédy. Now elevated to the position of Prime Minister, Imrédy apparently hoped very much that England did not regard Hungary as already sold in bondage to Germany and therefore not worth helping, particularly if some small and unobtrusive help could be given for supporting Hungarian exports. Norman was quick to pass on the request, to the Chancellor of the Exchequer, that Hungarian exporters to Britain might be treated with 'especial kindness during the present difficult period'. The Governor argued that both from the point of view of British creditors—who might see more resources devoted to covering the service of Hungary's financial obligations—and on wider grounds, there was much to be said for showing favour to Hungary whenever the opportunity arose. Indeed, as Norman himself told Imrédy, 'I have always taken a very special interest in the National Bank of Hungary'.[43]

Even in the last months of peace, therefore, the Bank of England and its Governor continued to try to find ways to support the Hungarian state. The preferred channel for this purpose was through contact with fellow bankers, especially those associated with the National Bank of Hungary. Imrédy was believed still to be accessible and sensitive to Western European influence. It may well have been the case that no financial expert in interwar Europe had been left completely untouched by Norman's vision for what could be achieved through the agency of central banks. But, however carefully designed, no international financial architecture could have withstood the impact of the ideological extremism in Europe.[44] By 1939, practical ways of making use of any lingering influence Britain might have had over Hungary were severely limited: the flows of international finance followed the political alignments of nations in a world that was soon to be at war.

Notes

1 A version of this study was presented as a paper at "Public Policies & the Direction of Financial Flows"—the Annual Conference of the European Association for Banking and Financial History (EABH) e.V.—Bucharest, Romania, 7th–9th June, 2012. The author gratefully acknowledges EABH's permission to reproduce here parts of that paper.

2 Liaquat Ahamed, *Lords of Finance: 1929, the Great Depression, and the Bankers who Broke the World* (London: Windmill Books, 2010), 464, 487–88.

3 Adam Tooze, *The Deluge: The Great War and the Remaking of Global Order, 1916–1931* (London: Allen Lane, 2014), 517.

4 See, Patricia Clavin, "Defining Transnationalism," *Contemporary European History* 14, no. 4 (2005).

5 Among the literature, see, for example, Charlotte Natmeßnig, "The Establishment of the Anglo-Czechoslovak Bank: Conflicting Interests," in *Universal Banking in the Twentieth Century*, eds. Alice Teichova et al. (Aldershot: Elgar, 1994).

6 Miklós Lojkó, *Meddling in Middle Europe: Britain and the 'Lands Between' 1919–1925* (Budapest: Central European University Press, 2006), 6.

7 Ann Orde, "Baring Brothers, the Bank of England, the British Government and the Czechoslovakian State Loan of 1922," *English Historical Review* CVI 418 (1991): 27–40. See, also, Alice Teichova, *An Economic Background to Munich: International Business and Czechoslovakia 1918–1938* (Cambridge: Cambridge University Press, 1974); Gerald D. Feldman, Carl-Ludwig Holtfrerich, Gerhard

A. Ritter and Peter-Christian Witt (eds.), *Die Erfahrung der Inflation Im Internationalen Zusammenhang und Vergleich* (Berlin: de Gruyter, 1984).

8 Youssef Cassis, *Capitals of Capitalism: A History of International Financial Centres, 1780–2005* (Cambridge: Cambridge University Press, 2006).

9 For a fuller consideration of this, see Neil Forbes, "Family Banking in an Era of Crisis: N.M. Rothschild & Sons and Business in Central and Eastern Europe between the World Wars," *Business History* 55, no. 6 (2013): 963–80.

10 Philip L. Cottrell (ed.), *Rebuilding the Financial System in Central and Eastern Europe, 1918–1994* (Aldershot: Scolar Press, 1997), 62.

11 Bank of England Archive, London (hereafter BoE), G14/108, letters, Snowden to Norman, 7 & 29 May 1924.

12 Derek H. Aldcroft, *Studies in the Interwar European Economy* (Aldershot: Ashgate, 1997); see also by the same author, *Europe's Third World: The European Periphery in the Interwar Years* (Aldershot: Ashgate, 2006).

13 Lojkó, *Meddling*, 130.

14 Pierre L. Siklos, "Interpreting a Change in Monetary Policy Régimes: A Reappraisal of the First Hungarian Hyperinflation and Stabilization, 1921–28," in *Monetary Régimes in Transition*, eds. Michael D. Bordo et al. (Cambridge: Cambridge University Press, 1993), 274–311.

15 BoE G14/108, cablegram, Norman to Harrison, 10 May 1929.

16 BoE G1/306, note, "Instructions given by the Governor to Mr Siepmann on the eve of his journey to Paris and Munich the 11th June 1929."

17 BoE OV33/46, letter, Popovics to Norman, 17 September 1929.

18 Ibid., copy of the Credit Agreement, 29 June 1929; note, "Hungarian Credit," by Siepmann, 9 January 1930.

19 BoE G1/306, "Secret Memo" by Siepmann, 15 October 1929.

20 BoE G14/108, letters, Norman to Lionel de Rothschild, 13 September & 24 October 1930.

21 BoE G14/108, note by Siepmann, 25 March 1931.

22 BoE C40/171, extract from the agenda for the meeting of BIS Board of Directors, 13 July 1931.

23 BoE G14/108, extract from the Minutes of the Committee of Treasury, 26 June 1931; C40/171, letter, GW McGarrah (President, BIS) to Norman, 7 July 1931.

24 BoE G14/108, Extracts from the Minutes of the Committee of Treasury, 8 July 1931; cablegrams, Norman to Harrison, 3 & 4 July 1931.

25 BoE G1/306, letter, Norman to Popovics, 8 July 1931.

26 BoE ibid., note by Siepamnn, 10 July 1931; letters, Norman to Vansittart, 22 July and reply 25 July 1931; copy letter, Sir Orme Sargent to Ladislas de Bárdossy, 18 July 1931.

27 BoE C40/171, note dated 22 December 1931, "Hungarian Credit Renewal Agreement, 18 December 1931."

28 BoE OV33/80, copy of cablegram, 18 January 1932, Hungarian sub-committee (Joint Committee of British Short-Term Creditors) to Goodhue (Chairman, American sub-committee); Memo, 20 January 1932, of meeting between Anthony de Rothschild and Governor; cablegram, 29 January 1932, Niemeyer to James Speyer & Co, New York.

29 BoE G14/108, letter, 2 July 1932, BIS to Chief Cashier, Bank of England.

30 BoE G1/306, Memo by Siepmann, 2 March 1933, "Central Bank Credits to Hungary."

31 BoE C40/171, note, 12 October 1933, by Siepmann, on meeting in Basle on 8 October 1933; also note, 2 November 1933, by Chief Cashier's Office.

32 BoE G1/306, letter, 17 November 1933, Popovics to Norman.

33 BoE C40/171, note, 19 February 1935, by Siepmann for Peppiatt.

34 P. Geddes, *Inside the Bank of England* (London: Boxtree, 1987), 61; P.L. Cottrell, "The Bank of England in its International Setting, 1918–1972," in *The Bank of England. Money, Power, and Influence, 1694–1994*, eds. Richard Roberts et al. (Oxford: Clarendon Press, 1995), 95; Neil Forbes, *Doing Business with the Nazis: Britain's Economic and Financial Relations with Germany, 1931–1939* (London: Frank Cass, 2000), 192.
35 BoE G1/306, letter, 16 November 1934, Norman to Fraser.
36 BoE G14/108, "Report on Hungary, November 1934." The report, dated 3 December 1934, is anonymous but is assumed to be by Siepmann.
37 BoE G14/108, "Confidential Note," 25 February 1935, of Hungarian Proposal, 21–22 February 1935.
38 Ibid., letter, 23 February 1935, Siepmann to Imrédy.
39 BoE G1/306, "Secret Note," 7 June 1935, by Cobbold, of Imrédy's visit, 5–7 June 1935.
40 BoE G14/108, Extracts from the Minutes of the Committee of Treasury, dated 26 February 1936, 17 June 1936, 18 November 1936.
41 BoE C40/171, "Secret Memo," 11 May 1937, by Siepmann for Norman and Cobbold; note, 18 May 1937, by Niemeyer for Norman.
42 BoE G14/108, Extracts from the Minutes of the Committee of Treasury.
43 BoE G1/306, note, 13 May 1938, by Cobbold for Governor, of meeting with Imrédy, 10 May 1938; letter, 19 May 1938, Norman to Sir John Simon; G14/108, letter, 10 August 1938, Norman to Imrédy.
44 Albrecht Ritschl and Tobias Straumann, "Business Cycles and Economic Policy, 1914–1945," in *The Cambridge Economic History of Modern Europe, 2: 1870 to the Present*, eds. Stephen Broadberry et al. (Cambridge: Cambridge University Press, 2010), 180.

Bibliography

Ahamed, Liaquat. *Lords of Finance: 1929, the Great Depression, and the Bankers Who Broke the World*. London: Windmill Books, 2010.
Aldcroft, Derek H. *Europe's Third World: The European Periphery in the Interwar Years*. Aldershot: Ashgate, 2006.
———. *Studies in the Interwar European Economy*. Aldershot: Ashgate, 1997.
Cassis, Youssef. *Capitals of Capitalism: A History of International Financial Centres, 1780–2005*. Cambridge: Cambridge University Press, 2006.
Charlotte, Natmeßnig. "The Establishment of the Anglo-Czechoslovak Bank: Conflicting Interests." In *Universal Banking in the Twentieth Century*, edited by Alice Teichova, Terry Gourvish and Agnes Pogány, 96–115. Aldershot: Elgar, 1994.
Clavin, Patricia. "Defining Transnationalism." *Contemporary European History* 14, 4 (2005): 421–39.
Cottrell, Philip L., ed. *Rebuilding the Financial System in Central and Eastern Europe, 1918–1994*. Aldershot: Scolar Press, 1997.
———. "The Bank of England in Its International Setting, 1918–1972." In *The Bank of England: Money, Power, and Influence, 1694–1994*, edited by Richard Roberts and David Kynaston, 83–139. Oxford: Clarendon Press, 1995.
Feldman, Gerald D., Carl-Ludwig Holtfrerich, Gerhard A. Ritter, and Peter-Christian Witt, eds. *Die Erfahrung der Inflation Im Internationalen Zusammenhang und Vergleich*. Berlin: de Gruyter, 1984.

Forbes, Neil. "Family Banking in an Era of Crisis: N.M. Rothschild & Sons and Business in Central and Eastern Europe between the World Wars." *Business History* 55, 6 (2013): 963–80.

———. *Doing Business with the Nazis: Britain's Economic and Financial Relations with Germany, 1931–1939*. London: Frank Cass, 2000.

Geddes, P. *Inside the Bank of England*. London: Boxtree, 1987.

Lojkó, Miklós. *Meddling in Middle Europe: Britain and the 'Lands Between' 1919–1925*. Budapest: Central European University Press, 2006.

Orde, Ann. "Baring Brothers, the Bank of England, the British Government and the Czechoslovakian State Loan of 1922." *English Historical Review* CVI 418 (1991): 27–40.

Ritschl, Albrecht and Tobias Straumann. "Business Cycles and Economic Policy, 1914–1945." In *The Cambridge Economic History of Modern Europe, 2: 1870 to the Present*, edited by Stephen Broadberry and Kevin H. O'Rourke, 156–80. Cambridge: Cambridge University Press, 2010.

Siklos, Pierre L. "Interpreting a Change in Monetary Policy Régimes: A Reappraisal of the First Hungarian Hyperinflation and Stabilization, 1921–28." In *Monetary Régimes in Transition*, edited by Michael D. Bordo and Forrest Capie, 274–311. Cambridge: Cambridge University Press, 1993.

Teichova, Alice. *An Economic Background to Munich: International Business and Czechoslovakia 1918–1938*. Cambridge: Cambridge University Press, 1974.

Tooze, Adam. *The Deluge: The Great War and the Remaking of Global Order, 1916–1931*. London: Allen Lane, 2014.

11 Weimar's Capitalist Spring

A Liberal Exception to Corporate Germany's *Sonderweg*[1]

Leslie Hannah

One little-noticed result of Weimar liberalisation was a massive increase in corporate numbers in post-Versailles Germany, which more than compensated for the transfer of 10% of its corporations to France and Poland. Guinnane et al. (2008) have argued that Germany's corporate law was already superior, particularly for SMEs, before 1914.[2] Both longitudinal and international cross-section comparisons of the numbers of corporations suggest that, on the contrary, law and politics in both the Kaiserreich and the Third Reich were spectacularly unconducive to incorporation, even with the addition of GmbHs to its menu of corporate forms. What was required for the development of Schumpeterian creative destruction and competitive diversity in limited liability companies was a liberal and open economic order, as Weimar Germany briefly—and the later *Wirtschaftswunder* more sustainably—demonstrated. Germany's smaller neighbours for long felt no need to copy the GmbH form, because they had open political and economic orders and more flexibility in their basic corporate forms. This analysis supports those who see civil law as no barrier to successful corporate development if accompanied by a liberal order and those who argue for continuity between Weimar and post-1945 Germany.

Imperial Germany, like many other industrialised countries, had moved away from the individual concession system for chartering business corporations. From 1870/1, companies could be formed by registration (as long permitted in the *Handelsregister* for partnerships), relatively simply and cheaply. However, nervousness about corporate fraud and defaults in the *Gründerboom* led in 1884 to a tightening up of the rules for *Aktiengesellschaften* (AGs, which is something close to the English public company). This may have helped stabilise widely held companies quoted on stock exchanges but was inappropriate for small and medium-sized AGs without traded shares. In 1892, therefore, a more flexible and less regulated corporate form was created for unquoted enterprises: the *Gesellschaft mit beschränkter Haftung* (GmbH, something close to the private company in England).[3] Guinnane et al[4] hail the German menu of organisational forms that resulted, which also had long included *Kommanditgesellschaften* (KGs or limited partnerships),[5] as superior to that of the US. The German menu, they argue, allowed a better choice between the needs to protect minority interests (easier in KGs and other partnerships) and the need to lock in capital for the longer term (easier in AGs), with the GmbH offering better compromises as a hybrid. Their reinterpretation called into question the view of La Porta et al.[6] that common law jurisdictions were more conducive to modern business development than German (or French) civil law jurisdictions, a critique that was widely shared by business historians sceptical that laws had the decisive impact alleged by La Porta and his World Bank research teams.[7]

The argument advanced here is that incorporation in Germany nonetheless remained rather restricted compared not only with common law countries such as England and the US, but also with many neighbouring civil law countries. Whatever merits the German organisational menu had, in principle, German businessmen were, in practice, surprisingly loth to savour its delights. Yet wartime defeat had a spectacularly liberalising effect. In the early years of the Weimar Republic, there was a massively expanded embrace of corporate forms (both GmbHs and AGs). However, this petered out in the depression and under Nazi rule. Indeed, after the Weimar spring, Germany is the *only* large non-communist industrialised country to have systematically and consistently *reduced* its corporate numbers *over more than two decades*.[8] Such extraordinary trends do not sit well with the view that the organisational menu concocted by German legislators was especially attractive. Instead, they suggest that—irrespective of the state of corporate law—corporations prosper in an atmosphere of liberalism and openness—such as early Weimar or Germany's post-war *Wirtschaftswunder*—an interpretation consistent with the analysis based on wider samples advanced by Rajan and Zingales,[9] Foreman-Peck and Hannah,[10] and Hannah and Kasuya.[11]

German Corporate Development

In the early twentieth century, common law countries had a distinctive lead over most civil law countries in the use of the classic corporate form. Indeed, in 1910, four of the world's wealthiest countries, all in the "Anglosphere" and with largely common law systems[12]—the US, the UK, Canada and Australia—together accounted for more than three-quarters of all corporations in the world.[13] In evaluating the use of the various corporate forms, it is therefore useful to abstract from any legal—or national wealth and income—advantages which might have privileged corporate development in these "Anglo-Saxon" countries. I thus confine comparisons initially to the statistics for civil law countries with some geographical proximity and/or living standards similar to Germany's (about two-thirds of the "Anglo-Saxon" level).

Table 11.1 compares levels of corporate development for 1910 and 1937, evaluating the situation before the two world wars and post-war settlements

Table 11.1 Corporatisation: Germany and Its Neighbours, 1910 and 1937.

Country (date of "GmbH-style" legislation in brackets)	Corporations per million population		Corporate stock values at par/ GDP % (figures in brackets at market)	
	1910	1937	1910	1937
Austria (1906)	70	336	26	17
Belgium (1935)	561	n/a	80 (104)	29*
Czechoslovakia (1920)	102†	214	30†	15
Denmark	998	1904	42 (45)	29
Finland	850	3616	41	29
France (1925)	306	1192	51 (76)	–
Germany (1892)	403	507	44 (71)**	27**
Hungary (1930)	134	347	34 (54)	34
Latvia	30†	187	33†	
Lithuania	30†	59	33†	
Netherlands (1971)	1262	948	85 (149)	20
Norway (1997)	2117	3685	49 (61)	35 (42)
Poland (1919)	154†	137	34†	
Russia (1922‡)	10	0	33	0
Spain (1919)ᵃ	106	199	27 (52)	39
Sweden (1995)	1055	1742	66	
Switzerland (1937)	1060	4678	75 (127)	80
European Average[1]				
Mean	477			
Median	251			
World Average[2]				
Mean	328			
Median	61			

Sources: for 1910 Hannah, "Global Census."; for 1937. unpublished paper, mainly based on *Statistisches Jahrbuch 1938* data.

* The *Statistisches Jahrbuch figure* for 1937 is based on Brussels-quoted companies only and is not comparable to the 1910 data.

** Hoffmann (1965, pp. 503, 508) reports a very similar share of profits in German corporations.

† Some countries did not exist in 1910: for Czechoslovakia, the reported figure is the mean of Austria and Hungary, and for Poland, the mean of Russia, Austria, Hungary and Germany. For Latvia and Lithuania, I have assumed that their level of corporatisation in 1910 was three times Russia's (for a justification for Latvia, compare the data in Meyer (*Latvia's*, p. 127) with that for Russia in Hannah's online statistical appendix 2 to "Global census").

‡ The new Soviet code of 1922, which replaced the liberal corporate law of the (pre-Bolshevik) 1917 revolution, allowed in article 138 a restricted form with multiple liabilities and state supervision, but private users effectively disappeared after Lenin's NEP was abandoned.

ᵃ The 1885 Commercial Code left open the possibility of SRLs (Spain's equivalent of SARLS), but few were formed before the category was separated in clause 108 of revised commercial register regulations in 1919, and precise terms were not statutorily specified until 1953 (T Guinnane and S M Rodriguez, "Choice of Enterprise Form: Spain, 1886–1936," *Yale Economic Growth Center discussion paper no 1049*, 2015.

[1] Including the countries in the table (except those with an asterisk), plus the UK, Bulgaria and Romania.

[2] Including 83 countries in 1910 (as in Hannah, "Global Census").

whose destructiveness and exploitative occupation controls handicapped enterprise throughout Europe. These dates are also likely to show any beneficial effects of the introduction of the allegedly advantageous "hybrid" form of the private limited company[14]—the GmbH (in Germany from 1892) and the SARL (in France from 1926)—while countries which made this innovation later might be expected to reflect the disadvantages of delayed adoption. In fact, the only countries featured in Table 11.1 which had legislated for that form well before the second relevant date (1937) were Austria (leading to similar post-war adaptations in Hapsburg offshoots: Poland, Hungary and Czechoslovakia) and Spain. The changes in Belgium and Switzerland only slightly pre-dated the 1937 data point. It appears from the table that introducing GmbH-equivalent forms was not particularly advantageous—at least by the crude measure of take-up compared with countries that lacked the form—anywhere.[15]

Growth in corporate numbers was generally maintained, decade by decade, in most countries, and a more complex reality is seriously obscured in Table 11.1 only in the German case. The shift to increased incorporation in the liberal, creative, competitive and inflationary atmosphere of early Weimar Germany is absent from the table. The territorial transfers of the 1919 Versailles settlement shifted to France and Poland nearly 10% of Germany's corporations (by numbers and capital values), but, with new foundations, the extant numbers increased by more than eight times those lost over just three years to 1922.[16] This remarkable efflorescence of corporate enterprise occurred during what is generally characterised as a period of confidence-sapping financial ruin and existential uncertainty for many bourgeois families. Political accounts of Weimar focus on big business and bankers, jointly with the social democrats, attempting to forge a viable new social and political order on corporatist lines,[17] which included the first moves to requiring worker directors on the supervisory boards of AGs.[18] Some among the German managerial and banker class—demonstrating a self-interested rapacity rivalling that of more recent exponents—also used the cover of economic disruption, inflation and the *Ueberfremdung* (foreign takeover) scare to renounce bond obligations and deprive small shareholders of pre-emption rights and reduce their voting rights, while generously lining their own pockets, in many quoted corporations.[19]

For the rank-and-file bourgeoisie, the imperatives of these years were also starkly personal and financial: the values of their bank accounts and bond holdings had been destroyed by inflation. Still rich in human capital (and with some real assets in shares and housing preserved), those who survived wartime and post-war horrors urgently understood the need to remake their lives and fortunes in a new Germany and for many that meant founding a business. All forms of new enterprise (not just corporations) proliferated on the *Handelsregister*—despite disruptive inflation, the occupation of the Ruhr by Belgian and French troops and Germany's loss (from victors' expropriations, accentuated by political and economic disruptions) of people, stable markets, patents and transportation assets. AGs and GmbHs with limited liability had the advantage in these desperately uncertain times that any remaining family assets could be shielded from further depredations if the business failed (as a high proportion did).

There were now few constraints on pursuing such objectives. Hyperinflation negated the minimum size constraint on GmbHs, not to speak of straining *Handelsregister* capacity for accurate recording (higher figures were initially reported but corrected in later editions of the *Statistisches Jahrbuch*). The year 1923 marked a high point of corporatisation, with more IPOs on Berlin than at any other time between 1875 and 1935[20] and many more off-exchange foundations. At the end of 1923, there were 16,262 AGs (three times the 1919 level) and 71,343 GmbHs (more than double the 1919 level). This took the total stock to 87,705 corporations, or 1,424 per million people.[21] This rich country norm—that Germany had fallen well short of in the pre-war years (Table 11.1)—was attained without any major legislative change or income increase, but during a period when Germany could even more clearly stake a claim to being an open access political and economic order than before the war.[22] However, as Reckendrees has speculated,[23] this was arguably a rare case: an open access order—of the kind praised in the new institutional economics—that actually failed, a misfortune he traces to lack of legitimacy stemming from failed coordination, so that authoritarians could claim to offer better prospects.

It was in this period also that the German corporatist consensus began to be forged, replacing an earlier and different German consensus (that shareholder value was paramount) with the view that quoted corporations had to recognise a broader public purpose and responsibility to other stakeholders.[24] This was advocated in multiple published works by Walther Rathenau, the ex-head of AEG and Jewish minister assassinated by rightists in 1922, whose ideas, paradoxically, were taken up by both Weimar and later Nazi legislators. In the Nazi period, after a decade in which many new Weimar corporations were forced into liquidation or simply ceased to operate, the promiscuous Weimar corporate foundations were sternly castigated as "unhealthy."[25] Yet they were arguably no more so than those founded in other countries or, with less casually lamentable outcomes, still waiting to be founded in Germany's celebrated 1950s *Wirtschaftswunder*. What differentiated the later *Bundesrepublik* from Weimar was not such planting of the microeconomic roots of a disciplined, pluralist capitalism, manifested in corporate multiplication and creative destruction, but their more effective post-1945 fertilisation by support for Germany's macroeconomic stability and state legitimacy than the Dawes plan had earlier offered to the 1920s recovery.

In the harsher climate of its earlier currency stabilisation, Germany from May 1924 experienced something unprecedented outside the communist world: for many years, its scant foundations of new AGs and GmbHs were numerically overwhelmed by corporate disappearances, so that its stock of corporations consistently declined over more than two decades.[26] This partly followed from the chill of a restored M20,000 minimum size (following stabilisation on the new Reichsmark at the pre-war gold parity), though existing companies below that size in real terms were allowed to continue.[27] The depression killed more companies and destroyed faith in the post-war polity. Thus, in 1933, it took only six months for Hitler to rub out Weimar multi-party democracy, but a little longer to re-arm, hamstring capitalism, occupy and economically plunder most of Europe and systematically murder millions. Some Nazis argued that good "Aryan" entrepreneurs should not hide behind an artificial corporate entity and wanted to abolish the GmbH and restrict AGs, but Schacht (the Reichsbank president) and others successfully made the case for caution against such radicalism. Although some writers treat Nazi economic planning as indistinguishable from Stalin's, the Nazis refrained from nationalising industries (with a few exceptions, such as Junker and the Reichswerke Herman Goering) and actually privatised some companies that had earlier required state rescue (for example, in 1936/7 the major banks and Vereinigte Stahlwerke). Nazi policy was not, of course, derived from respect for private property as a human right, but from the strong belief of many Nazi leaders, the military and bureaucrats in the efficiency of private contracting even if mainly under state (rather than free market) direction.[28] Many Nazis considered shareholders (and, *a fortiori*, Jewish owners) as unnecessary or undesirable.[29] Yet this curious Nazi ambivalence about key institutions of capitalism (or arbitrary imprisonment of the Aryan hotelier whose property rights offended Hitler's view of Berchtesgaden) was not incompatible with a firm commitment to private enterprise—and particularly government contracting under the institution of private law with creative, profit-making entrepreneurs efficiently producing armaments and ersatz materials—as the preferred instrument of economic mobilisation.

Thus, while there was much hot air opposing the corporate form (and much invective about destroying English/Jewish capitalism), the new 1937 corporate laws merely required AGs to have at least RM500,000 capital, encouraged existing corporations to convert to partnerships and strengthened the rhetorically favoured (if largely economically empty) "Führerprinzip," increasing managerial (and correspondingly reducing shareholder) prerogatives.[30] The already restored proscription of new GmbH foundations below RM20,000, the bankruptcy or deregistration of many earlier companies and the expropriation or abandonment of many Jewish firms, combined with severe economic depression and Nazi military imperatives, further contributed to the more than halving of the number of corporations between 1923 and 1937, to a level *below that of 1919* in terms of both numbers and capital.[31] The prolonged and massive decline from the post-war peak—shared by both public (AG) and private (GmbH) companies—was as exceptional as the early Weimar rise, with few parallels in other (non-communist) large economies for which we have data.[32] The decline of the corporation further

continued during wartime. Of course, wartime industrial concentration policies (designed to release workers for combat and armaments production)
temporarily restricted the number of operating small enterprises (including
corporations) in many countries, but Germany's elimination of corporations
was more than ordinarily extensive.[33] With minor blips during depression
or wartime defeat, other major authoritarian economies—like Italy and
Japan—experienced continued growth in corporate numbers in the 1930s
and the 1940s, as did democratic, free-market economies.[34]

Germany's Neighbours: Slow Adopters?

Germany's curious *Sonderweg* in corporate matters thus—after the unchar-
acteristic Weimar interval—long remained resistant to the supposed attractions of its corporate organisational menu, praised by Guinnane et al.
Moreover, other civil law countries in Table 11.1 where the penetration
of the corporate form was even *lower* than in Germany are other GmbH
adopters plus Russia (which abolished the capitalist corporation in December 1919, tolerated the constrained private forms permitted under its 1922
legal code during Lenin's NEP, before again eliminating it under "socialism in one country"). All these slow adopters were relatively backward
in terms of living standards and/or liberal-democratic credentials, so such
comparisons may not be a good test of the inherent attractions of introducing Guinnane et al.'s "new" hybrid GmbH-style organisational option.
For example, the Austrian GmbH introduced in 1906 liberalised a much
tougher administrative and tax regime even than Germany's, yet its terms,
other than a lower size limit, remained quite illiberal.[35] Nonetheless, and
despite the removal of its economic hinterland by the 1920 dismemberment
of the Hapsburg Empire, Austria escaped Germany's marked interwar corporate reversal and so was nearer to Germany's level of corporatization
just before the *Anschluss*: the full impact of introducing GmbHs was more
evident (allowing for Austria's reduced population) by 1937 than in 1910.[36]

What other factors might have driven the large divergences in Table 11.1
that cannot be explained by the GmbH size restriction? German registration and notarial fees were relatively high, though it is difficult to believe
that even small firms would have begrudged a few hundred marks for the
advantages of GmbHs extolled by Guinnane et al., especially as similar fees
applied to attaining only partially limited liability in KGs (limited partnerships). Many GmbH owners were less interested in the "hybrid" governance advantages stressed by the revisionists than in full managerial limited
liability (relative to KGs, where managing partners had full personal liability) or accounts secrecy (relative to AGs, which had to publish accounts).[37]
The small northwest European countries—who with only the AG (or NV/
AS etc.) form created more corporations per capita—possibly faced richer
economic opportunities than Germany,[38] and their small domestic markets
were arguably only a modest constraint on corporate size, for their firms

also enjoyed relatively unimpeded access to larger open markets.[39] Perhaps their businesspersons were also more inherently commercial and entrepreneurial and their banks and trade creditors more familiar and comfortable with limited liability entities, conditioned by earlier more liberal commercial practice.[40] It may have been such historical and cultural factors that stimulated their lead, not primarily that their corporate laws were (even after 1892) still significantly more accommodating to the needs of SMEs than Germany's.

Moreover, the once-independent parts of the federal *Kaiserreich* that most resembled the smaller countries of northwest Europe—the three "free" Hanseatic states—had early argued for a more liberal regime than Prussia's[41] and registered proportionately more corporations than the rest of Germany, though all were constrained by the same Reich legislation.[42] It was perhaps a combination of the continuing weight of Prussian caution on incorporation and fear of financial instability,[43] residual conservative Berlin bankers' distrust of limited liability SMEs[44] and the high minimum size specified throughout the Reich for GmbHs, not primarily the law's governance provisions, that earlier held back Germany's corporatisation. As we have noted,[45] when such forces were in retreat—in the more frenetically liberal pressure-cooker atmosphere of early 1920s Weimar—there was an efflorescence of corporate formations, which (temporarily) propelled Germany's corporatisation above the pre-war levels of some of its neighbours in per capita terms, even without any relevant change in corporate law. This shortfall appears to have deep historical roots. Even before Germany's 1884 tightening of its AG law, the Reich already lagged its neighbours, especially in incorporating SMEs, and this was also discernible in Prussian data before 1870.[46]

Within civil law frameworks, Norway, Switzerland and the Netherlands had also *not* tightened up their—already on some dimensions more liberal—AG (NV) laws,[47] and initially saw absolutely no need for GmbHs.[48] Yet in 1910, even without this (supposedly superior) form, they had, respectively, 2,117, 1,062 and 1,262 AGs (NVs/ASs) per million population, several times the figure for GmbHs, AGs and *Gewerkschaften combined* in Germany (Table 11.1).[49] Germany's neighbours at this time could be forgiven for seeing the GmbH as an imperfect substitute for the flexible civil law that their corporations *already* enjoyed. On many dimensions they, quite justifiably, did not see that the new form "in all countries allowed firms to do things that neither a partnership nor a corporation could do."[50] Although many countries, including the Netherlands and Sweden, insisted on shareholders having the right to remove directors, entrenching them for as long as five (Sweden) or six (Belgium) years was permissible and judicious use of share distributions and voting rules (though problematic in the Netherlands, given its statutory cap on large shareholder votes)[51] could often in practice extend that.[52] Sweden was restrictive on several other issues,[43] while Denmark was almost as free as Norway. Even Sweden allowed close companies to control share transmission (for example, limiting sales to existing holders or new ones approved by the board), provided only that the share certificates specified such terms. Critically, a major factor driving German businesspersons from the AG to the GmbH form—the AG's stringent accounts publication requirements—simply did not apply to AG equivalents in many civil law countries.[54]

The argument that such freedoms simply made the GmbH unnecessary was even made in France,[55] though two pieces of evidence (in addition to France's lower 1910 number of corporations than Germany in Table 11.1) suggest caution in extending the point that far. First, when France did introduce the SARL in 1925 (partly in response to the existence of GmbHs in annexed—formerly German—Alsace-Lorraine), within a year they outnumbered new SA registrations, and, indeed (as Table 11.1 suggests) France then soon overtook *all* corporate forms in a Germany which remained less appreciative than its—initially reluctant—pupil of the form.[56] It is true that the French corporate law of 1867 (as mildly modified in 1893 and 1902) already before 1925 permitted French *sociétés par actions* private company characteristics like accounting secrecy, share transfer restrictions and even Norwegian-style entrenched directorships that were barred to German AGs,[57] but those using all such loopholes were probably a minority. In 1910–13, for example, 53% of the 6,726 new French SA registrations, accounting for 82% of their total capital, were "public" (in the sense they were required to conform to more stringent publicity requirements).[58] The flow of such "public" companies in those years was several times the accumulated *stock* of all companies then listed on French stock exchanges, so it is clear that most of them were actually not very "public": they were traded informally (off the bourses) or not at all. Yet this classification implies they could not as freely avoid some onerous public requirements as did private companies in other countries. French SA governance rules were also compromised by uncertainties about which provisions entrenched in their charters could be changed and on what terms, until the position was clarified by legislation in 1913.[59] Nonetheless, many French companies were *de facto* able to achieve outcomes similar to those in more liberal civil law countries.[60]

Conclusion

The new institutional economics emphasises that open access economic and political orders are mutually reinforcing and key to understanding the sources of prosperity in modern economies.[61] In many respects, pre-1914 Germany approximated such an open order and enjoyed its growing prosperity, but both in authoritarian control of foreign and defence policy by the Kaiser and in some aspects of its restrictive incorporation policy, it fell short of many of its neighbours. It is argued by some that Britain's decision to support France and Russia in 1914 was justified by the outcome: deposition of the Kaiser and reversal of (and punishment for) Germany's breach of Belgian neutrality. Those making such calculations in 1914 on both sides were, of course, not obviously concerned about the consequences for open access economic orders, but most assessments of the actual consequences of the war for capitalist economies and liberal orders are negative. They emphasise the destruction of markets and private ownership by Soviet communism, and, even in countries more fortunate, an increased role of the state and wider parliamentary franchises (which further entrenched state interventions): both stimulated by total war and its inevitably illiberal features. The analysis here suggests that more liberal consequences—more usually celebrated in Weimar's artistic and design achievements than in the institutions of capitalism—also sometimes followed defeat and the recasting of bourgeois Europe. That Weimar's capitalist spring was reversed by the unfortunate failure of (mainly American) capital flows consistently to support recovery[62]—and, more deliberately, by Nazism—should not blind us to the similarities between early Weimar capitalism and more successful versions. The modern capitalist order later developed in Erhardt's *Wirtschafts-wunder* also saw corporate proliferation, but was based on more determined rooting out of illiberalism and more effective international macroeconomic support. Neither the Weimar spring, nor the post-war *Wirtschaftswunder*, required a change in corporate law, reinforcing the view that it was not legal family which fundamentally determined the degree of corporatisation, but the support of an open and liberal political order.[63] More generally, this analysis supports those—like Paqué, Eichengreen and Ritschl[64]—who doubt the Olsonian view of post-war German recovery based on destruction of sclerotic institutions and see significant continuities between Weimar and the *Wirtschaftswunder*. Germans were initially (and to a mild extent still remain) resistant to the corporate form, but, given the right conditions, German businesses became—like ordinary capitalists everywhere—increasingly inclined to incorporate.

Notes

1 Thanks to Carsten Burhop, Timothy Guinnane, Sibylle Lehmann-Hasemeyer, Chris Kobrak and participants in this volume's pre-conference and editors for helpful discussion of the issues. The usual disclaimers apply.
2 "Pouvoir et propriété dans l'entreprise: pour une histoire internationale des societies à responsabilité limitée," *Annales* 63, 1 (2008): 73–110.
3 Literal translation of AG (joint-stock company) and GmbH (limited liability company) is unhelpful since both had stocks (though, technically, called *Anlei-hen* or quotas in GmbHs) *and* limited liability. Private companies, in the sense of those closely held by few shareholders and not publicly tradable, were already well established in the UK, though not given formal legal definition until 1907, when they were defined as those having no more than 50 shareholders, not publicly traded and not required to publish balance sheets. German GmbHs were similar, but there was no restriction on numbers of shareholders. I use the terms corporations and company (both used in American and British English, but with the former predominating in the US) interchangeably, except where the

context makes clear that I am using company (like *Gesellschaft, vennootschap* or *société*) in the broader sense to include non-corporate forms such as limited partnerships (KGs, CVs, SCs) or all firms. American English lacks the distinction made in European laws between the public (AG, NV, SA etc.) and private (GmbH, BV, SARL etc.) corporate forms, though the legally unrecognised term "close corporation" is roughly equivalent to private company in British English. In all cases these should be considered very rough—sometimes utterly misleading—translations. As the exposition below stresses, a German AG, Swiss AG, Dutch NV and British public company were historically very different in their four independent legal systems, especially before recent EU harmonisations.

4 T.W. Guinnane, R. Harris, N. Lamoreaux and J.-L. Rosenthal, "Putting the Corporation in its Place," *Enterprise and Society* 8 (September 2007): 687–729; Ibid., "Pouvoir et propriété dans l'entreprise: pour une histoire internationale des societes à responsabilité limitée," *Annales* 63, 1 (2008): 73–110. While I define corporations as including GmbHs and AGs in what follows, they see the GmbH as a hybrid rather than pure corporate form.

5 In KGs, general partners had unlimited liability, while sleeping partners had limited liability.

6 R. La Porta, F. Lopes-de-Silanes and A. Shleifer, "The Economic Consequences of Legal Origins," *Journal of Economic Literature* 46, 2 (June 2008): 285–332.

7 For a summary, see A. Musacchio and J.D. Turner, "Does the Law and Finance Hypothesis Pass the Test of History?" *Business History* 55, 4 (June 2013): 524–42.

8 The nearest contemporary parallels were in smaller interwar eastern European nationalist dictatorships.

9 R.G. Rajan and L. Zingales, "The Great Reversals: The Politics of Financial Development in the Twentieth Century," *Journal of Financial Economics* 69 (2003): 5–50.

10 J. Foreman-Peck and L. Hannah, "The Diffusion and Impact of the Corporation," forthcoming, *Economic History Review*, 68, 3 (2015): 962–984.

11 L. Hannah and M. Kasuya, "Twentieth Century Enterprise Forms: Japan in Comparative Perspective," *Enterprise and Society*, 17, 1 (2016): 80–115.

12 (Civil Law) Louisiana, Quebec and Scotland were the exceptions.

13 L. Hannah, "A Global Corporate Census: Publicly-Traded and Close Companies in 1910," *Economic History Review* 68, 2 (May 2015): 548–73.

14 I do not use their abbreviation for the private limited liability company—"PLLC"—since that is not a recognised legal abbreviation anywhere and is equally suited to (and confusingly reminiscent of) its opposite (officially sanctioned) abbreviation, the "PLC" or *public* limited (liability) company in some jurisdictions today. It seems equally unhelpful to refer to the distinctive form as an "LLC"—as do some English writers (directly translating the original German designation of the GmbH)—since other corporate forms (notably the AG) also had limited liability.

15 I am grateful to Tim Guinnane and Naomi Lamoreaux for pointing out that these comparative statistics omit some limited liability forms, notably KGs (limited partnerships), which may bias the result. KGs clearly fulfil some, but not all, the functions of corporations (and differentially in different countries). Although there is less data on them, such data as we have from intermittent censuses and registration flows suggest there would be few—and only modest—changes in rank among civil law countries as a result of including them (though, for example, France might rank higher than Germany in 1910 as well as 1937) and that some common law jurisdictions also had numerous limited partnerships.

16 Capital values increased by more but are meaningless, given inflationary distortions.

17 C.S. Maier, *Recasting Bourgeois Europe* (Princeton, NJ: Princeton University Press, 1975).

18 Though the one or two required were easily sidelined in large supervisory boards.

19 Holtfrerich, *Great Inflation*; A.B. Levy, *Private Corporations and their Control*, 1950, 168–76; Neumann, *Behemoth*, 233–36; M. Fiedler, "Business Scandals in the Weimar Republic," *European Yearbook of Business History* 2 (1999): 155–78.

20 C. Burhop, D. Chambers and B. Cheffins, "Law, Politics and the Rise and Fall of German Stock Market Development, 1870–1938," University of Cambridge Legal Studies Research paper no 4/2015, February 2015, 11.

21 AGs and GmbHs combined, but without adding *bergrechtliche Gewerkschaften*.

22 The major early Weimar change in the AG law was a new requirement to appoint one or two employee members to the supervisory board in certain companies, an early move towards the co-determination more widely mandated after the Second World War. This probably made the AG form less palatable to capitalists, though in fact it was easy to swamp employee members in large supervisory boards.

23 Alfred Reckendrees, "Weimar Germany: The First Open Access Order that Failed?" *Freiburger Diskussionspapiere zur Ordnungsökonomik*, 14 May 2014. His article focuses on political and legal issues and ignores 1920s corporate formations, though he recognises Germany's pre-war numerical backwardness (relative to the US/UK) in corporate formations, despite freedom of corporate registration.

24 Philipp Klages, "The Contractual Turn: How Legal Experts Shaped Corporate Governance Reforms in Germany," *Socio-Economic Review* 11, 1 (2013): 159–84 (at p. 168), who sees the recent move towards reasserting shareholder value principles in Germany as a return to the nineteenth-century German norm. See also Burhop et al., "Law."

25 "ungesunden," Statistisches Reichsamt, "Die Gesellschaften mit Beschränkter Haftung am 31 Dezember 1936," *Statistik des Deutschen Reichs* 502: 4. Schacht and the Reichsbank had also (erroneously) considered the Weimar investment boom as irrational exuberance as early as 1927, see H.-J. Voth, "With a Bang, Not a Whimper: Pricking Germany's 'Stock Market Bubble' in 1927 and the Slide into Depression," *Journal of Economic History* 63, 1 (March 2003): 65–99.

26 Anon, "Gründungstätigkeit:" 65 and later issues of *Statistisches Jahrbuch*. The latter were not published between 1941–2 and 1952.

27 As late as 1936, 23% of the (then much reduced) number of GmbHs had less than the revalued RM20,000 capital and a further 49% RM20,000–50,000 (Statistisches Reichamt, "GmbH": 6. (Berlin, 1937)). In 1980 the minimum was raised to DM 50,000 (€25,000) and in 2008 reduced to a nominal figure.

28 Christoph Buchheim and Jonas Scherner, "The Role of Private Property in the Nazi Economy: The Case of Industry," *Journal of Economic History* 66, no. 2 (June 2006): 390–416. Earlier writers like Franz Neumann, Tim Mason, Richard Overy and Peter Temin had tended to downplay the surviving role of private property rights, free contracting and entrepreneurial initiative, though one can see elements of this reinterpretation in their work.

29 By 1944, the divorce of ownership from control was less obvious in Germany than the US or UK. Most shares were held by majority owners, the state or other companies: the general public owned only 20–25%. A 1944 Ministry of Justice order suppressed all AGMs of shareholders (Levy, *Private Corporations*, 217).

30 F.A. Mann, "The New German Company Law and Its Background," *Journal of Comparative Legislation and International Law* Third Series 19, no. 4 (November 1937): 220–38.

31 Moreover, the capital invested in GmbHs (but not their numbers) was below even that of 1913.

32 For the decline in companies in Ancient Rome following the collapse of the republic, see Ulrike Malmendier, "Law and Finance 'at the Origin'," *Journal of Economic Literature* 47, no. 4 (2009): 1076–1108. For that in India's post-independence "license Raj," see Hannah and Kasuya, op. cit.

33 E.g. Franz Neumann, *Behemoth: The Structure and Practice of National Socialism* (London: Gollancz, 1942), 231–32.

34 The nearest European parallels to Germany were in those Baltic republics whose corporations were in the 1930s initially suppressed by authoritarian nationalists and, thereafter, even more decisively, by Stalin.

35 J. Liebmann, "Die Vereinheitlichung des deutschen und österreichschen Rechts der Gesellschaft mit beschränkter Haftung," *Zeitschrift für das Gesamte Handelsrecht und Konkursrecht* 73 (1913): 1–44; Paul Pic and F. Baratin, *Des sociétés à responsabilité limitée: étude critique et commentaire pratique de la loi du 7 mars 1925, mise en parallèle avec les principales lois étrangères avec formules* (Paris: Librairie des Juris-Classeurs editions Godde, 1929), 21.

36 G. Drouets, *Traité Théorique et Pratique des SARLs* (Paris, 1927). In 1938, Germany's corporate law was extended to Austria.

37 In 1936, nearly two-thirds had only one (28% of GmbHs) or two (38%) owners (Statistisches Reichsamt, *GmbH*, 9). A voluntary Berlin *Handelskammer* survey of 1905—with a 73% response rate at a time when some reformers advocated eliminating the one-man company—suggested that only 10% then had one owner (F. Fränkel, *Die Gesellschaft mit beschränkter Haftung: eine volkswirtschaftliche Studie* (Tübingen, 1915), 149), but the proportion was soon higher, perhaps peaking around 1923, judging by the periodic reports of *Einzelfirmen* converting to GmbHs and vice versa in *Wirtschaft und Statistik* and the high number of companies with the M20,000 minimum capital (which were more likely than larger GmbHs to have one-owner). In terms of the Guinnane et al. menu, one-man companies (and some two-man companies) had no "minority" to protect; there was scant likelihood of any outsider being able (or wanting) to buy shares and/or the supposedly "non-personal" entity theoretically "shielded" could—as many were—in practice be dissolved at will. There were some GmbHs (more than 13% in 1936, see *Statistisches Jahrbuch 1938*, 446) that were subsidiaries of AGs, foreign multinationals etc., or were vehicles for organising cartels, uses for which the Guinnane et al. entrepreneurial menu considerations were also (largely) irrelevant. Compare T. Shimizu ("Management and Control in Small and Medium-sized Enterprises: The Case of Private Limited Liability Companies in Japan before World War II," Paper at World Business History Conference, Frankfurt, 2014, p. 10) on the 1941 Osaka survey suggesting 23.8% had 10 or more shareholders, from which he deduces that attracting outside capital was not a major motive (p. 13) but could be biased sampling. France allowed one-man companies from the beginning of SARLs in 1925, though the UK only followed in 1992, under pressure for EU homogenisation, and many Latin American companies continued to ban them (M.-H. Monserie-Bon and 6 others, "Les sociétés unipersonelles," in *Qu'en est-il du Code de Commerce 200 ans après?*, ed. C. St-Alary-Hovin (Presses de L'USST, Toulouse, 2009), 257–65.

38 An argument made by Guinnane et al. in relation to higher US corporatisation. In the case in Switzerland (and probably some others), including KGs (limited partnerships) would probably widen its lead over Germany in all limited liability entities.

39 Making market size less of an explanation of the difference than it became in later decades. Antwerp and Rotterdam handled almost as much trade as Germany's largest ports before 1914, and the five countries were nearer than most of

Germany to the largely tariff-free British market, as well as being large exporters to (only moderately protected) Germany and France (L. Hannah, "Logistics, Market Size and Giant Plants," *Journal of Economic History* (March 2008)).

40 One possible test of this is the emerging liberal approach to bankruptcy (P.-C. Hautcoeur and P. Di Martino, "The Functioning of Bankruptcy Law and Practices in European Perspective (c.1880–1913)," *Enterprise and Society* 14 (September 2013): 579–605. J. Sgard, "Do Legal Origins Matter? The Case of Bankruptcy Laws in Europe 1808–1914," *European Review of Economic History* 10 (2006): 389–419), though in fact the five small countries do not show noticeably greater liberalism than Germany. Although Scandinavian countries initially led (Sgard, 402), they (and the Netherlands) retained imprisonment for debt a little longer than Germany and Belgium (Sgard, 407), and the treatment of debtors by Germany's 1877 law was more remarkably free of moral stigma than sometimes sterner German discussions of corporate limited liability.

41 P. Muchlinski, "The Development of German Corporate Law until 1990: An Historical Reappraisal," *German Law Journal* 14, 2 (2013): 347–49.

42 The law was standard, but the *Handelsregister* remained a regional responsibility. In 1909, the free states of Hamburg, Bremen and Lübeck accounted for just over 2% of the Reich's population, but 5% of its GmbHs and 7% of its AGs. (*Statistisches Jahrbuch 1911*, 1, 406; E. Moll, "Private Unternehmungsformen," in *Die Statistik in Deutschland*, vol. 2, ed. F. Zahn (Munich, 1911), 428–67, at p. 457). The overall phenomenon persisted, despite world depression and Nazism: in 1936, Bremen and Hamburg alone had 7% of Germany's GmbHs (by number and capital) and 5% of AGs. (*Statistisches Jahrbuch 1937*, 418, 426).

43 Note the liberal bank chartering policy of the free city of Frankfurt, before its 1866 annexation by Prussia (L. Hannah, "Corporations in the US and Europe, 1790–1860", *Business History* 56, no. 6 (September 2014): 865–99).

44 Fränkel, *GmbH*; R. Dalberg, *Kreditversicherung bei der GmbH* (Berlin, 1911), 32.

45 Above, and for the rapid multiplication of small GmbHs: Zahn, *Statistik*, 457; Anon, "Die Gründungstätigkeit im Deutschen Reich im Jahre 1924," *Wirtschaft und Statistik* 5, no. 2 (28 January 1925): 63–66.

46 Hannah, "Corporations."

47 Though, when the Netherlands did so in 1928, particularly tightening up publicity requirements—remarkably, without providing the BV (*besloten vennootschap*) private company form as a safety valve until 1971—the numbers of NVs declined proportionately to population or GDP (Table 1).

48 H.M.A. Schadee, "De L'Inutilité de la Création en Hollande d'une Forme Nouvelle de la Société," in *Documents du Congrès Juridique International des Sociétés Anonymes*, ed. L. Mahieu (Louvain: Van Linthout, 1910), 181–85; M. Lüpold, "Der Ausbau der 'Festung Schweiz': Aktienrecht und Corporate Governance in der Schweiz, 1881–1961," 2008, Zürich, Ph.D. thesis, published online 2010 at http://opac.nebis.ch/ediss/20111015_003417152.pdf.

49 Switzerland did not introduce the GmbH form until 1937 and, even today, has more AGs than GmbHs, while in Germany, GmbHs are overwhelmingly numerically dominant, as is also true of Dutch BV (*besloten vennootschap*) equivalents (despite their late 1971 introduction).

50 T.W. Guinnane and J.-L. Rosenthal, "Making do with Imperfect Law: Small Firms in France and Germany, 1890–1935," *Entreprises et Histoire* 87 (December 2009): 79–95, at p. 80. Even in some among the four countries on which the revisionist four focus, the "things" they specify in this context—entrenching managers, restraining share sales, differential voting, supermajority requirements in corporations, as well as attaining modest entity-shielding in partnerships (contractually or using trusts)—were possible elsewhere, though rarely standard default conditions.

51 However, the limit on any NV shareholders exercising more than three or six votes could be overcome by the use of nominees by dominant shareholders.

52 And this was, of course, the position in German GmbHs too (not to speak of American corporations), though in France and Britain, entrenching directors directly (in corporate statutes) was possible.

53 J. Guinchard, *Sweden: Historical and Statistical Handbook*, Stockholm Government Printing Office, 1914, 698–701. Under the 1895 law, accounts had to be presented at the AGM, various minority rights were protected and foreign directors (up to one-third) required government permission, though the general meeting otherwise had quite wide powers over the articles of association (*bolagsordnung*). Note that what Guinchard arguably mis-translates as a "private company" (*enkelt bolag*) was not one in the Guinnane et al. (or our) sense.

54 For example, the Dutch code of 1838 (effective until 1928) required only that shareholders be able to consult the accounts at the corporate office prior to the AGM. This provision allowed *de facto* close companies to preserve secrecy, though companies seeking funds from the public, of course, increasingly found voluntary accounts publication to be advantageous (J. Jonker and K. Sluyterman, *At Home in the World Market: Dutch International Trading Companies from the Sixteenth Century until the Present* (The Hague, 2000), 178). On accounting practice more generally, see Edouard Folliet, *La Vérification des comptes dans les sociétés par actions: Thèse . . . par Edouard Folliet,...* (E. Froreisen, 1911).
It was quite common for some sectors (railways, banks, insurance) or some categories (public companies in Germany and Britain) to have seriously strong compulsory reporting requirements, but almost unknown (apart from Germany 1884–1892, the UK 1900–07 and some US states where the provisions were easily avoided) for companies in general.

55 J. Escarra, "Les restrictions conventionelles de la transmissibilité des actions," *Annales de droit commercial* 25, nos. 5–6 (1911): 335–58, 425–70 at pp. 467–70; F. Laurent, *Etude Comparée des Législations Française et Britannique en matière de sociétés par actions*, (Paris, 1919), 151.

56 The delay from 1919 to 1925 in introducing the SARL was partly induced by post-war distaste for all things German, and the GmbH had been less popular than the AG in German parts of Alsace-Lorraine (Pic and Baratin, *Sociétés*, 75), oppositely to the norm in Germany proper. The lack of clarity about what was included in the French registration statistics, and German enthusiasm for weeding the *Handelsregister* of defunct companies, may also exaggerate the 1937 French lead over Germany.

57 E.g C. Vivante, *Traité de droit commercial*, vol. 2 (Paris: Les sociétés commerciales, 1911), 183.

58 *Handwörterbuch der Staatswissenschaften*, 1923, vol. 1, 173. Freedeman gives somewhat higher figures for the public company share for 1913. In 1907, legislation had required publicity for companies appealing to the public for funds, except where the company raised capital from subscribers they knew without advertising (Leon Batardon, *Memento des Fondateurs de Societes*, (Paris: Dunod, 1923), 31–32). All SAs and *commandites par actions* also had to provide their shareholders with accounts a fortnight before the AGM, though the content was not prescribed (on the grounds that good faith was better than excessively detailed prescription, see Alfred Neymarck, *Les bilans dans les sociétés par actions* (Paris: Marchal et Godde, 1911), 14).

59 Laurent, *Etude Comparée*, 132–34 for the clearer English rules.

60 Hervé Joly ("La Direction des Sociétés Anonymes depuis la Fin du Xixe Siècle: Le Droit entretient la Confusion des Pratiques," *Entreprises et histoire* 57 (December 2009): 111–25) summarises the French legal situation and the evolution of practical governance arrangements in *large* companies. It was illegal to entrench

director's positions: these had to be formally revocable by shareholders in an SA. However, that did not apply to *commandites* with tradable shares (easily formed until 1931, by which time SARLs offered simpler alternative facilities) and in practice, even SA governance positions were extended for life by convention or private agreement (and also, presumably, especially in smaller SAs, through dominant shareholdings). There was no legal bar in French SAs to excluding small shareholders from voting, limiting directorships to those with high numbers of shares, reserving some profits to founders or having a board with one member. Plural votes for controlling entrepreneurs and other governance complexities suiting controlling managers were also possible (Joly, "Le Capitalisme Familial dans les Entreprises Moyennes: un Déclin Réversible," *Entreprises et Histoire* 28 (2001): 64–76) Plural votes became much more common in Europe after 1919 to protect incumbents in quoted companies: J. Percerou, *Régime Juridique des Sociétés par Actions au point de vue du Vote Privilégié et de la Protection des Minorités* (Paris: Rousseau, 1932), 4–11.

61 D.C. North, J.J. Wallis, and B.R. Weingast, *Violence and Social Orders: A Conceptual Framework for Interpreting Recorded Human History* (New York, 2009).

62 Olivier Accominotti and Barry Eichengreen, "The Mother of All Sudden Stops: Capital Flows and Reversals in Europe, 1919–1932," in *Economic History Review* 69, 2 (2016): 469–492. They see the disruptive withdrawal of macroeconomic support for Germany's recovery as driven by domestic factors in lending countries (notably the US), not primarily by weaknesses in Germany (and they note its more deleterious effects than recent German reduction of support for peripheral Eurozone economies).

63 Even so, Germany used the corporate form less than other rich countries (Hannah and Kasuya, Table 1) and public companies continued to account for much less of Germany's output (and family firms of the *Mittelstand* more) than the Anglosphere's (W. Carlin, "West German Growth and Institutions," in *Economic Growth in Europe since 1945*, eds. N. Crafts and G. Toniolo (Cambridge: Cambridge University Press, 1996), 455–97, at p. 488).

64 K.H. Paqué, "How clean was the slate? Some notes on the Olsonian view of the postwar German economic miracle," Kiel Working Papers, No. 588, Kiel Institute of World Economics, 1993; B. Eichengreen and A.O. Ritschl, "Understanding West German Economic Growth in the 1950s," *Cliometrica* 3, no. 3 (2009): 191–219.

References

Accominotti, O. and B. Eichengreen. "The Mother of All Sudden Stops: Capital Flows and Reversals in Europe, 1919–1932." *Economic History Review* 69, 2 (2016): 469–492.

Anon. "Die Gründungstätigkeit im Deutschen Reich im Jahre 1924." *Wirtschaft und Statistik* 5, no. 2 (January 28, 1925): 63–66.

Batardon, Leon. *Memento des Fondateurs de Societes*. Paris: Dunod, 1923.

Buchheim, Christoph, and Jonas Scherner. "The Role of Private Property in the Nazi Economy: The Case of Industry." *Journal of Economic History* 66, no. 2 (June 2006).

Burhop, C., D. Chambers, and B. Cheffins. "Law, Politics and the Rise and Fall of German Stock Market Development, 1870–1938." University of Cambridge Legal Studies Research paper no 4/2015, February 2015.

Carlin, W. "West German Growth and Institutions." In *Economic Growth in Europe since 1945*, edited by N. Crafts and G. Toniolo. Cambridge: Cambridge University Press, 1996.

Dalberg, R. *Kreditversicherung bei der GmbH*. Berlin, 1911.

Drouets, G. *Traité Théorique et Pratique des SARLs*. Paris, 1927.

Eichengreen, B., and A. O. Ritschl. "Understanding West German Economic Growth in the 1950s." *Cliometrica* 3, no. 3 (2009): 191–219.

Elster, L., A. Weber, and F. von Friedrich Wieser (eds.) *Handwörterbuch der Staatswissenschaften*, vol .1. Jena: G. Fischer, 1923.

Escarra, J. "Les restrictions conventionelles de la transmissibilité des actions." *Annales de droit commercial* 25, nos. 5–6 (1911): 335–58, 425–70.

Fiedler, M. "Business Scandals in the Weimar Republic." *European Yearbook of Business History* 2 (1999): 155–78.

Folliet, Edouard. *La Vérification des comptes dans les sociétés par actions: Thèse . . . par Edouard Folliet,...* Paris: E. Froreisen, 1911.

Foreman-Peck, J., and L. Hannah. "The Diffusion and Impact of the Corporation," forthcoming, *Economic History Review*, 68, 3, (2015): 962–984.

Fränkel, F. *Die Gesellschaft mit beschränkter Haftung: eine volkswirtschaftliche Studie*. Tübingen, 1915.

Guinchard, J. *Sweden: Historical and Statistical Handbook*. Stockholm: Stockholm Government Printing Office, 1914.

Guinnane, T. W., R. Harris, N. Lamoreaux, and J. -L. Rosenthal. "Pouvoir et propriété dans l'entreprise: pour une histoire internationale des societes à responsabilité limitée." *Annales* 63, 1 (2008).

———. "Putting the Corporation in its Place." *Enterprise and Society* 8 (September 2007).

Guinnane, T., and S. M. Rodriguez. "Choice of Enterprise Form: Spain, 1886–1936." *Yale Economic Growth Center discussion paper no 1049*, 2015.

Guinnane, T. W., and J. –L. Rosenthal. "Making Do with Imperfect Law: Small Firms in France and Germany, 1890–1935." *Entreprises et Histoire* 87 (December 2009).

Hannah, L. "A Global Corporate Census: Publicly-Traded and Close Companies in 1910." *Economic History Review* 68, 2 (May 2015): 548–73.

———. "Corporations in the US and Europe, 1790–1860." *Business History* 56, no. 6 (September 2014): 865–99.

———."Logistics, Market Size and Giant Plants." *Journal of Economic History* (March 2008).

Hannah, L., and M. Kasuya. "Twentieth Century Enterprise Forms: Japan in Comparative Perspective." *Enterprise and Society*, 17, 1, (2016): 80–115.

Hautcoeur, P. –C., and P. Di Martino. "The Functioning of Bankruptcy Law and Practices in European Perspective (c.1880–1913)." *Enterprise and Society*, forthcoming, online publication, July 2013;

Hervé Joly. "La Direction des Sociétés Anonymes depuis la Fin du Xixe Siècle : Le Droit entretient la Confusion des Pratiques." *Entreprises et histoire* 57 (December 2009): 111–25.

Hoffmann, W. *Das Wachstum der Deutschen Wirtschaft seit der Mitte des 19 Jahrhunderts*. Berlin: Springer-Verlag, 1965.

Holtfrerich. *Great Inflation*; A. B. Levy, *Private Corporations and Their Control*.

Joly. "Le Capitalisme Familial dans les Entreprises Moyennes : un Déclin Réversible." *Entreprises et Histoire* 28 (2001): 64–76.

Jonker, J., and K. Sluyterman. *At Home in the World Market: Dutch International Trading Companies from the Sixteenth Century until the Present*. The Hague, 2000.

242 *Leslie Hannah*

Klages, Philipp. "The Contractual Turn: How Legal Experts Shaped Corporate Governance Reforms in Germany." *Socio-Economic Review* 11, 1 (2013): 159–84.

La Porta, R., F. Lopes-de-Silanes, and A. Shleifer. "The Economic Consequences of Legal Origins." *Journal of Economic Literature* 46, 2 (June 2008): 285–332.

Laurent, F. *Etude Comparée des Législations Française et Britannique en matière de sociétés par actions*, 151. Paris, 1919.

Levy, *Private Corporations and their Control, 1950*. Routledge, 1950.

Liebmann, J. "Die Vereinheitlichung des deutschen und österreichschen Rechts der Gesellschaft mit beschränkter Haftung." *Zeitschrift für das Gesamte Handelsrecht und Konkursrecht* 73 (1913): 1–44.

Lüpold, M. "Der Ausbau der 'Festung Schweiz': Aktienrecht und Corporate Governance in der Schweiz, 1881–1961." 2008. Zürich Ph.D. thesis, published online 2010 at http://opac.nebis.ch/ediss/20111015_003417152.pdf.

Maier, C. S. *Recasting Bourgeois Europe*. Princeton, 1975.

Malmendier, Ulrike. "Law and Finance 'at the Origin'." *Journal of Economic Literature* 47, no. 4 (2009): 1076–1108.

Mann, F. A. "The New German Company Law and Its Background." *Journal of Comparative Legislation and International Law* Third Series 19, no. 4 (November 1937): 220–38.

Moll, E. "Private Unternehmungsformen." In *Die Statistik in Deutschland*, vol. 2, edited by F. Zahn, 428–67. Munich, 1911.

Monserie-Bon, M. –H., and 6 others. "Les sociétés unipersonelles." In *Qu'en est-il du Code de Commerce 200 ans après?* edited by C. St-Alary-Hovin, 257–65. Toulouse: Presses de L'USST, 2009.

Muchlinski, P. "The Development of German Corporate Law until 1990: An Historical Reappraisal." *German Law Journal* 14, 2 (2013): 347–49.

Musacchio, A., and J. D. Turner. "Does the Law and Finance Hypothesis Pass the Test of History?" *Business History* 55, 4 (June 2013): 524–42.

Neumann, Franz. *Behemoth: The Structure and Practice of National Socialism*, 231–32. London: Gollancz, 1942.

Neymarck, Alfred. *Les bilans dans les sociétés par actions*, 14. Paris: Marchal et Godde, 1911.

North, D. C., J. J. Wallis, and B. R. Weingast. *Violence and Social Orders: A Conceptual Framework for Interpreting Recorded Human History*. New York, 2009.

Paqué, K. H. "How Clean Was the Slate? Some Notes on the Olsonian View of the Postwar German Economic Miracle." *Kiel Working Papers*, No. 588, Kiel Institute of World Economics, 1993.

Percerou, J. *Régime Juridique des Sociétés par Actions au point de vue du Vote Privilégié et de la Protection des Minorités*, 4–11. Paris: Rousseau, 1932.

Pic, Paul, and F. Baratin. *Des sociétés à responsabilité limitée: étude critique et commentaire pratique de la loi du 7 mars 1925, mise en parallèle avec les principales lois étrangères avec formules*. Paris: Librairie des Juris-Classeurs editions Godde, 1929.

Rajan, R. G., and L. Zingales. "The Great Reversals: The Politics of Financial Development in the Twentieth Century." *Journal of Financial Economics* 69 (2003): 5–50.

Reckendrees, Alfred. "Weimar Germany: The First Open Access Order that Failed?" *Freiburger Diskussionspapiere zur Ordnungsökonomik*, May 14, 2014.

Schadee, H. M. A. "De L'Inutilité de la Création en Hollande d'une Forme Nouvelle de la Société." In *Documents du Congrès Juridique International des Sociétés Anonymes*, edited by L. Mahieu, 181–5. Louvain: Van Linthout, 1910.

Sgard, J. "Do Legal Origins Matter? The Case of Bankruptcy Laws in Europe 1808–1914." *European Review of Economic History* 10 (2006): 389–419.

Shimizu, T. "Management and Control in Small and Medium-sized Enterprises: The Case of Private Limited Liability Companies in Japan before World War II." Paper at World Business History Conference, Frankfurt, 2014.

Statistisches Jahrbuch für das Deutsche Reich, Schmidt, Berlin, *1911, 1937* and *1938*.

Statistisches Reichsamt, "Die Gesellschaften mit Beschränkter Haftung am 31 Dezember 1936," *Statistik des Deutschen Reichs*, 502 (Berlin, 1937).

Vivante, C. *Traité de droit commercial*, vol. 2, 183. Paris: Les sociétés commerciales, 1911.

Voth, H. –J. "With a Bang, not a Whimper: Pricking Germany's 'Stock Market Bubble' in 1927 and the Slide into Depression." *Journal of Economic History* 63, 1 (March 2003): 65–99.

12 The Impact of the First World War on British and French Management Thought and Practice

Trevor Boyns

Introduction

The working definition of globalisation used in this volume is the integration of previously self-sufficient economies through the development of global markets for commodities, capital, labour, knowledge and other factors of production. Management expertise, which is the focus of this chapter, falls into the knowledge category. This chapter assesses the extent to which the First World War promoted the international diffusion of US management practices across the Atlantic to Britain and France. Determining the degree to which management techniques and other business know-how diffuses across borders is, therefore, one way of determining whether globalisation is taking place. It is undoubtedly true that, since the end of the nineteenth century, management thought and practice in all countries has undergone a process of scientification, though the precise nature of such development has varied due to cultural, amongst other, factors. Within Europe it was not simply a case of accepting, without questioning, the American 'scientific management' of Taylor.[1] Moreover, as a global phenomenon, although the scientification of management began before the First World War, it was undoubtedly influenced by the war, and continued on its inexorable path thereafter. Examining the path of this process, however, is complicated by two factors: first, the loose use by writers of the term 'scientific management' and, second, the limited survival of evidence relating to managerial practice.

The research question informing this chapter is whether the First World War encouraged or retarded the scientification of management in Britain and France. Within the existing secondary literature, the broad consensus of opinion appears to be that it speeded it up, leading to a more rapid development in the 1920s and 1930s. This chapter, which will examine the validity of this view for Britain and France, shows that war had a complex, non-linear impact on the development of managerial practices in the two countries. It certainly did not result in the wholesale Americanisation of British and French management or the rapid adoption of Taylorism. However, this chapter discusses instances in which the war did promote the rise of American-style scientific management in Britain and France. The chapter thus provides tentative support for the view that the First World War influenced the nature of globalisation of management knowledge without stopping the process.

Management Thought and Practice Before the War: The General Context

JoAnne Yates dates the emergence of modern, systematic management, i.e., the development of a focus on managing through information, often presented in written reports and comprising the graphical presentation of statistical/accounting data, to the 1870s.[2] Over the next 60–70 years, the development of this new management ideology reflected the growing informational needs of those managing increasingly larger businesses and supply-side technological developments, including typewriters, duplicators and analytical machines.[3] While the focus of Yates's analysis is the US, systematic management developments also occurred in European countries such as Britain[4] and France[5] before the First World War. Within this 'broad but amorphous' development,[6] from the 1880s there emerged a more narrowly focused movement, scientific management, most closely associated with the work and writings of Frederick Winslow Taylor (1856–1915), especially his *Shop Management* and *Principles of Scientific Management*.[7]

While Taylorism has been seen as a 'creative synthesis of elements already known',[8] Kreis has warned against treating scientific management and Taylorism as synonymous.[9] Indeed, during the Great War, Hoxie pointed out that scientific management was not a single, consistent body of thought, identifying three main schools: those of Taylor, Henry Gantt and Harrington Emerson.[10] While there was much disagreement (sometimes outright hostility) between the adherents of each school, Witzel has argued that they were united in their common goal of trying to develop a coherent system of management, founded on a shared, fundamental basis 'that management, like work, can be broken down into sub-disciplines, procedures and tasks. By following these in methodical manner, managers can become more efficient and more effective'.[11] Whereas Emerson took a holistic view of each business, other American efficiency engineers, such as Taylor, Gantt, and the Gilbreths, focused their attention on 'micro-level management', while Europeans adopted a more 'macro-level' version of scientific management.[12] Thus, in contrast to the American focus on labour control and improving shopfloor efficiency through, for example, establishing performance benchmarks via stopwatch based time-study and the re-engineering of tasks, Europeans focused on issues such as industrial administration, i.e., on organisation, structure and the role of top management. Indeed, for classical management writers such as Lyndall Urwick (1891–1983), the 'minute subdivision of labour . . . has nothing to do with scientific management'.[13]

Contemporary critics, both in Britain and France, objected to the narrow approach to scientific management of US efficiency engineers. To many workers, trade unionists and others, including notable businessmen, the treatment of labour as a mere cog in the machine rendered scientific management inhumane. Recognising that workers, and indeed managers, had minds and wills of their own, members of what came to be known as the human relations school took a different perspective to improving efficiency, one that recognised the importance of human interactions. While many past authors have seen this welfare-oriented approach, with its reliance on the newly emerging sciences of psychology and sociology, as an alternative or as a direct response to the growth of scientific management, Kiechel sees the two approaches as complementary.[14] However, it would be wrong to see either Taylorism or scientific management as necessarily ignoring employer-employee relations. In the last few years of his life, Taylor emphasised that scientific management itself was a philosophy which required a mental revolution by both workers *and* managers.

Management Thought in Britain and France

Discussing British management, Craig Littler has suggested that the 'wall of indifference and lack of understanding of Taylorism . . . was finally breached in the run-up to the War'.[15] However, he goes on to note that the reactions were 'largely hostile', not least in a series of leaders published in *The Engineer* from 1911 through to 1914. The "crude and harsh 'engineering' approach to higher productivity which . . . was associated with some less enlightened sections of the American 'efficiency movement'"[16] grated with the views of British managers, whose approach was based around not simply the search for efficient performance, but also that of "service, which was intended to point to a solution of [contemporary] industrial unrest".[17]

In France, Taylorism had been introduced in 1907, when translations of some of Taylor's works by Henry Le Chatelier (1850–1936) were published in the *Revue de Métallurgie*, a review which Le Chatelier had founded in 1904.[18] Le Chatelier, a graduate of the Ecole Poyltechnique, and the engineer and naval architect Charles de Fréminville (1856–1936) were to be the chief proponents of Taylor's ideas throughout France over the next twenty years.[19] According to Fréminville, Taylor found a receptive audience in France for his ideas, not least because his emphasis on the scientific approach echoed the long-held French concern with method.[20] Conforming to this natural bent of the French, de Fréminville noted that Taylor's ideas represented the 'missing link' which French polytechnicians had been seeking, and especially appealed to those engineers and technicians who had been developing similar ideas at around the same time as Taylor.

The ideas of Taylor, however, were not the only new managerial ideas to emerge in France at this time. Henri Fayol (1841–1925) who, alongside Taylor and the German, Max Weber, is seen as an originator of twentieth-century management, developed a scientific approach to administration.[21] A mining engineer who subsequently became managing director of the coal, iron and steel combine of Commentry-Fourchambault and Decazeville, Fayol wrote about administrative or managerial efficiency, both within business and at the state level. While Fayol's main work, 'Administration industrielle et générale' (*AIG*), did not appear in print until 1916,[22] his writings on administration first appeared c.1900, pre-dating Le Chatelier's translations of Taylor's work. Furthermore, while *AIG* was strongly influenced by Taylor's *Shop Management*, it was not born out of it, and Fayol was critical of certain aspects of Taylor's ideas, not least that of the functional foreman, since he considered this undermined the central principle of uniqueness of command.[23]

Fayol's emphasis, however, was on the higher levels of administrative control within an organisation rather than shopfloor management. In his endeavour to develop a theory of administration, he devised fourteen management principles which were linked 'to the component activities of an organisation—technical, commercial, financial, security, accounting and managerial'.[24] Central to Fayol's elements of administration were the activities of planning, organising, commanding, co-ordination and control, the last of these being conceptually broader than Taylor's concept of control over labour and the work process. While Taylor's ideas appealed to French engineers, Fayolism, since it reinforced the existing 'caste system of command' and provided a justification for the 'position of the "directing" class', represented the natural organisational philosophy of employers.[25] It has been suggested, however, that French interest in scientific management was more intellectual than practical, its greatest impact being 'on the theoretical appreciation of industry by intellectuals'.[26]

In Britain, despite the lack of interest in Taylorism, there began to emerge from the late nineteenth century a growing literature on administration/management.[27] This included notable works by authors such as Emile Garcke, John Manger Fells, J. Slater Lewis and Edward Tregaskiss Elbourne, together with lesser-known ones by Francis G. Burton and Harvey Preen.[28] Such works emphasised a strong link between organisation, factory administration and accounting, something which became known in Britain as 'industrial administration'. The development of this field reflected, in part, the growth in business size and the increasing divorce of ownership from control, and the influence of not only engineers but also accountants.[29] Chandler and Daems, however, have criticised the British literature of the period for focusing on improving administrative monitoring rather than dealing with administrative coordination and control.[30]

Whatever their individual limitations, such works clearly reflected a more systematic approach to management, emphasising the benefits of the application of science, especially in achieving efficient business performance. Preen, for example, attempts to show how, through internal reorganisation, the elimination of waste, factory accounting and efficient costings, any manufacturer or merchant could increase his profits through the determination of which goods yielded him a profit and which did not. For Preen, a scientific approach to the recording of business transactions was paramount, though he lamented the contemporary lack of knowledge of 'the science of business economics'.[31] In *Factory Administration and Accounts*, aimed at factories or works engaged in the engineering and machine making industries, Elbourne also favoured an analytical approach. However, while admitting that his ideas 'may hardly be said to reduce administration to a science', they did demonstrate 'the desirability and feasibility of a critical treatment of every routine essential to the well-being of a factory'.[32]

Management Practice

Although French engineers may have been enthusiastic about Taylorist methods, 'most employers remained skeptical, especially when early experiments to apply them resulted in a number of strikes, as was the case in the automobile industry'.[33] Louis Renault and André Citroën, amongst the most notable French businessmen interested in Taylorism before the war, found their attempts to introduce it were far from smooth. Not especially impressed by the attempts of Georges de Ram to introduce scientific management at a workshop employing 150 workers at the company's main Billancourt plant in 1907 and 1908, Louis Renault resisted de Ram's treaties to introduce it more widely.[34] However, following a visit to the US in 1911, where he met both Henry Ford and Taylor, Louis saw scientific management as a means of restoring the company's dominant position within the French car industry. Despite warnings from Taylor, Renault attempted simply to increase worker productivity and reduce labour costs, which led to widespread strikes in 1912 and 1913, causing 'the spread of scientific management in French industry to slow down temporarily'. As a result, 'Taylorism retreated, vanquished, until France entered the First World War'.[35]

Knowledge of the implementation of Taylorist ideas in pre-war Britain, as in France, is limited to a small number of well-known concerns, including Cadburys, Lever Brothers and Mather & Platt. Although he undoubtedly distrusted certain elements of Taylorism, in *Some Principles of Industrial Organization*, published in 1912, Edward Cadbury revealed that this firm's Bournville works used Taylorist practices including the scientific selection of workers, the recording of results, the standardisation of tools and equipment, the use of careful cost estimates and of time study, the key symbol of scientific management for many observers.[36] The most complete application of Taylorist ideas, however, occurred at the Manchester chain-manufacturing concern of Hans Renold Ltd., encompassing time study, the use of Alexander Hamilton Church's system of costing (based on the notions of production centres for operational cost control and the machine hour rate for the allocation of overhead expenses),[37] the drawing up and regular revision of organisation charts and even functional foremen, although the latter were abandoned during the war due to their impracticability.[38]

Despite the increasingly widespread development of systematic management, the implementation of Taylorism in Britain before the war does not seem to have been extensive. One reason for this was the absence of any individuals or an organisation specifically devoted to its adoption. Other factors cited include the development of an alternative, proto-human relations approach, reflecting a concern for the welfare of workers,[39] and that it was inappropriate in the market conditions prevailing in pre-war Britain, especially in sectors like engineering, where the limited mass market provided fewer opportunities for standardisation and the specialisation of tasks than in the US.[40] Indeed, British engineers, despite their familiarity with Taylor's ideas, as indicated by vigorous debate in the journals, failed to show the same interest in Taylorism as did their French counterparts, only being willing to concede the suitability of the premium bonus system, based on accurate time study, as a means of improving industrial output.[41]

The British and French experiences before the war were therefore not dissimilar: an ever-increasing dissemination of scientific management ideas but limited application within private-sector businesses. Piecemeal adoption, especially as a means of attempting to save failing firms, tended to give scientific management a bad name, and may go some way to explain its limited practical appeal. Nevertheless, it has been claimed that, by 1914, in both countries, nearly half of all engineering employees worked under some form of incentive wage system, a key component of Taylorism.[42] While British state-operated arsenals had introduced piecework systems to a certain degree before the end of the nineteenth century, it was amongst French military officers that the potential of scientific management for improving the efficiency of operations within arsenals was most widely recognised, Taylor's methods being used in at least one plant prior to the outbreak of war.[43] It should be noted, however, that an amendment to the US Army Appropriation Act introduced in 1914, however, forbade the use of the stopwatch and premium bonus systems in any establishment under the control of the US government. This prohibition continued for 33 years.[44]

Wartime Developments

According to Nelson,[45] the scientific management movement was shaped by 'the exigencies of war, more than the work of Taylor, Le Chatelier or others'. However, the nature and impact of the war differed between countries: France was invaded and much of the productive capacity in the east and northeast of the country was lost for the duration; Britain, by contrast, although suffering some aerial bombardment, did not suffer ground fighting on its territory. A key requirement, in both France and Britain, however, was the need to produce as much as possible from the resources available, to which end the elimination of waste became the greatest priority. As men entered the armed forces, the resulting shortages of skilled workers led to a much greater use of less conventional types of labour, including unskilled workers, women and handicapped persons. Such changes were only made possible through the introduction of machinery that either saved labour or could be operated by unskilled workers, a change which required trade union co-operation. Both in France and Britain, the war ultimately led to widespread state control of productive assets, which often increased in size to meet the demands placed upon them. This expansion of government, however, meant the state became increasingly reliant on individuals from the private sector to manage such assets, while the increasing size of productive units placed a growing emphasis on the need to develop appropriate managerial systems. The result of this process was 'an amalgamation of scientific and personnel management . . . a new emphasis on the compatibility of time study, incentive wage plans, and collective bargaining . . . [and] an unprecedented degree of production planning and coordination'.[46] In Nelson's view, everything, therefore, was set for scientific management to take centre stage. But did it?

In both Britain and France, the war was initially seen as likely to be of a short-term nature, and little pre-war planning had taken place. However, such expectations were quickly and rudely shattered. The Great Shell Scandal of early 1915 dramatically illustrated the deficiencies of the 'business as usual' approach of the British government. The failure to ensure munitions supplies through the market mechanism resulted in the creation of the Ministry of Munitions which, together with the Ministries of Food, Shipping and Labour, became responsible for controlling sixty percent of employment by 1918. 'Under the Munitions of War Act hundreds of establishments were declared to be 'controlled', manufacturing methods, as well as wages and profits, coming thereby under State regulation'.[47] In France, the impact of war on production was more immediate and acute: the German invasion severely restricted the country's productive capabilities, many important mines and factories lying in the occupied zone. The state quickly began to requisition output, but the lack of pre-war planning resulted in paralysis. To overcome the situation, consultative economic action committees, organised by military region and *département*, were introduced.[48] Although Bhimani has claimed that the war provided 'a totally new industrial landscape for altering the structure of the workplace in those industries engaged in the war effort',[49] the initial impact of the war in France was negative; on the occasion of the memorial meeting for Taylor in October 1915, de Fréminville commented that, 'The [scientific management] movement then launched, which seemed so full of promise, has been arrested by the war'.[50]

A key figure, alongside individuals such as Le Chatelier, who sat as an expert on government committees on the manufacture of explosives and military equipment, and de Fréminville, in the development of scientific management in France was Albert Thomas. In October 1914, Thomas was given the task of intensifying munitions production, subsequently becoming Under Secretary for Munitions in May 1915 and later Minister of Armaments.[51] From 1916, together with Minister of Commerce Etienne Clémentel, Thomas strongly advocated the use of scientific management.[52] Alongside other former students from the *Ecole normal supérieure*, Thomas reorganised munitions production in state-owned factories, co-ordinated and controlled the activities of private industries and managed the man-power problems of the French war industry.[53] Thomas had learned of sci-entific management through his close links with Louis Renault and André Citroën, especially the latter, who had 'established the highly efficient mass production of shells in Paris',[54] believing that both workers and capital-ists could gain through its implementation, via higher wages, shorter work-ing hours and lower product prices.[55] While advocating the use of scientific management, Thomas was mindful of the need to keep workers onside, and it was for this reason that he denied Le Chatelier any meaningful role within the Ministry of Armaments and War Production, fearing his social conser-vatism would have raised serious objections within the labour community.[56] The French labour movement, antagonistic towards scientific management before the war, moved from a position of hostility to one of qualified sup-port under Alphonse Merrheim and Leon Jouhaux.[57] To help ensure labour support, in late 1916 and early 1917 Thomas experimented with a version of the British government's successful welfare work program alongside the provision of support for 'trade-unionist initiatives for establishing arbitra-tion commissions and, in government-controlled factories, shop stewards'.[58] Although Thomas resigned his position in late 1917, the development of the use of scientific management was continued under his successor, Louis Locheur.

One example of a significant wartime development is that of the Penhoët naval shipyard where, in 1915, Guillet, an associate of Le Chatelier, intro-duced a planning department, time study and a bonus wage system. After his departure in late 1915, this work was continued by de Fréminville.[59] Elsewhere, powder production was reorganised under the Taylor system in 1916 [60] and scientific management was increasingly relied upon for the manufacture of shells, arms, explosives and airplanes.[61] Merkle points out,[62] however, that it was not until 1918 that official recognition was given to the 'growing tide of Taylorism in war industries', when Georges Clémenceau, in a circular dated 28 February, 'emphasized that all heads of military estab-lishments must study methods of work suitable to the exigencies of the moment, in particular, the works of Taylor'. This process was undoubt-edly assisted by the 'broadcast' distribution of Taylor's books by the French government.[63]

One industry significantly altered during the war was motor vehicle manu-facture. At the French truck and car manufacturer, Berliet, scientific manage-ment was introduced from late 1915 by a Briton, Edward Banks, who was engaged as assistant manager, having gained experienced of Taylorism at the US firm Westinghouse.[64] Other French car manufacturers which had already dallied with scientific management before the war utilised it further in an attempt to cope with the demands generated by a rapid increase in size during the war: the workforce of Renault, for example, rose from 4,400 to 22,000 by 1918, while that of Citroën increased from 3,500 to 11,700 between 1915 and 1918, making them 'among the country's very largest companies' at the time.[65] By the end of the war Renault had been transformed into an organisation in which productive units 'could be monitored, assessed and controlled numerically' as a result of the application of scientific management procedures and the provision of data by the *Service de statistique*.[66]

In Britain, the process by which a more scientific approach to management was adopted was boosted during the war by the establishment of 'National' factories, designed to increase the supply of munitions and armaments. Given the requirement for large numbers of the same type of product, National Factories could utilise large-scale production techniques, implement standardization and improved labour conditions and be operated through scientific management.[67] Such factories were also used to establish 'bogey' costs for private manufacturers, providing benchmarks to help them improve efficiency, thereby lowering the cost of supplies to the state. In operating National Factories, three managerial approaches were adopted: agency management, i.e., the use of existing firms, local Boards of Management and direct management by the Ministry of Munitions.[68] In the early part of the war, 'about one-third of the national factories were run . . . by private firms on an agency basis. The proportion would have been higher but for the lack of technical knowledge where Explosives and Filling Factories were concerned'.[69]

Assessments of the relative efficiency of the different managerial régimes are made difficult by the complexity of factors involved but, despite the reluctance to use it, there was some slight evidence in favour of direct control, possibly reflecting its adoption at larger factories where private sector expertise was limited and/or unavailable (e.g., filling factories). However, it was recognised that if 'the Ministry had assumed direct control of all factories, they would probably have met with far greater difficulties in the quest for efficient managers than they experienced in dealing with experts on local Boards and private firms'.[70] In the final analysis, it was concluded that '[s]uccess in administration is seen to be largely independent of any particular system or method of management'.[71] Whatever the managerial regime adopted, control by the Ministry involved supervision of production methods and plant layout and, it was claimed, this led to 'a general levelling up of standards of accomplishment in the engineering trade, more economical use of material and of labour, the increased adoption of labour-saving and automatic machinery, more accurate costings, and a higher standard of accuracy, attained by the use of precision gauges on a scale hitherto unknown in England'.[72] Other gains claimed included progress in the standardisation of parts and a greater specialisation by each business on a smaller range of products. As in France, the impact could be clearly seen in motor vehicle manufacture, the war moving British car manufacture from a 'cottage industry', in which only William Morris used standardised parts, to one where standardisation was common.[73] Between August 1914 and November 1918, at its Longbridge plant, the Austin Motor Company produced over eight million shells, 650 guns, over 2,000 aeroplanes, nearly 500 armoured cars and vast quantities of other equipment.[74] However, as will be seen below, the long-term consequences of the war with respect to standardisation were not always positive.

Literature also played a role in helping to promote increased efficiency in Britain, the Ministry of Munitions distributing copies of Elbourne's *Factory Administration and Accounts*, possibly explaining its prodigious sales of 10,000 copies between the autumn of 1915 and mid-1919.[75] Texts specifically devoted to scientific management also began to appear in Britain from 1917, the most prominent amongst these being authored by Margaret McKillop and Alan Dugald McKillop, Herbert Newton Casson and Dwight Thompson Farnham.[76] Casson, a Canadian who had previously worked as a consultant in America, having arrived in Britain during the early months of the war, became a significant figure in the British efficiency movement. In 1915 he founded the journal *Efficiency*, which he wrote and published, and during the war presented lectures on factory management to workmen and staff at various companies, including Mather & Platt in July 1917 and Cadburys between January and July 1918.[77] Like other efficiency experts, including Edward Purinton and T. Sharper Knowlson, Casson sold 'diluted forms of Taylorism injected with liberal doses of the moral efficiency of Harrington Emerson'.[78]

Despite the claims made in the official history of the Ministry of Munitions, McKillop and McKillop noted that the ideas and methods of the American efficiency engineers were not always embraced enthusiastically within British establishments: 'Many individuals find in the methods a complete new gospel for industry; others dismiss them as either worthless or injurious, or already known and practised'.[79] Elbourne went so far as to question whether scientific management gave 'much inspiration to us in this country'.[80] However, in the context of the scientific study of efficiency, Kreis has suggested that the war years provided the 'real impetus' in Britain, as a result of the activities of 'a mixed bag of industrial psychologists, medical doctors, industrial hygiene experts and social researchers' who 'discovered the relationship between the health and fatigue of industrial workers and industrial efficiency'.[81] While wartime exigencies necessitated the maintenance of production at high levels, there was also a well-recognised need for workers to be treated fairly, in part reflecting the pre-war paternalistic concerns of British managers. The health and welfare of workers was considered paramount to the maintenance of the war effort and, in the opinion of Merkle, '[t]he real growth of the indigenous British management philosophy based on the study of health and psychology of industrial workers dates from the First World War'.[82] In this regard, Kreis singles out the role of the Health of Munitions Workers' Committee (HMWC), established in late 1915 by David Lloyd George at the Ministry of Munitions. Although the committee's work came to an end in late 1917—its final report was published in April 1918—its activities were taken over from December 1917 by the Industrial Fatigue Research Board. Through its impact on this later body and others, the HMWC helped to 'institutionalize' a form of scientific management which was more scientific than Taylorism, i.e., one which embodied the human factor in industry, and as a result, industrial psychology was poised to come of age during the interwar years.[83]

This emphasis on treating labour as a human entity rather than as a market commodity represented one of the three major influences in 'hastening the spread of new thinking on industrial control which . . . had its foundations before 1914, the other two being a recognition of 'a wider public responsibility in the form of service to the community' and a renouncing of 'autocratic methods of managing employees'.[84] Championed by prominent Quaker employers such as Lord Leverhulme and Seebohm Rowntree, this approach reflected a widespread desire not to return to the conflicts between capital and labour that had occurred in the run up to war. While many employers failed to embrace this defensive approach towards labour, there was an emphasis in British management thought during the war and immediately afterwards on welfare issues and profit sharing, which led ultimately to a human relations/industrial psychology approach to management.[85]

Another approach which was to develop in Britain was that focused on the higher levels of management administration. Developed during the interwar years by Lyndall Urwick (1891–1983), Britain's foremost management thinker and writer of the twentieth century, it was, moreover, an approach built upon both Taylorism and the ideas of Henri Fayol.[86] Through the activities of the firm which he controlled, Fayol had experienced first-hand the early French wartime military and state administration, being less than impressed by it. Writing in April 1916, Fayol attributed France's military and industrial inferiority to the administrative weaknesses of its government, pointing to the country's leaders being ill-informed and incapable of governing, forecasting or organising. Fayol's explanation for such failings was that the nation erroneously believed that eloquence, mathematical science and 'quality of the elected' implied administrative capability.[87] Fayol's view of French national leaders, however, contrasted with his view of the French nation as a whole, which he considered to be forward-looking, echoing the view of de Fréminville, expressed six months earlier, that 'France is thinking of the future, and of the necessity, greater than ever before, of undertaking a systematic organization of her resources and of her work'.[88]

Assessing the Impact of War

Any assessment of how the war influenced management thought and practice must consider its role in the process by which the ideas associated with scientific management came to underpin modern management ideas. How-ever, as noted earlier, a complicating factor is the lack of consensus amongst either contemporaries or historians as to what actually constitutes 'scien-tific management'. As Smith and Boyns have indicated, 'difficulties face any attempt to develop a comprehensive and definitive picture of management thought and its impact on management practice and education in the early years of the twentieth century'.[89] Moreover, any assessment of the impact of the war depends on whether the focus is on the war years themselves, or the longer term.

Considering the war years, moves in the direction of a scientific approach to management were already underway in both Britain and France prior to the outbreak of hostilities. In France, the views of Taylorists had begun to permeate the ranks of the engineers, who had been developing home-grown approaches, while Fayolism was also emerging; across the Channel, a Brit-ish management movement was under development from the 1890s. Child suggests that the war provided 'added impetus' to the British movement, a view recently reiterated by Wilson and Thomson.[90] Whitston puts it stron-ger, emphasising the 'sharp impetus' given by the war to scientific man-agement, both ideologically and in practice.[91] Whitston stresses that the war merely helped 'to complete the process by which Taylorism became accepted rather than mark any fundamental break in development', and going on to suggest that, by the end of the war, Taylorism 'had achieved the status of conventional wisdom'.[92] A similar position appears to have existed in France, where Vanuxem and Wilbois suggested in 1919 that the 'Taylor system' was being defended in the widest circles as 'gospel'.[93] Thus, in both countries, the war is seen as either bringing scientific management to the fore and/or cementing its place within the mainstream of management thought and practice.

But how realistic is such an assessment? If we focus on certain tools or techniques closely associated with scientific management, then the case would indeed seem to be a positive one. Thus, Kreis has suggested that, by 1920, British scientific managers had made great strides in streamlining pro-duction through attention to the mechanical aspects of labour, i.e., routing, planning, stores, layout, machine feeds and speeds.[94] Similarly, Whitston has emphasised the development of production planning, at the same time not-ing that the official history of the Ministry of Munitions points to the devel-opment of the use of the premium bonus system,[95] a comment that seems inconsistent with George Douglas Howard Cole's suggestion in 1928 that wage payment systems changed little during the war.[96] In France, the war has been seen as having 'enabled the integration of Taylorism into the gen-eral organisation of the enterprise . . . [allowing] industrialists to discover new possibilities of enhancing their firms' efficiency in terms of quality and productivity'.[97] Rials has suggested that, from an administrative perspective, the war provided both an audience and a justification for the development of administrative doctrine within France,[98] while Merkle has stressed that the wartime reorganisation of production helped to root 'Taylorism and Fayolism firmly in French productive and governmental organisation'.[99]

However, war can generate both positive and negative impacts. Towards the end of his life, Taylor placed the emphasis of scientific management not on a specific set of tools or techniques, since he recognised these could change with time, but on the achievement of the necessary 'mental revolution', suggesting that this could take up to five years to effect within an organisation. While it is possible that the specific conditions and priorities of war may have speeded up the mental revolution process, the peculiar pressures engendered by the war are just as likely to have generated delays.[100] While the war undoubtedly provided an opportunity for new developments within firms, the governments' strategic requirements distorted economic activity, engendering negative consequences and thereby delaying change. At a board meeting of the ammunition and explosives manufacturer Kynoch Ltd. in January 1915, it was noted that the war had prevented the implementation of scientific management reforms which had been under investigation prior to the war, while the introduction of scientific management was delayed at Rowntrees until the early 1920s, not simply due to the antipathy of Seebohm Rowntree, but also the 'immediate demands on managerial time' made by the war.[101] Similarly, Sir Herbert Austin blamed the war for having to shelve plans to use budgets and standard costing as a means of perfecting 'a scheme of works control',[102] although the war did not prevent Hans Renold Ltd., a company which had diverted all its energies to producing materials to aid the war effort, from adopting budgets for control purposes from 1915, which was itself part of a longer-term developmental process, or to experiment with standard costing in its shell department in 1918.[103] In France, although Marius Berliet had indicated a desire to implement standard costs in April 1917, he seems to have been thwarted by the demands of war.[104]

If the war both generated change and delayed its introduction during the war years, what of its longer-term impact? Reflecting on British wartime developments, the official historians of the Ministry of Munitions expressed the view that, once experienced in practice, efficient methods would spread, where applicable, 'to industries other than those in which they were first used'.[105] However, they also warned against expecting too much by way of long-term change, pointing out that the wartime experience of National Factories was not necessarily applicable to peacetime conditions or readily generalisable. Indeed, much of the plant and equipment installed during the war which aided standardisation was scrapped once hostilities ceased, having no peacetime use. Moreover, the benefits of standardisation could be limited. While engineering firms such as Austin and BSA in Britain and the major car companies in France embraced standardisation during the war, attempts to subsequently employ the lessons learnt did not always prove successful. BSA, for example, found that concentrating 'on producing as many as possible of the machines which had been developed during the

War, making full use of the skills which had been learned in the efficient mass-production of precision weapons'[106] proved inappropriate and detrimental to the company's fortunes in the 1920s.[107] Perhaps it was such experiences that led Cole, ten years after war had ended, to comment that British industry was less standardised than in 1918.[108]

Views as to the extent to which managerial developments occurred in Britain during the 1920s differ greatly. Cole, for example, considers that while the slump following 1921 presented a 'matchless opportunity' for the introduction of scientific management, it was not taken because British manufacturers rejected it, having no faith in its results.[109] Furthermore, Child has remarked that, in the depressed conditions of 1920s Britain, managerial attitudes reverted back to the pre-1914 *status quo* despite attempts, such as the inauguration of the Oxford 'management conferences' in 1919 and the formation of the Management Research Groups (MRGs) from 1926, both supported by Seebohm Rowntree, to encourage the wider dissemination of knowledge of both new ideas and management practices.[110] Nevertheless, Kreis has claimed that the war stimulated a managerial approach based on industrial psychology, one which was reflected in *Scientific Business Management*, a pamphlet published by the Ministry of Reconstruction in 1919, and one whose further development in the 1920s was exemplified by the activities of companies such as Rowntrees and Renolds.[111]

In France, as in Britain, welfare issues took on a growing prominence during the war, and helped inform the concept of scientific management championed by Clémentel as part of the new post-war order.[112] However, despite the immediate post-war period being seen as ripe for further developments in scientific management, progress was far from smooth. Differences between the Taylorists and Fayolists undermined the extent of its impact and by 1926, when the two groups joined to form the Comité National de l'Organisation Française (CNOF), it has been argued that scientific management, while penetrating many French industries, had done so only in form rather than substance. Thus, at Renault, it was only in 1937 that widespread use of time and motion studies and standards was advocated.[113] In the view of Merkle, what emerged in France after the war was a specifically French system of scientific management: one which emphasised planning and order, but which also allowed traditional French management patterns, based on 'general inspiration and financial control' to survive.[114] Indeed, many French engineers began to view scientific management as an 'alien culture complex', and by the 1930s had embraced a corporatist approach to political, social and economic matters, reflecting some of the ideas of the German rationalisation movement of the early 1920s.[115]

The growth of rationalisation undoubtedly impacted more heavily in France than in Britain. In Europe generally, the dissemination of scientific management ideas and practices was encouraged by the International Management Institute (IMI), an International Labour Organisation (ILO) body based in Geneva and supported financially by the League of Nations and American money. The brainchild of Albert Thomas, the Director of the ILO, it was led initially by Thomas's fellow countryman, Paul Devinat and, from November 1928 to its demise at the end of 1933, by Lyndall Urwick. Despite Urwick taking up the IMI reins following his overseeing of the establishment of the MRGs, the IMI had little impact in Britain. Indeed, much to his chagrin, Urwick failed to encourage the development in his native country of an organisation dedicated to the promotion of scientific management, such as CNOF in France. Nevertheless, after 1926, the introduction of bastardised versions of Taylorism did gain some success in Britain, and to a lesser extent in France, due to the activities of a small number of, mainly American, management consultants, not least Charles Bedaux.[116]

In summing up, the war clearly impacted on managerial thought and practice in Britain and France, both during the war years and thereafter. However, as this chapter has shown, the developmental process of the scientification of management from the late nineteenth century onwards was not a simple, linear one, and the impact of the Great War on this process cannot be seen as simply speeding up the introduction of Taylorism or scientific management. Indeed, the impact of the war on the increasingly complex process of the scientification of management was multifaceted.

Notes

1 Daniel Nelson, "Scientific Management in Retrospect," in *A Mental Revolution: Scientific Management since Taylor*, ed. Daniel Nelson (Columbus, OH: Ohio State University Press, 1992), 5–39.
2 JoAnne Yates, "Evolving Information Use in Firms, 1850–1920: Ideology and Information Techniques and Technologies," in *Information Acumen: the Understanding and Use of Knowledge in Modern Business*, ed. Lisa Bud-Frierman (London: Routledge, 1994), 26–50.
3 Alfred D. Chandler, *The Visible Hand: The Managerial Revolution in American Business* (Cambridge, MA: Belknap Press, 1977).
4 Margaret McKillop and Alan Dugald McKillop, *Efficiency Methods—an Introduction to Scientific Management* (London: Routledge, 1917).
5 Anne Pezet, "The History of the French tableau de bord (1885–1975): Evidence from the Archives," *Accounting, Business & Financial History* 19, no. 2 (2009): 103–25.
6 Yates, "Evolving Information Use," 47 fn.40.
7 Frederick Winslow Taylor, *Shop Management* (New York: American Society of Mechanical Engineers, 1903) and *Principles of Scientific Management* (New York: Harper & Brothers, 1911).
8 John Child, *British Management Thought: A Critical Analysis* (London: Allen & Unwin, 1969).
9 Steven Kreis, "Early Experiments in British Scientific Management: The Health of Munitions Workers Committee, 1915–1920," *Journal of Management History* 1, no. 2 (1995): 66.
10 Robert Franklin Hoxie, *Scientific Management and Labor* (New York: Augustus M. Kelly, 1966;—reprint of 1915 edition), 7.

11 Morgan Witzel, *Management History—Text and Cases* (London: Routledge, 2009), 21.
12 Ibid.
13 L.F. Urwick, "A general survey" in the L.F. Urwick Archive, PowerGen Library, Henley Business School, ms. 34/6/15, f.1, undated, c.1968.
14 Walter Kiechel, "The Management Century," *Harvard Business Review* 90, no. 11 (2012): 61–75.
15 Craig R. Littler, *The Development of the Labour Process in Capitalist Societies; a Study of the Transformation of Work in Britain, Japan and the USA* (London: Heinemann, 1982), 94–95.
16 Child, *British management Thought*, 40.
17 Ibid, 41.
18 Jean-Louis Peaucelle, *Henri Fayol—Inventeur des outils de gestion* (Paris: Economica, 2003), 86.
19 Nelson, "Scientific Management in Retrospect," 18.
20 Charles de Fréminville, "The Response of France to Scientific Management: Paper Read at Memorial Meeting for F.W. Taylor, Philadelphia, 22 October 1915" (translated by E.B. Cooke)—available online at http://stevens.cdmhost.com/cdm/ref/collection/p4100coll1/id/624 — accessed 9 January 2015, 4.
21 Kevin Whitston, "Scientific Management and Production Management Practice in Britain between the Wars," *Historical Studies in Industrial Relations* 1, no. 1 (1996): 47–71.
22 In the *Bulletin de la société de l'industrie minérale*; it was published in book form in 1917: Henri Fayol, *Administration industrielle et générale; prévoyance, organisation, commandement, coordination, controle* (Paris: H. Dunod et E. Pinat, 1917).
23 Peaucelle, *Henri Fayol*, 37.
24 Ian G. Smith and Trevor Boyns, "British Management Theory and Practice: The Impact of Fayol," *Management Decision* 43, no. 10 (2005): 1322.
25 Judith A. Merkle, *Management and Ideology: The Legacy of the International Scientific Management Movement* (Berkley, CA: University of California Press, 1980), 160.
26 Ibid., 168.
27 The relatively small number of texts published in Britain compared to the US has often been commented on. For example, see Joseph August Litterer, *The Emergence of Systematic Management as Shown by the Literature of Management from 1870 to 1900* (New York: Garland Publishing, 1986), 177.
28 Emile Garcke and John Manger Fells, *Factory Accounts: Their Principles and Practice* (London: Crosby Lockwood, 1887); J. Slater Lewis, *The Commercial Organisation of Factories* (London: E & F.N. Spon, 1896); Edward Tregaskiss Elbourne, *Factory Administration and Accounts* (London: Longmans, Green & Co., 1914, 1916). Francis G. Burton, *The Commercial Management of Engineering Works* (Manchester: Scientific Publishing Co., 1899); Harvey Preen, *Reorganisation and Costings: A Book for Manufacturers and Merchants* (London: Simpkin, Marshall, Hamilton, Kent & Co. Ltd, 1913).
29 Fells and Preen were accountants, while Garcke, Slater Lewis, Burton and Elbourne were engineers who had moved into managerial roles.
30 Alfred D. Chandler and H. Daems, "Administrative Coordination, Allocation and Monitoring: A Comparative Analysis of the Emergence of Accounting and Organization in the U.S.A. and Europe," *Accounting, Organizations and Society* 4, no. 1/2 (1979): 11, 16.
31 Preen, *Reorganisation and Costings*, 2.
32 Elbourne, *Factory Administration and Accounts*, v.

33 Matthias Kipping, "American Management Consulting Companies in Western Europe, 1920–1990: Products, Reputation, and Relationships," *Business History Review* 73, no. 2 (1999): 196.
34 Alnoor Bhimani, "Indeterminacy and the Specificity of Accounting Change: Renault 1898–1938," *Accounting, Organizations and Society* 18, no. 1 (1993): 11.
35 Merkle, *Management and Ideology*, 154.
36 Michael Rowlinson, "The Early Application of Scientific Management by Cadbury," *Business History* 30, no. 4 (1988): 377–95.
37 Church was a protégé of Slater Lewis, see John F. Wilson and A. Thomson, *The Making of Modern Management: British Management in Historical Perspective* (Oxford: University Press, 2006), 178.
38 Trevor Boyns, "Hans and Charles Renold: Entrepreneurs in the Introduction of Scientific Management Techniques in Britain," *Management Decision* 39, no. 9 (2001): 719–28.
39 Merkle, *Management and Ideology*, 226–29.
40 Littler, *The Development of the Labour Process*, 95.
41 Kreis, "Early Experiments" 65–66.
42 Nelson, "Scientific Management in Retrospect," 17.
43 Ibid., 21.
44 Hugh Aitkin, *Taylorism at Watertown Arsenal: Scientific Management in Action, 1908–1915* (Harvard: Harvard University Press, 1960), 233.
45 Nelson, "Scientific Management in Retrospect," 21.
46 Ibid.
47 *History of Ministry of Munitions*—Vols. VII, Part 1, and VIII, part 1 (London: HMSO), vol. VII, Pt. I: 2.
48 Peaucelle, *Henri Fayol*, p. 82.
49 Bhimani, "Indeterminacy and the Specificity of Accounting Change," 14.
50 De Fréminville, "The Response of France," 10.
51 E. Walter-Busch, "Albert Thomas and Scientific Management in War and Peace, 1914–1932," *Journal of Management History* 12, no. 2 (2006): 214.
52 Nelson, "Scientific Management in Retrospect," 22.
53 Walter-Busch, "Albert Thomas," 214.
54 Ibid., 216.
55 Ibid., 214.
56 Bhimani, "Indeterminacy and the Specificity of Accounting Change," 15, fn.8.
57 Nelson, "Scientific Management in Retrospect," 22.
58 Walter-Busch, "Albert Thomas," 217.
59 Nelson, "Scientific Management in Retrospect," 21–22.
60 Merkle, *Management and Ideology*, 157.
61 Nelson, "Scientific Management in Retrospect," 21.
62 Merkle, *Management and Ideology*, 158.
63 H.W. Allingham, "The Determination of Standards in Scientific Management," *The Accountant* LX (1919): 345–52. The claim was made on p. 350 by J.F. Butterworth who, in 1917, was described as the representative of Frank Gilbreth in England by McKillop and McKillop, *Efficiency Methods*, v. Butterworth noted, in contrast, that only about 800 copies had been published in London.
64 Henri Zimnovitch, "Berliet, the Obstructed Manager: Too Clever, Too Soon?" *Accounting, Business & Financial History* 1 (2001): 43–58.
65 Youssef Cassis, *Big Business—the European Experience in the Twentieth Century* (Oxford: Oxford University Press, 1997), 55–57.
66 Bhimani, "Indeterminacy and the Specificity of Accounting Change," 25.
67 *History of Ministry of Munitions*, vol. VIII, Pt. I: 84.
68 *History of Ministry of Munitions*, vol. VIII, Pt. I: 73–81.

69 *History of Ministry of Munitions*, Vol. VIII, Pt. I: 83.
70 Ibid.
71 Ibid.
72 *History of Ministry of Munitions*, Vol. VII, Pt. I: 94–95.
73 Roy A. Church, *Herbert Austin: the British Motor Car Industry to 1941* (London: Europa Publications, 1979), 32.
74 Ibid., 42–43.
75 Edward F.L. Brech, "Management History: An Introduction," *Contemporary British History* 13, no. 3 (1999): 4.
76 McKillop and McKillop, *Efficiency Methods*; Herbert Newton Casson, *Factory Efficiency* (London: Efficiency Magazine, 1917); D.T. Farnham, *Executive Statistical Control* (London: A.F. Bird, 1917).
77 Herbert Newton Casson, *Lectures on efficiency, etc* (Manchester: Mather & Platt, 1917); Rowlinson, "Early Application of Scientific Management," 390.
78 Kreis, "Early Experiments in British Scientific Management," 66.
79 McKillop and McKillop, *Efficiency Methods*, 2.
80 E.T. Elbourne, *The Costing Problem* (London: The Library Press, 1919), 5.
81 Kreis, "Early Experiments in British Scientific Management," 66.
82 Merkle, *Management and Ideology*, 230.
83 Kreis, "Early Experiments in British Scientific Management," 67, 73.
84 Child, *British Management Thought*, 44, 46.
85 Ibid., 50–51.
86 Ian G. Smith and Trevor Boyns, "British Management Theory and Practice: The Impact of Fayol," *Management Decision* 43, no. 10 (2005): 1317–34.
87 Manuscript version of first, and only, page of the unpublished fourth part of *AIG*, quoted in Peaucelle, *Henri Fayol*, 82.
88 De Fréminville, "The Response of France to Scientific Management," 10.
89 Ian G. Smith, and Trevor Boyns, "Scientific Management and the Pursuit of Control in Britain to c.1960," *Accounting, Business & Financial History* 15, no. 2 (2005), 188.
90 Child, *British Management Thought*; Wilson and Thomson, *Making of Modern Management*, 179.
91 Kevin Whitston, "Scientific Management Practice in Britain: A History." (Unpublished Ph.D. thesis, University of Warwick, 1995) (available online at wrap.warwick.ac.uk/3981/—accessed 31 January 2015), 116.
92 Kevin Whitston, "Worker Resistance and Taylorism in Britain," *International Journal of Social History* 42, no. 1 (1997): 2.
93 Paul Vanuxem and Joseph Wilbois, *Essai sur la conduit des affaires et la direction des hommes* (Paris: Payot, 1919).
94 Kreis, "Early Experiments in British Scientific Management," 94.
95 Whitston, "Scientific Management Practice in Britain," 106.
96 George Douglas Howard Cole, *Payment of Wages: A Study in Payment by Results under the Wage-System*, Rev.ed (London: Allen & Unwin, 1928).
97 Aimée Moutet, "La première guerre mondiale et le Taylorisme," in *Le Taylorisme*, eds. Maurice de Montmollin and Olivier Pastré (Paris: La Découverte, 1984), 73.
98 S. Rials, *Administration et organisation 1910–1930: de l'organisation de la bataille à la bataille de l'organisation dans l'admninistration française* (Paris: Editions Beauchesne, 1977), 89.
99 Merkle, *Management and Ideology*, 161.
100 Howard F. Gospel has argued that scientific management had only permeated British management to a limited extent as late as 1939. See his *Markets, Firms and the Management of Labour in Modern BRITAIN* (Cambridge: University Press, 1992), 52.

101 Kynoch Archives, Birmingham Central Library, MS1422; Robert Fitzgerald, *Rowntree and the Marketing Revolution, 1862–1969* (Cambridge: University Press, 1995), chapter 8.

102 L. Perry-Keene, "Cost Control in the Motor Car and Allied Industries," *The Cost Accountant*, 2 (1922/23). The comments by Sir Herbert Austin appear on pp. 284–285,

103 Basil H. Tripp, *Renold Chains; A History of the Company and the Rise of the Precision Chain Industry, 1879–1955* (London: Allen & Unwin, 1956); Trevor Boyns, "Hans and Charles Renold: Entrepreneurs in the Introduction of Scientific Management Techniques in Britain," *Management Decision* 39, no. 9 (2001): 719–28.

104 Zimnovitch, "Berliet, the Obstructed Manager," 47–48.

105 *History of Ministry of Munitions*, Vol. VIII, Pt. I: 84.

106 Barry Ryerson, *The Giants of Small Heath: The History of BSA* (Yeovil: Haynes, 1980), 41.

107 Trevor Boyns, John Richard Edwards, and Mark Matthews, "A Study of the Interrelationship between Business, Management Organisation and Accounting Developments: Budgets and Budgetary Control in Britain between the Wars," in *Accounting and History* (Madrid: Ortega, 2000), 80.

108 Cole, *Payment of Wages*, vii.

109 Cole, *Payment of Wages*, ix–x.

110 Child, *British Management Thought*, 50–51.

111 Kreis, "Early Experiments in British Scientific Management".

112 Nelson, "Scientific Management in Retrospect," 22–23.

113 Bhimani, "Indeterminacy and the Specificity of Accounting Change," 32.

114 Merkle, *Management and Ideology*, 166.

115 Ibid., 168–69; Nelson, "Scientific Management in Retrospect," 23.

116 Kreis, "The Diffusion of Scientific Management".

Bibliography

Aitkin, H. G. T. *Taylorism at Watertown Arsenal*. Cambridge, MA: Harvard University Press, 1960.

Allingham, H. W. "The Determination of Standards in Scientific Management." *The Accountant* 60 (1919): 345–49 (the article), 349–52 (the discussion).

Bhimani, A. "Indeterminacy and the Specificity of Accounting Change: Renault 1898–1938." *Accounting, Organizations and Society* 18, 1 (1993): 1–39.

Boyns, T. "Hans and Charles Renold: Entrepreneurs in the Introduction of Scientific Management Techniques in Britain." *Management Decision* 39, 9 (2001): 719–28.

Boyns, T., J. R. Edwards, and M. D. Matthews. "A Study of the Interrelationship between Business, Management Organisation and Accounting Developments: Budgets and Budgetary Control in Britain between the Wars." In *Accounting and History*, 71–90. Madrid: Ortega, 2000.

Brech, E. F. L. "Management History: An Introduction." *Contemporary British History* 13, 3 (1999): 1–9.

Burton, F. G. *The Commercial Management of Engineering Works*. Manchester: The Scientific Publishing Company, 1898.

Cassis, Y. *Big Business—the European Experience in the Twentieth Century*. Oxford: Oxford University Press, 1997.

Casson, H. N. *Lectures on Efficiency, etc.* Manchester: Mather & Platt, 1917a.

———. *Factory Efficiency*. London: Efficiency Magazine, 1917b.

Chandler, A. D. Jr. *The Visible Hand: The Managerial Revolution in American Business*. Cambridge, MA: Belknap Press, 1977.

Chandler, A. D. Jr., and H. Daems. "Administrative Coordination, Allocation and Monitoring: A Comparative Analysis of the Emergence of Accounting and Organization in the U.S.A. and Europe." *Accounting, Organizations and Society* 4, 1–2 (1979): 3–20.

Child, J. *British Management Thought: A Critical Analysis*. London: Allen & Unwin, 1969.

Church, R. A. *Herbert Austin: The British motor Car Industry to 1941*. London: Europa Publications, 1979.

Cole, G. D. H. *Payment of Wages: A Study in Payment by Results under the Wage-System*. Revised edition. London: Allen & Unwin, 1928.

The Cost Accountant. Vol. 1. London: Institute of Cost and Works Accountants, 1921/22.

de Fréminville, C. "The Response of France to Scientific Management." Paper read at Memorial meeting for F.W. Taylor, Philadelphia, 22 October 1915 (translated by E.B. Cooke)—available online at http://stevens.cdmhost.com/cdm/ref/collection/p4100coll1/id/624—accessed 9 January 2015.

Elbourne, E. T. *The Costing Problem*. London: The Library Press, 1919.

———. *Factory Administration and Accounts*. London: Longmans, Green & Co, 1914, 1916.

Farnham, D. T. *Executive Statistical Control*. London: A. F. Bird, 1917.

Fitzgerald, R. *Rowntree and the Marketing Revolution, 1862–1969*. Cambridge: University Press, 1995.

Garcke, E., and J. M. Fells. *Factory Accounts; their Principles and Practice*. London: Crosby Lockwood, 1887.

Gospel, H. *Markets, Firms and the Management of Labour in Modern Britain*. Cambridge: Cambridge University Press, 1992.

History of Ministry of Munitions—Vols. VII, Part 1, and VIII, part 1. London: HMSO.

Hoxie, R. F. *Scientific Management and Labor*. New York: Augustus M. Kelly, 1966—reprint of 1915 work.

Kiechel, W. "The Management Century." *Harvard Business Review* (November 2012)—available online at http://hbr.org/2012/11/the-management-century—accessed January 10, 2015.

Kipping, M. "American Management Consulting Companies in Western Europe, 1920–1990: Products, Reputation, and Relationships." *Business History Review* 73, 2 (1999): 190–220.

Kreis, S. "Early Experiments in British Scientific Management: The Health of Munitions Workers Committee, 1915–1920." *Journal of Management History* 1, 2 (1995): 65–78.

———. "The Diffusion of Scientific Management: The Bedaux Company in America and Britain, 1926–1945." In *A Mental Revolution: Scientific Management and Taylor*, edited by D. Nelson, 156–74. Columbus, OH: Ohio State University Press, 1992.

Littler, C. R. *The Development of the Labour Process in Capitalist Societies; A Study of the Transformation of Work in Britain, Japan and the USA*. London: Heinemann, 1982.

Litterer, J. A. *The Emergence of Systematic Management as Shown by the Literature of Management from 1870 to 1900*. New York: Garland Publishing, 1986.

McKillop, M., and A. D. McKillop. *Efficiency Methods—An Introduction to Scientific Management*. London: Geo. Routledge & Sons, 1917.

Merkle, J. A. *Management and Ideology: The Legacy of the International Scientific Management Movement*. Berkley, CA: University of California Press, 1980.

Moutet, A. "La première guerre mondiale et le Taylorisme." In *Le Taylorisme*, edited by M. de Montmolin and O. Pastré, 67–81. Paris: La Découverte, 1984.

Nelson, D. "Scientific Management in Retrospect." In *A Mental Revolution—Scientific Management since Taylor*, edited by D. Nelson, 5–39. Columbus, OH: Ohio State University Press, 1992.

Peaucelle, J. L. *Henri Fayol—Inventeur des outils de gestion*. Paris: Economica, 2003.

Perry-Keene, L. A. "Cost control in the motor car and allied industries." *The Cost Accountant* 2 (1922/23): 104–07, 132–38, 170–74, 220–24, 252–56, 284–85.

Pezet, A. "The History of the French tableau de bord (1885–1975): Evidence from the Archives." *Accounting, Business & Financial History* 19, 2 (2009): 103–125.

Preen, H. *Reorganisation and Costings: A Book for Manufacturers and Merchants*. London: Simpkin, Marshall, Hamilton, Kent & Co, 1907; 1913.

Rials, S. *Administration et organisation 1910–1930: de l'organisation de la bataille à la bataille de l'organisation dans l'admninistration française*. Paris: Editions Beauchesne, 1977.

Rowlinson, M. "The Early Application of Scientific Management by Cadbury." *Business History* 30, 4 (1988): 377–95.

Ryerson, B. *The Giants of Small Heath—the History of BSA*. Yeovil: Haynes, 1980.

Slater Lewis, J. *The Commercial Organisation of Factories*. London: E & F. N. Spon, 1896.

Smith, I. G., and T. Boyns. "Scientific Management and the Pursuit of Control in Britain to c.1960." *Accounting, Business & Financial History* 15, 2 (2005): 187–216.

———. "British Management Theory and Practice: The Impact of Fayol." *Management Decision* 43, 10 (2005): 1317–34.

Tripp, B. H. *Renold Chains*. London: Allen & Unwin, 1956.

Urwick, L. F. *A general survey*. L.F. Urwick archive, PowerGen Library, Henley Business School, ms. 34/6/15, (undated, c.1968).

Vanuxem, P., and J. Wilbois. *Essai sur la conduit des affaires et la direction des hommes*. Paris: Payot, 1919.

Walter-Busch, E. "Albert Thomas and Scientific Management in War and Peace, 1914–1932." *Journal of Management History* 12, 2 (2006): 212–31.

Whitston, K. "Worker Resistance and Taylorism in Britain." *International Journal of Social History* 42, 1 (1997): 1–24.

———. "Scientific Management and Production Management Practice in Britain between the Wars." *Historical Studies in Industrial Relations* 1, 1 (1996): 47–71.

———. "Scientific Management Practice in Britain: A History." Unpublished Ph.D. thesis, University of Warwick, 1995 (available online at http://wrap.warwick.ac.uk/3981/—accessed January 31, 2015).

Wilson, J. F., and A. Thomson. *The Making of Modern Management—British Management in Historical Perspective*. Oxford: Oxford University Press, 2006.

Witzel, M. *Management History—Text and Cases*. London: Routledge, 2009.

Yates, J. "Evolving Information Use in Firms, 1850–1920: Ideology and Information Techniques and Technologies." In *Information Acumen: The Understanding and Use of Knowledge in Modern Business*, edited by L. Bud-Frierman, 26–50. London: Routledge, 1994.

Zimnovitch, H. "Berliet, the Obstructed Manager: Too Clever, Too Soon?" *Accounting, Business & Financial History* 1 (2001): 43–58.

Index